Phronesis

Phronesis

Retrieving Practical Wisdom in Psychology, Philosophy, and Education

Kristján Kristjánsson
Jubilee Centre for Character and Virtues, University of Birmingham, UK

and

Blaine J. Fowers
University of Miami, Florida, USA

Great Clarendon Street, Oxford, OX2 6DP,
United Kingdom

Oxford University Press is a department of the University of Oxford.
It furthers the University's objective of excellence in research, scholarship,
and education by publishing worldwide. Oxford is a registered trade mark of
Oxford University Press in the UK and in certain other countries

© Oxford University Press 2024

The moral rights of the authors have been asserted

First Edition published in 2024

All rights reserved. No part of this publication may be reproduced, stored in
a retrieval system, or transmitted, in any form or by any means, without the
prior permission in writing of Oxford University Press, or as expressly permitted
by law, by licence or under terms agreed with the appropriate reprographics
rights organization. Enquiries concerning reproduction outside the scope of the
above should be sent to the Rights Department, Oxford University Press, at the
address above

You must not circulate this work in any other form
and you must impose this same condition on any acquirer

Published in the United States of America by Oxford University Press
198 Madison Avenue, New York, NY 10016, United States of America

British Library Cataloguing in Publication Data

Data available

Library of Congress Control Number: 2023942221

ISBN 978–0–19–287147–3

DOI: 10.1093/oso/9780192871473.001.0001

Printed and bound by
CPI Group (UK) Ltd, Croydon, CR0 4YY

Oxford University Press makes no representation, express or implied, that the
drug dosages in this book are correct. Readers must therefore always check
the product information and clinical procedures with the most up-to-date
published product information and data sheets provided by the manufacturers
and the most recent codes of conduct and safety regulations. The authors and
the publishers do not accept responsibility or legal liability for any errors in the
text or for the misuse or misapplication of material in this work. Except where
otherwise stated, drug dosages and recommendations are for the non-pregnant
adult who is not breast-feeding

Links to third party websites are provided by Oxford in good faith and
for information only. Oxford disclaims any responsibility for the materials
contained in any third party website referenced in this work.

Acknowledgements

This book is the product of cross-disciplinary work between a philosopher (Kristján) and a psychologist (Blaine). Crossover work is not always successful; recall the cringeworthy duet by Placido Domingo and John Denver, 'Only Love'. However, we have enjoyed our collaboration enormously and found it mutually productive. We hope those feelings will be shared by readers. We began work on this book during the Covid-19 pandemic and finished it in April 2023. As readers will glean from the content of each of the 12 chapters, one of the authors made more of a contribution to some of them and the other to others. However, every chapter went through many rewrites by both of us as it was carried by email across the pond again and again. We consider ourselves, therefore, jointly responsible for the book as a whole.

We are grateful to current and past colleagues and friends for their advice, support, and comments on earlier drafts of many of the following chapters. We are most of all grateful to the following authors who co-operated with us on some of the papers and reports on which individual chapters are built, and gave us permission to draw on their work, as well as our own: Cat Darnell, Liz Gulliford, Fransisco Moller, Panos Paris, David Pollard, and Steve Thoma. We would like to single out a few additional names of colleagues who helped us refine some of our thoughts: James Arthur, Laura Blackie, David Carr, David Civil, Philip Cushman, Igor Grossmann, John Haldane, Tom Harrison, Sabena Jameel, Eeva Kallio, Andrew Maile, Shane McLoughlin, Andrew Peterson, Matt Stichter, Aidan Thompson, Maria Silvia Vaccarezza, and Jonathan Webber. Kristján is particularly indebted to the John Templeton Foundation for funding the work of the Jubilee Centre. Martin Baum at OUP deserves thanks for being unreservedly supportive of the book project throughout its gestation. Two anonymous reviewers provided generously extended feedback, which was much appreciated. Dr Kristian Guttesen conscientiously helped us compile the index.

We thankfully acknowledge permissions to recycle material from the following articles and reports:

- *Phronesis* as an Ideal in Professional Medical Ethics: Some Preliminary Positionings and Problematics (K. Kristjánsson), *Theoretical Medicine and Bioethics*, 36(5), 2015.

- *Phronesis* and the Knowledge–Action Gap in Moral Psychology and Moral Education: A New Synthesis? (C. Darnell, L. Gulliford, K. Kristjánsson, & P. Paris), *Human Development*, 62(3), 2019.
- *Phronesis*: Developing a Conceptualisation and an Instrument (K. Kristjánsson, C. Darnell, B. Fowers, D. Pollard, F. Moller, & S. Thoma). Research Report, 2020, https://www.jubileecentre.ac.uk//userfiles/jubileecentre/pdf/Research%20Reports/Phronesis_Report.pdf
- *Phronesis*: Using an Aristotelian Model as a Research Tool (K. Kristjánsson, D. Pollard, C. Darnell, & S. Thoma). Research Report, 2021, https://www.jubileecentre.ac.uk/userfiles/jubileecentre/Phronesis%20Report.pdf
- Twenty-Two Testable Hypotheses about *Phronesis* (K. Kristjánsson), *British Educational Research Journal*, 47(5), 2021.
- *Phronesis* (Practical Wisdom) as a Type of Contextual Integrative Thinking (K. Kristjánsson, B. Fowers, C. Darnell, & D. Pollard), *Review of General Psychology*, 25(3), 2021.
- The Need for *Phronesis* (K. Kristjánsson) in *Values and Virtues for a Challenging World: Royal Institute of Philosophy Supplementary Volume*, 92, eds. Anneli Jefferson, Orestis Palermos, Panos Paris, & Jonathan Webber (Cambridge: Cambridge University Press, 2022).
- Collective *Phronesis* in Business Ethics Education and Managerial Practice: A Neo-Aristotelian Analysis (K. Kristjánsson), *Journal of Business Ethics*, 181(1), 2022.
- Post-*Phronetic* Pain (K. Kristjánsson), *Acta Philosophica*, 31(2), 2022.
- The Primacy of Civic Virtue in Aristotle's Politics and Its Educational Implications (K. Kristjánsson), *History of Political Thought*, 43(4), 2022.
- A Multifunction Approach to Assessing Aristotelian *Phronesis* (Practical Wisdom) (C. Darnell, B. Fowers, & K. Kristjánsson), *Personality and Individual Differences*, 196(October), 2022.
- Teaching *Phronesis* to Aspiring Police Officers: Some Preliminary Philosophical, Developmental and Pedagogical Reflections (K. Kristjánsson), *International Journal of Ethics Education*, forthcoming, 2023 (available online).
- *Phronesis* as Moral Decathlon: Contesting the Redundancy Thesis about *Phronesis* (K. Kristjánsson, & B. Fowers), *Philosophical Psychology*, forthcoming, 2023 (available online).

Contents

1. **Aims and Scope: Getting *Phronesis* Right**   1
   1.1 The *Phronesis* Bandwagon: Aligning Divergent Tracks   1
   1.2 The Background Context: Character-and-Virtue Research on the Rise   12
   1.3 A Neo-Aristotelian 'Standard Model' of *Phronesis*   15
   1.4 Alternative *Phronesis* Concepts   20
   1.5 Summary of Subsequent Chapters   26

2. **A Neo-Aristotelian *Phronesis* Model and Some Philosophical Alternatives**   31
   2.1 Elaborating the 'Standard Model' of *Phronesis*   31
   2.2 A Four-Componential Model of *Phronesis*   35
   2.3 The Contentious Blueprint Component   48
   2.4 Two Philosophical Counter-Positions   54
   2.5 Some Remaining Philosophical Alternatives   58

3. **The History of Wisdom Research in Psychology and the New Common Model**   63
   3.1 The Early History of Wisdom Research in Psychology   63
   3.2 *Phronesis* in Psychology: Some Nonmainstream Voices   70
   3.3 The New Common Wisdom Model   74
   3.4 Initial Critiques of the Common Wisdom Model   78
   3.5 Concluding Remarks   81

4. **Comparing Our *Phronesis* Model with the New 'Common Model' and Other Psychological Alternatives**   83
   4.1 Three Issues in Wisdom Research   83
   4.2 Three Primary Critiques of the CWM   87
   4.3 Comparing the CWM and the APM   93
   4.4 Is *Phronesis* Redundant with Respect to Existing Psychological Concepts?   98
   4.5 Concluding Remarks   110

5. **The 'Gappiness Problem' in Moral Psychology and the Relevance of *Phronesis***   111
   5.1 The Historical Backdrop: From Kohlberg Onwards   111
   5.2 Moral Identity as a Gap-Stopper   115
   5.3 Moral Emotions as a Gap-Stopper   121
   5.4 Comparing the APM with the Neo-Kohlbergian Four-Componential Model of Moral Functioning   126
   5.5 The Prospects of *Phronesis* as a Gap-Stopper   130

6. A New Measure of *Phronesis*: Empirical Findings — 133
- 6.1 Introduction — 133
- 6.2 Methods — 135
- 6.3 Results and Discussion — 143
- 6.4 A Replication of the Proof of Concept Study — 147
- 6.5 Concluding Comments — 151

7. *Phronesis* in Professional (Medical) Ethics — 155
- 7.1 The *Phronesis* Bandwagon — 155
- 7.2 *Phronesis* in Medical Ethics: Aristotle or MacIntyre? — 160
- 7.3 Relativist or Universalist *Phronesis*? — 165
- 7.4 The Two Remaining Binaries — 169
- 7.5 Which Conception of *Phronesis* in Medical Ethics and Education? — 172

8. *Phronesis* and the Civic Virtues — 177
- 8.1 Why the Lack of Engagement with Civic *Phronesis*? — 177
- 8.2 *Phronetic* Method, Teleological Axiology, and Civic Primacy — 180
- 8.3 Interlude: Actual Constitutions and the Ideal State — 188
- 8.4 Moral and Civic Virtue, and the Role of *Phronesis* — 191
- 8.5 Some Educational Implications — 201

9. Collective *Phronesis* — 203
- 9.1 Why Collective *Phronesis*? — 203
- 9.2 What Is Aristotle's Take on Collective *Phronesis*? — 209
- 9.3 Interpreting the Accumulation Argument for Collective *Phronesis* — 213
- 9.4 The Components of Collective Managerial *Phronesis* — 217
- 9.5 Some Practical Business Applications — 220

10. Difficult Decisions and *Post-phronetic* Pain — 227
- 10.1 What Is *Post-phronetic* Pain? — 227
- 10.2 The Mystery of the Missing Motivation — 232
- 10.3 Some Possible Aristotelian Rejoinders — 236
- 10.4 Types of Moral Sadness — 239
- 10.5 Does PPP Have Any Redeeming Features? — 242

11. Educating *Phronesis* — 247
- 11.1 Aristotle's Reticence about *Phronesis* Education—and a First Look at the Developmental Picture — 247
- 11.2 Developing towards Virtue: Mining and Transcending Aristotle's Model — 256
- 11.3 Some General Educational Hypotheses and Observations — 265
- 11.4 Professional *Phronesis* Education and the Limited Role of Teaching — 273
- 11.5 Civic Education and Civic *Phronesis* — 280

12.	**Concluding Remarks**	**285**
	12.1 An Overview of the Main Conclusions Reached	285
	12.2 Some Further Reflections on the Role of *Phronesis* in the Overall Flourishing Life	289
	12.3 Some Further Reflections on Measuring *Phronesis*	292
	12.4 Interdisciplinary Work on *Phronesis*: The Pros and Cons	301
	12.5 Future Research on *Phronesis*	307

References   *309*
Index   *333*

1
Aims and Scope

Getting *Phronesis* Right

1.1 The *Phronesis* Bandwagon: Aligning Divergent Tracks

This is a book about *phronesis*, or practical wisdom, as excellence in moral decision-making, co-written by a philosopher and a psychologist who have both devoted considerable attention to themes within broadly Aristotelian Virtue Ethics. In this introductory chapter, we first outline our motivations, as well as the aims and scope of the work (in the present section). We then move to a brief overview of the wider theoretical terrain: recent theorizing about character and virtues (in Section 1.2). This leads us (in Section 1.3) to an exploration of the recent theoretical literatures about *phronesis* and in particular the so-called standard neo-Aristotelian model that has been developing gradually and that we aim to analyse further and augment in various ways in what follows. Section 1.4 discusses a number of alternative concepts of and approaches to *phronesis* that we have, for different reasons, mostly decided to eschew in the following chapters. The present chapter then ends with a summary of the remaining parts of the book.

   This chapter ended up being considerably longer than we anticipated at the beginning. Our excuse is that much of what we aim to contribute, in terms of novel insights about *phronesis*, can only be understood against the background of substantial discourses that already exist. We consider it crucial that readers are aware of those preliminaries and are taken on a fairly comprehensive sightseeing tour of the surrounding theoretical landscape before they can begin to assess whether our contribution adds significantly to that terrain.

Initial orienting thoughts

Here are some initial insights that served as the starting point of our journey. For ordinary people, morality has frequently been about choosing virtues over vices, as Aristotle famously assumed. In the words of Scottish philosopher Alasdair MacIntyre (1998), most laypeople have been, and still are, 'proto-Aristotelians'. This is reflected both in historical sources and in major works of arts throughout the ages, transcending temporal or cultural boundaries. In those sources, moral heroes are seen as people with an abundance of virtues; moral villains are those succumbing to vice. Through most of human history, this understanding informed the dominant moral theories of the day. Those have been, broadly speaking, *virtue ethical* (as specified, e.g., by Aristotle, Aquinas, or Confucius), according to which an action is, broadly speaking, right if it exemplifies virtue.[1] The last 200–300 years, since the Enlightenment, constitute an exception—an aberration or a 'blip' (Russell, 2009, p. 43) if you like—during which moral theorizing aimed to move beyond the perceived messiness of virtue language, with all its inevitable shades of grey, to algorithms that would give us more definitive and precise answers to moral quandaries. To cut a long story short, however, Virtue Ethics—the plain person's moral philosophy—has been undergoing a revival in the last half a century or so and now constitutes (again) a formidable competitor to the more easily codifiable Enlightenment frameworks.

This history will be familiar to most readers of this book; we only expand upon it briefly below. What matters for present purposes is that for Aristotle—the veritable progenitor of contemporary Virtue Ethics—the development and personal administration of virtue goes through two fairly distinct phases. Children first develop broad dispositions or, better put, states of character (*hexeis*), comprising virtues or vices. For example, if fortunate enough to be influenced by positive role models whom they can emulate and who habituate them into the virtues, children internalize a broad disposition of kindness towards other people rather than cruelty. A broad tendency of this kind will stand a child in good stead in simple encounters with friends and family. The child will come to be known as, and be consistently rewarded for being, kind and compassionate. Without this broad state of character—which Aristotle called 'habituated virtue'—the child cannot move on to a more fully developed moral life. However, at the same time, mere habituated virtue is fairly undifferentiated and coarse, and without further polishing, children will

---

[1] In other words, 'right action' is defined in terms of virtue but not vice versa (cf. Russell, 2009, p. ix).

quickly grind to a halt once they encounter more complex exigencies, especially those involving an apparent conflict of virtues. Given that children have also developed other habituated virtues than kindness, such as honesty and justice, what shall they do when two or more seemingly conflicting virtues are called for in the same situation? The morally agreeable child, once she enters dilemmatic space, is no King Solomon yet.[2]

To move beyond the merely rudimentary, if necessary, initial stage of habituated virtue, Aristotle posited a specific, later developing, intellectual virtue, namely *phronesis*, or practical wisdom, that oversees the other virtues (moral or civic[3]) and provides them with the necessary checks and balances to secure overall morally wise decisions. It is concerned both with finding the correct 'golden mean' of a single virtue,[4] when applied in complex contexts, and the proper interactivity, or balancing, of different virtues where those seem to call for different responses in the same situation. For instance, is it possible to reconcile somehow the demands of honesty and compassion in situation *S*, by being compassionately honest or honestly compassionate, or does this particular situation *S* call for the abandonment of one of the two virtues? Whatever the eventual decision may be, it is the faculty of *phronesis* that is meant to do the adjudicative heavy lifting. At the same time, it turns simple dispositions to be good along various independent paths into a coherent way of life: a comprehensive moral journey, guided by 'right reason'.[5] And only then can the person be said to possess proper moral virtues, or moral virtues in the strict sense

---

[2] Some philosophers reserve the term 'dilemma' for moral quandaries of the *Sophie's Choice* kind where both or all options seem morally unacceptable or 'equally bad'. In Psychology, however, 'dilemmas' and 'quandaries' tend to be used mostly interchangeably. In this book, we follow the latter precedent.

[3] Most of the academic literature focuses on Aristotle's account in the *Nicomachean Ethics* of *phronesis* as adjudicating on the proper application of, and conflicts between, moral virtues. It tends to be forgotten that *phronesis* plays an equally important part in his *Politics*, regarding the balanced administration of civic virtues, although Aristotle believed that the simplest civic virtues do not need *phronesis* (see further in Chapter 8). For convenience of exposition, we talk about 'moral' versus 'civic' virtues in this book because that is the standard terminological way in modernity of denoting those two categories of virtue (see, e.g., Jubilee Centre, 2022). This terminology is slightly misleading, however, from an Aristotelian perspective, because Aristotle did not have at his disposal any word corresponding to 'moral' in modern English. Anscombe's (1958a, p. 2) observation on this is trenchant: 'If someone professes to be expounding Aristotle and talks in a modern fashion about "moral" such-and-such, he must be very imperceptive if he does not constantly feel like someone whose jaws have somehow got out of alignment: the teeth don't come together in a proper bite.' Aristotle's distinction was between virtues that have to do with individual character (*ethos*) and those that have to do with social associations in the state. A more accurate terminology would thus be to talk about ethical/characterological versus political/communal virtues. Moreover, in current Psychology, 'moral' is often used interchangeably with 'prosocial', but 'prosociality' is a behaviouristic concept, and Aristotle had no academic interest in a behaviouristic conception of right action, except for persons at the early (uncritical) stage of habituation into virtue. Therefore, we do not use the term 'prosocial' except in very limited ways.

[4] We take it that readers are familiar with the standard Aristotelian architectonic of a virtue as a medial state between two extremes, an excess and a deficiency, and we will not expand on it further in what follows. For an enlightening modern variation on this theme, see Ng and Tay (2020).

[5] As noted by Russell (2009, p. 19), Aristotle treats *phronesis* and 'right reason' as interchangeable.

(Aristotle, 1985, p. 170 [1144b4–17]; cf. Müller, 2004). The mediating, overseeing, and orchestrating role of *phronesis* gives it a clear status as a higher-order intellectual virtue, variably termed 'practical reason', 'good sense', 'good judgement', or 'practical wisdom', although we mostly avoid those terminological variations in English by simply talking about *phronesis*.

Different theorists use different characterizations to describe this faculty. Burbules (2019) talks about *phronesis* as helping us figure out what to do when we 'get stuck'. Hursthouse (2006) describes the *phronimos* (the person possessing *phronesis*) as 'wisely worldly' rather than just 'worldly wise', and Swartwood (2020) defines 'practical wisdom' as 'a grasp (1) of what one ought to do, (2) all things considered, (3) in particular situations'. However, all these different theorists understand *phronesis* in a broadly Aristotelian way as a meta-level (i.e., metacognitive) virtue helping the moral and civic virtues find the right means to their ends.[6] Indeed, the most uniquely identity-conferring feature of Aristotelian and neo-Aristotelian forms of Virtue Ethics (as well as their educational incarnation as Character Education) is the invocation of *phronesis*, or practical wisdom, as an intellectual *meta-virtue* of this sort that orchestrates the moral and civic virtues and ultimately guides mature decision-making in those areas. This uniqueness is best seen by comparing Aristotelian Virtue Ethics with other forms, such as Platonic or Thomistic that, contra Aristotle, both rely on a specific *master virtue* among the moral virtues trumping others[7] (justice in the former and love as *agape* in the latter), or with the reigning social scientific virtue paradigm of the day, Positive Psychology (Peterson & Seligman, 2004), which makes do without either a master or a meta-virtue for adjudication, assuming rather that the more of each virtue is better (critiqued by Grant & Schwartz, 2011; Ng & Tay, 2020).[8] This is a point worth harping on and bearing in mind through all the subsequent chapters: there is no master moral virtue in Aristotle and not even any priority list of cardinal virtues.[9]

---

[6] As will become clear in Chapter 2, *phronesis* also influences the ends themselves through backward loops.

[7] When virtue ethicists talk about a 'master virtue', they mean that one of the moral virtues overrides or 'trumps' others if there is a virtue conflict. A 'meta-virtue' is, in contrast, a virtue of another kind, at a higher level, that adjudicates conflicts between the lower-level moral (and possibly other kinds of) virtues.

[8] McGrath and Brown (2020) argue that three of the 24 positive psychological virtues, namely prudence, judgement, and perspective, can collectively execute the adjudicative function that Aristotle ascribes to *phronesis*. We return briefly to their thesis in Chapter 3.

[9] Aristotle does make the odd remark about some moral virtues being weightier than others are, but those are mostly unsystematic. The same goes for his account of the much-debated moral virtue of great-heartedness (*megalopsychia*). Although it is described as some sort of a master virtue that incorporates other moral virtues and makes them greater, this virtue is reserved for a special group of agents (public benefactors) enjoying unusual moral luck, in the form of riches and social positions, and taking on unique philanthropic responsibilities in society (Kristjánsson, 2020, chap. 4). Hence, it is not a general master virtue in the same sense as, say, justice is for Plato.

Because of the context-dependence of moral life and the complexity of the situations in which we find ourselves, there is no single overriding moral concern that can serve, so to speak, as our moral compass; only the intellectual virtue of *phronesis* can.

Aristotle's troubling vagueness

Aristotle's historical importance notwithstanding, those wanting to carve a fully-fledged account of *phronesis* out of Aristotle's texts will be disappointed. Some of the things Aristotle himself says about *phronesis* are cryptic, and he is frustratingly reticent, as we rue at later junctures, on various issues that one would have expected him to address: for example, on exactly when and how (i.e., through which means) *phronesis* develops (cf. Curzer, 2012, p. 351). Because of Aristotle's own patchy treatment, Aristotelian scholar Sarah Broadie refers to *phronesis* as having a 'rougher terrain' than most other Aristotelian concepts: one 'densely thicketed with controversy' (1991, p. 179). In one sense, that is an unfortunate situation. It would be easier if *phronesis* constituted an unambiguously defined Aristotelian concept that philosophers and social scientists could either embrace or reject through a set of clearly specified, competing arguments. In another sense, however, the variations in the way *phronesis* is understood, even by Aristotelians, allow for a more nuanced grasp of its moral and methodological salience and make it more easily amenable to new conceptual revisions and updated empirical findings.

In all events, however radically we think Aristotle needs to be updated, there is but one natural place to start any exploration of *phronesis*—namely, in his own texts—and that we propose to do, although this book does not aspire to an exercise in orthodox Aristotelian scholarship (i.e., textual exegesis). At the same time, we remain mindful of the dangers of reading modern concerns into ancient accounts or of imposing an ancient philosophical concept on current psychological and educational research in order to ameliorate practical lacunae, as is our aim. Philosophizing the social sciences can appear as revanchist, even reactionary (cf. Kristjánsson, 2018b, chap. 10), and this appearance will be compounded when the philosophy in question is more than 2000 years old and, as some may think, empirically *passé* (Lapsley, 2016; 2019; 2021). We return to the question of the proper use of Aristotle—and the extent to which our account in this book is neo-Aristotelian rather than Aristotelian—in Section 1.3.

Motivating contemporary *phronesis* research

What would be the motivation for studying *phronesis* in the present day and age? The first and most obvious thing to note is that people spend considerable part of their waking hours reflecting upon and discussing the moral dilemmas they face with their significant others, friends, and work colleagues (Narvaez, 2010). In many cases, that deliberation focuses on how to deal with conflicting considerations: for example, about how to respond to clashing demands of honesty versus loyalty to friends (Thoma et al., 2019). The perennial importance of good deliberation clarifies why *phronesis* has historically attracted attention. However, this interest gradually faded in Enlightenment and post-Enlightenment theorizing, with *phronesis* being brushed off as both too moralistic and indeterminate as a decision procedure, and indeed as part of a naive 'bag-of-virtues' conception of moral life, according to Kohlberg (1981). The decline of interest in *phronesis* developed in tandem with the erosion of Virtue Ethics as a paradigm in Moral Philosophy (MacIntyre, 1981) and the replacement of 'character' with a conception of human 'personality' as 'character devaluated' in Psychology (Allport, 1937) and in Western societies (Sussman, 1973). *Phronesis*, with its emphasis on making wise moral decisions based on the specifics of a context, cannot be formulated via the kind of algorithmic principle-based decision-making typically favoured by Enlightenment and post-Enlightenment thought.

As a decision process, *phronesis* thus became replaced by top-down procedures that fit the post-Enlightenment frame of mind better. There are many historical influences cast in the mold of that thought, including an instrumentalist cost-benefit analysis of the utilitarian kind (Mill, 1972; Weber, 1949), a formalistic deontological procedure emphasizing purely rational arbitration of decision-making (Kant, 1964; Kohlberg, 1981), a sentimentalist philosophy that views desires and emotions (not reason) as the sources of all decision-making (Haidt, 2001), and a logical positivist philosophy of science that eschews values and ethics in science (critiqued by Richardson et al., 1999). These influences on Psychology can be parsed many ways, but they were all unfriendly to the concept of *phronesis*. In the flow and ebb of intellectual opinion, these post-Enlightenment positions have more recently come under heavy criticism for their uncritical bifurcation of facts and values (Anscombe, 1958a, 1958b; Carr, 2002a; Fowers, 2005; Sayer, 2011). At the same time, the rationalistic approach in early Moral Psychology (Kohlberg, 1981) also suffered a major setback when it transpired that correlations between developmental stages of moral reasoning and actual moral action were low (Blasi, 1980), as we chart in Chapter 5.

Phronesis and the current political climate

In addition to academic motivations for retrieving *phronesis*, there is also a political driver. It is not a complete coincidence that we hit upon the topic of *phronesis* at the beginning of the third decade of the twenty-first century. It has become almost a platitude to say that the twenty-first century has witnessed increased political and ideological polarization as well as a surge in populism from both the right and the left. Phrases such as 'post-truth', 'fake news', and 'alternative facts' have become household terms, and after the divisive Brexit campaign in the UK, for example, parents take much worse to it than before, if an offspring dares form amorous bonds with an individual from the 'other' side of the political spectrum (Guardian, 2016). Conspiracy theories have garnered increased popularity: some of them so bizarre, such as QAnon, that they make far-fetched figments of the medieval imagination seem positively reasonable by comparison.

There are conflicting views on whether recent technological advances, especially in the field of social media, have simply taken the lid off a discourse that hitherto had been confined to the locker room, the staff room, and the kitchen table, or whether there has actually been a radical turn for the worse (or at least for the more radical, divisive, and inflammatory) in the way people discuss hot topics of the day. In any case, the worldwide pandemic that broke out in early 2020 helped crystallize many of the above-mentioned developments. As well as bringing existing polarizations into sharper relief, it created new ones, such as the one between public health and economic prosperity—dividing people both along and across traditional conflict lines. The socio-moral and economic reverberations of the pandemic led to a proliferation of debates in public media that closely connect—albeit in new and unforeseeable ways—to proverbial debates about the virtues and possible trade-offs between them.

Consider the debate between lockdown adherents and sceptics during the pandemic. To be sure, pro-lockdown arguments teemed with references to compassion and care towards the vulnerable and the need to protect those at all costs. However, the language of the typical anti-lockdown argument tended to be strewed with virtue-signalling references to the loneliness of the locked-up old, the misery of the furloughed or unemployed middle-aged, the despair of the studies-deprived and desolate young, and heavily referencing personal 'freedom' and choice. All in all, the language of both lockdown supporters and deniers was steeped in moral language in general and virtue language in particular. Yet what struck us here was the complete elision of any master or meta-virtue meant to secure a balance between the competing first-level virtues. Wisdom was seldom, if ever mentioned, still less *phronesis*.[10] The 'good people' advancing those conflicting arguments all seemed to be 'excessively good' in the Aristotelian sense of people who simply try to enhance individual virtues as much as possible without paying attention to a balance of virtues within a life ordered according to a golden mean.

As scholars interested in the role of virtues and character strengths in the good life (Fowers, 2005; Fowers et al., 2021; Kristjánsson, 2015; 2020), we found those debates fascinating and infuriating in equal measure. What characterizes the present age, in our view, is a strange discordance between, on the one hand, the reduction in vice across the world as measured by objective criteria, such as the extent of serious crime and warfare (Rosling et al., 2018),[11] as well as the increased eagerness to at least pay lip service to virtue (Tosi & Warmke, 2020), versus, on the other hand, the increased polarization and fierceness of debates about values and virtues. Could it be that what we are seeing is a situation in which the development of the meta-virtue of *phronesis* has simply not kept up with the advancement of moral virtues?[12]

We were reminded of an old work by G. K. Chesterton. Although his text was written from a fairly orthodox Christian perspective, there is a lot to be learned from it in the current intellectual climate, irrespective of one's religious views. 'A man was meant to be doubtful about himself, but undoubting about the truth; this has been exactly reversed' (1908, chap. 3), Chesterton remarks in a way that seems to anticipate the current era of post-truth coupled with inflated narcissistic expressions of subjective identities. What he says about virtues is no less timely and topical:

> The modern world is not evil; in some ways the modern world is far too good. It is full of wild and wasted virtues. When a [moral] scheme is shattered [. . .], it is not merely the vices that are let loose. The vices are, indeed, let loose, and they wander and do damage. But the virtues are let loose also; and the virtues wander

---

[10] Yet a report compiled during the pandemic by Harrison and Polizzi (2021) indicated that the virtue that most adolescents wanted their friends to show on social media was wisdom, and this virtue was also prioritized in a parental survey.

[11] They also point out how abject poverty, often considered a breeding ground for vice, is being reduced around the world.

[12] Schwartz and Sharpe complained that *phronesis* is rarely mentioned in academic debates or public discourse (2010, p. 11). While that situation has changed dramatically in academia in the last decade, public discourse has not yet followed suit.

more wildly, and the virtues do more terrible damage. The modern world is full of the old [. . .] virtues gone mad. The virtues have gone mad because they have been isolated from each other and are wandering alone. (Chesterton, 1908, chap. 3)

Chesterton goes on to reminisce about a lost system that 'could to some extent make righteousness and peace kiss each other. Now they do not even bow.' This is precisely what we noticed in the lockdown debates during the pandemic. The virtues upheld by the adherents and sceptics did not even bow to one another, let alone kiss or aim for any affective union. The former simply celebrated one kind of care and compassion and their counterparts another kind. All these virtues 'wandered alone', however, like a group of novice scouts on an excursion without any guide to lead them. The diverse moral values touted seemed to represent a world that is 'far too good', to use Chesterton's words, in the sense of being out of balance. Perhaps the best way to summarize the aim of our book is to say that it aims to gather together again some of those wandering virtues and lend coherence to them.

A renaissance of *phronesis* research—and our aims

To return to the academic story again, despite its absence from political agendas, *phronesis* has been undergoing a significant academic revival of late. What we could call the new '*phronesis* bandwagon' is not only driven by philosophers (e.g., Annas, 2011; Curzer, 2012; Russell, 2009) but also psychologists (Darnell et al., 2019; Fowers et al., 2021; Schwartz & Sharpe, 2010) and theorists working within various branches of Professional Ethics, such as medicine (Jameel, 2022; Kaldjian, 2014), nursing (Flaming, 2001), and business (Ames et al., 2020): branches where *phronesis*-guided Virtue Ethics is gradually becoming the dominant moral theory. Various educationists are also jumping on this bandwagon (e.g., Bohlin, 2022; Burbules, 2019; Harðarson, 2019).

Most recently, a long-standing discourse on general wisdom within Psychology has been swaying significantly in the direction of *phronesis*—away from both *sophia* (theoretical wisdom) and *deinotes* (wisdom understood as mere instrumentalist calculation) (Grossmann, Weststrate, Ardelt et al., 2020).[13] Even more radically, *phronesis* has been suggested as nothing

---

[13] One of the major themes in this book is how our model of *phronesis* compares with that of Grossmann, Weststrate, Ardelt et al. (2020) and whether these two models are competing or complementary. See esp. Chapters 3 and 4. Not all wisdom researchers in psychology have been impacted by this recent rapprochement with *phronesis*, however. For example, in the recent semi-popular (but quite comprehensive) overview book by Sternberg and Glück (2022), neither 'Aristotle' nor '*phronesis*' feature in the index.

less than a comprehensive research paradigm for the whole of Social Science (Flyvbjerg, 2001, 2004; Flyvbjerg et al., 2012). However, on closer inspection, this new *phronesis* discourse is characterized by frequently unrecognized tensions, lacunae, and ambivalences. Finding convergence in the sea of divergence is a tall order.

In a nutshell, the present book purports to work through some of the most relevant puzzles created by the recent *phronesis* discourse(s), ameliorate various lacunae in the current literatures, and push the research agenda in new directions. It will do so in a way that is radically cross-disciplinary and draws in equal measure on insights from Psychology, Philosophy, Professional Ethics, and Education. More specifically, this book has five primary aims. The *first* is to set the recently surging interest in *phronesis* in Psychology, Philosophy, Professional Ethics, and Education in historical and theoretical contexts. The *second* is to analyse and elaborate upon Aristotle's standard model of *phronesis* in a way that is both philosophically credible and allows for a psychologically serviceable and empirically tractable conceptualization. The *third* is to juxtapose our new Aristotelian *phronesis* model with the recent consensual model of wisdom in Psychology (Grossmann, Weststrate, Ardelt et al., 2020) and with various other alternatives, as well as responding to different kinds of scepticism about the usefulness of the *phronesis* construct. The *fourth* is to elicit a number of practical implications of our model for the development and education of *phronesis* and its application in areas of professional practice and daily conduct. The *fifth* and final aim is to explore the relevance of *phronesis* in areas that have mostly eluded investigation so far, including the spheres of civic/political virtues and collective (managerial) decision-making.

In our initial draft, the title of the present scene-setting section was 'Getting *Phronesis* on the Right Track'. However, we eventually found that title misleading. Currently, the *phronesis* discourses within different disciplines follow divergent tracks with scant mutual interaction. None of those tracks is 'wrong' in our view; rather they are incomplete individually. Our aim is not so much to *correct* them as it is to *align* them. By comparing the different tracks with the original source in Aristotle and juxtaposing them with one another, we hope that we can bring them into line: at least make them all head in the same direction, if not necessarily merge into a single mega-track. Put more simply, we are looking for synergies between the different discourses: how they can strengthen and inform one another in the service of the overall aim of aiding wise moral decision-making.

Although we are unapologetic about our cross-disciplinary aspirations, we realize that there is a trade-off between depth and breadth. Our broad-brush strategy will not allow for the same exegetical devotion as that offered by true Aristotelian doyens (e.g., Broadie, 1991); it will not be as philosophically nuanced as Russell's (2009) classic study; nor as meticulously attentive to previous psychological accounts of wisdom as Grossmann, Weststrate, Ardelt et al. (2020); and it will not offer as many illuminating case studies and practical examples as Schwartz and Sharpe's (2010) exemplary introduction. Finally, this book will not provide as much depth in terms of tightly focused explorations of discrete aspects of practical wisdom, in different philosophies and contexts, as many of the individual chapters in the two volumes, edited by De Caro and Vaccarezza (2021) and Frey (2024). However, what we lose in depth we hope to make up in breadth and scope, by writing a through-composed monograph aiming to synthesize and supplement the already existing literature, as described above.[14]

Since we hope that this book will be found to be an accessible reading for a broad range of academics, students, and interested intellectually minded non-academics, we have tried to write it in a way that presupposes as little background theoretical and research methods knowledge as possible. This means that we have decided to reduce quite a few academic detours and references to footnotes. Ordinary readers should be able to follow the main thread of the argument without bothering with the footnotes; however, those will hopefully add academic gravitas and nuance for readers who want to dig deeper. We must admit that neither of us is a particular friend of footnotes, but those do serve a purpose in a crossover work like this.

We would like to warn psychologists and other readers with a Social Science background that the remainder of the current chapter and Chapter 2 are denser theoretically, referencing multiple philosophical positions. Because this is an interdisciplinary book, we deemed it necessary to deal with important philosophical questions and positions first before exploring the psychological implications of *phronesis*. Readers who find this a challenging slog have two options. They can persevere with us through Chapters 1 and 2, and perhaps learn important nuances. Or, for those who simply want to skip the philosophical preliminaries, an alternative is to move now straight to Chapter 3. In either case, we promise practically minded readers that Chapters 3–6 are mostly psychological.

---

[14] The work that perhaps comes closest to ours in terms of methodological aspirations is the recent book, *Understanding Virtue*, by Wright et al. (2021). Although its remit is much more general than ours is, it also discusses *phronesis* in various places, synthesizing psychological and philosophical insights.

1.2 The Background Context: Character-and-Virtue Research on the Rise

The *phronesis* bandwagon has not been set in motion in an intellectual vacuum. It would be incomprehensible outside of the context of the recently rising interest in character and virtues within Philosophy, Psychology, and Education. 'Character' is here meant to denote the morally evaluable, reason-responsive, and educable part of human personhood, consisting, inter alia, of stable and robust (if necessarily context-sensitive and flexible) multi-componential traits called 'virtues' or 'vices'. A typical virtue consists of a bundle of interrelated components (e.g., beliefs, values, emotions, perceptions, and motivations) relevant to a discrete sphere of life that are collectively conducive to both the agent's wellbeing and the wellbeing of other people.[15]

The reasons for this surge of interest are multi-faceted and cannot be discussed in any detail here. They are related, briefly speaking, on the one hand, to the disillusionment in philosophical circles with non-virtue-based moral theories (Anscombe, 1958a; MacIntyre, 1981) and, on the other hand, with the realization, in Social Science, that a rich and thick account of human beings—their motivations and explanations of actions—cannot be given without invoking character traits in general and the virtues in particular.[16] The importance of recent philosophical insights notwithstanding (e.g., Annas, 2011; Curzer, 2012; Russell, 2009), we consider the recent resurgence of interest in *phronesis* to have been more directly inspired by a latter-day retrieval of character-and-virtue research in Psychology (McGrath & Brown, 2020; Narvaez, 2010; Ng & Tay, 2020; Wright et al., 2021). That retrieval, often referred to as a new 'science of virtue' (Fowers et al., 2021), has been encouraged by the advent of Positive Psychology in general and in particular its research into universal character strengths, virtues, and the flourishing life (Peterson & Seligman, 2004[17]; McGrath, 2019; Seligman, 2011), although neo-Aristotelians often look askance at various aspects of Positive Psychology (Fowers, 2005; Kristjánsson, 2013). The new science of virtue suggests that virtues are the habitual traits that make it possible to live a good or

---

[15] There is no overall consensus among virtue theorists about what exactly this bundle includes. Yet, for the moral virtues, at least, there will be broad agreement about some of the main components that need to be identified and evaluated; see, for example, Morgan et al. (2017) on gratitude. Cf. Fowers et al. (2021).

[16] Various other reasons suggest themselves, although those will not be pursued here, such as a deep sense of loss among practitioners within the domain of professional ethics as it has become more formulaically code-and-rule based, compliance-oriented, and more divorced from any characterological concerns. See further in Chapter 7. Cf. Schwartz and Sharpe (2010); Arthur et al. (2021).

[17] McGrath (2022) notes that of references in PsycINFO that include 'virtue' in both title and subject heading, 85% have appeared since Peterson and Seligman's book came out in 2004.

flourishing (*eudaimonic*) life, and *phronesis* is then considered to encompass the wisdom an individual recruits to recognize what virtues are appropriate to a specific situation so that action conduces to that flourishing life. *Phronesis* is, in other words, central because *eudaimonia* has typically been seen to include the actualization of virtues of character and the correct balancing of those virtues within a well-rounded life. In a sense, then, 'flourishing' is the ultimate grounder of the new science of virtue, rather than '*phronesis*' or even 'character', just as it was for Aristotle.[18] However, 'flourishing' is a devilishly complex concept and will not be addressed further at this point, although we return to it obliquely when we explore the blueprint component of *phronesis* in Chapter 2[19] and in Chapter 12, where we hypothesize about the relationships between *phronesis* and *eudaimonia*.

Unfortunately, recent developments in the 'science of virtue' have not led to any single conceptual model of virtue, which suggests that the current state of virtue research is a 'patchwork' that lacks an agreed-upon 'framework' (Fowers et al., 2021; Kristjánsson, 2018a). Under threat from decades of psychological research indicating situational malleability of character traits (e.g., Doris, 2002) and, more recently, from the revival of a social intuitionist model that reduces the role of reason in moral decision-making to *post hoc* rationalizations (e.g., Haidt, 2001), the new character scientists in Psychology have tried out various models that are meant to avoid those misgivings. For example, some theorists emphasize cross-situational consistency as evidenced by 'density distributions' of virtue-relevant actions (Jayawickreme & Fleeson, 2017), while others insist on within-situation-type consistency only (Ng & Tay, 2020).

---

[18] Critics often claim that the flourishing at which *phronesis* aims is just the agent's own flourishing and that the 'standard model' of *phronesis* therefore represents little more than an exercise in rational egoism. However, the terms 'egoism' and 'altruism' carry little weight in neo-Aristotelian theory, or in antidotes to such a theory, because Aristotelian self-theory is deeply relational, such that our friends and close relatives count as our 'other selves' (Sherman, 1987). The idea of self-sacrifice is alien to the *phronesis* model not because *phronesis* never asks the individual to give up personal goods for the sake of others but because such 'sacrifice' (when guided by *phronesis*) is seen as self-enhancing rather than self-diminishing. From a neo-Aristotelian perspective, it is a disparagement of contemporary psychology that its inherent individualism has created the need for quasi-moral designators such as 'prosociality' and 'altruism', symptomatic of an overly restrictive conception of selfhood (cf. Fowers, Novak, Calder, & Sommer, 2022). We reiterate this point in note 6 in Chapter 4.

[19] For extensive accounts of flourishing, see Haybron (2016) and Kristjánsson (2020). As an example of how complex the concept of (Aristotelian) flourishing is, see this specification from Kristjánsson (2020, chap. 1): 'Human flourishing is the (relatively) unencumbered, freely chosen and developmentally progressive activity of a meaningful (subjectively purposeful and objectively valuable) life that actualizes satisfactorily an individual human being's natural capacities in areas of species-specific existential tasks at which human beings (as rational, social, moral and emotional agents) can most successfully excel.' For a psychological approach, see Fowers, Novak, Kiknadze, and Calder (2022b).

What the science of virtue needs is (1) a conception of character and virtue that is both theoretically sound and empirically testable (updating Aristotle where needed), (2) a developmental account of virtue that can ground educational interventions (either in the form of simply good upbringing or more formal educational programmes for schools and professional training), and (3) feasible strategies for measuring virtue and character development.[20] The nature of the character-and-virtue model needed depends on perceived priorities among requirements (1)–(3). For example, if the main focus is on the educational goals of (2), the model can be allowed to be fairly light on psychological theory and foreground more the relevant practical elements (see, e.g., the Jubilee Centre's Framework, 2022). If the model aspires, however, to make serious inroads into Psychology, two options present themselves. One is to integrate the model with some existing psychological theory. This is, for instance, what Wright et al. (2021) aim to do, by integrating their essentially neo-Aristotelian take on character and virtue with Fleeson and Jayawickreme's (2015) 'Whole Trait Theory'. The other option is to create a new model by synthesizing elements of neo-Aristotelianism with various (diverse) current empirical findings from developmental science, and from both Personality and Social Psychology. The latter option was pursued, for instance, by Fowers et al. (2021) in their creation of the STRIVE-4 model, according to which virtues are scalar traits that are role-sensitive, include situation-by-trait interactions and are related to important values that help constitute *eudaimonia*. All the variables in this model are then considered to require empirical validation.

There is no space here to explore all the possible general models of character and virtue and how those relate to *phronesis*. It suffices to note that the two prominent models mentioned above are meant to be compatible with a broad Aristotelian outlook, and both give pride of place to *phronesis*.[21] The STRIVE-4 model, for instance, is neo-Aristotelian in that it portrays virtues as acquired traits whose expressions are deeply contextualized in relations with situational factors and social roles. In its most recent iteration (Fowers et al., in press), the model incorporates *phronesis* to provide guidance in properly appraising situations, understanding which virtues are called for in concrete situations, recognizing how to harmonize various virtues, harmonizing

---

[20] As explained in their Introduction, for example, Wright et al. (2021) focus on (1) and (3). However, they consider (3) to be still in its infancy.

[21] Although the two models have much in common, they differ in how they view the personality–virtue relationship, with Wright et al. (2021) seeing virtues as aspects of Whole Trait Theory and Fowers et al. (in press) viewing virtues as traits that differ substantially from personality traits as typically defined. In addition, Wright et al. demur about the virtue–*eudaimonia* relationship, whereas Fowers et al. hypothesize that this relationship is positive and substantial.

reason and emotion in action, and how virtue expression will contribute to a flourishing life. For virtue enactment to be fitting, it requires the context sensitivity of *phronesis*.

1.3 A Neo-Aristotelian 'Standard Model' of *Phronesis*

It is now time to delve deeper into an Aristotelian conception of *phronesis*. There is already a large theoretical literature on practical wisdom in general (e.g., Russell, 2009) and the Aristotelian concept in particular (e.g., Curzer, 2012). However, most of that literature is either exegetical or purely philosophical in orientation, and hence outside of our immediate cross-disciplinary interests. What matters for present purposes is that in philosophy there has gradually evolved what Miller (2021) calls a neo-Aristotelian 'standard model of *phronesis*', which carries independent interest, whatever one may think of some of Aristotle's own controversial claims. This model owes a lot to Russell's (2009) meticulous analysis of the concept of practical wisdom, although the model he excavates is not meant to be exclusively Aristotelian. The various advocates and detractors of the 'standard model' do not always agree about its details. In this section, we elaborate upon some aspects of it about which there seems to be reasonable agreement. Our discussion here is highly selective; we only highlight aspects that we consider relevant to the subsequent development of our own version of the 'standard model'. That specific version does not materialize until Chapter 2, however, along with comparisons and contrasts with other variants of the 'standard model' (e.g., Wright et al., 2021), as well as other non-Aristotelian models (e.g., Grossmann, Weststrate, Ardelt et al., 2020), and a discussion of scepticism about all *phronesis* models (e.g., Lapsley, 2021): an exploration that continues through Chapters 3–4.

As a prelude, however, it is instructive to add a few more words about the use that philosophers (e.g., Russell, 2009), as well as some of the psychologists engaged in the new science of virtue (e.g., Fowers et al., 2021), typically make of Aristotelian theory, to avoid misunderstandings. Some have worried that invoking Aristotle leads to an argument from authority, or 'special pleading' (Lapsley, 2016; McGrath & Brown, 2020). We suggest that this worry is mostly unfounded. Today's Aristotle-inspired virtue ethicists and character educationists (e.g., Annas, 2011; Kristjánsson, 2015) are mostly neo-Aristotelian reconstructors, drawn to Aristotle's theory precisely because of Aristotle's naturalistic method, according to which all moral theorizing needs to be answerable to empirical research and hence constantly updated. What may create the impression of Aristotelian theory as authoritative is that the theory is often treated as a placeholder for 'common sense'. This is both because Aristotle was, so to speak, the first common-sense philosopher, and because his theories have become so influential over the centuries that they have themselves informed common sense, such that today's plain persons are often, to a significant degree, 'proto-Aristotelians', as noted in Section 1.1. Aristotle's own conceptualizations, for instance of *phronesis*, thus serve a function in neo-Aristotelian theories as the 'first word' that should not be departed from unless a demonstrably better alternative is found, although it is never the 'last word'.

A neo-Aristotelian approach

We consider our development of the 'standard model' in this book to be *neo-Aristotelian* rather than *Aristotelian* for four reasons. First, although Aristotle famously discussed *phronesis* at significant length in the *Nicomachean Ethics*, he did not do so in the detailed way that we approach this topic, much less in a way that is amenable to contemporary measurement and empirical research. Developing a model of *phronesis* that can be studied empirically is one of the primary aims of this book. Second, because of his excessive deference to the views of 'the many' and 'the wise', where those agreed, Aristotle included some prevalent but problematic opinions in his ethics, such as about the inferiority of women, slaves, manual labourers, and non-Greeks. These opinions are unacceptable today, as well as unnecessary for his ethics. Therefore, we have expunged those opinions from our appropriation of his philosophy. Third, because Aristotle recognized that he did not have the last word on ethical questions and that ethics must always be contextualized historically and culturally, it is up to authors to adapt his philosophy to fit the contemporary norms and expectations of their time and place. We do not see our 'neo-' version here as unduly relativistic, however, because we expect ethical formulations to have a family resemblance to one another, but that is a very large topic that we cannot address in a book focused on *phronesis* rather than on the universalism–localism debate about virtue.[22] Fourth, we do not prioritize *sophia* (wisdom related to unchanging matters) over *phronesis* (wisdom about tangible and everyday matters) as Aristotle seems to do in Book 10 of the *Nicomachean Ethics* (1985).

---

[22] For that debate, see various chapters in the volume edited by Darnell and Kristjánsson (2021).

Differentia of *phronesis*

Although Aristotle is not the only ancient philosopher to have discussed intellectual virtues, the distinctions he made between different modes of thinking and the respective intellectual virtues have proven so durable that they have served as the starting point of almost all historical accounts of intellectual virtues. Aristotle (1985) analysed various modes of thinking but let us focus presently on the three main categories. One is contemplation (*theoria*) about abstract and unchanging things, such as god (in Aristotle's deistic sense) and the laws of physics. The intellectual virtue representing excellence in this area is theoretical wisdom (*sophia*), which operates mostly at the vantage point of secure distance from practical concerns. It speculates about issues that would nowadays be referred to as 'metaphysical'. Thales, the 'first philosopher', had an abundance of theoretical wisdom, but he lacked practical wisdom (Aristotle, 1985, p. 158 [1141b3–6]), as witnessed by well-known anecdotes about his awkwardness.

Diametrically opposed to *theoria* is *poiesis*: thinking and acting in the area of production. The intellectual virtue in this area is *techné*: excellence or refined practical skill in making things. While expertise in *techné* is often straightforward and codifiable (you just follow a predetermined plan to succeed, for example, producing a standard *crème brûlée*), some areas of *techné* are contingently (if not necessarily) uncodifiable, for example the skills of a ship captain, an army general, or a teacher (Dunne, 2022; Kristjánsson, 2007, chap. 11).

Placed in between *sophia* and *techné*, but significantly closer to the latter, is the virtue of *phronesis*, operating in the sphere of *praxis*: of (thinking about) action, which is about 'doing' as distinct from 'making'. Although Aristotle likes to compare *phronesis* to a skill, such as playing the flute, in particular regarding how it is picked up (namely experientially) and internalized (through repeated practice), he remains clear on the distinctions between the two. One key difference is that the excellence of *techné* lies in the product or outcome of actions, but the excellence of *phronesis* lies in the process of thinking and acting. Moreover, unlike a skill, *phronesis* cannot be misused (Russell, 2009, p. 17).[23]

---

[23] Some have revised the concept of skill to make it a capacity to seek constitutive or intrinsically valuable ends, and thereby see virtues and *phronesis* as skills (Annas, 2011; Stichter, 2018). However, we find Aristotle's distinction between skills and virtues to be valid and useful, so we will not follow these philosophers' revision of skills. See further in Chapter 2.

To complicate matters, Aristotle describes *phronesis* as a subspecies of a more general cognitive capacity that he calls 'cleverness' or 'calculation' (*deinotes*): the intellectual virtue of being able to figure out the proper actions 'that tend to promote whatever goal is assumed and to achieve it. If, then, the goal is fine, cleverness is praiseworthy, and if the goal is base, cleverness is unscrupulousness; hence both [*phronetic*] and unscrupulous people are called clever' (Aristotle, 1985, p. 169 [1144a23–8]).[24] As distinct from general *deinotes*, *phronesis* only concerns issues that fall under the moral sphere, which for Aristotle (who did not have a modern concept of 'the moral', recall note 3) meant the sphere of ethical character.

Preliminary explications of the 'standard model'

It will be instructive to begin by clarifying a few concepts.

Functions and components

In the standard neo-Aristotelian model, the task of *phronesis* is complex (Tiberius & Swartwood, 2011), and a common suggestion from the literature is that it has at least three components. First, in the constitutive function of single-virtue-application, *phronesis* helps the (budding) *phronimos* to spot situations where the relevant virtue is required and how to execute it. For example, courage is the virtue that is appropriate to situations involving risk. Second, the integrative function of conflicting-virtues arbitration allows the *phronimos* to integrate different virtues that seem to come into conflict in the same situation, such as being courageously generous. This arbitration can also lead to enacting one virtue that is a higher priority and in unresolvable conflict with a second virtue (e.g., mercy versus justice). Only through *phronesis* do the virtues become a 'package deal' (Russell, 2009, p. 26). Third, the function of emotion regulation builds on emotional dispositions cultivated through habituation, in that the *phronimos* re-evaluates those early dispositions critically, infusing them with reason and justification (Curzer, 2017). Others have added a fourth, the function of 'deep understanding' (Tiberius & Swartwood, 2011) of the human condition, to this mix: more specifically, an understanding of what constitutes human flourishing as an irreducibly moral activity. We have followed that lead and refined it in our detailed

---

[24] Given the practical, experiential nature of both *deinotes* and *phronesis*, Hursthouse (2006, p. 298) advises us not to be taken aback by the realization that some of the wicked (e.g., 'successful conmen') may be better at deliberating cleverly than those with mere habituated virtue.

four-componential model, explained in Chapter 2.[25] However, our elaborations of those components there go well beyond—and will be more controversial than—the sparse detail typically on offer in the 'standard model'.

Specificity and individualization

There seems to be consensus among psychologists that wisdom is context-sensitive and perspectival (e.g., Grossmann, Weststrate, Ardelt et al., 2020). Here the explanatory power of the 'standard model of *phronesis*' is particularly strong, given Aristotle's own emphasis on the individualization and context-dependence of all virtue as relative to individual constitutions, social roles, and developmental levels. Let us focus here on individualization because the contextualization of virtue is already widely recognized. The following four examples illustrate individualization in Aristotle: (1) Following role models is a virtue for young people whereas adults have less of a need to emulate role models.[26] (2) Large-scale generosity and great-heartedness (*megalopsychia*) are virtues for people blessed with unusually abundant material resources but not for ordinary folks. (3) Temperance in eating is not the same for a professional athlete as for a novice. (4) From an educational perspective, a sports coach will not impose the same training regime on all trainees.[27] There is thus no *one* best way across individuals to be, say, virtuously generous as opposed to be being stingy or wasteful. It all depends on one's individual circumstance and the specific context. This does not apply only to representations of individual virtues. How different virtues cluster and gain greater expression and dominance in each individual's life—yet being constrained by the *phronimos*' overarching arbitration of the virtues—depends on the individuality of the virtuous person. This emphasis on the particularities of individuals and situations fits well with current psychological models of characterological development (Lerner, 2019). We return to some of those insights in Chapter 11.

---

[25] We sometimes refer to the different features of *phronesis* as 'components' and sometimes as 'functions'. While the terminology of components will be more familiar to philosophers and functions to psychologists, we mostly use these terms interchangeably in what follows. The reason why we retain both in the text is that 'components' sounds a more felicitous expression to describe different features of a single concept, whereas 'functions' fits better to describe different psychological tasks that *phronesis* is meant to perform.

[26] When Aristotle says that emulation is not a virtuous emotion for adults, he seems to be focusing his attention on fully developed *phronimoi* who need no further learning from exemplarity. We disagree with him on this point; in our view even the most developed human beings keep learning from role models and friends throughout life.

[27] For a fuller discussion and various textual references to Aristotle, see Kristjánsson (2022b, chap. 4).

1.4 Alternative *Phronesis* Concepts

Readers may have gained the impression from the preceding discussion that the current *phronesis* discourses, insofar as those are seen to hark back to Aristotelian sources, are simply variations on the 'standard model' and that the only remaining work to be undertaken in this book is to develop the arguably 'best' version of the 'standard model' among many. However, this is slightly misleading, not least if we examine the most extensive of the discourses currently taking place about *phronesis*, and we will identify three such alternatives: a version of *phronesis* presented by MacIntyre, a postmodern version, and Williams's concern about ethical filters.[28]

MacIntyre's *phronesis*

The first alternative *phronesis* concept draws on MacIntyre's (1981) view of practical wisdom as excellence in deliberation within human 'practices'. This view is especially prominent in Professional Ethics (e.g., relating to medicine, business, nursing, teaching, social work, policing, and the army). While paying lip service to Aristotle, most of that discourse is not about the 'standard model' at all and, as we argue below, hardly about a recognizably Aristotelian concept.[29] We will not be able to avoid some engagement with those alternative *phronesis* concepts in our chapter on *phronesis* in Professional Ethics (Chapter 7), but to motivate our decision to see them as mostly outside the remit of the present work, we need to say something about them here at the outset.

MacIntyre defined a 'practice' as 'any coherent and complex form of socially established cooperative human activity through which goods internal to that form of activity are realised' (1981, p. 175). This is quite different from an Aristotelian *praxis* (the sphere in which *phronesis* is enacted), because 'practice' here presumably includes a wider range of intrinsically valuable activities than would fall under the sphere of the ethical. To give an example that fit within a MacIntyrean definition, but not a neo-Aristotelian one, consider

---

[28] We postpone discussion of a recent Socratic/Platonic model until Chapter 2 (De Caro et al., 2021).

[29] It may seem churlish to reject the label 'neo-Aristotelian' for the concepts that we explain below. For instance, regarding the first one, the MacIntyrean concept, MacIntyre himself considers any departures from Aristotle in *After Virtue* as 'a strengthening rather than a weakening of the case for a generally Aristotelian standpoint' (1984, p. 197). We do not claim any monopoly on the term 'neo-Aristotelian'. However, MacIntyre's concept is clearly not the same as Aristotle's, and it is not neo-Aristotelian in the sense of constituting a mere variation on the 'standard (neo-Aristotelian) model' of *phronesis*.

the complex decisions by a team of cancer specialists on the mixture of cancer drugs to prescribe to an individual patient, depending on her constitution and condition.[30] Such decisions are not unambiguously *phronetic* in character.

More specifically, in Aristotle, *praxis* is an exclusively 'moral' domain in the discrete Aristotelian sense of having to do with the development and exhibition of moral character. MacIntyre's notion is wider than Aristotle's in incorporating paradigmatic examples of what Aristotle would specify as *techné*; indeed, it seems to include all complex public projects with socially defined points and internal goods. It is narrower, however, in excluding individual conduct and self-development that does not have socially relevant repercussions. So, for example, while MacIntyre will say that the reflective decision of the wise farmer about complex, uncodifiable farming issues (which need have nothing to do with the ethics of farming) can best be understood along the architectonic of *phronesis*; he will however, presumably, refrain from categorizing the deliberation of Robinson Crusoe on a desert island, about whether or not to exhibit temperance in eating, as an instantiation of a *phronetic* activity. MacIntyre's concept is also less universalist than Aristotle's is and more sociological or Hegelian (as most, if not all, practices are historically and culturally conditioned). The incentive in Professional Ethics for preferring MacIntyre to Aristotle often seems to be that of making sense of the uncodifiability of a range of professional activities that do not, strictly speaking, fall under the category of ethics. Yet this departure was never necessary, in our view, because Aristotle already had at his disposal, as noted earlier, a subconcept of *techné* that allows for uncodifiability,[31] for instance the expertise of a ship's captain, an army general, or a doctor.[32]

---

[30] This is what draws professional ethicists specifically to MacIntyre, because they are now able to say that their whole domain of study—say teaching, medicine, or business—is a 'practice', with *phronesis* as its characteristic (or at least ideal) mode of thinking (see, e.g., Beadle & Moore, 2018, on business). MacIntyre himself completely baffled his followers, however, long after writing *After Virtue* (1981), by claiming that teaching essentially involves *techné* rather than *phronesis* because it aims at external rather than internal goods, namely student learning (MacIntyre & Dunne, 2002, pp. 8–9); and he has made similar deflationary remarks about business. One could even say that MacIntyre himself is not a 'MacIntyrean' about professional ethics in the same sense as his followers, whose views we scrutinize in more detail in Chapter 7. Paradoxically, therefore, the person most immediately responsible for the retrieval of *phronesis* research within professional ethics, MacIntyre, appears to have steered the discourse off course in a number of ways.

[31] We strongly recommend Dunne's (1993; 2022) writings about this subconcept, which he calls Aristotle's 'unofficial' *techné* concept. In fact, those inclined to a MacIntyrean position would do well to study Dunne's version, which is in many ways more subtle and nuanced than MacIntyre's. That said, Dunne goes further in the direction of moral particularism and perspectivism than the present authors would accept (see, e.g., Kristjánsson, 2007, chap. 11).

[32] In her—in many ways ground-breaking—doctoral thesis on medical *phronesis*, Jameel (2022) nevertheless prefers to couch her understanding in terms of MacIntyrean *phronesis*; her point being that in medicine, all major decisions concern the patient's overall flourishing (indeed, often questions of life and death) and hence inevitably draw on the ethical character of the practitioner. This point is worth taking seriously, although Aristotle himself was content with specifying medicine as a *techné*, and we return to it in Chapter 7.

Postmodern *phronesis*

More inimical to the task of reviving the Aristotelian concept of *phronesis* has been what we referred to above as a 'postmodern impulse'. That impulse is evidenced in accounts of *phronesis* reducing it to some sort of mysterious intuitive artistry that does not admit of any truths and falsehoods and, in the end, comes down to nothing more than individual subjective discretion (or even aesthetic appreciation).[33] On those accounts, *phronesis* is a fuzzy and indeterminate concept, referring to an elusive capacity 'to think on one's feet [. . .] experiment [. . .] and let one's logos hang loose' (Caputo, 1993, p. 101). Kemmis (2012), who is perhaps the most coherent representative of this view, talks about *phronesis* as belonging to an enigmatic 'negative space for knowledge' (2012, p. 155), rather than being a construct that can be given a positive, objective specification.

What goes amiss in these postmodern interpretations is that Aristotle was a moral realist, believing that *phronetic* ethical judgement admits of true or false answers (1985, p. 151 [1139b12–13]). For him, such judgements do not evaluate subjectively an independent realm of facts but rather describe an objectively existing realm of ethical truths. The perfect *phronimos*, described in Aristotle's *Politics* as 'a god among men' (1944, p. 241 [1284a10–11]), and the ideal ruler in a utopian monarchy would always know how to get things right in ethically tricky or dilemmatic situations.[34] Thus, such situations are not essentially uncodifiable. However, because no perfect *phronimos* of this kind exists in the real world, and because of how messy that world is in terms of varied situational contexts and individual dispositions, we can only aspire to *phronetic* best guesses about the ultimate objective truths. Hence, in the world in which we happen to live, *phronesis* is contingently uncodifiable. One way to put this is to say that *phronesis* signals the epistemological acknowledgement of a tenuous access to an ontological reality that nonetheless exists. To be sure, the theorists who seem to wish to fetishize moral uncertainty and ambivalence in the name of *phronesis* would complain that this realist assumption betrays a 'hope for another version of *techné*' (Kemmis, 2012, p. 153) in the ethical sphere. However, what they fail to appreciate is that the main

---

[33] As a helpful antidote to this anti-intellectualism, we recommend Russell's sobering insights (2009, p. 23) about how *phronesis* 'turns out to be nothing mysterious' but is simply a settled ability that is in many ways analogous to various technical competences representative of expertise. For a clever stab at dispelling the myth of a mysterious capacity underlying expertise in general, see Pálsson and Durrenberger (1990). For a very different, and eye-opening, take on the aesthetic dimensions of Aristotle's own concept of *phronesis*, however, see Brewer (2021).

[34] In some cases, it could of course turn out that two options have exactly the same value or disvalue.

variable distinguishing *phronesis* from *techné* was never, for Aristotle, that of uncodifiability. As already noted repeatedly above, he made space for areas of (contingently) uncodifiable *techné* also. The crucial difference lies rather in the products of *techné* only being extrinsically valuable whereas the products of *phronesis* are intrinsically valuable (in terms of the activity itself, independent of further external benefits for, say, prosociality or favourable business outcomes).

It is worth noting here, however, that one of the motivations behind the postmodern concept seems to be to account for the apparently arational spontaneity of much of moral decision-making—by reducing it to some sort of mystical intuitive aha moments. In that sense, the postmodern concept bears a certain academic resemblance to a dual-process social intuitionist model of moral decision-making (Haidt, 2001). However, the insights of the neo-Aristotelian 'standard model' are far removed from this recently fashionable form of intuitionism also (Kristjánsson, 2022a). While *phronetic* decision-making will wind up being automatic to a large extent in a mature person encountering familiar situations, this is not because reason has been circumvented by arational, intuitive emotional thrusts, but rather because the *phronimos* has, through precedents and prospection, anticipated (most often unconsciously) the proper reactions to future scenarios. Our affective system seems to be constantly active in the business of evaluating and adjudicating alternatives—and in doing so, it draws on previous experiences, stored implicit knowledge, and important aims. It thus recruits the human capacities for reflection, simulation, and metacognition. What is more, it does not only do so at crunch moments when we meet with unexpected quandaries, rather more like the Google search engine, it prepares 'answers' to 'possible questions' long before we ask them—by processing all the information that is already in the system: metabolizing the past to simulate possible futures (Railton, 2016, pp. 45–6). We will not be allocating further space in this book to responding to Jonathan Haidt and his followers, as we consider there to be more serious psychological challenges to our version of the neo-Aristotelian 'standard model' worthy of our responses (Chapters 3–4).

Williams's worry about ethical filters

We will end by mentioning briefly a view that is in a way internal to Aristotelian Virtue Ethics, but which betrays, in our view, an underappreciation of the role of *phronesis*. This is the view, famously espoused by Bernard

Williams (1981), that Virtue Ethics distinguishes itself from both deontology and utilitarianism by not requiring 'one thought too many'. Those two latter moral theories fail, in Williams's view, an adequacy test for a similar reason: by compelling us to subject our obvious natural choice to prioritize the needs of a close friend (or a loved one) over those of a stranger, in times of moral danger, to a theoretical decision procedure before coming up with the 'right' reaction. Such requirements of reflective calculation rob us, according to Williams, of psycho-moral reasons to live at all by attacking the source of any integrity-grounding prime motivation that makes us tick. The decision procedure required by these two moral theories—be it the categorical imperative or the utility calculus—inserts a *filter* (which Williams seems to think of as an artificial gadget or fetish) between the natural moral motivation of any normal person and the decision to act on it. But this interjects 'one thought too many' into the moral reaction mechanism and fetishizes it in the service of a psychologically overbearing theory.

Now, Williams is obviously right in the sense that there are certain kinds of considerations that the *phronimos* does not need to dwell upon whereas, say, the utilitarian chooser does: for example, demands about the maximization of overall value for humankind in each moral decision (Kristjánsson, 2022b, chap. 4). However, this does not mean that there is no 'filter' between the virtues and the eventual moral decision of the *phronimos* and that it just comes automatically to her. It is worth acknowledging—although this is not the crux of Williams's argument—that Aristotelian Virtue Ethics tells a more detailed developmental story of how moral decisions solidify into habitual responses, so that the *phronimos* does not need to go through the same *phronetic* process each time a similar decision comes her way. Yet the deontologist and the utilitarian must be expected to develop some habitual and spontaneous responses also; otherwise, their lives would be impossible to live, as they would be spending too much time on constant repeated deliberations. The main point that Williams is making is much more radical than this: namely, that the virtue ethical agent can make do without any filter and can act effortlessly and un-interruptedly on a moral motivation emanating from a virtue like friendship.

In our view, Aristotle blows away any such illusions in the *Eudemian Ethics* when he says that those who unreflectively 'give everything' to a friend 'are good-for-nothing people' (1935, p. 433 [1244a17–19]). So even in the case of such an important moral virtue as friendship, there is no justifiable unreflective decision. In the simplest of cases, say, ingenuous childhood friendship, we may be able to act quite spontaneously on the needs of a close friend. However, as soon as the situation becomes more complicated, the decision process slows down, as *phronesis* needs time to kick in and evaluate the situation. Do the needs of the friend conflict with those of another friend, or perhaps a large group of strangers? Furthermore, once we are acting through the mediation of *phronetic* rather than just habituated virtue, the filter becomes much more demanding, as it requires not only that we comply with the demands of the most immediate virtue relevant to the given situation (in this case, friendship) but that it also takes account of claims proper to other virtues—say, compassion and justice (cf. Müller, 2004).

Friendship as a simple habituated childhood virtue may be compatible with your helping the friend for a foolish cause. However, from the perspective of *phronesis*-guided virtue, the critical dimensions of the virtue of friendship are not determined by the architectonic of that particular virtue only but also by the demands of other virtues. All these different requirements need to be synthesized through *phronesis*, and although that synthesis may appear to proceed fairly quickly and reliably in the case of an experienced moral agent, to get things right, the agent still needs to apply the filter of *phronesis* correctly to the concrete situation. There is no room in Aristotelian theory for a *phronetic* decision that is, in principle, unfiltered (see further in Kristjánsson, 2022b, chap. 3).

Phronesis therefore imports an additional thought into the decision process. Whether that counts as 'one thought too many' depends on whether we consider it to undermine the integrity of the moral agent to have to subject every motivation derived from a moral virtue to the arbitration of a separate intellectual capacity. Williams clearly thinks so, but we do not agree. *Phronesis*-based Aristotelian Virtue Ethics requires an extra thought here, but we deem it to be an invaluable thought, not one 'too many'. This means, however, that there is no essential *structural* difference of the kind Williams envisages between Virtue Ethics and the other two major contenders for the moral theory of choice: deontology and utilitarianism. The choice between them depends on our *substantive* assessment of the nature of the filter they propose between motivation and decision, not on the presence or absence of a filter.

We engaged in this brief detour into 'departures' from the neo-Aristotelian 'standard model' as a reminder that there are differing concepts of *phronesis* swirling around in the academic literature. Despite the preponderance of alternative conceptions in the current Professional Ethics literature in particular, we will leave those out of further reckoning until Chapter 7.

1.5 Summary of Subsequent Chapters

Some readers like an introductory chapter to contain a detailed roadmap of what is yet to come in a book. For the benefit of those, we summarize the following chapters below. For those who do not want 'spoilers', we suggest skipping this section and going straight to Chapter 2.

Chapter 2: A Neo-Aristotelian *Phronesis* Model and Some Philosophical Alternatives

In this chapter, we explain the need to advance a 'standard neo-Aristotelian model' in light of contemporary research in Psychology and Philosophy. We detail and argue for a four-componential neo-Aristotelian *phronesis* model that is formulated through the integration of neo-Aristotelian philosophical understandings and the best available moral psychological research and measurement. This conceptualization allows for empirical as well as theoretical scrutiny. The chapter ends by looking at other philosophical accounts of *phronesis* (e.g., De Caro et al., 2021; Wright et al., 2021) and scepticism (e.g., that expressed by Miller, 2021) about the philosophical need for a *phronesis* model.

Chapter 3: The History of Wisdom Research in Psychology and the New Common Model

Wisdom research in Psychology has soared in recent years, culminating in a new 'common [consensual] wisdom model' (Grossmann, Weststrate, Ardelt et al., 2020) that has brought the discourse to a new level of precision and nuance. Their short definition of 'wisdom' is the 'morally-grounded application of metacognition to reasoning and problem-solving'. Although the new common model aims successfully at integrating common denominators of the wisdom construct from previously diverging theorists, various sceptical and heterodox voices remain amongst wisdom researchers. The two primary threads of disagreement with the new model seem to be (1) its neglect of emotionality and (2) the vagueness of its depiction of the morality inherent in wisdom. Although the common model is, in many ways, a culmination of previous theory and research on wisdom, it remains just a first step and more conceptual work is needed. In general, this chapter gives readers an overview of the current state of play of wisdom research in Psychology since the time of the Berlin Model, and the positionality of the new common model.

Chapter 4: Comparing Our *Phronesis* Model with the New 'Common Model' and Other Psychological Alternatives

This chapter compares the Aristotelian *phronesis* model, developed in Chapter 2, with the new common model explained in Chapter 3. The former offers a philosophically grounded, psychologically practicable model of wise (*phronetic*) decision-making that conceives of morality in realist terms and sees moral considerations as reason-informed. It incorporates the emotional and motivational aspects of *phronesis* by explicating two main sources of moral motivation, one emerging from specific virtues and one that emerges from the blueprint function of *phronesis*; how those motivations are synergistically integrated; and how the blueprint function is gradually refined in the light of experiential knowledge. It also provides an account of the balancing of reason and emotion. In a similar vein, the new common model makes significant progress in the Psychology of Wisdom by circumscribing the sort of wisdom under scrutiny (as practical, nonabstract), and by foregrounding the role of moral aspirations as grounding the perspectival metacognition in this approach to wisdom. However, the venture of the common model into the moral realm goes awry by lacking vital substantive content. We argue in this chapter the Aristotelian *phronesis* model offers a more detailed and overt take on a number of wisdom considerations and variables; and at least in the context of wise moral decision-making, it carries substantial explanatory power *qua* theoretical construct beyond the common model. The chapter ends by exploring why other constructs in Psychology, such as metacognition, do not render *phronesis* redundant, as well as responding to Lapsley's (2021) *phronesis* scepticism.

Chapter 5: The 'Gappiness Problem' in Moral Psychology and the Relevance of *Phronesis*

This chapter has two aims. First, to offer a critical review of the literatures on two well-known single-component solutions to the proverbial problem of a gap between moral knowledge and moral action: moral identity and moral emotions. Second, to take seriously the lessons from the rising interest in Aristotle-inspired Virtue Ethics and character development within the social sciences: lessons that may indicate that the development of *phronesis* bridges the gap in question. The idea of a neo-Aristotelian multi-component solution to the 'gappiness problem' invites comparisons with another multi-component candidate, the neo-Kohlbergian four-component model, with which it shares at least surface similarities. We argue for the theoretical uniqueness of a *phronesis*-based multi-component model vis-à-vis the neo-Kohlbergian one. Our main conclusion is that the neo-Aristotelian model holds significant promise of solving the 'gappiness problem'.

Chapter 6: A New Measure of *Phronesis*: Empirical Findings

This chapter describes two empirical 'proof of concept' studies (one conducted with an adult sample and the other with an adolescent sample) that evaluated our new neo-Aristotelian *phronesis* model via a *phronesis* assessment battery based on the best available validated measures in empirical Moral Psychology to approximate the components of the *phronesis* model. In both studies, the hypothesized *phronesis* model fitted the data well. The four first-order components were found to be structurally related to a predicted second-order latent *phronesis* variable, and, promisingly, this variable was strongly associated with a prosocial behaviour variable. Finally, some implications of these findings are elicited, and future research steps are charted.

Chapter 7: *Phronesis* in Professional (Medical) Ethics

Phronesis has become a buzzword in contemporary Professional Ethics. Yet the use of this single term conceals many significant conceptual controversies, based on divergent philosophical assumptions. This chapter explores three of those divergences: on *phronesis* as universalist or relativist, generalist or particularist, and natural/painless or painful/ambivalent. It also, fourthly, explores further the tensions between MacIntyre's and Aristotle's concepts on *phronesis*. Turning the lens specifically to medical ethics (as a case in point), the chapter offers those binaries as a possible analytical framework to classify accounts of *phronesis* within medical ethics.

Chapter 8: *Phronesis* and the Civic Virtues

While there is renewed interest in *phronesis* in educational circles, *phronesis* is almost exclusively discussed in the context of adjudicating between conflicting moral virtues, not between moral and civic virtues, or between civic virtues internally. Although *phronesis* is a standard topic within Character Education, it is rarely invoked in the Civic Education literature. This chapter begins by unpacking the association between the civic and the moral virtues in Aristotle's writings and drawing some relevant lessons about how to alleviate the tension between them. The chapter then shows how the civic is (teleo) logically prior to the moral, while secondary in a developmental and analytical sense. The ultimate aim of the chapter is to shed light on the relationship between *phronesis* (practical wisdom) and the civic virtues: a hitherto underdeveloped topic.

Chapter 9: Collective *Phronesis*

Most of the discourses on *phronesis* treat it as a personal strength of character, possessed by an individual. But is it possible to widen its scope to the collective level? The aim of this chapter is to provide an overview of various discourses relevant to developing a construct of collective *phronesis*, with implications for professional practice. Aristotle made some intriguing remarks about *phronesis* at the collective level in his *Politics* that encourage elaboration, and some revisionary thinking about neo-Aristotelian *phronesis*. The lion's share of this chapter is, therefore, devoted to making sense of Aristotle's somewhat unsystematic remarks and the lessons we can draw from them about collective *phronesis* and Professional Ethics education.

Chapter 10: Difficult Decisions and *Post-phronetic* Pain

Phronesis oversees and adjudicates moral decisions in various difficult, dilemmatic situations. But what happens after a *phronetic* decision has been made? The aim of this chapter is to refute the standard assumption in orthodox Aristotelian virtue theory that a fully *phronetic* decision is always characterized by psychological unity and freedom from ambivalent emotions, without eliciting any *post-phronetic* pain (PPP). Yet the presence of nonoptimal emotions after a *phronetic* decision creates a mystery for Aristotelian virtue theory. We then examine three unsuccessful attempts to defang the PPP puzzle. The fourth section delineates the nature of PPP (when it occurs) by arguing that it comprises several distinguishable emotions of moral sadness, and frankly acknowledging the imperfections of human reasoners. The final section probes several neo-Aristotelian resources for reconceptualizing PPP as beneficial to a certain extent.

Chapter 11: Educating *Phronesis*

This chapter begins by charting the vagaries of educational discourses on *phronesis*, and by eliciting some developmental insights from Aristotle, along with their shortcomings. Mindful that making progress in the educational study of *phronesis* is not only a conceptual or philosophical endeavour but also an empirical one, the chapter then elicits and illustrates several testable hypotheses about the development of *phronesis* from the Aristotelian and neo-Aristotelian literatures. A serviceable conceptualization (e.g., the one introduced in Chapter 2) will need to offer ways to evaluate the educational credibility of each hypothesis in real life, rather than just serving as a new philosophical plaything. We then review the educational literature on *phronesis*. We finally explore some lessons learned from a study of a *phronesis* intervention for Police Science students.

Chapter 12: Concluding Remarks

This chapter offers some concluding and complementary reflections on the various hypotheses and suggestions made in this book. Special attention is paid to evaluating the incremental value of the neo-Aristotelian model proposed and to the role of *phronesis* in the good life. Final observations are offered about the fruitfulness of the radically cross-disciplinary approach adopted in this work. Comparisons are made with recent efforts at charting the terrain of virtue research, for instance by Fowers et al. (2021) in *Perspectives on Psychological Science*, later in *Virtue Science* (in press), and Wright et al. in *Understanding Virtue* (2021). The concluding section addresses the question of where *phronesis* research should ideally head next.

2
A Neo-Aristotelian *Phronesis* Model and Some Philosophical Alternatives

2.1 Elaborating the 'Standard Model' of *Phronesis*

The aim of this chapter is to develop a new substantive neo-Aristotelian *phronesis* model (APM for short) out of the basics of the 'standard model' introduced in Chapter 1. The present discussion will focus on the philosophical content and credentials of the APM and juxtapose the model with some philosophical alternatives. In Chapters 3–4, however, we place the APM in the context of psychological accounts of (practical) wisdom. It is not until Chapter 5 that it becomes fully clear what we hope this new model can achieve—namely, to bridge the proverbial gap in Moral Psychology between knowing the good and doing it—and in Chapter 6 we chart some apparent achievements along those lines.[1] Chronologically speaking, our personal explorations began with the considerations spelled out in Chapter 5. However, the most logical way to present an argument is not always the chronological one, and we deem it more instructive to present here at outset the proposed content of the APM before delving into the uses that can (hopefully) be made of it.

To recap some of what already emerged in Chapter 1, Aristotle's *phronesis* is an intellectual virtue (virtue of thought[2]) that serves the purpose of living well by monitoring and guiding the moral virtues. Building on emotional dispositions cultivated through early years habituation, *phronesis* re-evaluates those dispositions critically, allowing them to truly 'share in reason', and it provides the agent with proper justifications for them. In addition to latching itself on to every 'habituated' moral virtue, and infusing it with systematic reason, the function of *phronesis*, as 'a state grasping the truth', is to 'deliberate finely' about the relative weight of competing values, actions, and emotions in the

---

[1] We say 'apparent' here because Chapter 6 just presents findings from proof-of-concept studies rather than results of comprehensive empirical research into the APM.
[2] We need to understand 'intellectual' fairly broadly here, as *phronesis* includes, for example, perceptual discernment, along with deliberation (*bouleusis*), see below.

context of the question of 'what is good or bad for a human being' in the sense of 'what promotes living well in general'. A person who has acquired *phronesis* has thus, inter alia, the wisdom to adjudicate the relative weight of different virtues in conflict situations and to reach a measured decision (*prohairesis*) about best courses of (re)action (Aristotle, 1985, pp. 153, 154, 159, 164, 171 [1140a26–9, 1140b4–6, 1141b30–1, 1143a8–9, 1144b30–2]).[3] We know further from Aristotle's text about *phronesis*, and the more general contours of his virtue ethics, that the 'best' course is the one that tracks the 'golden mean' of an individual virtue—hits the bull's eye like an archer's arrow—or finds the medial overall way of reacting when there is a conflict between virtues. The briefest definition of '*phronesis*', on Aristotle's own understanding, could thus be *excellence in ethical decision-making about the 'mean'*. It is precisely *phronesis* that is meant to secure the consistency of a person's character, because *phronesis* acts (ideally) as the organizational principle of character as a whole, rather than just regulating individual virtues in specific contexts (Kamtekar, 2004).

The 'standard model' and its critics

Exegetical disputes among Aristotelian scholars notwithstanding,[4] as well as various differences within the neo-Aristotelian camp, Miller (2021) is correct in identifying a consensus on a neo-Aristotelian 'standard model'. However, his specification of it is sketchy: simply stating that *phronesis* is 'a character trait which is distinct psychologically from the moral virtues, but which is necessary for them to count as virtues' (p. 53). De Caro et al. (2018, p. 291) had earlier proposed a very similar definition of what they call the 'standard Aristotelian view', except adding the consideration that the moral virtues must be 'shaped by *phronesis* itself'. Although these characterizations of the 'standard model' are even more sketchy than the one we proffered in Section 1.3—which assumed, among other things, that *phronesis* comprises distinct if inter-related *components* or *functions*—these skeletal definitions still suffice

---

[3] We have sometimes tried to convey the nature of *phronesis* to students by talking about its four 'Ds': discernment, deliberation, discretion, and decision. While catchy, this string of words does not quite capture the components of *phronesis* as we analyse them in Section 2.2. Another folksy way to convey the role of *phronesis* to students is by comparing it to that of a conductor of a symphony orchestra standing on a pedestal above the instrument players and making sure that the sound coming from the orchestra is harmonious. However, this analogy may be criticized for invoking a homunculus fallacy; *phronesis* is obviously not a 'little person' inside the agent's head.

[4] Some of those become apparent in the discussion in Section 2.3 about the blueprint component of *phronesis*. However, we steer as far away as possible in this book from disputes that are mainly of philological or exegetical interest.

to help us distinguish between two sources of moral failings. The *primary* moral failing is that of a lack of individual virtue called for in the relevant circumstances—say, courage for a situation of danger—in a person lacking wholly in this trait as a habituated virtue or having it insufficiently developed. The *secondary* moral failing is that of a person with some degree of the given habituated virtue but lacking the required *phronesis* to apply it correctly in the situation, or not knowing how to balance it with other competing virtues in the same situation. This secondary kind of failing can be even more devastating than the first, as the apparent possession of habituated virtue gives the agent more agential power and, at the same time, more scope for disastrous error. For example, as Rorty (1986, p. 153) points out, merely habituated courage may be a very dangerous virtue when it is not measured by its ends, bounded by other moral virtues, and subjected to the checks and balances of *phronesis*. Nevertheless, as Russell (2017) rues, even virtue ethically minded people, who should be mindful of the importance of *phronesis*, typically seem to underestimate the secondary failings, which Russell calls 'vices of practical unintelligence'—for example various policy miscalculations by otherwise well-meaning people in public office—perhaps because it is easier to pinpoint primary vices where the agent lacks the relevant moral virtue(s) *tout court*.[5]

Most proponents of the 'standard model' want to distance themselves from Aristotle's (apparent) view that one either has or does not have *phronesis* (e.g., Ferkany, 2020; Fowers et al., 2021; Russell, 2009).[6] Aristotle had an unfortunate penchant for defining concepts with respect to their most fully realized instances (Cooper, 1977). However, Aristotle's own idealistic specification of what counts as *phronesis* would make the group of actual *phronimoi* vanishingly small: a possibility that understandably turns some psychologists off the concept (Lapsley, 2019; McGrath & Brown, 2020). Aristotle's notorious reciprocity or unity thesis about virtue—that when one has *phronesis*, one has 'all the [moral] virtues as well' (1985, p. 171 [1145a1–3]), and that they mutually support each other in a psycho-morally unified way—is even

---

[5] This is what makes literary writings better sources of real-life examples of moral failings than academic texts. Accomplished writers such as Shakespeare or Dostoevsky are rarely interested in persons with simple moral failings (vices), but rather in people torn by inner conflict and lacking in *phronesis*—or being placed in tragic situations in which *phronesis* seems unattainable: the situations which Aristotle considered to rule out *eudaimonia* but where the *phronimos* would still not become totally 'miserable' (Aristotle, 1985, pp. 25–6 [1100b5–1101a10]).

[6] Interestingly, Ferkany (2020) argues that in our imperfect world with imperfect people, some of the strategies used by the *phronimos* may be representationally inseparable from those used by the 'continent' person: for example, not keeping tubs of ice cream in her fridge for fear that she might eat them all when feeling peckish and frustrated. We summarize Aristotle's developmental account—which posits an essential difference between continence and *phronesis*-guided virtue—in Chapter 11.

more problematic. We think this unity only makes sense, at best, as an idealization.[7] If taken literally, as a thesis about the real world and the people in it who actually make the grade as *phronimoi*, it would make mincemeat of much of Aristotle's own discussion of hard moral dilemmas and his frequent concessions of how even the *phronimoi* sometimes fail to find the best option (Curzer, 2005).[8] We are not sure that the reciprocity thesis works even as an idealization—for a world without value conflicts simply seems incomprehensible *qua* human world—and we will mostly pass over this thesis in silence in what follows until Chapter 10 where it forces itself onto the agenda again.

In contrast to an idealized conception of perfect *phronesis*, proponents of the 'standard model' typically understand *phronesis* as a 'scalar concept': namely, as referring to a set of individual differences whose actualization varies over time, domain, and context (Fowers et al., 2021). No *phronesis* at all and full *phronesis* will then be seen as statistical outliers on a scale of actualization that can (in principle, at least) be assessed with qualitative or quantitative methods (Wright et al., 2021).

Phronesis as a 'satis' concept

Russell's specification of *phronesis* as a satis concept (2009, chap. 4.2), also referred to as a 'threshold concept' (see, e.g., Curzer, 2012, pp. 400–1), is helpful here as well. A 'satis concept' belongs to a subset of threshold concepts: one with a vague, rather than a sharp, boundary. 'Satis concepts' are such that, for the concept C, something can satisfy it simply by being 'C enough' rather than being 'absolutely C' or 'as C as can be'. Unless we understand *phronesis* as a satis concept, the number of actual *phronimoi*—already curtailed by Aristotle's fairly strict criteria—would shrink to zero. Notably, for a person P to satisfy the conditions of *phronesis*, it is not only sufficient that most people think P does. In addition to being a satis concept, *phronesis* is thus also what Russell helpfully calls a 'model concept': a concept that models the matter of interest,

---

[7] Cf. Cokelet and Fowers (2019). Nevertheless, we agree with Annas that it lies in the very nature of Aristotelian *phronesis* that it develops over one's character as a whole, in a holistic way (Annas, 2011, p. 68). As Annas explains clearly, life itself it not compartmentalized, descriptively or evaluatively, and the unity of the virtues is, in a certain sense, 'no odder or more mysterious than the fact that a pianist does not develop one skill for fingering and another, quite separate skill for tempo, only subsequently wondering how to integrate the results' (2011, p. 87). However, Aristotle's reciprocity thesis is typically understood in a much stronger sense than this holistic, developmental one—and it is from that stronger sense that we wish to distance ourselves.

[8] Aristotle conveniently forgets his unity thesis of virtue from time to time and gives plausible examples of unevenly virtuous persons who are, say, generous but cowardly (1985, p. 71 [1115a20–2]).

but allows for the possibility of serious error about what counts as a central case of falling under the concept (Russell, 2009, pp. 117–22).[9] Because it is a model concept subject to error, *phronesis* needs a theoretical account, such as the one aspired to in the present book, to undergird it. It is not a concept that is just immediately recognizable by a perceptive observer.

Russell's (2009) account of the way in which Aristotelian *phronesis* needs to be understood as an idealization has been influential in informing the 'standard model'. However, in a recent chapter (Russell, 2021), he added an important clarification. Conceptual idealizations are mental tools: regulative ideals that guide our thinking about the real world. In some cases, we should aim for approximations of those idealizations. However, for something to count as a proper and helpful idealization, it is not necessary that it resembles the real world and allows for any appropriate approximations.[10] Russell (2021) thinks full Aristotelian *phronesis* is an example of an idealization that illuminates the real world precisely in virtue of 'not resembling it' (p. 22). It refers to a world of boundless cognitive and material resources, which can never be the human world. Trying to approximate it would represent both folly and hubris in trying to transcend the human condition. However, it is precisely by attending to the gap between *phronesis* in an ideal world and what *phronesis* can be at its best in the real world of scarce resources and human finitude that we can learn to make the most serviceable use of the potentialities of real-world *phronesis*.

2.2 A Four-Componential Model of *Phronesis*

Proponents of the 'standard model' agree that *phronesis* needs to perform a set of functions and that it includes different components that deal with those functions. However, as came to light in Section 1.3, there is no consensus on how many those components are or exactly how to characterize their functions. Our initial task in this section is to explain what we consider to be the components in question, which allows us to lay the conceptual basis of the APM. While we believe that what we propose is, in all essentials, in line with Aristotle's texts, it goes beyond them in various ways, for instance by being attentive to current empirical evidence; hence, this is a neo-Aristotelian model, with a stress on the 'neo'.

---

[9] Notably, on this account, other key concepts of virtue ethics that we introduced in Section 1.2, such as (good) *character* and *virtue*, are also satis model concepts.
[10] Wolbert et al.'s (2019) distinction between *utopian* and *realistic* ideals is also salutary here.

Two further caveats are in order here. First, the APM is a *pragmatic* model. It does not aim at unearthing essential structures of the human mind. We are simply interested in what roles *phronesis* is called upon to perform and how those can best be characterized for *explanatory purposes* and, subsequently, for purposes of *development* and *measurement*.[11] Second, the components do not refer to psycho-moral capacities that are completely independent of one another and can be turned 'up' or 'down' in isolation.[12] For example, the cultivation of moral sensitivity is likely to have impact in various ways upon the capacity for moral reasoning about the situations identified with greater sensitivity, and the results of the reasoning will, in turn, influence the way things appear to us in the future (Rabinoff, 2018, p. 133). Nevertheless, a componential model highlights the fact that a developmental intervention may, for example, tap most specifically into one component while having less direct influence on the others.

For practical purposes of measurement and intervention, we embarked on a two-level effort. First, the standard model of *phronesis* would have to be elaborated upon and populated with sufficient specificity to constitute a psychological model (Darnell et al., 2019), which we call the APM. Second, instruments would have to be found or designed to measure the various components of the model (see later in Chapter 6). We decided on a four-component model of *phronesis* with the following functions, which Wright et al. (2021) subsequently endorsed broadly,[13] as have Polizzi and Harrison (2022), with minor variations, for online contexts.[14] The order in which we present the components of the APM below is not crucial, although it is not entirely random. The resolution of a moral issue will begin with the appreciation that there is

---

[11] Krettenauer (2019) may be right that, from a structural point of view, as well as the point of conceptual parsimony, two of the components identified below might better be seen as preconditions rather than constituents of *phronesis*, which would leave two essential components only. The only essential components would, then, be the constitutive and integrative ones, as delineated presently. Cf. Cokelet's (2022) distinction between 'deliberative' and 'nondeliberative' practical wisdom, where only these two count as 'deliberative'. Nevertheless, from a pragmatic perspective—as the two 'preconditions' are also necessary for *phronesis* to function—we include them as components. We are in good company here. Aristotle was, for example, notoriously ambiguous himself about some variables in his concept of *eudaimonia*, sometimes speaking of good friends and good health as preconditions of *eudaimonia* but sometimes as constituents. More generally, nothing precludes the same item x from being seen simultaneously as instrumentally (precondition) and intrinsically (component) related to y, when looked at from different perspectives.

[12] This interdependence is captured with the direction of the arrows in Figure 2.1, later in this section. Cf. also Curzer's discussion of the organic structure of a good, in Aristotle's account, where one cannot understand the full value of each component without understanding its relation to the other components (2012, p. 298).

[13] Yet see their caveats about the blueprint component, explained below in Section 2.3.

[14] Their model is slightly different from ours, drawing on insights from Monika Ardelt also. They argue that *phronesis* in cyber-contexts will assume slightly different features from ordinary off-line *phronesis*.

a moral issue at stake; hence it is reasonable to begin with the perceptive faculty.[15] We label the components below in terms of the *functions* they perform within the overarching *phronesis* construct. The constitutive component is the component in charge of the constitutive function, for example.

Constitutive function/component

Phronesis involves the cognitive discriminatory ability to perceive the ethically salient or central aspects of a situation and to appreciate these as calling for specific kinds of responses. In the *phronimoi*, this becomes a cognitive excellence in that, after having noted a salient moral feature of a concrete situation calling for a response, they will be able to weigh different considerations and see that, say, courage is required when the risk to one's life is not overwhelming but the object at stake is extremely valuable; or that honesty is required when one has wronged a friend (cf. Russell, 2009, p. 21).[16] We also refer to this function as *moral sensitivity* or *moral perception*, in order to link it more directly to the standard Moral Psychology literature (see Chapter 5).[17]

There is a close association between conceptualization and perception. One cannot see *x* as *y* unless one has a concept of *y*. This is why the cultivation of what has been called 'virtue literacy' (the capacity to conceptualize, understand, and spot virtues; see, e.g., Jubilee Centre, 2022[18]) needs to be a primary

---

[15] Psychologists may be surprised that metacognition is not one of the components delineated below. The last three components, however, clearly involve metacognition in (a) integrating emotion with reason, (b) evaluating cognition, emotion, and action in view of the agent's understanding of how to live well, and (c) harmonizing the requirements of a set of virtues We recognize that metacognition is a very important topic; see Dinsmore et al. (2008) and Ohtani and Hisasaka (2018) for reviews. Thorough investigations (conceptual and empirical) of the relationships between *phronesis* and metacognition will be important for future work on *phronesis*, and we anticipate such work with further discussions in Chapters 4 and 11.

[16] Stichter (2021, p. 111) is hesitant about categorizing the constitutive component as part of wisdom because it does not take place in the 'goal-striving phase'. However, one cannot possess the wisdom to strive for the right goal unless one is able to read the situation correctly in terms of available goals and means to those goals. Therefore, we are not prepared to hive off moral perception from *phronesis*, as Stichter seems inclined to do. For some of the intricacies of combining goal-striving (which sometimes requires narrower attention) with the broadening-of-attention requirements of *phronesis*, see Waggoner (2021). Her conclusion is that 'cultivating [phronetic] virtue requires a balancing of broadened and narrowed attention' (p. 1237).

[17] Possibly another descriptor could be 'moral attention'. Jacobs (2017) considers attention to be a seriously underappreciated feature of virtue and worries that some people, lacking it, are virtue-deaf in the same sense as others are tone-deaf. One of the reasons why openness to experience is the only one of the Big Five personality traits consistently correlated with wisdom (Sternberg & Glück, 2022, chap. 7.2) could be that open-minded people are more attentive to new ways of looking at their surroundings.

[18] There is some ambiguity in writings from the Jubilee Centre (cf. Jubilee Centre, 2022 versus Carr & Harrison, 2015) about exactly what 'virtue literacy' means and whether 'virtue reasoning' is part of it. In this book, we understand 'virtue literacy' as an amalgam of virtue understanding and virtue perception only. We include 'virtue reasoning' in the integrative function of *phronesis*, rather than in moral perception, because we think that it is better to see virtue literacy (here positioned in the constitutive function of *phronesis*) as the first step in any such reasoning process.

step in all virtue/character education, including education towards *phronesis* (Carr & Harrison, 2015; Vasalou, 2012).[19] A child who is not in command of the concept of gratitude will not see acts of benefaction through the lens of this virtue, nor be able to distinguish between all its nuances and possible overlaps or conflicts with other virtues (Gulliford, 2018); similarly, a person who is not aware of all the components of *phronesis* may fail to bring those to bear on her decision-making. There is also a close connection between moral perception and imagination, such that a person lacking in the constitutive function of *phronesis* may not be able to engage in the imaginative leaps required to think through the possibilities of different courses of action. A true *phronimos* will, for example, often be able to see through simplistic depictions of situations as tragic dilemmas with only two available options, doing x or not doing x, where other opportunities (for doing y or z) are actually lurking in the background (cf. Hursthouse, 2006, pp. 294–5).[20]

Aristotle (1985) himself does not explicitly define sensitivity or perception as part of *phronesis*; this is one of many reasons why we call the APM 'neo-Aristotelian'. However, he posits a subsidiary intellectual virtue of comprehension (*sunesis*) which is about reading or correctly grasping the essentials of a situation (p. 164 [1143a1–18]). Moreover, he does refer to *phronesis* as *the eye* of moral experience, typically in the context of explaining how appreciation of individual circumstances cannot be captured simply by general moral truths. Unfortunately, this focus on what we call here the constitutive function of *phronesis* has led to some over-the-top particularist interpretations of Aristotle, according to which moral decision-making is only about 'thats', not 'whys', to use McDowell's (1998) famous terms.

In Dunne's (1993) words, in the sphere of *phronesis*, 'practical-moral universals cannot unproblematically cover or include particular cases' because the former contain 'an element of indeterminateness which is removed only through confrontation with particular cases' (p. 311). This is, in Dunne's view, so far from being a defect that it is, rather, 'the great merit' of *phronesis* (p. 314). Phrases such as 'particularist discernment', 'intuitive discrimination', 'perceptual capacity', 'illative sense', and 'situational appreciation' abound. For example, the particularists are fascinated by Aristotle's analogy of *phronesis* to

---

[19] In Chapter 11, we explain, for instance, how an intervention to enhance *phronesis* among police-science students needs to begin with a class explicating the concept of *phronesis* and its components. In our work with much younger students (at the primary/elementary school level), we have noticed that presenting them with dilemmas to ponder often does not work, simply because they are not able to 'see' or identify what the conflicting virtues are. This is why virtue literacy has to precede virtue reasoning.

[20] Carroll (2016) helpfully describes the capacity to be trained here as that of being able to recognize something heretofore unnoticed or unremarked: to bring something into the foreground, 'previously tucked recessively into the background, as if in soft focus, a blur, effectively hidden in clear sight' (p. 386).

vision. Experience is, for Dunne, a comprehensive situating process of which knowledge and virtue are specific moments and to which *phronesis* contributes 'an eye'. *Phronesis* is, in other words, the discernment of particular situations that enables, say, the experienced doctor faced with a moral dilemma 'to see aright' every time, but which remains ultimately experiential rather than universal 'since the universals within its grasp are always modifiable in the light of its continuing exposure to particular cases' (pp. 280, 293, 297, 361).

We see ourselves as Aristotelian generalists,[21] who, along with others, find fault with this particularist interpretation of *phronesis* because it sits loosely with, or even radically diverges from, essential elements of Aristotle's moral system. Of course, Aristotle warns us against looking for the same precision in matters of moral judgement as we would find in mathematics. Nor do we deny that he takes *phronesis* to be concerned with situated particularities that are difficult to capture in a general account. Neither of these concessions, however, is sufficient to warrant a particularist interpretation of *phronesis*. What must be shown for that interpretation to hold is that Aristotle thought that (1) any generalizing (moral) truth must be abandoned in favour of particular (moral) truths or at least reduced to a mere summary of such truths and (2) the perception of particulars is epistemologically prior to the guidance of general moral truths. However, as we and others have argued at length elsewhere, neither of those assumptions has any substantive grounding in Aristotle's texts (Irwin, 2000; Kristjánsson, 2007, chap. 11; cf. Vaccarezza, 2018). Our final word on this particularism debate derives, most fittingly, from Hursthouse (2011). She explains conclusively what the 'priority of perception' means and does not mean in Aristotle's virtue ethics. It does mean that (a) our assessment of complex situations begins with the perception of specific moral facts; (b) there is no substitute in moral education for induction into virtue literacy through personal engagement with situated moral perceptions; and (c) there is no theoretical language in which *phronesis*-relevant dilemmas can be couched that could somehow replace (a) and (b). However, none of this means that becoming a *phronimos* is just about mastery of particularist moral perceptions (Hursthouse, 2011, pp. 52–3). We need further components.

---

[21] See, for example, our focus on the general blueprint function of *phronesis* below. We are content to be labelled 'qualified generalists', however, as Vaccarezza (2018) labels herself in her excellent anti-particularist interpretation of Aristotelian *phronesis*. This is seen, for example, in our reluctance to endorse a full 'grand-end view' of *phronesis*; see Section 2.3.

Emotional regulative function/component

Individuals foster their emotional wellbeing through *phronesis* by harmonizing their emotional responses with their understandings of the ethically salient aspects of their situation, their judgement, and their recognition of what is at stake in the moment. This is both because they will have already acquired habituated virtues, that is, have shaped their emotions in ways that motivate them to behave as the virtuous person would, and because having formed these habits and consolidated them through understanding and reasoning, they will have a robust intellectual basis for them; hence, enabling them to be emotionally intelligent.[22] For example, a *phronimos* might recognize that her appraisal of the situation is problematic, giving rise to an emotional response that is inappropriate to the situation. The emotional regulative function can then help her adjust her appraisal and emotion by, for instance, giving herself an inner 'talking to' or asking herself questions about what is prompting the ill-fitting emotional response. For this reason, we can also refer to this function, in a more standard Aristotelian way, as infusing emotion with reason (see below).

The emotional motivations *phronesis* feeds on from the moral virtues may lead in conflicting directions (e.g., the pain of sympathy may clash with pleasure of satisfied indignation when an evildoer receives comeuppance), or the relevant emotions may be disproportionate to a holistic assessment of the situation. An implication of this, insofar as emotions are our prime motivational anchors, is that the *phronimos*' emotions must be in harmony with her rational judgement and virtuous outlook and motivate her to behave accordingly. That is, she sees the dangerous as fearsome, is horrified by injustice, pained by others' undeserved suffering, and so on, and these emotions are felt in due proportion to their object and in turn offer reasons for responding in certain ways.

Because 'emotion regulation' in Psychology has sometimes been seen as equivalent to 'emotional control', or more specifically to the cognitive policing of wayward noncognitive emotions, it is easy to understand why this function of *phronesis* may be misunderstood by some psychologists to involve emotional suppression (Jeste et al., 2020), or to invoke an outdated

---

[22] Yet for a distinction between Aristotelian emotional virtue and the modern amoral and instrumentalist idea of 'emotional intelligence', see Kristjánsson (2007, chap. 6); cf. Kristjánsson (2018b, chap. 9). One of the features of emotional intelligence is about understanding others' emotions and 'managing' other people. Hursthouse (2006, p. 306) explains well how this sort of 'people management' is essentially different for the *phronimos* versus the merely emotionally intelligent ('clever') person.

reason–emotion dichotomy (Lapsley, 2019).²³ Nothing is further from the truth, however, as Aristotelians understand emotion regulation in terms of reason-infusion rather than suppression by reason. Those considerations matter, and we will return to them once we begin to compare our model with the recent 'common wisdom model', regarding the role of emotion regulation, in Chapter 4.

Wright et al. (2021, p. 9, note 6) take the reason-infusion to imply that the emotional regulative function can be subsumed under the other functions of *phronesis* (e.g., the integrative one), which will require us to tone the relevant emotions up or down according to the considered reflective view of the responses fit for the given situation. However, we see a separate role for emotional regulation within the *phronesis* construct, apart from simply that of finding the golden mean of the eventual moral response (including expressed emotion as well as action). Rather, we are primarily thinking here in terms of what often happens in the decision procedure after a moral quandary has been perceived/identified. Often, the situation will evoke such strong emotions that those 'get in the way' (Briggs & Lumsdon, 2022) of decision-making. Or, alternatively, we try so hard to denude our assessment of the situation of emotion that we end up approaching it in an unnaturally detached way. What we mean by the emotional regulation function of *phronesis* is, thus, what we called above the initial 'inner talking to' needed to make sure the emotions feeding into the moral decision process are neither too weak nor too strong for the given situation.

Blueprint function/component

The synthesizing work of *phronesis* operates in conjunction with the agent's overall understanding of the kinds of things that matter for a flourishing life: the agent's own ethical aims and aspirations, her understanding of what it takes to live and act well, and her need to live up to the standards that shape and are shaped by her understanding and experience of what matters. This amounts to what we call a blueprint of flourishing. A 'blueprint', in our view, has more similarity to what psychologists call 'moral identity' than a full-blown theoretical outline of the good life.²⁴ *Phronetic* persons possess a

---

²³ Lapsley (2019) worries about the invocation of a 'pyramidal model' of the mind, with noble reason at the top and uncouth emotions at the bottom. However, such a model is singularly inept at capturing Aristotle's view of virtuous emotions (see Kristjánsson, 2018b, chaps 1 and 2).

²⁴ That said, the problem with the concept of moral identity in Moral Psychology is that it is an anti-realist concept. It simply refers to the beliefs that one has about oneself as a moral agent and the aspirations that one attributes to oneself. However, one could be thoroughly self-deceived about that identity: think, for

general justifiable conception of the good life (*eudaimonia*) and adjust their overall reactions to that blueprint, thus furnishing it with motivational force.[25] This does not mean that each ordinary person needs to have the same sophisticated comprehension of the 'grand end' of human life as a philosopher or an experienced statesperson might have, in order to count as possessing *phronesis*. Rather than being an 'elite sport', the sort of grasp of a blueprint of the aims of human life informing practical wisdom is within the grasp of the ordinary well-brought-up individual and reflected in ordinary acts (cf. Broadie, 1991, esp. pp. 198–202). It draws upon the person's standpoint on life as a whole and determines the place that different goods occupy in the larger context and how they interact with other goods. This blueprint is ideally 'on call' in every situation of action (Segvic, 2009, pp. 105, 158).

Here we see the source of our previously declared (qualified) Aristotelian generalism. Because of the blueprint component, *phronesis* is not only about resolving tricky particularist situations, but about what 'promotes living well in general' (Aristotle, 1985, p. 153 [1140a25–8]). For morality, as for medicine, 'there is a ruling [science]'[26] (1985, p. 159 [1141b22–3]).[27] More specifically, this science is encapsulated in the very ungrounded grounder of virtue ethics, the concept of human flourishing and, through the blueprint component, in

---

example, that the driving force behind one's business dealings is philanthropy when it is actually just love of money. The blueprint component in the APM is, on the other hand, a realist construct: it is about your de facto overall conception of what you want your life to look like. The psychological concept that is closer to blueprint than moral identity is, therefore, *moral selfhood* (see further in Chapter 5; cf. Kristjánsson, 2010a). However, it is not a widely entrenched concept in Psychology, and we will therefore continue to avail ourselves of the concept of moral identity in what follows. Cf. Haldane (2022) on the elision of true self-knowledge in contemporary Character Education.

[25] Stichter worries that our account is 'ambiguous as to whether a blueprint needs to meet a certain threshold of justification to count' (2021, p. 112). To count as a 'blueprint' as such it does not. To count as a blueprint that makes the grade as a component of an overall *phronesis* capacity it obviously does, however. Otherwise, the APM would be completely out of sync with the sort of Aristotelian moral realism to which we subscribe. This was perhaps not made clear enough in the original Darnell et al. (2019) paper. Similarly, there was some lack of clarity about the motivational role of the blueprint component, upon which Lapsley (2021, p. 153) fastens, which we hope to clarify in the present chapter. For example, it is not as if we consider moral identity inert motivationally until prompted by *phronesis*; rather what we mean is that in the *phronimos*, moral identity does not begin to motivate *phronetically* until the blueprint component and the other components have settled sufficiently and have begun to inform one another.

[26] The empirical science of flourishing is rather preliminary at this point (Fowers, Novak, Kiknadze, & Calder, 2022) and riddled with disagreement. The beginnings of a scientific account of flourishing are beginning to emerge, however (Fowers et al., 2023). Owen Flanagan calls the current burgeoning empirical-normative inquiry into the nature and conditions of human flourishing '*eudaimonistic scientia*': scientific inquiry aimed at capturing deep structural features of *homo sapiens*, based on testable hypotheses (Flanagan, 2007, pp. 1, 38, 112). Cf. Kristjánsson (2020).

[27] Likening *phronesis* to the autofocus mechanism on a camera is catchy (Garver, 2006, p. 101), but slightly misleading as the autofocus mechanism is based on a complicated set of general engineering principles: a 'ruling science'. In the case of good character, that ruling science provides 'a target' on which the *phronimos* focuses, and 'there is a definition of the mean' which is 'between excess and deficiency' because it expresses 'correct reason' (Aristotle, 1985, p. 148 [1138b20–2]).

how the agent identifies with such a conception for herself.[28] As Russell (2009, p. 27) explains well, the blueprint guides deliberation about particular cases by bringing this overall flourishing conception to bear on details of the given situation.[29]

The blueprint component contains the solution to an old puzzle about *phronesis*: whether it is itself a source of moral motivation or whether it simply feeds on motivations drawn from the moral and civic virtues that it synthesizes. The answer in the APM is *both*. The *phronimos*' primary source of moral motivation continues to be derived from the specific moral virtues.[30] For example, she acts honestly primarily because of the motivational component of the virtue of honesty. However, that primary motivation is reinforced and shaped by the overall blueprint motivation of the agent to be an honest person. This secondary *phronetic* motivation is brought into sharper relief when there is a conflict between virtues: say, when both honesty and compassion are motivating the person in the same situation but where those motivations seem to call for opposite reactions.[31] Then the secondary background motivation derived from the blueprint component becomes crucial. It demands coherence and prompts the agent to seek for the golden mean of reaction that best accords with her sense of who she is and wants to be overall as a person.[32]

Because of the currently reigning liberal model of value in Western democracies, according to which there is no best comprehensive view of the good life to which the wise person (or, by implication, the state) can be privy, the

---

[28] As we have explained at earlier junctures, this conception of human flourishing has implications for the good of the whole community, not only the agent herself. Although Aristotle was not a utility maximizer (believing that every decision has to take into account the collective interests of humankind in the long run), he was even less a rational egoist. His self-concept was more other-entwined than the modern Western one, for example, and included friends and family; in some cases (esp. for statespersons) even all the citizens in your state.

[29] However, Russell (2009, p. 30) plausibly warns against the interpretation that *phronesis* is, therefore, nothing but the application/implementation of general truths to/in particular cases. This is both because the general truths are too general and because they continue to be mutually informed by experiences garnered in the special cases. Cf. Navarini et al.'s (2021) preference for the term 'adaptation' over 'application' in this context (p. 116).

[30] This primary motivational source is not visualized in Figure 2.1 below, which is only about *phronesis* itself and its outcome.

[31] Despite their misgiving about the way in which we categorize the blueprint component (see the following section, 2.3), Snow et al. (2021, p. 88) agree that *phronesis* 'cannot exist unless it is motivated by the desire to be virtuous and to pursue the kinds of goods that virtue enables us to attain'.

[32] We leave it open whether this was Aristotle's own view. On Curzer's (2012, p. 311) account, the sole moral motivation still comes only from the individual moral virtues, but *phronesis* simply adds pieces of knowledge about the good life, which then help to inform and develop the yearnings of the moral virtues. To account for Aristotle's non-Humean view of motivation (see later in this chapter; cf. Irwin, 1975), we find the role of the blueprint component (and hence of the *phronesis* construct itself) as a secondary motivator more helpful. It also seems to tally with the Aristotelian general notion of human beings having a natural inclination to actualize their potentialities. However, we refrain once again from getting embroiled in primarily exegetical quibbles.

blueprint component may the 'hardest sell' of all the *phronesis* components. This difficulty is compounded by enduring textual debates about Aristotle's own interpretation of the conception of the good life: debates which, in this instance, carry substantive rather than just exegetical weight (Snow et al., 2021). Nevertheless, we do not (and we believe that Aristotle did not) recommend any single form of the good life, because individuals' circumstances, capacities, and visions of good life can vary considerably, yet still conduce to a good way of living. We think those forms of good living will have sufficient 'family resemblances' to count as instances of an overall conception of what it is to live well. At this point, these family resemblances are a promissory note rather than an established, cohesive fact.[33] As this issue opens up a can of worms, we have decided to devote a separate section to the blueprint debate (Section 2.3), postponing further discussion of it here.[34]

Integrative function/component

Let us assume that we have identified a moral problem correctly as one potentially requiring input from two apparently conflicting moral virtues. Let us further assume that we have infused our relevant emotions with reason and that they are not obstructing the decision process. Finally, let us assume that we have a clear, non-self-deceptive, justifiable identity of who we want to be—a blueprint of the good life—and an overall motivation to bring our reactions into line with that identity. That leaves just the final component of the APM construct: the integrative one—which we could also call its adjudicative function or, in line with standard Moral Psychology, denote as a form of 'moral reasoning'.

Through this component, an individual integrates different virtue-relevant considerations, via a process of checks and balances, especially in circumstances where different ethically salient considerations, or different kinds of virtues or values, appear to be in conflict and agents need to negotiate

---

[33] See Fowers et al. (2023) for an initial attempt in this direction.
[34] There is another complication that we have, however, decided to circumvent completely here for reasons of space. It has to do with the relationship between the blueprint component and *self-knowledge*. If this section had been written in ancient Greece, self-knowledge would have figured prominently in the discussion. However, self-knowledge (as well as other 'self-talk') has lost credibility in the contemporary era after having found itself squeezed from opposite sides: from a pervasive anti-self-realism in Philosophy, on the one hand, derived from Hume, and on the other hand from inflated views of the relevance of self-concept in some pockets of Psychology (criticized in Kristjánsson, 2010a). For an enlightening account of this historical turbulence and (an implicit) plea for the retrieval of self-knowledge in contemporary discussions of virtue and character, see Haldane (2022). Recall also note 24 above.

dilemmatic space.³⁵ Imagine, for instance, a situation in which honesty calls for revealing to a dying friend the life-long unfaithfulness of the friend's partner, while compassion pulls in the opposite direction, with perhaps specific features of the friend's personality and considerations stemming from your relationship to them further complicating the matter. In a situation like this, it may be unclear even for the relatively practically wise person what should be done. But the thought is, it is *she* who will be best-placed to weigh such considerations in a way that manifests due concern for all of them and to integrate them alongside everything else that she deems valuable in life overall. In some cases, such integration may call for a 'blended' or 'synchronized' virtuous response, such as being honest but expressing the honestly in a particularly compassionate way; in other cases, a virtue may have to be put on hold completely in a given situation in light of the overriding requirement of a conflicting virtue, such as in a case of a compassionate white lie. The point is that this function allows the person to engage in the adjudication of moral matters when conflicting desiderata arise (cf. Russell, 2009, pp. 22, 262).³⁶

Some would say that, by turning attention to this final component, we have entered that part of the *phronesis* territory where the APM is bound to encounter its severest trials, especially because the reasoning strategies of which the *phronimos* must avail herself are not essentially codifiable, like for example Bentham's utility calculus or Kant's categorical imperative are meant to be.³⁷ Our own view is, in short, that people and virtues are suited for different circumstances, and that the *phronimos* will need to draw on diverse reasoning strategies depending on the nature of the moral problem at hand. We agree with Navarini et al. (2021) that the best logical term to describe this process is probably *abduction*, rather than either *deduction* or *induction*.³⁸ However,

---

³⁵ Cf. Railton's (2017) helpful notion of 'foraging for value', and how such foraging requires having representational capacities that replicate the structure of the world, as well as assessing the magnitude of risk versus magnitude of value corresponding to importantly different structural features. This also explains why the Jubilee Centre (2022) explains the *phronesis* phase of virtue development as being about 'character sought' rather than simply 'taught' or 'caught'.

³⁶ As this function is highly situation-specific, in seeing the general through the lens of the particular, traditional wisdom research in Psychology, which homes in on more explicitly global capacities, is not well suited to capture the components of APM. A notable exception here, however, is the Situated Wise-Reasoning Scale (SWIS), developed by Brienza et al. (2018). The SWIS assesses the elements of wise-reasoning, by shifting from global, decontextualized reports to state level reports about concrete situations (cf. also Grossmann, 2017b). See further in Chapters 3 and 6.

³⁷ As argued in Section 1.4, we do not take *phronetic* adjudications to be essentially uncodifiable, but rather contingently so. However, that does not make the practical problem of finding the best solution any less demanding. Notably, contingent uncodifiability does not imply that the *phronimos* cannot make use of a set of fairly determinate ranking rules, which apply 'for the most part' (Hursthouse, 2011, p. 44), or that the *phronimos* cannot accept any categorical prohibitions (Vogler, 2020).

³⁸ 'Abduction' refers to syllogistic reasoning in which the major premise is given but the minor premise and, therefore, the conclusion are only probable. Basically, it involves forming a conclusion from the information that is known. Abduction will lead you to the best explanation through the formation of hypotheses that are then tested through action. However, Navarini et al. (2021) are alert to standard biases created

simply characterizing the process in that way yields limited information about its content.

In order not to turn this into a book about moral reasoning strategies—which is an important topic but outside of our current remit—we will only offer a couple of pointers about how the integrative deliberative function of *phronesis* might work in different situations,[39] but mostly shelve any further discussion of this issue until later chapters.[40] First, we warn *phronesis* advocates against simply looking down their noses at utilitarian cost-benefit analyses (cf. Russell, 2014). Much of the virtue ethics literature is about distancing it from utilitarianism—and rightly so (Anscombe, 1958a).[41] However, some large-scale social problems are so complex and broad—take the Israel-Palestine dispute, the issue of global warming, or even various sweeping trade-offs elicited by the recent COVID pandemic—that it is difficult to envisage how an individual *phronimos*, or even a group of dedicated *phronimoi*, could come up with a reasonable solution without drawing on some fairly mechanical calculations of benefits and costs. Just focusing on individual virtues and how to balance them will not suffice.

Second, at the other end of the scale, some problems seem to be so clear-cut that the integrative function of *phronesis* will be able to come up with a virtually spontaneous answer. We believe that, in most cases, this spontaneity may

---

in abductive reasoning. Another factor that must be studied is that of *time* (Wright et al., 2021, chap. 5). Abductions take place in time and can be quite time-consuming, although they may in some cases seem spontaneous. For further thought-provoking reflections on *phronesis* and time, see Curzer (2022).

[39] For a detailed overview, we recommend the article by Zheng (2021). Zheng helpfully reminds us that the Greek term for 'deliberation' ('*eboulia*') can also be sensibly rendered as 'good counsel' (p. 219). Phronetic adjudication is thus best understood as involving the agent giving herself the same kind of advice as a good counsellor would, and going through the same steps in her mind as such an external adviser would recommend. Cf. also Tiberius and Swartwood (2011) on reflective and problem-solving capacities as parts of *phronesis*.

[40] To fulfil the aims of this book, we need to figure out what a *phronimos* would look like in real life if we are to concretize *phronesis* in a psychologically serviceable way, in order not only to identify the *phronimoi* (or those 'more *phronimoi*' than the next person), but also envisage ways in which to trace the development of *phronesis*, and thereby form better informed hypotheses and predictions concerning how it may be acquired and subsequently taught. We return to those issues in Chapters 6 and 11.

[41] That said, there are versions of utilitarianism that are extremely flexible with regard to empirical evidence and actual psychological capacities. According to some such versions (perhaps even Mill's 1972 version), relying on *phronesis*—rather than the 'utility calculus' as understood in cruder but more mainstream versions—could be the utility-maximizing and hence the right thing to do—if it is, in fact, empirically true that this will be conducive to people's overall wellbeing. Similarly, such versions could endorse Aristotle's assumption that ordinary people (as distinct from rulers applying civic *phronesis*, see Chapter 8) do not need to take the interests of the whole of humankind into account in their moral decision-making, given that such a demand places unrealistic psychological burdens on them and makes their lives impossible to live. Of course, from the perspective of *all* utilitarians, it would be *better* if all moral decisions could accommodate the longstanding interests of humankind. Yet, demanding of people something they cannot psychologically do is arguably inimical to utility.

be an illusion, in the sense that the rapidity of the decision-making is a result of previous (possibly time-consuming) decisions about similar issues that have already been internalized and then simply being replicated automatically (Railton, 2016). We agree, however, with Warren et al. (2022) in their partial acceptance of Cokelet's (2022) suggestion that conscious deliberation may not be the only pathway to *phronesis*. There may be individuals who acquire *phronesis* in a more bottom-up, intuitive manner, without a great deal of conscious deliberation, but we think that conscious deliberation facilitates the acquisition and practice of *phronesis* however one acquires it. Debates about which is primary—conscious or nonconscious deliberation—are best answered empirically, and we are content to simply recognize that both are possible, while also asserting that conscious deliberation is invaluable. At a minimum, we see a clear role for 'nonconscious deliberation' as part of *phronetic* decision-making, when it refers to a replication of a manoeuvre already tried and tested in similar-enough situations in the past. We see the role of nonconscious deliberation in the development of *phronesis* as an exception to its standard development rather than the typical pathway.

Although most moral psychologists would feel more comfortable referring to our 'integrative function' simply as '(sound) moral reasoning'—and we have alluded to that terminological temptation above—that is slightly misleading because *some* moral reasoning also inevitably takes place at the *prephronetic* stage of mere habituation. Decisions reached about the exhibition of virtue at that stage are not simply 'subrational knacks' (Annas, 2011, p. 25) or mere repetitions of previous decisions internalized by the agent through habituation—for who encounters exactly the same moral situation twice? Even a 7-year-old child may need to reflect on the best way of showing gratitude to her grandparents, although the child is incapable of dealing with complicated and ambivalent virtuous motivations. Snow (2006) worries that habituated virtue is incompatible with virtue for which the agent is responsible, as the deliberative element is missing, and she comes up with a fairly complicated manoeuvre, involving unconscious virtue-relevant goals, to explain how habituated virtue is compatible with acting for reasons that make the agent accountable. We do not see this as a problem in an Aristotelian model unless one assumes that no deliberation takes place until the *phronesis* level. But that was never Aristotle's view, nor is this view plausible from a developmental science viewpoint (Kingsford et al., 2018; Tomasello, 2019). *Nonphronetic* agents can avail themselves of calculation (*deinotes*) and various other reasoning strategies to figure out what to do. What is habituated is only the motivation to exhibit a given virtue in relevant circumstances, not exactly how this should be done. What the *nonphonetic* agent lacks is thus not deliberation (and responsibility for the outcome of such deliberation) per se, but rather the kind of blueprint-infused coherent deliberation that *phronesis* allows and that is specifically alert to virtue conflicts.[42]

Choice

What the whole *phronetic* process, involving four components/functions, aims at is obviously choice/decision/election (*prohairesis*). We do not consider choice, however, a separate fifth component of *phronesis*, but rather as the way in which *phronesis* is enacted. To clarify, individuals engage in *phronesis* to guide their moral action, not 'behaviour' as the latter term is typically used in behavioural science (Ng & Tay, 2020). By 'moral action' we mean here behaviour under a certain characterological description, or a behaviour-motivation combination (e.g., giving money out of generosity, or not giving money because of thrift). This is also why equating 'moral action' with 'prosocial action' is misleading, because 'prosocial' is a term derived from behavioural science attempting to describe mere behaviour that happens to benefit the agent's socio-moral environment, whether or not chosen for the right (*phronesis*-guided) reasons.[43]

Figure 2.1 illustrates our overall conceptualization of *phronesis*. Notice that we try to couch the components there in a language that will be more familiar to psychologists (entirely capitalized words) than the names of the four 'functions'. Notice also the central role accorded to the blueprint component, to which we return in Section 2.3.

2.3 The Contentious Blueprint Component

The blueprint component comes with a set of philosophical issues of its own, and we feel it would be inapposite to ignore those completely, although some of them would require a fuller treatment than we have space for here (see, e.g., Kristjánsson, 2020) to satisfy philosophically savvy readers.

---

[42] See Asma (2022) for a detailed discussion. She comes up with her own solution, based on Anscombe's account of the inherently rational structure of all actions. However, as Asma herself seems to acknowledge towards the end of her article, this solution may rescue the responsibility of habituated actions at the cost of obliterating the distinction between habitual and nonhabitual (e.g., *phronetic*) actions.

[43] Recall also note 3 in Chapter 1.

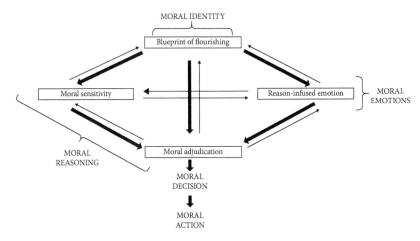

Figure 2.1 A Neo-Aristotelian Model of Wise (*Phronetic*) Moral Decision-Making

The Humean interpretation of the blueprint component

The first issue is whether Aristotle's motivational model is Humean or not. This is an important question not only for philosophers but also for psychologists, as a Humean approach to motivation has exerted a deep influence on Social Science, contributing to Psychology's overarching instrumentalism (Fowers, 2010). The 'Humean' approach includes two theses: first, that reason alone (independent of desires) does not motivate, and second, that reason is irrelevant to the choice of ultimate ends, which is based on nondeliberative desires (usually in contemporary Psychology understood primarily as subjective desires or 'preferences').

It seems natural to elicit the first Humean thesis from the 'standard model' of *phronesis* and, indeed, from Aristotle's own words that 'thought by itself [. . .] moves nothing' (1985, p. 150 [1139a36–7]) unless driven by a goal-directed desire. While we know from Aristotle's developmental account that there comes a time in our lives, presumably during adolescence, when we are morally expected to turn our habituated virtues into *phronetic* ones, after having re-evaluated them and reinternalized their content critically, there is a way to interpret this process which does not require deliberation about ultimate ends. The teenager on the path to *phronesis* may not question ultimate truths, such as that *eudaimonia* is the final end of human life and requires virtues, but rather aim for a deeper understanding of them. She may realize that certain means that she had naively considered to be conducive to *eudaimonia* in an unproblematic sense are only so in complex and nuanced ways, and she may need to reconsider and reconceive her view of the relative value of certain virtues for the good life. But all these considerations can presumably stay within the area of deliberation about means, and do not necessarily undermine the interpretation of Aristotle as a Humean.

The second thesis may also seem consistent with Aristotle's (1985) explicit claim about *phronesis* only constituting reasoning about means to ends (pp. 168, 171–2 [1144a6–9, 1145a4–6]). Yet, importantly, Aristotle elaborates and corrects the notion that *phronetic* reasoning is concerned with means only. His considered view is that nonintellectual habituation of virtues picked up uncritically from the environment is insufficient for full virtue; full virtue requires a decision to choose virtue *for itself*; and that decision requires *phronesis*. So, although a virtuous person grasps the right ends because she has the right desires, those desires require *phronesis* for their development precisely in order to count as the right desires in the first place (Aristotle, 1985, pp. 39–40, 168–9 [1105a28–32, 1144a13–22]). In other words, the transition from habituated virtue to *phronesis*-guided virtue is one of essence: the previously nonintellectually founded desires become deliberative desires, and they are no longer the *same* desires as before, simply with a fancy intellectual embellishment, but rather *new* desires, *reformulated* by *phronesis*.[44] Hence, Aristotle cannot be categorized as a Humean with respect to Hume's second thesis: that all practical thought depends on nondeliberative desires (Irwin, 1975; Kristjánsson, 2018b, chap. 2). *Phronesis* is thus a dynamic motivational concept: a synthesizing one in a constructivist (creating a new motivation) rather than just a coherentist (integrating existing motivations) sense.[45]

These non-Humean considerations are reflected in the backward arrows in Figure 2.1 of the APM above. Once new experience has been garnered and a moral decision adjudicated upon, this experience feeds back into the understanding of the good life (the 'blueprint') and alters desires about both means and ends. However, since Figure 2.1 does not include the individual moral and civic virtues, it does not visualize the more important part of this non-Humean Aristotelian picture: namely, that the blueprint gradually informs and changes the underlying virtues also. For example, person *P* takes a

---

[44] Miller (2021, p. 56) calls this the 'end-setting function' of *phronesis*, noting that many proponents of the 'standard model' subscribe to it. We do not consider this a discrete 'function', however, in the same sense as the four functions delineated in Section 2.2, but rather a functional implication of the APM as a whole.

[45] We are not sure if Curzer would agree with this interpretation insofar as it is meant to be Aristotelian rather than simply reconstructively neo-Aristotelian. However, Curzer (2012, pp. 309–10) does point out that *phronesis* helps us build and maintain the right state of mind and acts as a corrective against corruption. It could hardly do this if it were concerned with means to ends only. The most detailed and meticulous argument against attributing the anti-Humean argument to Aristotle himself is to be found in Moss's (2011) article. Yet even she acknowledges that *phronesis* helps clarify existing ends. There may not be a huge difference, however, between determining already existing indeterminate ends and identifying new ends.

significant moral decision about the administration of justice in a complex situation by utilizing strategies drawn from the integrative function of *phronesis*. This decision subtly changes her blueprint of the good life, insofar as justice is concerned, and this altered blueprint then feeds back into the underlying moral virtue of justice, shifting its characteristic desires slightly. What we end up with, therefore, in the APM, is an account of motivation that is essentially non-Humean in at least one crucial aspect.[46]

The elitist objection to the blueprint component

Let us now turn to the second topic of this section: whether our blueprint component is overdetermined and elitist. Snow et al. (2021) express serious doubts about our specification of this component in their recent chapter, although they had broadly endorsed our version of the 'standard model' in their book, which came out in the same year (Wright et al., 2021). They agree that the 'blueprint view' is less rigid than the grand-end view of the good life that some Aristotelians support (see later in this section); yet they also want to depart from it for two reasons (Snow et al., 2021, pp. 74–5). First, they wish to allow for *phronesis* in the lives of people who do not yet have a fully articulated comprehensive vision of the good. In other words, they want to give *phronesis* a constructive role in the creation of a blueprint rather than presupposing a ready-made blueprint. Second, they reject the Aristotelian assumption that only well-brought-up people can develop a conception of the good life and hence acquire *phronesis*. In contrast, in their view, even people exposed to and inculcated into vice in their early years can cultivate in themselves *phronetic* reflections about the kind of person they want to become.

The first point Snow et al. (2021) make is conceptual and the second developmental. In response to the first point, recall that we take *phronesis* to be a scalar concept, and a 'satis' concept. It is not just the case that people either possess or do not possess *phronesis*. Rather, candidates for *phronesis* are (hopefully) somewhere on the way to developing it, and at some point in that trajectory, there is a threshold point where we would be comfortable with calling them *phronimoi*, although they are still not fully developed as such. There may be a slight difference between our APM and Snow et al.'s preferred model of where that threshold point lies, in particular concerning the

---

[46] The strong sense of personal agency that Kumagal (2014), for one, attributes to *phronesis* would only be half-baked if *phronesis* did not have the power to inform the underlying moral virtues. Insights from Aristotle-friendly self-determination theory (Ryan et al., 2013) could also be brought to bear here.

development of the blueprint component. However, we are not even sure that there really is. Our reason for preferring a blueprint component to a grand-end component is precisely that we want to allow for a blueprint as part of *phronesis* that is not yet comprehensive, fully articulated, nor includes an explicit ordering of all the person's ends and aims. While the idealized blueprint of the *phronetic* philosopher or statesperson includes all those elements, the blueprint of the ordinary *phronimos* need not. The latter is work in progress. Nevertheless, to count as a blueprint, it needs to have some essential elements in place that are typically ascribed to moral identity (see, e.g., Hardy & Carlo, 2005), not just a budding open-ended desire to reflect on what kind of person you want to be, as one can often see developing in late-childhood–early adolescence. Moreover, the blueprint must—as Krettenauer (2022) has shown for moral identity more generally—be fairly abstract, long-term oriented, and hypothetical, rather than too concrete and situation-specific, in order to motivate moral actions.[47] So, to repeat, Snow et al. (2021) may be slightly less demanding than we are about the required level of the formation of a moral self-identity for it to count as a genuine blueprint component of a person's *phronesis*. However, we find the label 'elitist' for our interpretation of the blueprint component to be inappropriate.

The second point our blueprint sceptics make is developmental, and it so happens that we mostly agree with it. We are no fans of Aristotle's early years determinism about moral development and we have argued elsewhere that neo-Aristotelians had better find ways to get round it (see, e.g., Fowers et al., 2021; Kristjánsson, 2015, chap. 5; 2020, chap. 6). In other words, we think that, even for the very 'badly brought-up' person, there are avenues open (through epiphanies inspired by character friends and mentors; even perhaps solitary theoretical reflections) to develop *phronesis*. However, we still need to find some way of overcoming the obstacle, identified by Aristotle, that the typical badly brought-up person simply does not have the conceptual repertoire at her disposal to see the need for change. Snow et al. (2021, p. 75) take an example of a young woman born into a troubled home environment and getting involved in drugs and crime. In prison, however, she takes a hard look at her life and develops a motivation to improve, aided by encouragement from others who are benevolent and supportive. Her reflections on how to improve

---

[47] Krettenauer's (2022) integrative review, which we mention again in Chapter 5, will be music to the ears of neo-Aristotelians, as he shows that moral identity must be fairly abstract, internally motivated, and promotion-focused rather than prevention-oriented in order to motivate moral actions. The blueprint component, as we have described it here, obviously satisfies all three criteria.

are, in their view, an example of *phronesis* at work—something that our blueprint component of *phronesis* would allegedly rule out.

As we see it, Snow et al. (2021) are conflating two points with their example, one developmental and the other conceptual. Regarding the developmental point, we fully share their anti-Aristotelian optimism that, through mentorship and support, badly brought-up people can find their way onto the path of *phronesis* development. The conceptual point, however, is whether the woman prisoner can be said to be exhibiting *phronesis* through her reflections. As the example is articulated, the woman already has a blueprint, which states that getting out of prison and improving her life would be conducive to her *eudaimonia*. It is not as if she has no blueprint at all! The remaining question is whether she has already got a *sufficiently developed* blueprint for us to be able to say that her reflections count as exercises in *phronesis*, rather than just as rudimentary preliminaries to *phronetic* thinking. As acknowledged above, it may be that we are slightly more demanding here than our sceptics. Yet we see no serious challenge implicated in the counter-arguments launched by Snow et al. that threaten to undermine a blueprint component of *phronesis* as such, especially because the same authors have later rejected a much more radically open-ended and theoretically neutral conception of the content of the reflections required for *phronesis* (see Warren et al.'s, 2022 response to Cokelet, 2022).

In order to settle the question of whether our blueprint component is overdetermined or not, it helps to set it in the context of the well-known exegetical debate between Broadie (1991) and Kraut (1993) on whether or not Aristotle subscribed to a grand-end view of the human *telos* required for *phronesis*. Broadie objects to the view that Aristotle demanded 'a comprehensive, substantial vision of that good', seeing it as an exalted and unrealistic demand (p. 198). Kraut defends what he calls a grand-end view, however, and he sees it as essential to a justification of moral decisions: 'if a person of practical wisdom is asked to state his reasons for making a decision, then the full justification must begin with a substantive and correct conception of happiness [*eudaimonia*]' (p. 362). For Broadie, such a grand-end view would require the sum of everything that matters, supplemented perhaps by an assignment of weights. In arguing that this was not Aristotle's view, Broadie has a hard time explaining away Aristotle's own stringent demand from the *Eudemian Ethics* that we 'must enjoin every one that has the power to live up to his own choice to set up for himself some object for the good life to aim at [. . .] with reference to which he will then do all his acts, since not to have one's life organized in view of some end is a mark of much folly' (Aristotle, 1935, 1214b6–11; we are here using Broadie's own translation, 1991, p. 4).

Much of the exegetical debate revolves around the issue of whether Aristotle simply assumed this grand-end view in the *Nicomachean Ethics*, without stating it (as Kraut believes), or whether he had abandoned it for a less determinate and more particularist view, as Broadie argues. Although we take Kraut to make a stronger case about what was Aristotle's own view—and we agree with him, contra Broadie (1991), that there is nothing logically odd about the idea that the practically wise person's grand end includes 'a portrait of practical wisdom' (p. 200)—most of this debate is outside of our present interests. Underlying our specification of the blueprint component of *phronesis* is the belief that while Kraut (1993) may be right about the historical Aristotle, neo-Aristotelians need not go as far as him in assuming that 'if one lacks a fully developed and correct conception of happiness, one's decisions are apt to go astray' (p. 371). The demand for 'full' development and correctness would surely make the grand-end view too 'elitist' for current consumption, to use Snow et al.'s (2021) label. This is precisely why we have opted for the idea of a blueprint component situated somewhere between Kraut's grand-end view and Broadie's much more rhapsodic conception. Our blueprint component may be closer to Kraut's than Snow and et al.'s (2021) conception is, on that spectrum. But even their view, as we see it, is closer to Kraut than to Broadie.[48] In sum, we agree with Wright et al. (2021) that *phronesis* entails 'having a conception of what is valuable in life, what goods we think are worth having, and the ability to step back to take inventory on how our lives align with these ideals and what virtues we need to cultivate to give us a better chance at attaining those goods' (p. 277). However, rather than contrasting this, as they do, with a 'full-fledged blueprint of the good life', we would see it as constituting nothing less than such a blueprint.

2.4 Two Philosophical Counter-Positions

Despite the current enthusiasm for *phronesis* within diverse academic circles, *phronesis* enthusiasts have recently been experiencing considerable blowback, both from philosophers and psychologists, who dispute the construct from two opposing perspectives. The critics argue either that *phronesis* is asked to bite off more than it can chew in moral decision-making, or that the role

---

[48] Interestingly, MacIntyre, whose view was understandably, in *After Virtue* (1981; recall our Section 1.4), closer to Broadie's, had moved closer to Kraut's grand-end view by the time he later wrote his 1998 paper, in which he demands of plain-person *phronimoi* that they retrospectively examine what overall good their lives are aimed towards (MacIntyre, 1998, p. 8). Cf. Wolfe (2016).

accorded to it within the neo-Aristotelian 'standard model' is still not prominent enough.

Phronesis eliminativism

Let us start with the *phronesis* eliminativists who argue that *phronesis* has been given an inflated role in recent theorizing and that the functions it is meant to perform can more readily and parsimoniously be accorded to less complex—and better researched/understood—psycho-moral constructs. We refer to this as 'the redundancy thesis' about *phronesis*, and we draw upon two recent incarnations of it, by a philosopher (Miller, 2021), to whom we respond briefly in this section, and a psychologist (Lapsley, 2021), a more thorough response to whom awaits the psychologically oriented Chapter 4.

Miller initially 'flirts with' (as he puts it) but then apparently endorses what he calls 'Practical Wisdom Eliminativism' (2021, p. 65). It posits that rather than appealing to one intellectual virtue that is supposed to carry out the functions neo-Aristotelians ascribe to *phronesis*, we should appeal to a distinct trait performing each function. *Phronesis* is, then, at best a helpful shorthand for a collection of those specific functions, at worst an intruder or a red herring. Miller does not indicate precisely which functions are, in fact, performed by which processes or traits. He seems to leave room for either (or both) of (a) what he calls the 'Fragmentation Model', according to which all the functions of *phronesis* can be reduced to those of the individual moral virtues (although he considers that model to face difficulties, and that no one presently subscribes to it), or (b) the idea, closer to Lapsley's (2021) and probably Miller's considered view, that there are discrete psychological processes performing each function on behalf, so to speak, of one or more virtues.[49]

Miller's (2021) scepticism of *phronesis* is motivated by a number of concerns, the most salient of which are the 'Unity Concern': of why one should believe that a single trait, such as *phronesis*, should be able to carry out all the miscellaneous functions typically ascribed to it, and the 'Subsumption Concern': of what is left of a moral virtue once the various roles of *phronesis* are factored out: namely, apparently nothing except *phronesis* itself (pp. 58–9).

---

[49] Miller identifies six of those functions, not only four (2021, p. 57). For example, as we mentioned earlier in this chapter, he lists the 'end-setting function' of *phronesis* as a special function, whereas we consider 'end-setting' as just an implication of the other functions of *phronesis* (esp. the blueprint one). However, Miller may simply be highlighting here how varied the functions are that different proponents of the 'standard model' have ascribed to *phronesis*.

In the end, Miller's practical wisdom eliminativism concludes that 'on metaphysical grounds, practical wisdom does not exist' (p. 66).[50]

Let us briefly mention two initial conceptual responses to the redundancy thesis, although we do not think either of them suffices fully to counter it. The first response involves an appeal to ordinary language. It seems as if a unified concept of (practical) wisdom is fairly entrenched in everyday discourse. Most people would, for example, describe the capacity that King Solomon applied when making good choices as 'wisdom'. They would not say that he used a battery of independent functions to arrive at his wise decisions. Obviously, appeals to ordinary language have fallen out of favour in recent decades in Philosophy; however, psychologists tend quite eagerly to honour distinctions that ordinary people (and standard dictionaries) make, and philosophers used to take them as at least 'the first word' also (Austin, 1964). Yet no theorist would hold that every concept used as part of 'folk psychology' has ultimate authority, so an appeal to ordinary people operating with a unitary concept of practical wisdom does not suffice to combat Miller's (2021) eliminativism. Indeed, Miller admits that *phronesis* may be used in ordinary language as just a matter of convenient labelling. But his claim is that this label, as convenient for pragmatic purposes as it may be, does not pinpoint a real character trait (psychologically and metaphysically speaking). The second counterargument would be that 'first is not always the best'. Although there are decades of research available from the twentieth century to the present day within Moral Psychology (both as practised by philosophers and psychologists) on the functions that neo-Aristotelians ascribe to *phronesis*, without making any use of such an integrative concept, there is no reason to believe that the already presented constructs are either definitive or exhaustive.

Those initial responses notwithstanding, Miller's 'Unitary Concern' is a valid misgiving. Although we consider ourselves to have parried it indirectly in this chapter already by explicating the synergic motivational role that

---

[50] Lapsley is even more explicit in his critique and more direct in offering empirically researched alternatives to the functions that *phronesis* is—vaguely, in his view—supposed to perform. See our response in Chapter 4. Apart from Lapsley's and Miller's, there are other, more tentative and less radical, version of *phronesis* eliminativism around, for example Gulliford's (2017). She cleverly deconstructs the common metaphor of *phronesis* as a conductor of a symphony orchestra, replacing it with the metaphor of moral decision-making as the workings of a mutually correcting and inter-harmonizing jazz group that operates without a specific conductor. Gulliford likens her 'mutual interpenetration model' to the relationship between the persons of the Trinity in Christian theology. In her model, the moral virtues—just like the Father, Son, and the Holy Spirit—permeate each other and dwell in each other. Although Gulliford claims to be taking Occam's Razor to *phronesis*, she presents her alternative model in terms of 'scaling back' the contribution made by *phronesis*, rather than replacing it completely. Clever as the metaphor of the jazz group is, jazz groups seem to operate, so to speak, with a covert or speculative conductor whose 'orders' are conveyed through a long tradition of how to play jazz classics. Notably, Schwartz and Sharpe—ardent advocates of *phronesis*—liken *phronesis* itself to the orchestration of 'moral jazz' (2010, pp. 41, 101).

phronesis plays, above and beyond its four specific functions (both with respect to those functions and the underlying moral and civic virtues), we consider a more detailed response in order, explaining more fully the holistic nature of *phronesis*. However, for expository reasons, we leave that response until we have explored Lapsley's (2021) even more radical and explicit redundancy thesis in Chapter 4. In addition to the conceptual responses, there is a serious gap between the objections that both these scholars raise and the empirical evidence that is directly germane to the objections. That is, to some degree, both the APM and these objections are answerable to empirical evidence. We will elucidate this gap in Chapter 4.

Critics of the insufficiency of the APM

Now, as already noted, the new *phronesis* bandwagon has also come under attack from the other side: from philosophers who think that it does not, in fact, give *phronesis* sufficient priority with respect to the moral virtues (as traits), and that the only trait a truly virtuous moral agent needs to possess is simply *phronesis*. More specifically, on this view, all ethical virtues are ultimately unified within *phronesis* itself, understood as overall *moral expertise* (De Caro et al., 2021; cf. De Caro et al., 2018).[51] Miller (2021) refers to this view as the 'Socratic Model' because of its resemblance to the Socratic idea that virtue can be equated with *knowledge* (of a sort): here the practical wisdom that the *phronimos* presumably possesses. The Socratic Model simply bites the bullet of the 'Subsumption Concern' and turns it into a presumed advantage, although it intensifies Miller's 'Unity Concern' at the same time. De Caro et al. (2018, p. 292) worry that the only ultimate alternative to their Socratic Model is what Miller (2021, p. 54) calls a 'Fragmentation Model' (to which he says no one claims to subscribe), according to which each moral virtue occupies a discrete sphere of its own—siloed from other spheres, hence losing any sense of the unity of moral agency.[52] Notably, they do not present their model just as an attractive philosophical plaything but, rather, consider it to have salient practical implications, for instance, in Moral/Character Education, which on this model should primarily take the form of training in overall moral expertise rather than habituating the young into exercising specific virtues (p. 294).

---

[51] They aptly describe their version of *phronesis* as a master virtue, rather than a meta-virtue. It is a master virtue not only in the sense of trumping all other virtues, but in subsuming them. They also enlighteningly refer to their model as 'virtue molecularism' (De Caro et al., 2021, p. 31).

[52] De Caro, Marraffa, and Vaccarezza (2021, p. 32) refer to such a model as one of 'virtue atomism', as opposed to 'virtue molecularism'.

It should come as no surprise to perceptive readers that we are more sympathetic to this alternative to the Aristotelian 'standard model' than the eliminativist one espoused by Miller (2021). What we like here is the keen understanding in the Socratic Model of the orchestrating role of *phronesis*. However, we are mindful of Aristotle's own famous complaint about the original Socratic Model that, although it correctly implicates (*phronetic*) knowledge in every virtue, the virtues are more than just (*phronetic*) knowledge (Aristotle, 1985, p. 170 [1144b18-21]). We worry, just like Wright et al. (2021), that an extreme form of virtue unionism loses track of the uniqueness of each virtue, and in particular its unique form of moral motivation.[53]

On our understanding, the 'virtuous person' is not only the fully *phronetic* person. Any suggestions to that effect paint an unrealistic picture of actual Moral Psychology, as most (even overall virtuous) people possess a mixture of *phronesis*-guided and non-*phronesis*-guided traits. Even children can be considered proto-virtuous, in terms of their habituated virtues, before *phronesis* kicks in. Although the 'Socratic Model' allows that *phronesis* can be appropriately attributed to imperfect agents who possess a sufficient level of ethical expertise understood as a scalar trait, it does not account well for states of uneven virtue development. We have three further reservations about the Socratic Model. First, it seems to confine virtuous motivation to the motivation originating in *phronesis*. However, we believe the primary virtuous motivation stems from the individual moral virtues, as we have explained in detail. Second, the Socratic Model would need to exclude the civic virtues, if it is to remain even minimally faithful to Aristotle's original concept of *phronesis*, since he explicitly states in the *Politics* that all citizens can possess the civic virtues and that they do not require *phronesis*, except for the rulers of states (see Chapter 8 in the present book). Finally, the Socratic Model lacks direct empirical tests, leaving it stranded in conceptual space. All that said, we value the contribution made by De Caro et al. to the *phronesis* discourse, especially the warning signals they sound about the threat of virtue atomism.

2.5 Some Remaining Philosophical Alternatives

This chapter has basically traversed an Aristotelian terrain only: our four-componential elaboration of the neo-Aristotelian 'standard model' and a few philosophical alternatives, rooted within that same discourse. In the next two

---

[53] Importantly, Plato was a hard motivational internalist, believing that moral knowledge motivates intrinsically. Aristotle did not share that view (Kristjánsson, 2013, chap. 5).

chapters, we explore some psychological alternatives. However, before leaving the philosophical accounts of practical wisdom behind for a while, we want to mention briefly four important accounts that do not have the same Aristotelian provenance. We have no space to elaborate upon those accounts as meticulously as we have tried to develop the neo-Aristotelian ones, nor to introduce other historically prominent accounts. We simply want to give readers the sense that there is more to the philosophy of *phronesis* than adding footnotes to Aristotle.

Phronesis in medical decision-making

We are great admirers of the work that Lauris Kaldjian (2014; 2019) has done on *phronesis* in the context of medical decision-making—although we question some of its MacIntyrean presuppositions—and we return to it in Chapter 7. At the present juncture, we simply wish to highlight the 'core elements' that Kaldjian has elicited from historical accounts of *phronesis* and from his work with medical practitioners, in order to show how strikingly similar those are to the components of our model:

(1) pursuit of worthwhile ends (goals) derived from a concept of human flourishing;
(2) accurate perception of concrete circumstances detailing the specific practical situation;
(3) commitment to moral virtues and principles that are interdependent and form an integrated moral framework;
(4) deliberation that integrates ends (goals), concrete circumstances, and moral virtues and principles; and
(5) motivation to act in order to achieve the conclusions reached by such deliberation (2019, p. 706).

As readers will quickly see, (1), (3), and (5) are tasks that we attributed to the blueprint function; (2) is synonymous with our constitutive function; and (4) corresponds to our integrative function. The only of our functions missing is the emotional regulative one. However, Kaldjian includes that in his model under the rubric of 'associated virtues', and he considers empathy in particular as the 'feeling component' of *phronesis* (2019, p. 703), although, for some reason, he leaves it out of the list of 'core elements'.[54] It is heartening to see

---

[54] Interestingly, Svenaeus (2014) also refers to 'empathy' as the 'feeling component of *phronesis*'. In Aristotelian virtue theory, intellectual virtues (as distinct from moral ones) do not have a specific feeling

a theorist develop a model out of sources other than those we have mainly relied upon but ending up with more or less the same ingredients. Equally interesting is another medically derived model of *phronesis*, Jameel's recent 'fish-school' model (2022, chap. 8), comprising 33 ingredients derived from interviews with medical doctors and arranged under six themes. Jameel's emphasis on the synchrony of the ingredients in the model and how *phronesis* is more than a sum of its individual parts is, for us, an attractive feature of her model insofar as it confirms our own insights and helps alleviate misgivings by various above-mentioned theorists about virtue atomism. Another attractive feature is obviously the atheoretical provenance of Jameel's model in interviews with practitioners, most of whom had no ready-made Aristotelian Philosophy in their pockets.

Aquinas

Let us next say a few words about Aquinas. Historically, Aquinas obviously drew extensively on Aristotle, whom he simply referred to as the 'Philosopher' and whose insights he tried to reconcile as much as possible with a Christian framework. Aquinas chose to refer to practical wisdom as 'prudence', and that term has become entrenched in the extensive Christian literature on wisdom.[55] While Aquinas defined prudence very much in line with Aristotle's characterization of *phronesis*, as a filter of deliberation between ends and means,[56] Aquinas's concept was made to fit into a virtue theory that is in many ways different from Aristotle's, for example, in making use of a moral master virtue (Christian love or charity) and in invoking various psycho-moral concepts that were not part of Aristotle's arsenal, such as 'will' and 'conscience'. In a way, prudence becomes for Aquinas a capacity to execute coherently the dictates of Christian conscience. While Aquinas did not come up with a list of the functions of prudence, comparable to our list of the functions of *phronesis*,

---

component. However, empathy can perhaps serve as a proxy for the emotional regulative function of *phronesis*, and indeed we use it such in Chapter 6 for measurement purposes, but more in default of better existing measures than as a theoretically complete assessment.

[55] Prudence is also one of the 24 character strengths in the psychological VIA model (Peterson & Seligman, 2004), although it is not understood there as a meta-virtue. In our experience, young people in the English-speaking world have a limited understanding of the word 'prudence' and commonly confuse it with being 'prudish' or simply cautious. This is one reason why we avoid it and do not see it as a helpful translation of '*phronesis*'.

[56] Aquinas also shared Aristotle's disregard for mere utilitarian tactics.

his account of *phronesis* is almost certainly closer to ours than either Miller's or De Caro et al.'s, explored in the previous section.

Confucius

The final historical account we want to mention here briefly is that of Confucius: a virtue theorist who, for obvious reasons, cannot be accused of simply writing footnotes to Aristotle. Although there are striking structural similarities between the virtue theories of Aristotle and Confucius (Yu, 2007), it is not easy to juxtapose their views on practical wisdom. There are two (intellectual) virtues in Confucius that occupy a higher-status of the kind that Aristotle ascribes to *phronesis*, namely appropriateness/righteousness (*yì*) and wisdom (*zhì*). Yet the division of labour between them is not always clear, and neither seems to do all the work that *phronesis* does in Aristotle's theory. Wisdom is broader, sometimes so much so that it embraces the tasks of both *deinotes* and *sophia* in Aristotle, as well as *phronesis*. Yet, like *phronesis*, it is essentially meant to dispel moral confusion. Appropriateness is more about practical choices in daily affairs, and in that sense closer to *phronesis*, but it seems to need input from the more abstract considerations offered by wisdom (Yu, 2007, pp. 150–1). Confucius would thus probably have considered Aristotle's distinction between *sophia* and *phronesis* too clear-cut.[57]

The skill analogy

Before closing this chapter, a few words are in order about the extensive recent discourse on the so-called skill analogy: namely, the extent to which virtue in general and *phronesis* in particular can be understood, analogously or even literally,[58] as a skill (e.g., Stichter, 2018; 2021; Swartwood, 2013; Tsai, 2020; 2022; Zheng, 2021). We must admit that we have been rather underwhelmed by this

---

[57] For a completely different take on Confucius, in which benevolence/humaneness (*ren*) is seen as closest to practical wisdom, because it 'entails other moral virtues', see Sim (2024). However, we remain unconvinced that the role of *ren*, which is a moral virtue, can be compared with that of *phronesis*, which is an intellectual virtue, in Aristotle. While we do not claim competence in the field of Chinese Philosophy, *ren* seems to us more similar to a moral master virtue than an intellectual meta-virtue. We remain closer, therefore, to Yu's view that there is no virtue in Confucius that fully plays the role of *phronesis* in Aristotelian theory and that this may, indeed, be a potential weakness in the Confucian virtue system. While our expertise in African Philosophy is even more limited, we recommend Kayange's (2020) article for a thought-provoking discussion of the potential relationship between the African moral virtue of *ubuntu* and *phronesis*.

[58] Tsai (2020, p. 235) refers to these as distinct theses: an analogy thesis and an identity thesis.

discourse and are perhaps not the most motivated discussants of it. To recap, Aristotle himself often draws an analogy between moral or intellectual virtues and skills. However, he also notes an essential asymmetry between skills (*techné*) and virtues in that the former are only valuable in terms of their outcome whereas virtues have a value in themselves as a process. Stichter (2018) reinterprets skills in terms of constitutive rather than only instrumental ends, but we think it undermines the usefulness of the idea of virtues as skills because retaining the difference between extrinsically motivated skills and intrinsically motivated virtues is important. Some contributors to the debate focus on this difference (Hacker-Wright, 2015; cf. Tsai's 2020 rejoinder), and sometimes other differences, such as the more complex existential challenges involved in the exhibition of virtues rather than typical skills (Kristjánsson, 2015, chap. 4). Others find the skill analogy invaluable to articulate the nature of virtue, especially to novices (Annas, 2011), or to explain, say, the relationship between *phronesis* and wellbeing understood as 'attitude success' (Tsai, 2022).

We have mixed feelings about this discourse. On the one hand, we acknowledge that Annas's (2011) account of Virtue Ethics, explicated by dint of the skill analogy, is possibly the best initial reading about virtue and *phronesis* from an Aristotelian perspective that can be recommended to new students. Moreover, we do not exclude the possibility that by couching *phronesis* in terms of a skill, certain empirical sources on skill acquisition and skilful expertise, which are useful for understanding *phronesis*, will be consulted that would otherwise slip through the net. In other words, the skill analogy may help as a facilitator of cross-disciplinary work on *phronesis*, synthesizing diverse literatures and supporting crossover research projects: enterprises in which we see great merit. On the other hand, we do not share Zheng's (2021) enthusiasm for the skill analogy as a *necessary* steppingstone towards understanding the nature of, say, good deliberation. We believe that we succeeded in explicating our model of *phronesis* in preceding sections of this chapter without couching *phronesis* specifically in terms of a skill, and in the following two chapters we draw upon various relevant research traditions in contemporary Psychology that, again, can cast a helpful light on practical wisdom without understanding it, explicitly at least, as a skill. This seems to render the portrayal of *phronesis* in skills terms optional. However, if the pragmatic explanatory benefits of the skill analogy will be further borne out in future research, we are no die-hard foes of it either.

3
The History of Wisdom Research in Psychology and the New Common Model

We turn now to a discussion of the history of wisdom research in Psychology. Psychological research on wisdom has a lengthy and rich history that has set the stage for contemporary scholarship not only on general wisdom but also on practical wisdom. This history of empirically oriented wisdom research is vital to understanding the recent turn towards *phronesis*. We begin with the early history of this scholarship and recount many of the psychological models of wisdom that have been proposed in the last 40 years. We see this history culminating recently in the presentation of what has been called the 'common wisdom model', which has brought the general wisdom theories into closer alignment with the historical discourse on practical wisdom as *phronesis*. After discussing this model, we examine some of the most salient critiques that have been offered by other wisdom scholars.

3.1 The Early History of Wisdom Research in Psychology

Although wisdom research has been conducted in Psychology for over 4 decades, it has mostly followed its own distinct path, parallel to research trajectories in Philosophy but without significant interactions. This research began by inquiring about implicit or folk theories of wisdom (Clayton & Birren, 1980; Sternberg & Karami, 2021), after which it was transformed into a series of theories generated by psychologists and other social scientists. From the beginning, however, there has been confusion about what these researchers have meant by 'wisdom'. They often straddle the Aristotelian concepts of *sophia* and *phronesis*, portraying their construct sometimes in otherworldly and universalistic terms (akin to *sophia*) and sometimes pursuing the topic in very pragmatic terms (akin to *phronesis*). At other times, it is difficult to differentiate psychological theories and measures from *deinotes* ('cleverness'), largely because of the social scientific penchant for avoiding moral commitments. Recall that the difference between *phronesis* and *deinotes* is that the latter is not tied to moral or noble aims, whereas the former is inseparable from moral aims. A third common shortcoming—at least from the present perspective—is that when wisdom theorists offer the kind of moral account of action that differentiates wisdom and *deinotes*, the moral-discourse terms they use tend to be quite formal, which means that any morally relevant goods can be inserted into the theory, whether they are morally good, morally bad, or morally indifferent. We describe the major theories of wisdom in this section, beginning with the Berlin Wisdom Paradigm (BWP), and illustrate these shortcomings of the psychological literature on wisdom.

Berlin Wisdom Paradigm

Near the end of the twentieth century, several psychologists studying human development concluded that adding the concept of wisdom to psychological inquiry would be 'a worthwhile challenge' (Baltes & Staudinger, 2000, p. 132). One of the early models was the BWP, developed at the Max Planck Institute for Human Development. The BWP defined 'wisdom' as 'expertise in the fundamental pragmatics of life' (Baltes & Staudinger, 2000, p. 124). In this paradigm, 'wisdom' is an expert knowledge system, relating to persons' conduct and construction of meaning. Individuals develop expertise or extraordinary knowledge through years of training and practice. The expertise in question is measured with five criteria: the richness of relevant factual knowledge, the richness of relevant procedural knowledge, the extent of life-span contextualism and perspective, relativism of values and life priorities producing toleration of difference, and the recognition and management of uncertainty (Staudinger & Glück, 2011). In this approach, we see a focus on the practical, but the absence of any moral element, rendering the BWP, insofar as it is understood as a practical capacity, indistinguishable from cleverness. The fundamentally pragmatic nature of this paradigm means that one can 'wisely' pursue goals of any sort, including not only noble aims, but also reprehensible aims such as human trafficking or trivial aims such as ephemeral fame. By their very nature, amoral theories cannot rule out amoral or immoral pursuits. Although the BWP included an admirably rigorous interview-based rating system, that system has also lost favour because it is considered cumbersome, expensive, and overemphasizes cognition.

Balance model of wisdom

Contemporaneously, Sternberg (1998; 2003) proposed a balance theory of wisdom. He characterized wisdom as a meta-skill in applying tacit knowledge, mediated by values, to the integrative task of achieving 'the common good'—which he defined as balancing intrapersonal, interpersonal, and extrapersonal (e.g., humanity, God, and the universe) interests and adapting these to environmental contexts. Sternberg clarifies that the balance theory differs from other wisdom models in its focus on a wise person's accomplishments of ends rather than on personal traits. He therefore described his theory as functional rather than trait-based. According to Sternberg, persons are wise to the extent that they use their skills and knowledge to (1) achieve a common good, by (2) balancing intrapersonal (their own), interpersonal (others'), and extrapersonal interests over (3) the long term, as well as the short term, through (4) the utilization of positive ethical values, by (5) adapting to, shaping, and selecting environments.

From the beginning, Sternberg (1998) differentiated what he termed 'wisdom' from what he called 'practical intelligence', with the latter mapping onto cleverness. In addition, he has consistently used moral terms such as 'values' and 'good', thereby creating some distance from the concept of cleverness. Yet he has also consistently framed those moral terms in formal ways, leaving their content mostly undefined. Generally, he discusses the moral aspect of wisdom in terms of balancing 'interests'. The difficulty with this approach is that if one happens to value domination or exploitation, Sternberg has few resources for arguing that one could not or should not pursue such ends in a balanced way and hence wisely. Notably, Sternberg (1998) claims that wisdom always results in 'the common good', so he might argue that exploitation might violate the common good. This claim is undermined, however, because his version of 'the common good' is also formal, defined in terms of a balance of the interests of those concerned. An exploiter could simply claim that the proper balance or the best common good when it comes to 'wolves and sheep' is for wolves to take a larger proportion of goods, while sheep must accept that whatever division of goods is available once wolves have taken what they want.

Sternberg et al. (2022) are clear about the formal nature of the common good, stating: 'One achieves the common good by balancing one's own interests with the interests of others and of large entities, such as the community, a state or province, a country, the world, or even entities beyond the world, such as the universe' (p. 55). Sternberg (1998) explicitly demurs on fleshing out what makes an interest good or on how to define 'the common good', claiming that such matters are 'better dealt with by moral philosophy and religion' (p. 355). He also leaves the nature of 'balance' undefined, meaning that Sternberg's balance theory cannot differentiate among moral and immoral ends, after all. This penchant for highly abstract conceptualization also makes it difficult to separate Sternberg's concept of wisdom from *sophia*. He also claims that wisdom deals with highly abstract and extra-worldly concerns related to God or the universe, which are realms that are generally seen as matters of *sophia* more than *phronesis*. After all, what would it mean, in practical terms, to balance one's interests with the universe?

In addition, as Brienza et al. (2018) point out, 'there has been little effort to explicitly use balance-related criteria to evaluate the hypothesized effectiveness of wisdom-related cognitive processes' (p. 1094). Without clear empirical results supporting the balance concept of wisdom, it remains an abstract conception without clear ties to real-world decision-making and action.

Self-report measures of wisdom

Partly disillusioned with the methodological intricacy of the BWP (especially its reliance on qualitative interviews with fairly cumbersome analyses), partly motivated by theoretical misgivings about the BWP's exclusive focus on wisdom as knowledge rather than attending to the affective and reflective elements of wisdom, Ardelt (2003; 2004) developed a three-dimensional theory of wisdom. The three dimensions are: *cognitive* (measuring deep understanding of human life), *reflective* (measuring insightful perception of events from multiple perspectives), and *affective* (measuring sympathetic and compassionate love for others). Based on this theory, she produced her Three Dimensional Wisdom Scale (3DWS) Several researchers have concurred with Ardelt's criticism of the prominence of cognitive elements in wisdom research (e.g., Darnell et al., 2019; Glück & Bluck, 2013). In the 3DWS, Ardelt (2003) presents a set of statements about wisdom and asks respondents how true the statements are about themselves. Her scale has been used many times in wisdom research.[1]

---

[1] We particularly recommend Jameel's (2022) thesis for an ingenious use of Ardelt's scale, when combined with other measures.

Several authors have followed a similar self-report strategy for wisdom scales, including the Self-Assessed Wisdom Scale (Webster, 2003), and the Adult Self-Transcendence Inventory (Aldwin et al., 2019; Levenson et al., 2005). The core difficulty with self-report scales of wisdom is the apparent paradox wherein those who lack wisdom are likely to overestimate how wise they are, perhaps because of poor insight, and those who are wise are likely to underestimate their wisdom, perhaps because of intellectual humility. In addition, there are many well-known self-report biases, such as social desirability, memory distortion, confirmation biases, and the difficulties of summarizing vast swaths of experience in a single numerical response. In short, there are significant doubts about the construct validity[2] of an exclusive focus on self-reported wisdom. In a meta-analysis and a study of the prerequisites of wisdom, Dong and her colleagues (Dong & Fournier, 2022; Dong et al., 2023) found that self-report wisdom scales and performance scales (e.g., the BWP) load on different latent factors and have different correlates. This suggests that, although self-report and performance measures are correlated, they are assessing distinct aspects of a construct of wisdom.

In a measurement approach largely designed to reduce self-report biases, Brienza et al. (2018) designed the Situated Wise Reasoning Scale (SWiS) to assess wisdom as a contextualized state construct rather than as a global decontextualized trait construct.[3] They were interested in assessing how people adjust their reasoning to specific situations they have encountered rather than obtaining global summary responses about wisdom. Therefore, they asked respondents to reflect on a situation they have experienced and choose responses that reflect the quality of their reasoning about the situation. They cited several criteria for wise reasoning: 'intellectual humility, recognition of a world in flux and change, appreciation of different perspectives, application of an outsider's vantage point, consideration of and search for compromise and conflict resolution' (p. 1097). They reported excellent psychometric properties for their scale, and the SWiS has become a standard measure of wisdom alongside several other measures (Dong et al., 2023). The general difficulty is that there are several extant measures

---

[2] Psychologists use the term 'construct validity' roughly to refer to the degree to which a measure assess the construct it is intended to assess. In the case of self-report wisdom scales, the question is how well the respondent can evaluate her own wisdom.

[3] 'State constructs' are phenomena that occur at a particular time, that may or may not aggregate into a general characteristic. State constructs allow careful assessment of situational variables. In contrast, 'trait constructs' refer to general characteristics of a person that are likely to be manifested in many different contexts and are generally assessed with global, decontextualized measures.

of wisdom that are only mildly or moderately correlated, and there is little or no evidential guidance for researchers to pick one or the other beyond some simple form of preference.

A polyglot of models

In the last 10–15 years, various other new wisdom research methods and models have arrived on the scene (see Grossmann, Westrate, Ardelt et al., 2020, for a comprehensive overview). However, characterizing most of those—as the previously mentioned ones—has been a focus on a broad and undifferentiated conception of wisdom, often in the context of exploring what sets apart the mature thinking of experienced people in general or in the context of adult Developmental Psychology in particular (cf. Kallio, 2020). Relying in turn on conceptions of wisdom derived from experts or from folk psychology, this discursive tradition has not paid special attention to what motivates wisdom cultivation to allow deliberation about ethical quandaries, leading to moral action. The lack of a motivational account of wisdom and the absence of a connection between deliberation and action have been highlighted by the *phronesis* discourses in Philosophy and Moral Education (Darnell et al., 2019), which have gradually been sedimenting around the proverbial post-Kohlbergian question of what bridges the gap between moral cognition and moral action (see our discussion in Chapter 5).

In addition to the theories of wisdom already discussed, there are others that have widely varying definitions, including: mastery, openness, reflectivity, emotional regulation, and empathy (Glück & Bluck, 2013); humour, emotional regulation, reminiscence/reflectiveness, openness to experience, and critical life experiences (Webster, 2007; 2019); a 4P Model of person, press, product, and process (Phan et al., 2021); integration, embodiment, and positive effects (Yang, 2008); and knowledge, reflectivity, self-regulation, prosocial behaviours, moral maturity, openness, tolerance, sound judgement, creativity, dynamic balance, and synthesis (Karami et al., 2020).

Although there are some commonalities in these models, this brief registry indicates the polyglot of proposals lacking cohesion, despite recent efforts at synthesis by Grossmann, Westrate, Ardelt et al. (2020) and Sternberg and Karami (2021). As Grossmann Westrate, Ardelt et al. (2020) put it,

> empirical wisdom researchers have prioritized different philosophical models of wisdom, without specifying a shared theoretical vocabulary or standards to allow for a clear comparison between them... This theoretical diversity can lead

researchers to use different terms for the same concept, or use the same term for different concepts, resulting in conceptual ambiguity (p. 104).

Sternberg and Karami (2021) concurred, stating that the 'various models of wisdom contain so many elements that it is not possible to incorporate each and every one in any single model without turning the model into a grab bag' (p. 136). This theoretical disarray is likely the result of the rather intuitive and idiosyncratic ways that most investigators have conceptualized wisdom, and the mixing up of metaphysical, moral, and instrumental considerations relating to the diverse functions of wisdom. They have seldom elaborated a systematic theory of wisdom, and there is a penchant for psychologists to rush to measurement prior to developing a well-grounded theoretical perspective on a construct. Even among highly intelligent and capable scientists, this is a recipe for theoretical disarray.

Potential solutions to theoretical disarray

Two notable solutions to this conceptual confusion have been recently proposed. Sternberg and Karami (2021) offered a '6P' approach to provide a minimalist framework for organizing multiple theories and models of wisdom. This approach identifies six elements to encompass the important components of the various wisdom theories and models: purpose, persons, processes, products, press, and problems. They also suggested which wisdom concepts fit within which categories. As they noted, the 6P framework is not a theory or even a model. Rather, it is a framework for understanding how different aspects of wisdom, and theoretical accounts of them, can be accounted for in a single framework (Sternberg & Karami, 2021, p. 5). Although it may have some benefit as an organizing framework or a taxonomical umbrella, the 6P approach is even more devoid of content than the wisdom models it is meant to organize. An organizational framework cannot provide the systematic theory that is generally missing in psychological scholarship on wisdom.

The second attempted solution was presented by Grossmann and his colleagues (Grossmann, 2017b; Grossmann, Westrate, Ardelt et al., 2020) as a 'common wisdom model'. These scholars attempted to combine features of other models, such as balancing viewpoints, practising epistemic humility and adaptability, and taking multiple perspectives. They defined 'wisdom' as 'morally-grounded excellence in social-cognitive processing' (Grossmann, Westrate, Ardelt et al., 2020, p. 133). In the common model, they highlighted two main elements: perspectival metacognition and moral aspirations. From our viewpoint, the most promising aspects of the common model are that it relates wisdom more directly to developments in the science of virtue and much closer to the concept of *phronesis*. Owing to the gravity and importance of this 'common model' of wisdom, we return to it in Section 3.3 for a more thorough discussion. Prior to that, it is important to survey several attempts to understand wisdom from a *phronetic* perspective.

3.2 *Phronesis* in Psychology: Some Nonmainstream Voices

Although the conceptual space surrounding wisdom seems to be overpopulated with psychological theories already, there are other important voices in this discussion that were inspired by neo-Aristotelian (more or less) thought rather than by standard psychological approaches that prioritize measurement. We begin with Positive Psychology, despite the fact that their debt to Aristotle regarding wisdom is quite shallow; then we discuss contributions by Fowers (2005), Schwartz and Sharpe (2010), Ng and Tay (2020), and Snow et al. (2021). This clarifies that Grossmann and his colleagues are not isolated in attempting to appropriate a more Aristotelian understanding of wisdom as *phronesis*.

The positive psychological alternative

The debt owed to Positive Psychology for putting character and virtues back on psychological agendas notwithstanding, positive psychologists have also been criticized for their lack of attention to *phronesis* or indeed to any intellectual meta-virtue for the integration and adjudication of character virtues (e.g., Fowers, 2008; Kristjánsson, 2013). Departing from the standard architectonic of virtue as a 'golden mean' between the extremes of excess and deficiency (Aristotle, 1985), positive psychologists normally take it for granted that 'more is better' and that a chain of virtues is as strong as its strongest links. This view has been criticized by numerous authors (e.g., Fowers, 2008; Grant & Schwartz, 2011; Ng & Tay, 2020) who have presented argument and evidence that more of many good things is not better.

Neither *phronesis* nor any reasonable analogue appears in the 24 proposed universal character strengths and virtues (Peterson & Seligman, 2004). Wisdom is one of the six virtues they catalogue, but it is made up of the 'character strengths' of creativity, curiosity, open-mindedness, love of learning, and perspective. This is an interesting collection, but it overlaps only slightly with the psychological wisdom scholarship we discussed in the beginning of this chapter and is quite distinct from a neo-Aristotelian viewpoint.

It is striking, from a neo-Aristotelian viewpoint, that wisdom is not given a special position among the virtues in Positive Psychology. There is no discrete 'meta' (integrative) or 'master' (overridingness) function in their model (Peterson & Seligman, 2004). Wisdom is just one of several virtues. The typical rationale given for those omissions is that psychologists would be abandoning their scientific credentials by positing a meta-virtue, because there is no universal consensus on the action-oriented arbitration of virtue conflicts in the same way as there is, arguably, regarding the perceived value of individual virtue traits, for which Peterson and Seligman (2004) claimed to have found universal endorsement. We have our doubts about the existence of universal consensus about many concepts, let alone the idea of taking consensus (either lay or academic) as a necessary basis for theoretical propositions.

There is an even more jarring lacuna in Positive Psychology in its efforts to render a good life as a mostly subjective matter. This was evident in Seligman's (2002) original concept of 'authentic happiness', and it remains prominent—albeit modified—in his later version of 'the good life' (Seligman, 2011), described as PERMA (positive emotion, engagement, relationships, meaning, and accomplishment). Although the concept of relationships could transcend the individual, Seligman focused his attention almost entirely on the perception of relationships from an individual's perspective and on the positive effects of relationships on individuals. Subjectifying the good life is important for Seligman to maintain the value-neutrality that he believes is necessary. Seligman seems to believe that making the good life purely a matter of an individual's self-assessment means that the researcher does not adopt any evaluative posture.[4] Like many psychologists, Seligman appears to have ignored the voluminous critiques of that sort of 'value-neutrality' (e.g., Brinkmann, 2011; Richardson et al., 1999).

The Values-in-Action (VIA) assessment approach grew out of Peterson and Seligman's (2004) seminal volume, and it was designed to assess the 24 character strengths originally proposed. As the primary contemporary analyst of and advocate for that approach, McGrath (2019) has suggested that the role we ascribe to *phronesis* can be played collectively by 3 of the 24 VIA character strengths: *prudence* (for the emotional regulative function), *judgement* (for the constitutive function), and *perspective* (for the integrative function; recall

---

[4] That said, Seligman (2011) is fairly sceptical about many standard self-report measures in Psychology and encourages theorists to find ways to go beyond them.

Chapters 1 and 2 for descriptions of these functions). Moreover, McGrath (2019) has made the rather sweeping claim that 'we have no empirical evidence to suggest practical wisdom' (p. 43). Unsurprisingly, McGrath was speaking only about evidence from studies of the VIA, which he recognizes does not attempt to measure anything like *phronesis*.

Although we applaud McGrath's efforts in trying to find space for the functions that we attribute to *phronesis* within the conceptual repertoire of Positive Psychology, we harbour two main worries about his proposal. One is that the central role of the blueprint component is missing—although McGrath and Brown (2020) venture that this role may, in some unspecified way, be satisfied by the focus of *perspective* on moral issues and the 'big picture'. Second, and more significant, we worry about the lack of an intellectual meta-virtue in the positive psychological system overall (cf. Schwartz & Sharpe, 2006). If the metacognitive role we ascribe to *phronesis* is to be taken over by 3 discrete virtues at the same epistemological and characterological level, how will conflicts between the requirements of judgement, perspective, and prudence be adjudicated? Which of the virtues calls the shots—and why? If the idea is that the virtues function more like a jazz group than a symphony orchestra, without the need for a conductor (Gulliford, 2017), it is incumbent on the proposers to provide a psychological account of how this coordination takes place, without invoking an arbitrator, and without ending up with an explanatory vicious regress—or moral paralysis.

What seems to be missing in the theory, Schwartz and Sharpe (2006) argue, is a moral integrator: the locus and terminus of justification. No attention is thus given in Positive Psychology to the problem of one virtue colliding with another or to the bigger picture of relevance: how different characteristics fit into a well-rounded life. Rather, individual strengths are treated as logically, empirically, and morally independent, and virtuous character as a smorgasbord where items can be picked or not picked at the individual's whim. This smacks more of post hoc reasoning than of systematic theory.

Neo-Aristotelian conceptualizations of *phronesis*

There have always been psychologists interested in virtue and *phronesis* who do not count themselves as members of the Positive Psychology movement. From the beginning of this century, Fowers (2001; 2005) has taken on the challenge of adapting psychological theory, research, and practice along neo-Aristotelian lines. He originally presented a three-component model of *phronesis* based on his reading of Aristotle at that time, which included moral perception, deliberation, and reasoned choice. In the second half of that book, this model was presented as the basis of an approach to psychological practice, research, and ethics. Fowers's initial model has been superseded by the four-component Aristotelian phronesis model (APM; Darnell et al., 2019; Fowers et al., 2021; 2022b), because the two models are rather compatible, and the four-component APM is more inclusive. Fowers and colleagues (in press) incorporated the four-component model into their discussion of the emerging science of virtue.

Schwartz and Sharpe (2010) have also made a strong appeal for the (re)appropriation of practical wisdom in psychological theory and practice, as well as within professional ethics (e.g., business, medicine, teaching, and nursing). Their book renders *phronesis* accessible to psychologists. In addition, they are clearly working with Aristotle's original concept of *phronesis*. Their book is an excellent introduction to the topic, chock full of rich examples.[5] That said, the book is written for a general audience and may not satisfy the meticulous academic.

Two recent and very thoughtful additions to this growing neo-Aristotelian literature on *phronesis* have come from the interdisciplinary team of Wright, Warren (psychologists), and Snow (a philosopher). They published a book that provided a detailed, in-depth analysis of *phronesis* and how it relates to virtue research and measurement (Wright et al., 2021). In addition, they expanded this analysis in a stand-alone chapter (Snow et al., 2021). In their view, *phronesis* has four functions: '(1) action guidance; (2) the regulation of a multiplicity of virtues within character; (3) emotion regulation; and (4) reflection on one's life as a whole' (p. 71). These roles are similar to the four components of the APM and are also in line with the 'standard' Aristotelian model of *phronesis* we discussed in Chapter 1.

They depart most strongly from the APM's 'blueprint' component in arguing that an individual can engage in *phronesis* without having a 'fully articulated comprehensive vision of their good' (p. 74). In particular, they want to leave room for *phronesis* to be part of the moral formation of the person. This difference is quite nuanced, in our view, because where Snow et al. (2021) suggest that *phronesis* plays a role in the moral formation of individuals, we might suggest that the development of *phronesis* and the moral formation of individuals are more dialectical. That is, in the early stages of forming oneself

---

[5] Schwartz has also produced a number of excellent online presentations (including a much-watched TED talk) on practical wisdom, available on YouTube, which we often recommend to students as a preliminary source of insights on the concept, even before we advise them to read more academic outputs.

morally, *phronesis* is as incomplete as one's moral character, and the development of one is part of the development of the other. In other words, a nascent or immature version of *phronesis* can be active in moral formation, but mature *phronesis* entails mature character. We refer readers back to Section 2.3 in which we offered a more detailed response to Snow et al. (2021). However, at this juncture we simply wish to applaud their carefully crafted discussion of *phronesis* and highlight the substantial overlap between their conceptualization and our APM.[6]

3.3 The New Common Wisdom Model

Disillusioned with the continued controversies among wisdom researchers in Psychology on the definition of 'wisdom' (Grossmann, 2017b), Grossmann, Weststrate, Ardelt et al. (2020), including many of Psychology's most prominent wisdom researchers, gathered a 'Wisdom Task Force' to try to carve out a 'consensus position' (p. 104) by inquiring into whether there were common threads in the heterogeneous psychological literature on wisdom. Furthermore, they conducted a mixed-methods survey of expert conceptualizations of wisdom. In this study, the two most prominent themes were that wisdom is morally grounded and that it deals with metacognition. 'Moral grounding' referred to general attributes (e.g., 'prosociality') and specific tendencies (e.g., compassion, sympathy). Grossmann, Weststrate, Ardelt et al. (2020) also emphasized balancing self-interest with common interests as their understanding of moral grounding. The metacognitive theme was comprised by references to considering multiple perspectives, searching for balance between varying interests, and epistemic humility. The authors suggested that the nonpropositional capacity can balance multiple perspectives in their understanding of metacognition.

Given the results of their survey of experts, a new Common Wisdom Model (CWM) was designed by this group of wisdom researchers to integrate the apparent 'common denominators' (Glück, 2020) of metacognition and moral grounding. The Task Force eventually redefined these terms as perspectival metacognition and moral aspirations, comprising its two main pillars. *Qua* intellectual virtue, the CWM depicts wisdom, therefore, as 'morally grounded

---

[6] Snow et al. (2021) have another aim in their discussion of *phronesis*, which is to integrate *phronesis* with the empirically oriented personality approach called Whole Trait Theory. Although they argue that Whole Trait Theory is hospitable to *phronesis*, we are not as sanguine about that integration as Snow et al. seem to be. However, developing an argument to that effect would take us too far afield here.

excellence in [a certain kind of] social-cognitive processing' (Grossmann, Weststrate, Ardelt et al., 2020, p. 103). They clarified that wisdom is a dimensional construct (i.e., that individuals have it in degrees) and that it has both trait and state properties, as found by Brienza et al. (2018). These authors also noted a long history of psychologists being interested in wisdom going back to Stanley Hall.

Grossmann, Weststrate, Ardelt et al. (2020) defined 'excellence in social-cognitive processing' as 'the application of certain forms of metacognition to reasoning and problem-solving in situational domains that have the potential to affect other people' (p. 103). In their response to the commentaries on their presentation of the CWM, Grossmann, Weststrate, Ferrari et al. (2020) clarified that they view perspectival metacognition, 'both in its orientation to different perspectives on the self and others' as 'necessary for any full appreciation of wisdom-related morality as well as its implementation in the context of real life' (p. 189). Grossmann et al. characterized moral grounding as a 'balance of self- and other-oriented interests, pursuit of truth, and orientation toward shared humanity' (Grossmann, Weststrate, Ardelt et al., 2020, p. 103) and commented that 'scientists chiefly define common good through a lens of shared humanity, as well as balance of self-protective-and other-oriented interests' (Grossmann, Weststrate, Ferrari et al., 2020, p. 189).

The article introducing the CWM (Grossmann, Weststrate, Ardelt et al., 2020) constitutes a tour de force of psychological scholarship, characterized by a deft handling of voluminous bodies of literature and a strongly conciliatory spirit that is rare in academia. In their review, they carefully differentiated the CWM from related constructs, including general intelligence, emotional intelligence, rationality, and perspective-taking.

One of the Task Force discussions was about whether to include emotions and emotion regulation in the CWM. Grossmann, Weststrate, Ferrari et al. (2020) noted that the group 'deliberately avoided including emotions as a component of wisdom, after a debate among the authors of our target article, as there was no consensus on their fundamental nature for the CWM' (p. 186). They declined to include emotion regulation in the CWM partly because adaptive emotion regulation does not entail the kind of self-reflection that many theorists see as central to wisdom. In addition, they noted that conceptualizations of emotion regulation are not univocal and differences in conceptions make it difficult to incorporate this concept in the CWM.

Grossmann, Weststrate, Ferrari et al. (2020) also clarified that they did not include actions in the CWM because they believed that the wisdom of actions require considerable interpretation and is dependent on context and outcome. They suggested that considering actions to be wise required attention to the contingencies of the outcome of the action. They believed that these considerations make 'postulating any action to be a priori wise ... challenging and impractical' (p. 187). We return to this choice in Chapter 4.

It is very difficult to attain a consensus position among a large group of eminent researchers, and the CWM has already experienced considerable blowback, as seen by the many critical commentaries in the same journal issue. Some divisions also remain among the co-authors of the target article themselves, especially on the 'moral aspiration' pillar (Grossmann, Weststrate, Kara-Yakoubian et al., 2020), as we explain presently. The difficulty of the task of producing the CWM is evident in the nine critical commentaries that accompanied it, along with a response by some authors of the target article (Grossmann, Weststrate, Ferrari et al., 2020). Moreover, the authors themselves deemed it necessary to report on subtle 'divergences' within their own conceptualization (Grossmann, Weststrate, Kara-Yakoubian et al., 2020). In their response to the commentaries, Grossmann, Weststrate, Ferrari et al. (2020) helpfully related their wisdom model to the then ongoing health crisis, presenting it as a contribution from the social and behavioural sciences to addressing the dilemmas caused by the new world-wide challenge (e.g., the health versus wealth tension). Even more importantly, Grossmann, Weststrate, Ferrari et al. (2020) evidenced the intellectual humility many wisdom theorists advocate by stating that '[t]he CWM represents only the first step toward a systematic and open science of wisdom' (p. 191). They follow this by highlighting some unanswered questions about wisdom (e.g., can training in metacognition increase wisdom?).

Although we will discuss the pros and cons of the CWM in considerable detail in Chapter 4, we want to highlight here the extent to which it can be seen as a game-changer in the wisdom discourse. The CWM was built partly upon the 'Aristotelian idea of practical wisdom' (Grossmann, Weststrate, Ardelt et al., 2020, p. 113). Its definition of 'wisdom' as 'morally-grounded excellence in certain aspects of meta-cognition' (Grossmann, Weststrate, Ardelt et al. 2020, p. 108) may not seem world-shaking. However, its uniqueness is multi-faceted. The CWM (a) synthesizes the conceptualizations of many of the most eminent researchers in the field, making it seem less fragmented and divisive than before; (b) is more accommodating than most previous conceptualizations of philosophical and theoretical insights; (c) attempts to do justice, in a way that most of its predecessors have not, to the moral function of wisdom; and (d) begins to build bridges between wisdom as a broad psychological concept and *phronesis*.

From an historical and philosophical perspective, previous conceptual work in Psychology has been hampered by attempts to reconcile (at best) or elide (at worst) the standard distinction between three discrete historical concepts of wisdom discussed earlier (Aristotle, 1985; Curnow, 2011): *sophia* (theoretical wisdom), *phronesis* (practical wisdom), and *deinotes* (instrumental wisdom or 'cleverness'). The new CWM comes, in many ways, closer to *phronesis* than earlier efforts in Psychology (Jeste et al., 2020) because it eschews the abstractness of *sophia*. Moreover, Grossmann, Westrate, Ardelt et al. (2020) pitched the CWM as unifying perspectival metacognition (PMC) and moral aspirations (*qua* 'morally-grounded PMC'), thereby potentially transcending *deinotes*. In our reading, the CWM seems to align with the *phronesis* construct which, since Aristotle, has been understood as a meta-virtue shaped by moral motivations (Darnell et al., 2019). This potential rapprochement, however, opens up various thorny questions—theoretical (conceptual), as well as practical—about a potential competition, or at least division of labour, between wisdom, as understood in the CWM, and *phronesis*. Does the new CWM make *phronesis* theoretically redundant? Or, given that the two main criticisms of the CWM focus on elements that the *phronesis* construct has traditionally aimed to account for (emotionality and moral grounding), is it perhaps time for a rehabilitation of *phronesis* into psychological research? Notice in this context that even the first author of the CWM acknowledged that 'the notion of moral grounding/aspirational motive' in the model is 'underspecified' (Grossmann, Weststrate, Kara-Yakoubian et al., 2020).

The most significant departures from previous psychological conceptualizations of wisdom—and at the same time a turn towards Aristotelian *phronesis*—lies in the deliberate omission of any traces of *sophia* (intellectual or abstract wisdom), and in the severing of links to religious and spiritual foundations or understandings, a point on which Jeste et al. (2020) objected. This move away from abstract domains towards a more practical wisdom is a significant narrowing of the typical folk conceptualizations of wisdom that previous wisdom researchers had been keen to capture. This move towards conceptual parsimony is motivated by the practical orientation of the authors and their scepticism of the possibility of conceptualizing and measuring the 'metaphysical or divine' (Grossmann, Weststrate, Ferrari et al., 2020, p. 187).

In addition, through its emphasis on moral aspirations, the CWM takes important steps towards the moral concerns that distinguish *phronesis* from *deinotes*. Recall once again that '*deinotes*' is the capacity to achieve one's goals without respect to their moral character, and that '*phronesis*' is a subtype of *deinotes* that is dedicated to good moral ends. By embracing the concept of moral aspiration, the CWM makes it clearer than some previous models that wisdom is much more than mere cleverness.

3.4 Initial Critiques of the Common Wisdom Model

The degree of commentary and disagreement about the CWM is impressive in its vibrancy, but, for the most part, each commentator focused on a narrow set of concerns that, at best, can only inform incremental progress. Nevertheless, it is important to note these divergences in the wisdom literature to begin to map the terrain that needs to be accounted for. The three primary threads of disagreement with the CWM and divergences among the authors seem to be (a) its neglect of emotionality (Glück, 2020), (b) the vagueness of its depiction of the morality inherent in wisdom (Lees & Young, 2020), and (c) the move away from transcendence (Jeste et al., 2020; Keltner & Piff, 2020). This degree of disagreement is unsurprising, given that wisdom research is in its infancy and that it is a very complicated domain. This disagreement also reaffirms that the CWM is no more than a first step and that more conceptual work is needed. We address these three domains of critique presently.

Does the Common Wisdom Model encompass emotion?

Several authors have critiqued the narrow cognitive focus on cognition in wisdom theory and research (Ardelt, 2003; Darnell et al., 2019; Glück, 2020; Glück & Bluck, 2013) This narrowness began with the BWP's overly constrained emphasis on 'expertise in the fundamental pragmatics of life', but has continued, with an unduly restricted focus on cognition, metacognition, and knowledge (e.g., Grossmann, Weststrate, Ardelt et al., 2020; Karami et al., 2020; Kunzmann, 2019). Although wisdom certainly has cognitive, metacognitive, and knowledge elements, these authors agree that scholars' limited focus on such processes leads to the neglect of affect.

Circumstances that require wise reasoning are generally strongly affectively laden, which means that emotional responses cannot be set aside, but rather necessitate a reasoned approach to affect so that emotions do not become disproportionate or misguiding. In contrast, the detached reason so often described in cognitive and metacognitive models is rarely described as being integrated with emotion. Glück (2020) argued that although perspectival metacognition and moral aspirations seem to be good candidates for wisdom components, they are very likely insufficient for dealing with strong emotion. She pointed out that real, potentially disorienting emotion may not appear in laboratory experiments, as it does in real life. In addition, 'seeing through illusion and self-deception requires emotional awareness, emotion regulation, and empathy' (Glück, 2020, p. 145).

Although a concept of wisdom may become too bloated by an overpopulation of its emotional elements, it can also be crippled by underpopulation. This is what we worry has happened with the CWM. Grossmann, Weststrate, Ardelt et al. (2020) use considerable space explaining why they do not include emotional regulation (or what they call 'emotional intelligence'), let alone individual emotions, in their CWM. In their target article, Grossmann, Weststrate, Ardelt et al. (2020) reason mainly on the grounds of consensus: None of the wisdom researchers they surveyed took 'emotional intelligence' (p. 112) to be sufficient for wisdom and only a few considered it necessary. However, it was typically considered a correlate of wisdom. In their response to critics, they give more substantive reasons. They accuse their critical commentators of not being clear on exactly what 'emotional aspects' are missing from the CWM. If it is 'emotion regulation', then that function is essentially subsumed under 'perspectival metacognition'; if it is 'empathy', then that is more or less synonymous with 'perspective-taking', which is already part of the CWM (Grossmann, Weststrate, Ferrari et al., 2020, p. 188). So, they claim to have included emotion under the guise of more cognitive-sounding terms, without explaining how emotion is integrated with these cognitive capacities. These responses are unlikely to satisfy their critics on this point.

Glück (2020) made a telling point by noting the well-known fact that people tend to make wiser choices on behalf of others than on their own behalf. The most likely reason for this is that they are led astray by unregulated emotions directed at themselves. 'Perspectival metacognition' and 'perspective-taking' are significant elements of many wisdom approaches. However, perspective-taking alone can only give us an indication of how others see things, not necessarily what is the most appropriate way to see things. The ability to construe matters properly is one key way in which the wise person ensures that their emotions can guide them properly through being infused with the right kind of reason. This emotion-reason combination seems necessary for emotions to be serviceably added to the balancing acts that the capacity of *phronesis* makes possible. At best, this should be an integration of cognition and emotion, rather than one controlling the other, as we discuss more fully in Chapter 4.

Do moral aspirations provide enough moral grounding?

A primary concern with the CWM is the remaining divergence of opinion among members of the 'Wisdom Task Force' themselves on the referents and precise value of its 'moral aspirations'. The first difficulty is that although peace has officially been declared, the debates on the place of morality in wisdom theory have not been resolved. The commentaries of the Wisdom Task Force members indicate some of these debates: Ardelt did not think the moral aspirations in the model cut deep enough and wanted to add a more distinct focus on 'compassionate love'; Brienza remained doubtful 'whether wisdom requires moral grounding, even in theory'; and Grossmann carved out a middle-ground position between the two by acknowledging that the 'moral grounding' factor in the CWM 'remains underspecified and requires further theoretical development' (Grossmann, Weststrate, Kara-Yakoubian et al., 2020). As we explain in Chapter 4, we are tempted to use words such as 'thin' and 'bloodless' about the current specification of 'moral aspirations' (*qua* moral grounder) in the model. We, unfortunately, have to agree with Lees and Young (2020) that the 'lack of clarity regarding the moral aspirations–PMC relationship is compounded by the vague definition provided for moral aspirations' (p. 168). Sternberg (2020) also argued that moral aspirations remain underspecified and vague.

Farb (2020) questioned whether there is a basis for integrating moral aspirations with PMC. He noted the paucity of suggestions for training in moral grounding, in contrast to specific suggestions for PMC training. In addition, Farb recognized that it is possible to have a highly cultivated PMC without moral regard, as in a high-PMC tyrant. He argued that contemplative traditions provide a direct link between PMC and moral grounding.

Loss of transcendence?

Aldwin et al. (2020) critiqued the CWM as neglecting self-transcendence and transformation. They suggested that although the CWM did not include self-transcendence explicitly, 'all the wisdom interventions reviewed by Grossmann, Weststrate, Ardelt, et al. [2020] fostered some aspect of self-transcendence, including mindfulness, self-distancing, and self-reflection' (p. 151).

Similarly, Keltner and Piff (2020) worried that the disenchantment in the move away from *sophia* may neglect the role of self-transcendent emotions (e.g., awe) as a moral grounding of wisdom. However, that worry is, in our view, misdirected. Proponents of the CWM could point out that there are two kinds of self-transcendence, *vertical* (pointing the self towards higher abstract ideals) and *horizontal* (pointing the self towards other people and the world around you). There are also different kinds of awe: *intellectual* elevation vis-à-vis abstract entities and *moral* elevation vis-à-vis exemplary people. Cutting the ties of wisdom to vertical self-transcendence and intellectual elevation still leaves scope for horizontal self-transcendence and awe as moral elevation. That said, those who have an appetite for higher and more enchanted understandings of wisdom are not likely take much comfort in the parsimony of the CWM, but rather consider it to tell only 'half the story' (Aldwin et al., 2020, p. 151). We do not share those worries in the specific context of the APM, and we will not elaborate further on them here.

3.5 Concluding Remarks

In this chapter, we have recounted the deep and broad interest in wisdom in Psychology. This interest has also been fuelled by a broad revival of virtue ethical scholarship and the recognition of the requirement for virtuous individuals to make intelligent decisions about how to act in the multifarious situations in which they find themselves. Psychological researchers have been grappling with this complex topic for over 40 years, and there have been many proposed models to account for wise reasoning. Many of the most prominent psychological accounts of wisdom have focused primarily on cognitive or metacognitive aspects of wisdom. Although we recognize that this domain is important to wisdom, we, along with some other scholars (e.g., Ardelt, 2003; Glück & Bluck, 2013), believe that an exclusive focus on cognition or metacognition falls short of a full account of wisdom, especially practical wisdom.

The multitude of models and concepts in the wisdom literature prompted a group of accomplished wisdom scholars to gather in a Wisdom Task Force to attempt to integrate the many models into a single model. This effort culminated in the CWM, a game-changer that represents several important accomplishments, three of which we recount here. First, it was highly collaborative, within the Task Force itself, in the wide survey of wisdom experts, and in the ways that the various models of wisdom were described in the inaugural CWM publication (Grossmann, Weststrate, Ardelt et al., 2020). Second, the Task Force enhanced the richness of wisdom concepts by explicitly addressing its moral element and including moral aspirations as one of its two core concepts. Third, Grossmann, Weststrate, Ardelt et al. (2020) moved wisdom closer to *phronesis* by reducing attention to the abstract and otherworldly concerns of *sophia* and by incorporating moral grounding to differentiate their concept from *deinotes*.

Interestingly, there was significant disagreement among the Task Force, especially about the inclusion of moral aspirations in the CWM. The reluctance to explicitly include moral questions in psychological theory and research has been very longstanding in the discipline and has taken the form of a dictum to maintain a sharp separation of facts and values (Richardson et al., 1999) although that dictum has been challenged repeatedly and without adequate response (e.g., Brinkmann, 2011). As we will discuss in the next chapter, we see *phronesis* as inextricably tied to living well as a human being and because of that understanding, we welcome the incorporation of moral aspirations in the CWM. In our view, this inclusion marks significant progress and brings wisdom research in Psychology closer to a neo-Aristotelian perspective.

As we discussed in this chapter, the CWM has also received considerable blowback from the very outset, with a variety of critics identifying issues with it and its premises. We rehearsed some of those criticisms, focusing especially on the critiques that the CWM does not attend sufficiently to emotion and motivation and that, despite the inclusion of moral aspirations, it is not sufficiently morally grounded. We will return to those topics in the next chapter in our own critical reflections on the CWM. But we wish to reiterate that we see the CWM as a significant accomplishment and a ground-breaking entry into the wisdom literature. Our critical comments should be seen in the light of our interest in adding to what Grossmann, Weststrate, Ardelt et al. (2020) accomplished.

4
Comparing Our *Phronesis* Model with the New 'Common Model' and Other Psychological Alternatives

4.1 Three Issues in Wisdom Research

As noted in the previous chapter, several authors have critiqued the narrow focus on cognition in contemporary wisdom theory and research (Ardelt, 2003; Darnell et al., 2019; Glück, 2020; Glück & Bluck, 2013), but we now want to take this a step further and discuss how this emphasis has led to four conceptual problems in most standard psychological wisdom research. This began with the Berlin Wisdom Paradigm's (BWP) emphasis on 'expertise in the fundamental pragmatics of life', but has continued, with ongoing concentration on cognition, metacognition, and knowledge (e.g., Grossmann, Westrate, Ardelt et al., 2020; Karami et al., 2020; Kunzmann, 2019). Although wisdom certainly has cognitive, metacognitive, and knowledge elements, scholars' restricted focus on such processes leads them to neglect the important roles of affect, aims, and action. The neglect of action is another instance of the much-bemoaned gap between moral reasoning and moral action that has bedevilled Moral Psychology since Kohlberg (Blasi, 1980).[1] In addition to these three areas of neglect, the focus on cognition and metacognition seems to have encouraged a questionable reliance on self-reports of wisdom. We presently discuss these areas of concern for wisdom research in general.

Affect and wisdom

First, although many scholars have focused almost exclusively on various forms of cognition, others have asserted that emotions or emotion regulation

---

[1] We address this issue specifically in Chapter 5.

is also important in wisdom (Ardelt, 2003; Aristotle, 1985; Darnell et al., 2019; Glück & Bluck, 2013; Sternberg & Karami, 2021; Webster, 2007; Wright et al., 2021). Circumstances that require wise reasoning can elicit strong, perhaps disproportionate affective responses, which may necessitate a reasoned approach to affect. It is also important to recognize that affective responses might guide cognition in attending to aspects of situations that would not be otherwise noticed.[2] As Sherman (1989) noted, 'We notice through feeling what might otherwise go unheeded by a cool and detached intellect' (p. 45) and without engaging our emotions, 'we do not fully register the facts' (p. 47). Identifying the proper emotion is important because emotions direct attention to specific elements of situations, and disproportionate or misguiding emotional responses misdirect attention. Yet several models of wisdom leave affect out in their emphasis on detached reason. This is a criticism of both the influential BWP and the recently developed Common Wisdom Model (CWM; Glück, 2020; Grossmann, Westrate, Ardelt et al., 2020; Kristjánsson, Pollard et al., 2021).

In contrast, Ardelt's (2003) model includes an affective dimension (along with cognitive and metacognitive processes) that assesses two specific emotions (sympathy and compassion). However, her choice of these specific emotions over others, or over a more general emotion-regulation capacity, is undermotivated because Ardelt does not explain why she singles out these particular emotions rather than some others, say, a healthy sense of pride at accomplishments or a sense of righteous indignation when encountering injustice. The worry here is about a possible slippery slope. If one includes one discrete emotion (rather than a more general capacity for integrating emotions with cognitions), why not more or perhaps all reasonably experienced emotions? However, that invites uncontrolled conceptual proliferation and threatens to turn 'wisdom' into a synonym for the whole of proper psycho-moral functioning; its uniqueness as a meta-construct would be lost. Moreover, if one emotion, such as compassion, is given a privileged place as part of wisdom, as distinct from being regulated by wisdom, does that mean it automatically trumps other emotions and is exempt from the integrative

---

[2] We emphasize the mutual influence of emotion and cognition here to distance ourselves from the outdated view that cognition and emotion are distinct, with a hierarchy of cognition controlling emotion. We thank Matt Stitcher for alerting us to the pitfall of inadvertently reinforcing this top-down understanding. See further in Kristjánsson (2018b, chap. 2), in which Aristotle is defined as a 'soft' rather than a 'hard' rationalist concerning the epistemology of emotion-derived knowledge. Emotions do not only 'track' independently accessible moral value but can also act as value-donors.

role of wisdom? Or is compassion somehow meant to regulate and integrate itself?

Glück and Bluck (2013) include two affective elements in their model: emotional regulation and empathy. Although they emphasize that 'regulation' does not simply mean suppression or avoidance, they frequently focus on 'managing' and 'limiting' affect, implying a top-down control process. Webster (2019) also includes emotional regulation in his model, focused on identifying and controlling emotion. Sternberg and Karami's (2021) 6P framework includes affect as one of five 'processes' in wisdom (e.g., affective skills, emotional regulation), and they group specific affects as 'person' variables (e.g., compassion, empathy). The inclusion of affect in wisdom theories and measurement remains controversial and inconsistent, as does the specifics of what scholars mean by 'emotional regulation', yet we agree with the many critics of general wisdom research and the new CWM that scholars often neglect to integrate emotions into their models of wisdom.

Aims and wisdom

A second common shortcoming of wisdom research is leaving the aims of the practically wise person unspecified or merely formal. Formal aims are ill-defined placeholders, such as 'optimal development' (Webster, 2007), 'balancing interests' (Sternberg & Karami, 2021), or 'moral aspirations' (Grossmann, Westrate, Ardelt et al., 2020). Virtually any content, even objectionable content, can be inserted into formal aims because they are agnostic about values by design. In other words, many theorists believe that selecting formal aims is necessary because a formal aim seems to give them an arms-distant way of referring to matters of value and leaving its definition to the target individual. The difficulty is that by avoiding any specific value commitments, they leave the door open to any commitments that can be fitted into their formal aims.

This focus on the process of reasoning without attention to its aims seems misguided, as though one could reason well regardless of the aims of the reasoning. The focus on cognition, metacognition, and knowledge emphasizes the means or process of wise reasoning but neglects its content and its ends. Formal aims can be invoked to facilitate disparate aims, including praiseworthy ends (e.g., vaccine development and distribution), blameworthy ends (e.g., illicit drug or human trafficking), or trivial ends (e.g., notoriety). Such inattention to the inherent relationship between wisdom and what is worthwhile means that a theory of wisdom cannot differentiate between praiseworthy and blameworthy actions. That is, wisdom guided by formal aims is more *deinotes* than *phronesis*.

Notably, the CWM incorporated moral aspirations as one of two core elements of wisdom (Grossmann, Westrate, Ferrari, et al., 2020).[3] They suggested that these moral aspirations could clarify the aims of wisdom. Although this seems like a promising development, Kristjánsson, Pollard et al. (2021) pointed out that moral aspirations are formal ends because they are never defined or given content. As noted in Chapter 3, Grossmann, Westrate, Ferrari et al. (2020) agreed that the 'moral grounding' of the common model 'remains underspecified and requires further theoretical development' (p. 188).

Sternberg and Karami (2021) also included aims in their 6P Framework under the rubric of 'purpose'. Like the common model, however, Sternberg and Karami did not clearly define purpose nor give it much content. They noted the purposes to 'achieve virtuous acts' and 'eliminate suffering', but they almost immediately reverted to a subjectivist approach in qualifying that 'What people consider to be virtuous acts differs, even to the extent that one person's virtuous act may be another's sinful act' (p. 139). They also attempted to 'finesse' this difficulty by stating that the purpose of wisdom is the 'common good' (p. 139), but they defined that formally as well by stating that it 'requires one to balance diverse interests' (p. 139). The balancing of interests is a very thin form of common good, as noted in Chapter 3, because interests are properties of individuals and subgroups, leaving the 'common good' as nothing more than an arena where such balancing somehow occurs (e.g., Sandel, 1996).[4]

Therefore, the two models that attempted to address the aims of wisdom have provided formal, contentless versions of those aims. These scholars did not create the research context in which defining aims and values has become so difficult and contentious, however, so the thinness of their concepts of worthwhile aims is part of a disciplinary commitment to value-neutrality, but it nevertheless leaves wisdom conceptualizations relatively aimless.

---

[3] This is also echoed in Sternberg and Glück's recent (2022) book: 'One cannot be wise in the absence of positive ethical values' (p. 9).
[4] Sternberg and Karami are not the only culprits here. In general, talk about the 'common good' has become increasingly ambiguous in Social Science discourse of late; see Arthur, Kristjánsson, & Vogler (2021).

Action and wisdom

Third, although wisdom researchers want to explain wise actions in the everyday world, their focus has been more on psychological processes than actions. The assumption has been that actions are an *outcome* of wise reasoning. However, the relationship between moral reasoning and moral action has been extremely weak, also known as the 'gappiness' problem (Blasi, 1980; Darnell et al., 2019). Various concepts of wise reasoning have been linked to moral action as a separate outcome variable (e.g., Brienza et al., 2018; Taylor et al., 2011), but these links have been weak.

The gappiness problem, which we discuss in detail in Chapter 5, may be primarily conceptual if moral action is incorporated into wisdom rather than seeing action as an outcome of wise reasoning, with both constructs defined independently. That is, moral action can be seen as partly constitutive of wisdom rather than being a separable outcome variable. We cannot resolve this complex conceptual question in this section, but we give this potential solution to the gappiness problem both conceptual and empirical attention in what follows.

In terms of measurement, one can build action into wisdom research by using 'performance' assessments (Kunzmann, 2019), wherein the research participant completes tasks and trained observers' ratings or experts' responses are used as performance criteria. That is, research participants' responses are themselves actions that can be incorporated into wisdom. The primary drawbacks of performance assessment are its complexity, time-intensity, and expense. The BWP uses performance measurement, and Sternberg (1998) and Brienza et al. (2018) also incorporated performance assessment in multiple studies, so it remains viable to entertain this option.

We see these three problems (affect, aims, and actions) as serious challenges for wisdom research. The three areas are pivotal for any psychological research, and are usually discussed in terms of behaviour, affect, motivation, and observations.

4.2 Three Primary Critiques of the CWM

The three problems we have just cited apply broadly to psychological research on wisdom. We now begin to zero in on the implications of three of those critiques with a clearer focus on the CWM (emotions, moral aspirations, and actions) and indicating some directions for how the Aristotelian *phronesis* model (APM) can address those critiques. These critiques are based on the description of the CWM we already provided in Section 3.3.

Emotions in the CWM

In Chapter 2, we explained the meaning of emotional regulation in Aristotelian theory and how it refers to the integration of emotion with reason rather than to the policing of emotion by reason. Aristotle was, in fact, the first known cognitivist about emotions, believing that every emotion has a cognitive (reason-responsive, educable) appraisal component to it. He argued that emotional dispositions can be experienced 'at the right times, about the right things, towards the right people, for the right end and in the right way' (1985, p. 44 [1106b17–35]), meaning that they can be evaluated for their level of reasonableness (or proper reason-integration). If a relevant emotion is 'too intense or slack' for its present object, we are badly off in relation to it, but if it is fitting to the object, we are 'well off' (1985, p. 41 [1105b26–8]). And persons can be fully virtuous only if they are regularly disposed to experience emotions in this reason-integrated way. Following Aristotle, we will add our views about the neglect of emotion in the CWM to the critics we discussed in Section 3.4.

As we noted in Chapter 3, the CWM is considerably closer to a concept of *phronesis* than previous wisdom models have been, but Grossmann, Westrate, Ardelt et al. (2020) have departed significantly from the Aristotelian tradition in neglecting the centrality of emotion. We discussed this point, as made by their critics in Section 3.4. In response to the critical comments on the lack of attention to emotion, Grossmann, Westrate, Ferrari et al. (2020) compound their difficulties because they believe their critical commentators were not clear on exactly what 'emotional aspects' are missing from the CWM. They stated that 'emotion regulation', is likely subsumed under 'perspectival metacognition' and that 'empathy' is more or less synonymous with 'perspective-taking' (Grossmann, Westrate, Ferrari et al., 2020, p. 188). The primary problem with this response is that they subsume emotional responses in a cognitive architecture. This suggests, intentionally or not, that the outdated idea that emotions can be subordinated and 'managed' by cognition.

Grossmann, Westrate, Ferrari et al. (2020) can be condoned for exploiting a common vagueness in claims about 'emotional aspects' of wisdom. Seen in that light, the CWM is at least no more vague or ill-equipped on emotion that some of the earlier wisdom models. Yet we do not think that Grossmann and colleagues parried the main concerns about emotion in wisdom. Recall that Glück (2020) pointed out a well-known fact about wisdom research, namely that people tend to make wiser choices on behalf of others than themselves, and that the most likely reason for this is that they are led astray by unregulated emotions related to themselves. Although 'perspectival metacognition' and 'perspective-taking' may help to recognize when emotional responses are problematic, they are less helpful when it comes to the positive role of emotions in wisdom. The ability to construe matters properly is one key way in which the wise person ensures that their emotions are informative about the situation, and this involves integrating emotion with the right kind of reason. This emotion–reason combination seems necessary for emotions to be serviceably added to the balancing acts that the capacity of *phronesis* makes possible. At best, this should be an integration of cognition and emotion, rather than one controlling the other. We agree with several authors (Ardelt, 2003; Glück, 2020; Lees & Young, 2020) who see the relationship between emotion and cognition as central to the question of wisdom. We have more to say about this relationship in the APM in Section 4.3.

Moral aspirations in the CWM

Our second concern with the CWM is that its perspectival metacognition seems inert, unmotivated, and unmotivating. In the CWM, perspective-taking has a dry, disengaged intellectuality about it that appears to be detached from decision-making and action. The CWM thus does not explain how perspectival metacognition guides wise action, arguably the central function of wisdom. This should come as no surprise because, as we just noted, perspective-taking can help us to see multiple points of view, but it does not, in itself, inform us about what the best viewpoint is, much less motivate us to be guided by that viewpoint.

That raises the question of whether this lacuna is filled with the other main pillar of the CWM, moral aspirations. We have been encouraged in this because the word 'moral' appears almost 100 times in the article introducing the CWM (Grossmann, Westrate, Ardelt et al., 2020). This is especially encouraging because academic psychologists have historically, since the days of Weber (1949) and Allport (1937), exhibited a great deal of nervousness about adopting a language of morality in general and virtue in particular. Psychological 'dichotomizers' (those who insist on a strict Humean dichotomy between facts and values) are still in the majority, although we now see an increasing number of psychologists becoming willing to discuss moral elements of Psychology more directly, at varying levels of commitment (Kristjánsson, 2018a). Even positive psychologists Peterson and Seligman (2004), who did so much to 'reclaim the study of character and virtue as legitimate topics of psychological inquiry' (p. 3), chose to engage in virtue-talk in an 'inverted-comma', arm's-length sense, reporting on people's subjective evaluations of a world of description, rather than acknowledging values as descriptions of an objective world of evaluation. Given this background, Grossmann, Westrate, Ardelt et al. (2020) must be applauded for wanting to steer clear of the amoral instrumentalism permeating so much of psychological theorizing (Fowers, 2010)—and thereby, in Aristotelian language, working to distinguish wisdom from mere calculated cleverness (*deinotes*).

As we discussed in Section 3.4, we, along with other wisdom scholars, are *not* encouraged by the divergence of opinion among members of the 'Wisdom Task Force' themselves on the referents and precise value of the 'moral aspirations', with opinions ranging from Ardelt's perspective that the moral aspirations in the model do not cut deep enough, Brienza doubting 'whether wisdom requires moral grounding, even in theory', and Grossmann diplomatically stating that the 'moral grounding' factor in the CWM 'remains underspecified and requires further theoretical development' (Grossmann, Weststrate, Kara-Yakoubian et al., 2020). Expressing the same sentiment as Grossmann, we are tempted to use words such as 'thin' and 'bloodless' about the current specification of 'moral aspirations' (*qua* moral grounder) in the model.

The problem with moral aspirations can be more sharply appreciated by noting Grossmann, Westrate, Ardelt et al.'s (2020) formal definitions of these aspirations as a balancing of self-and-other interests and an orientation towards a shared humanity. This is the same difficulty we pointed out regarding the BWP (Baltes & Staudinger, 2000) and Sternberg's (1998; 2003) Balance Model of Wisdom. Such terms are basically empty referents that cry out for elucidation. Instead of providing such an elucidation, the remainder of their article Grossmann, Westrate, Ardelt et al. (2020) and their rejoinder to critics Grossmann, Westrate, Ferrari et al. (2020) simply refer back to this specification without deepening it. Later (Grossmann, Westrate, Ardelt et al., 2020, p. 107), the word 'prosociality' is added to the mix, but as we explained in note 3 in Chapter 1, 'prosocial' is not the same as 'moral', or an elucidation of it. 'Prosocial' is a behavioural descriptor, and behaviour can be prosocial without being moral (e.g., uncritically and unreflectively following another person's lead to do a good thing) and moral without being prosocial (e.g., showing justified anger which happens to upset and alienate the persons who transgressed in a way that gave rise to the anger). 'Orientation toward a shared humanity' and a 'balance of self-and-other interests' can also mean several different things with radically different moral ramifications. For example, balancing interests could be pursued through a *phronesis*-guided virtue of justice, through an amoral group-centric ethos, through formal legal rights and duties, or through brute social exchange practices. Each of those is different in the gestalt and in the details of what one means by 'balance', and how one pursues it.

The core of the problem, as we see it, is that the lack of commitment in the CWM to any clear *ontology*, *epistemology*, or *methodology* of the science of morality, which leaves their description of moral aspirations empty or merely procedural. The emptiness of their version of moral aspirations can be filled in substantively in many different ways, meaning that it is seriously underspecified. For instance, does the talk about 'moral grounding' refer to a realist ontology of morality, as being about objective facts, or an antirealist one which sees all 'moral facts' as subjective or relative? Like most virtue ethicists, we favour moral realism. The fact that Grossmann, Westrate, Ferrari et al. (2020) expressed a preference for a virtue-ethical take on morality and wisdom, as opposed to a deontological (rule-based) or a consequentialist (utilitarian) one, may indicate an implicit commitment to moral realism. However, that is not explicitly born out in anything they happen to say about moral aspirations. For example, when they state that 'PMC appears to uniquely fulfil the chief mandate of practical wisdom which involves deeper understanding of how to live well' (p. 111), we are puzzled about how perspectival metacognition can fulfil this mandate on its own, without *substantive* moral aspirations. If moral aspirations are meant to be included in perspectival metacognition, why do the authors neglect to spell out a realist account of a virtue-based conception of 'living well'? Why, more generally speaking, do they become so vague here?

Turning from ontology to epistemology, the main contenders tend to be moral rationalism and moral sentimentalism. Rationalists believe that moral facts exist independently of our emotions, and that those facts can be tracked by human reason. Sentimentalists believe either that no moral facts exist at all or, alternatively, that moral facts are created by our emotions and exist in our minds (Kristjánsson, 2018b). Given that emotions are largely neglected in the CWM, one might deduce that the model assumes some sort of a rationalist epistemology. However, if that is the case, we remain uninformed about what that epistemology is, both because no such epistemology is elicited in the explanation of the CWM and because no prior ontology (explaining what sort of moral facts reason can track) is being offered as a prelude. In this book, we endorse a third epistemological alternative (sometimes referred to as 'soft rationalism'; Kristjánsson, 2018b) in which emotions can be integrated with reasons.

Our interpretation of the emptiness of Grossmann, Westrate, Ardelt et al.'s (2020) account of moral aspirations is that they are expressing ambivalence (whether collectively or individually) about biting the evaluative bullet

(Fowers et al., 2021; Kristjánsson, 2018a) by providing substantive meaning to their moral terms. They are in good company among psychologists in this reluctance to make moral commitments explicit. There are two common ways that psychologists avoid these commitments. The first is euphemizing the commitments with terms such as health, functionality, maturity, or adaptiveness. This veneer of neutrality is punctured, however, as soon as one asks what is specifically meant by any of these terms. When one asks, for instance, what is meant by maturity or adaptiveness, the specifications reveal what the scholar's values (e.g., ability to postpone gratification, or flexibly responding to difficulties). The second is to assume that moral substance is provided subjectively, meaning that the investigator can remain neutral about what is specifically considered moral while describing what the participants in the investigation see as moral. This subjectification of morality seems to give the scholar an arms-length relation to those moral commitments until one recognizes that assigning morality to subjective choice is part of the widespread and often implicit assumption of the value of individual autonomy in Psychology (Richardson et al., 1999). As we discuss in Section 4.3, the APM explicitly adopts moral commitments that help explain how a *phronimos* deliberates, decides, and is motivated to act in accordance with wisdom. In contrast, Grossmann et al.'s avoidance of substantive moral commitments leaves wisdom unmotivated and inert.

Action and the CWM

The lack of attention to wise action in the CWM makes its motivational inertness even more problematic. Although Grossmann, Westrate, Ardelt et al.'s (2020) flexibility about which methodological approach they prefer for assessing wisdom is laudably open-minded, it leaves wise action out of the CWM. This is perhaps understandable, given that psychological researchers may obviously be interested in various aspects and correlates of wisdom, including people's self-reports about how wise they take themselves to be. Yet, in view of the practical nature of the CWM and its explicit departure from *sophia* towards *phronesis*, one would have expected a primary focus of the CWM to be on how it explains and predicts actual wise actions rather than on what it tells us about the nature of wise thinking abstracted from actual performance, or about people's varyingly transparent conceptions of themselves as wise agents. The relationship between cognition and behaviour is perennially interesting to psychologists, and *phronesis* appears to be a promising way to bridge the well-known gap between moral judgement and moral action (Blasi, 1980; Darnell et al., 2019). The lack of attention to the behavioural performance of wisdom in the CWM leaves it stranded in the domain of disembodied cognition, and we discuss presently how the APM addresses this issue.

4.3 Comparing the CWM and the APM

To summarize the composition of the APM, it offers a philosophically grounded, psychologically practicable model of wise (*phronetic*) decision-making that conceives of morality in realist terms and sees moral considerations as informed by reason and emotion. It provides a nuanced account of the balancing of reason and emotion and incorporates action within the model instead of seeing action as a separable outcome of wise reasoning. It explicates two main sources of moral motivation, one emerging from specific virtues and one that emerges from the blueprint function of *phronesis*, as well as how those motivations are synergistically integrated and how the blueprint function is gradually refined in the light of experiential knowledge.

In our overall assessment of how the CWM and the APM compare, we are cognisant that the quality and topicality of the new CWM makes it somewhat odd to produce another wisdom model without juxtaposing it with the CWM. For the sake of comparisons and contrasts, therefore, we present the APM and argue that it ameliorates certain gaps in the CWM, especially having to do with cognitive-emotional integration, moral aims, and moral action. This comparison opens up various thorny questions—theoretical (conceptual), as well as practical,—about a potential competition, or at least division of labour, between wisdom, as understood in the CWM, and *phronesis*. Does the new CWM make *phronesis* theoretically redundant? Or, given that the three main criticisms of the CWM focus on elements that the *phronesis* construct has traditionally aimed to account for (emotionality, moral grounding, and action), is it perhaps time for a rehabilitation of *phronesis* into psychological research? We explained in Chapter 2 how the APM charts the moral motivations animating wise choices; indeed, the provision of action-guidance is arguably the greatest strength of the model. On the one hand, the *phronetic* capacity acts as a conduit and a filter for discrete moral motivations emanating from the individual moral virtues via their emotional components. *Phronetic* choice requires not only that agents comply with the demands of the most immediate virtue relevant to the given situation (say, honesty), but it also takes account of claims proper to other ethical virtues (say, compassion) to help us reach a measured decision (Müller, 2004). On the other hand, the blueprint component of *phronesis* provides its own additional (*phronesis*-internal) moral motivation, through the overarching deep understanding of the ultimate goal of leading a well-rounded *eudaimonic* or flourishing life.

Grossmann, Ardelt, Westrate et al. (2020) have displayed virtuous expansiveness in developing a consensual new model of wisdom, the CWM. They have thereby tried to end a fairly fruitless but turbulent factional strife among wisdom researchers, based partly on 'jingle-jangle fallacies' (Grossmann, Ardelt, Westrate et al., 2020, p. 123).[5] At the same time, they have assuaged worries sometimes expressed by philosophers that social scientists too often use imprecise definitions and uninformative linguistic descriptions of their concepts (Wittgenstein, 1973). In addition, they have narrowed the concept of wisdom down to avoid the common mix-up of *sophia* and *phronesis* elements, arguing persuasively that the concept of wisdom that lends itself best to psychological inquiry, measurement, and intervention, is that of *practical* wisdom. The CWM also makes significant progress on previous conceptualizations of wisdom in Psychology by circumscribing the sort of wisdom under scrutiny (as practical, nonabstract), and by foregrounding the role of moral aspirations as grounding the perspectival metacognition at work in (this kind of) wisdom.

In the stylistic context of divisive academic exchanges, we want to express our admiration for the work done by Grossmann and his colleagues without sounding like partisans, and we want to avoid sounding churlish in our critique of it. We repeat our earlier characterization of their target article as a tour de force of wisdom scholarship: a clear benchmark for any future work in the area. However, we cannot avoid the impression that the authors' venture into the moral realm goes awry by lacking vital substantive content on morality, emotions, and action.

They express sympathy and preference for an Aristotelian understanding of practical wisdom, and a virtue-ethical take on morality, but they hesitate to make the ontological, epistemological, or methodological commitments that would come with a neo-Aristotelian approach. That said, we appreciate the difficulties in fully committing to an Aristotelian approach, since the aim was for a 'common *denominator* model' (Grossmann, Westrate, Ferrari et al., 2020, p. 186), and we sympathize with Grossmann, Wesrate,

---

[5] A 'jingle fallacy' is when the same term is used to convey different concepts, and a 'jangle fallacy' is when different terms are used to convey the same concept.

Kara-Yakoubian, et al.'s (2020) own comment about the need for 'further theoretical development'.

In our neo-Aristotelian view, wisdom is about making good choices and helping others do the same in virtue of a deep moral understanding of complex human problems: an understanding arrived at through reflection and experience (Tiberius & Swartwood, 2011). As Grossmann, Westrate, Ferrari et al. (2020) acknowledge, the CWM is not primarily about behaviours or actions, but rather about wise thinking in a context (cf. Grossmann, 2017b). Nevertheless, the APM offers a more detailed and overt take on some variables that also play a role in the CWM, and at least in the context of wise moral decision-making, it seems to carry potential explanatory power *qua* theoretical construct above and beyond the CWM. This is why we maintain that the APM embodies some unique features (substantive moral motivation, emotional regulation, behavioural relevance) that psychologists studying wisdom ignore at their peril.

Emotion in the APM

We have critiqued the relative paucity of discussion of emotional elements of the CWM, which partly explain its apparent inertness. In contrast, the APM incorporates emotion directly into *phronesis* in two ways. First, emotions are recognized as potentially attention and action guiding. One's affective responses to situations are very important to the construal of the circumstances. Emotional responses are a key aspect of the constitutive component of the APM in that emotions help to alert the agent to what is important in the situation. Of course, the cognitive aspect of one's perceptions is also important, but we emphasize that it is both cognition and emotion that leads to the proper perception of what is important in a given situation.

Second, the APM explicitly includes the integration of the agent's reason and emotion in the 'emotion-regulation' component. Wise reasoning and action are predicated on this integration because cognition, on its own, can be abstract, dry, detached, and unmotivated, and emotion, on its own, can be unfocused and offer questionable guidance. The best appraisals of situations require the integration of the cognitive and emotional aspects of experience.

This perspective on emotion ties in with Aristotle's teleological view of psychosocial equilibrium, wherein emotion, cognition, and behaviour are attuned to the various social situations in which individuals will find themselves, inter alia by appropriately appraising those situations cognitively and emotionally. The capacity of *phronesis* is key to that psychosocial equilibrium, as we explained in Chapter 2 when introducing the component of emotional regulation as fulfilling one of its necessary functions. Because some social scientists are unfamiliar with well-sourced Aristotelian interpretations of practical wisdom and have erroneously claimed that this viewpoint has not 'taken the emotional sphere of human life into account' (Tynjälä et al., 2020, p. 170; cf. Glück, 2020), it is important to emphasize the critical role of emotion in *phronesis*.

Another interesting point about emotion was made by Lees and Young (2020), who suggest that wisdom requires a general capacity to understand other people's (negatively or positively valenced) emotions, and they cite the concept of 'theory of mind'. We agree, and we take understanding others' emotions to be part of the emotional regulation function of the APM because individuals frequently call upon *phronesis* in deciding how to respond to other people or coordinating one's actions with others. From the viewpoint of the actor, others' emotions are part of the situation they face.

As we have emphasized repeatedly, we do not subscribe to the notion that cognition and emotion are distinct, much less to the idea that there is a psychological hierarchy in which cognition serves to control emotion. Instead, we recognize that emotion and cognition are two aspects of virtually any experience, and both emotion and cognition contribute to how we construe situations. The most important point is that the APM explicitly focuses on the relevance and centrality of emotion in *phronesis*, whereas this remains implicit, at best, in the CWM.

Morality in the APM

Like the CWM, morality is central to the APM. The primary differences are that, in the APM, moral questions are treated substantively. In characteristically neo-Aristotelian fashion, the purpose of *phronesis* is to enhance the goodness of one's life. It is important to note that the neo-Aristotelian understanding of morality is focused on the goodness of one's life rather than on the rightness of an action. For neo-Aristotelians, the rightness of actions is found in its harmony with what it means to live a good life rather than being independent of that overall picture.[6]

---

[6] We recognize that the harmony between what is morally good and what is good for the actor is controversial, but our position is that the overall good and what is good for the actor are generally harmonious, although we will not take the space to defend that position here. For the historical Aristotle, at any rate, the idea that one can enhance one's own moral good without positively influencing others would have been an incomprehensible one, and he even thought of our closest and dearest others as our 'other selves', as

The centrality of moral concerns is apparent in all four components of the APM. The *constitutive* component is oriented to recognizing the morally salient elements of a given situation so that the agent can recognize which virtue(s) is(are) appropriate to that situation. The *integrative* component is focused on understanding how to harmonize the varying moral concerns that are relevant to the situation so that one can best address the most important concerns. The *emotion-regulation* component makes it possible for agents to integrate cognition and emotion in a way that facilitates moral deliberation and action. Finally, morality is deeply imbued in the *blueprint* component, on the basis of which the agent reasons, emotes, and acts so as to be in harmony with their best understanding of a good life.

One of the reasons that many psychologists prefer to avoid substantive moral commitments is that they believe that such commitments require one to make moral prescriptions that could impose one's values onto others. This is understandable given the common view that morality requires a set of rules or guidelines that have an imperative character. Aristotle (1985) introduced the concept of *phronesis* because he recognized that it is impossible to have a set of rules that is sufficient to guide action in the myriad concrete situations in human life. *Phronesis* is a form or reasoning that guides actions in response to the concerns of a given situation in light of an understanding of how to live well. Therefore, it is action-guiding rather than imperative in form. Given the fact that there are many different ways to live well, it is neither possible nor desirable to prescribe a single way of living.

Action in the APM

In contrast to all other models of wisdom, including the CWM, the APM incorporates action within its conception of wisdom. This follows directly from Aristotle and his conception of *practical* wisdom. From the APM perspective, reasoning is only wise if it is accompanied by wise action. The purpose of *phronesis* is wise action, not just wise reasoning or appropriate emotions and motivations. This emphasis on action is part of the reason for including performance measures in our initial assessment of the APM, to be described in Chapter 6.

The APM thereby provides an initially conceptual method for overcoming the reasoning-behaviour gap that has been so troubling in Moral Psychology.

---

can be seen in his theory of friendships (Kristjánsson, 2022b). Aristotle would thus be puzzled by the 'self-centredness objection' often lodged against modern forms of Virtue Ethics.

It seems that one reason for this gap is that reasoning and behaviour have been conceptualized as distinct. This is one of the outgrowths of the psychological insistence on classifying behaviour as a kind of observational primitive that can be assessed independently of an actor's cognitions, emotions, motivations, and intentions. We reject this characterization outright and understand overt behaviour as an element of action, which also includes the actor's cognitions, emotions, motivations, and intentions. Therefore, wise actions include the best sort of reasoning, emotions, motivations, behaviour, and moral aims. These elements are integrated in such a way that separating them is an artificial effort that may be undertaken to clarify them, but any distinctiveness that is attained will not represent the actuality of wisdom broken down into its basic elements. Instead, such an analysis would separate the constituent elements of *phronesis* in such a way that the wisdom of the *phronimos*' action is lost.[7] Of course, we look forward to the empirical assessment of our approach to *phronesis*, and we will measure its components, but look at them as the constituents of *phronesis* rather than as separable elements.

At the end of the day, the relative value of the APM and CWM depends on the investigator's aims. If one's research interest is in moral cognition, the CWM offers substantial resources. If one's research interest is in morally motivated action, then the APM offers greater explanatory possibility. Ultimately, the place and value of these two models must be subjected to empirical evaluation, with a demonstrated capacity to guide moral decision-making and action towards a good life as the key criterion, at least from a neo-Aristotelian perspective. We suggest some directions for future research in Chapter 12.

4.4 Is *Phronesis* Redundant with Respect to Existing Psychological Concepts?

Now that we have compared the APM to the CWM and outlined their distinctiveness and the ways that the APM addresses some of the criticisms of the CWM, it is important for us to consider whether pre-existing psychological concepts render the APM redundant. We begin with Lapsley's (2019; 2021) argument that three already existing psychological constructs tell us all we need to know about *phronesis*. Once we embark on the question of whether existing psychological constructs are sufficient, it makes sense to consider

---

[7] By analogy, attempting to study the components of *phronesis* separately is akin to attempting to understand what a cake is by separately examining its constitutive elements of flour or eggs.

other alternative psychological constructs that might render *phronesis* redundant (e.g., executive functions, expertise).

Lapsley's redundancy thesis

Lapsley's (2021) elaboration of the redundancy thesis is helpful in that it engages with the original version of the Aristotelian 'standard model' (Darnell et al., 2019). He argues that *phronesis* researchers need to learn from the extant psychological literature on metacognition, social-cognitive processes, and moral identity to inform their scholarship on *phronesis*. We are in full agreement with this reasonable proposal. Yet, he ultimately concludes that *phronesis* is a superfluous construct, playing a role much like that of 'ether in physics, once thought crucial but now expendable' (p. 154). Rather than accept this premature and rather puzzling conclusion, we think it better to examine his specific claims.

One of Lapsley's main criticisms is that *phronesis* fails because it lacks a complete developmental account with extensive research to support it. Of course, *phronesis* does not have such an account because empirical research on it is in its infancy. It is also widely known that Aristotle was mostly silent on how and when *phronesis* develops in the virtuous learner, apart from platitudes about it being picked up through 'experience and teaching' (1985, p. 33 [1103a14–16], but what kind of teaching? What sort of experience?). We agree with Lapsley that a fully adequate account of *phronesis* should have a developmental component, and we hope to see such an account formulated (i.e., the current absence of a developmental account does not imply the impossibility of one).

Lapsley (2021) suggests some reasonably widely accepted psychological constructs that he believes already covered the terrain mapped out in three of the four components in the Darnell et al. (2019) model.[8] His specific aim is to 'translate' the supposedly outdated Aristotelian lexicon into psychological categories that 'make sense in developmental and personality science' (p. 141). His suggestions for replacing Aristotelian concepts with concepts from contemporary Psychology are worth exploring in detail, and we presently examine each suggestion in turn.

---

[8] For some reason, Lapsley does not offer replacements for the emotional regulation component.

Cognitive-affective processes and the constitutive component

First, regarding the constitutive component (moral sensitivity), Lapsley (2021) argues that social-cognitive theories in Personality Science already provide the required theoretical framework to understand this presumed aspect of *phronesis*. He mentions, in that regard, well-known approaches such as CAPS ('cognitive-affective personality system') and KAPA ('knowledge and appraisal personality architecture'), which provide theoretical bases for understanding the sort of virtue perception ascribed to *phronesis*, discerning salient ethical features of situations. By comparison, Lapsley suggests that 'the value-added yield of *phronesis* is slight' (p. 151). We might add that Whole Trait Theory (Jayawickreme et al., 2019) includes similar social-cognitive processes. In contrast to Lapsley, Snow et al. (2021) provide a detailed argument that *phronesis* is a necessary aspect of Whole Trait Theory, at least as far as virtue expression goes.

There is extensive literature on social cognition and social reasoning that partly overlaps with but does not exhaust our concerns in this book. Lapsley (2019) advises us to connect to this literature, and he gestures at the appraisal processes contained in CAPS and KAPA. We think these are excellent resources for our work on *phronesis*, but he does not specify why *phronetic* theory cannot simply take this sensible approach and incorporate the relevant theory and research from these models. It seems obvious to us that the perceptions of the constitutive component involve appraisal processes, but that that appraisal is an integral part of wise reasoning and action aimed at the best kind of life that neither CAPS nor KAPA addresses.

At a more practical level, there is no denying the fact that the Social Cognition literature has yielded a number of interventions and measures that can, *mutatis mutandis*, facilitate practical and educational work in the area of *phronesis*. We are thinking here of research in the areas of problem-solving skills, critical thinking, and so-called social reasoning, understood as the social-cognitive capacity to consider, interpret, and determine between multiple aspects of a complex social situation. We are encouraged by Snow et al.'s (2021) attempt to integrate *phronesis* with Whole Trait Theory and its social-cognitive processes. They view the social-cognitive processes of Whole Trait Theory as hospitable to *phronesis*, citing especially the perceptual, goal-setting, goal-seeking, cognitive reappraisal, perspective-taking, and motivations. Theirs seems to be a significantly more ecumenical approach than Lapsley's.

Metacognition and the adjudicative function

Second, Lapsley aims to replace the adjudicative component of *phronesis* with metacognitions in Psychology. Here, again, Lapsley suggests that a somewhat vague and mysterious Aristotelian construct has been offered as a replacement of (and without taking account of) a well-established concept with decades of research behind it. We agree with Lapsley that one of the biggest advantages of metacognitive research in Psychology is that it connects to a credible developmental story about young people; and numerous interventions have shown how and when it is educable. In contrast, even Aristotelians acknowledge that Aristotle's story of the development of the adjudicative function of *phronesis* is skeletal at best, nonexistent at worst.

Everyone agrees that *phronesis* in the APM and wisdom in the CWM involve metacognition. But is this construct capable of accounting entirely for the adjudicative component of *phronesis*? Flavell (1979) first described metacognition as involving the monitoring and control of one's own cognitions, a description which is most commonly encapsulated as 'cognition about cognition' or 'thinking about thinking'. The processes of 'monitoring' and 'control' are thought to link two levels of cognition, a 'meta-level' and an 'object-level' (Nelson, 1990). The meta-level contains knowledge about both our own and others' cognitive processes as well as knowledge and understanding of tasks and strategies involved in actions. The monitoring component links the object-level to the meta-level, updating and assessing our own knowledge and regulating our behaviour (Nelson, 1990).

Helpfully for any model of wisdom, metacognition involves both propositional and nonpropositional aspects (Grossmann, Westrate, Ardelt et al., 2020). Although we have not made this clear so far, some of the components of *phronesis* clearly involve nonarticulated (if possibly articulable) aspects. For instance, moral sensitivity (i.e., what we called the 'constitutive function') may spot virtue-relevant situations in a flash without necessarily being able to define them propositionally, at least not unless prompted. Goal-setting has been identified as a core function of metacognition, and it is no coincidence that Aristotle's name frequently crops up in studies of it: for example, in a study which found that metacognition partly mediates the relationship between goal-striving and Aristotelian *eudaimonic* wellbeing (Klaei & Reio, 2014). Moreover, if one adds the designator 'moral' to metacognition, and then aims to design a scale to measure 'moral metacognition', the scale is likely to look similar to any prospective *phronesis* measure (as witnessed by McMahon and Good's (2015) 'moral metacognition scale').

One of the difficulties in responding to Lapsley's concern about metacognition is that it is an enormous and diverse area of theory and research. It is difficult to know quite what he means by metacognition beyond the simple, early definition of 'thinking about thinking' (Flavell, 1979). Metacognitive scholarship spans Educational, Clinical, Organizational, Cognitive, Geriatric, and Developmental Psychology, to mention just a few subdisciplines. In a reflection on the history of the concept of metacognition, Moshman (2018) states that 'The concept underlying what we now call "metacognition" is very old and diffuse, with complex and inconsistent terminology. Overlapping concepts include reflection, attribution, perspective-taking, and theory of mind' (p. 601). The field sprawls to such a degree that the term is virtually always qualified by its area of application, and scholars seldom refer to it generically (Lehman et al., 2022; Thomas et al., 2022).

From the perspective of our *phronesis* model, the construct of metacognition is in one sense too narrow and in another too broad to make it equivalent to *phronesis*. It is too *broad*, much in the same way as the executive functions (discussed below), in that it offers a sweeping take on various cognitive functions that entail awareness of cognitions, and a hierarchy of cognitions about cognitions, but may have little to do with what either experts or lay people would call wisdom (e.g., a skilled chef will have various cooking-relevant metacognitions). It is too *narrow* in that it does not incorporate a specific focus on moral aspirations. Consider once again the blueprint component of *phronesis*. It involves various beliefs about the good life. However, some of those are simply basic beliefs at the object-level without any 'monitoring', not beliefs about beliefs, and some of them are irreducibly moral. Hence, while *phronesis* cannot operate without metacognitions, it is not equivalent to metacognitions.

Moral identity and the blueprint component

Third, Lapsley (2021) sees the blueprint component of *phronesis* as somehow already explained by traditional psychological research agendas on the moral self and moral identity. However, whereas moral selfhood/identity forms a robust area of research in Psychology (indeed, Lapsley (2021) claims it has 'a better empirical record in the moral domain' (p. 152) than any other variable). Lapsley believes that the blueprint component of *phronesis* is underdeveloped conceptually and he sees it as motivationally inert (pp. 152–3).

The construct of moral identity, especially in its social-cognitive variant, may be his favourite topic because he has written about it as an important concept in Moral Psychology. However, moral identity is far from widely understood or accepted as a significant explanatory concept in Psychology more broadly (Kingsford et al., 2018; Krettenauer & Hertz, 2015). Moreover, there is more than one definition of moral identity (Aquino et al., 2009; Kingsford et al., 2018). It also competes with social-cognitive development theory, Haidt's Moral Psychology, and self-determination theory for explaining moral behaviour in the small subdiscipline of Moral Psychology. This contested position is made more complicated by the fact that although it is a developmental construct, there is very little truly developmental research on moral identity (Krettenauer & Hertz, 2015). The bottom line is that the empirical case for Lapsley's suggestion is rather weak. If that were not problematic enough, the idea that moral identity suffices for explaining an individual's understanding of a good life does not fit any extant definitions of 'moral identity', which tend to be focused on adherence to moral rules and guidelines, not living well as a human being. Therefore, the suggestion that moral identity has already covered the ground of the blueprint component is not only empirically weak, but also conceptually questionable.

We see Lapsley's suggestions to replace *phronesis* with extant psychological constructs as sufficiently weighty and specific to merit scrutiny. Nevertheless, we believe them to be ultimately flawed and puzzling for three reasons. First, he is decidedly generic in his claims when he gestures at metacognitive processes, but highly specific in pointing towards just two social-cognitive processes and a single contested definition of moral identity. This seems like a rather ad hoc collection of concepts to replace *phronesis.* Generally, none of them have been applied to what it means to live well as a human being, so they miss the mark rather significantly. There is, for example, a small amount of literature on moral metacognition (e.g., Mata, 2019), but most metacognition is about nonmoral topics such as learning. Similarly, most of the discussion of the social-cognitive processes Lapsley preferred is focused on nonmoral elements of personality and situations, with only a few recent and tentative forays into the moral realm (Jayawickreme et al., 2017; Wright et al., 2021).

Second, Lapsley wrote as if all psychologists accept the concepts he cites. In fact, there is little, if any, consensus about most of them. In the cases of metacognition and social-cognitive processes, the concepts are so expansive that they cannot be fully grasped. In the case of moral identity, it is best seen as a niche topic.

Third, it surprises us that Lapsley writes as if one must choose between his psychological concepts and *phronesis*. This seems like a false and unnecessary choice. As we have argued (Darnell et al., 2019; Kristjánsson & Fowers, 2023), there is a lot to learn about *phronesis* from psychological concepts, and our understanding of *phronesis* should be consistent with and informed by those psychological concepts. There is little doubt that constructs like social-cognitive processes, metacognition, and moral identity are relevant to *phronesis*, but *phronesis* requires a reinterpretation of what we mean by these constructs. Why does Lapsley insist on an unnecessary either/or choice when it seems much more sensible to take a both/and approach? Why does he advocate a premature closure and the elimination of the *phronesis* concept rather than seeking additional empirical clarification of the relations among these concepts?

We might add that there are many other psychological constructs that are relevant to *phronesis* (e.g., perspective-taking, empathy, humility, and emotion regulation). Given the breadth of psychological constructs relevant to *phronesis*, we are mystified by Lapsley's choice of such a limited range of constructs. We and other *phronesis* scholars (e.g., Wright et al., 2021) welcome the idea of empirically investigating *phronesis*, and the constructs Lapsley cites could contribute greatly to this research. We are puzzled, however, by the recommendation to simply substitute an ad hoc collection of existing psychological constructs for *phronesis* without pausing to study their roles or relationships with the concept of *phronesis*. Ultimately, this seems like a classic case of the value of examining psychological constructs, the concept of *phronesis*, and the relations among them, rather than being forced to choose one or the other prior to thorough empirical study. On our view, his objections simply suggest that there is work to be done.

The redundancy thesis about *phronesis* considered more broadly

As we just noted, there are other related psychological constructs related to *phronesis* that might render it redundant. We address three such prominent constructs in this section, without implying that we have considered all the possibilities. Since Aristotle's time, *phronesis* has been connected to adult thinking, or at least the sort of thinking that does not begin to develop significantly until late adolescence. Similar developmental age-constraints characterize much of the standard psychological literature on wisdom (Grossmann, 2017b). To get a better hold on *phronesis* as a psychological construct, it is therefore instructive to make some inroads into Developmental Psychology regarding the development of 'mature' thinking. By doing so, the aim is not only the positive one of grounding the *phronesis* construct better in the history and theory of Psychology but also potentially the negative one of looking for already-established constructs that might make the APM redundant. However, the explication of the full developmental account of *phronesis* is beyond the scope of this book. Indeed, such an undertaking is the work of several books in its own right.

Executive functions

'Executive function' (EF) is an umbrella term for another organization of 'higher' cognitive functions, which control and regulate 'lower-level' cognitive processes and goal-directed behaviour (Alvarez & Emory, 2006). Strictly speaking, EFs are self-directives, in that the agent directs themselves to act in particular ways that assist in decision-making, planning, problem-solving, and long-term goal pursuit. This is a kind of metacognition, of course, but these literatures are seldom combined. As with *phronesis*, executive functions tend to be explained componentially. For present purposes, the most relevant components are *updating*, *shifting*, and *inhibition*. 'Updating' refers to monitoring and changing active working-memory content by maintaining and manipulating information; 'shifting' represents the ability to change flexibly between tasks; and 'inhibition' means silencing otherwise dominant responses to avoid distraction (Miyake & Friedman, 2012). These cognitive processes are essential to the ongoing regulation of goal-directed processing: for example, inhibiting our own self-perspective when required to take the perspective of others.

To consider the executive functions as explanations for any or all of the intellectual virtues fully is doubtful, however. *Phronesis* is much more than an ephemeron of EFs because *phronesis* attends directly to the moral saliences of situations, whereas EFs are generic. In this generic character, EFs can serve moral or immoral acts, making EF skill more a matter of *deinotes* than of *phronesis*. Moreover, whereas *phronesis* requires some intellectual understanding also of the content of a flourishing life (for the blueprint component), EFs are agnostic about flourishing, focusing on goal pursuit and generic planning, whether or not those happen to contribute to a good life. That said, developmental studies of executive functions may help unearth some of the developmental precursors of *phronesis*, given a frequent focus on the early years and the extent to which the development of the components of executive functions can help to explain the early development of *phronesis* (Best & Miller, 2010).

Tacit knowledge

Another construct that frequently emerges in the literature on the development and nature of postformal adult thinking is tacit knowledge. We have already acknowledged that some of the knowledge involved in *phronesis* is nonpropositional and tacit. Polanyi's (1966) often-cited observation that 'we know more than we can tell' (p. 4) is apt but easily overinterpreted. For example, we need to avoid the implication that whenever knowledge is tacit, it is somehow arational (Narvaez, 2010; Vogler, 2020). We agree with Toom and Husu (2020) that research into tacit knowledge, as held and utilized by experts (e.g., expert professionals), may hold the key to a fuller understanding of advanced thinking in both general and practical wisdom (see also Tynjälä et al., 2020). Yet 'tacit knowledge' is more a descriptive than an explanatory term. It simply describes knowledge that operates in the background of action, in contrast to explicit, conscious, and propositional knowledge. However, it must be born in mind that much of the knowledge informing *phronesis* is explicit rather than tacit. Well-internalized knowledge and practices only remain tacit when they are sufficient for the situation. If obstacles to action arise that surpass the application of tacit knowledge and practices, then the agent must deliberate explicitly on how to proceed. This explicit deliberation will become less frequent as the *phronimos* develops, but it cannot be entirely eliminated. For example, the blueprint component of *phronesis* will be largely comprised of tacit knowledge about how to live well, but if challenges to that knowledge arise, they must be dealt with explicitly.

Expertise

'Expertise' is, in a sense, a success descriptor of *phronesis* rather than an explication of the concept. The *phronimos* is successful to the extent that she operates as a moral expert rather than a novice, but the concept of expertise does not explain what makes up *phronesis*. Both expertise and *phronesis* are believed to be acquired through experience, practice, and feedback. The notion of a '*phronesis* novice' may, however, sound paternalistic in a way that a 'novice car mechanic' may not. The latter may know next to nothing about car repairs before embarking upon a course of study, but even the '*phronesis* novice' has some of the fundamentals of moral functioning (namely the habituated moral virtues) already in place before fully developing her phronetic expertise. Just as with EFs, 'expertise' is a generic term that is applied to many domains, especially technical domains, and it has no special affinity for moral questions. But the *phronimos* is explicitly expert in moral matters.

All in all, a focus on *phronimoi* as moral experts may facilitate research on how *phronesis* develops and plays out in real life, just as the focus on wise people, rather than wisdom as a capacity, enlivened the wisdom discourse at the beginning of the century (Ardelt, 2004). A refocus on '*phronesis* exemplars' would also tally well with recent research trends in virtue ethics, philosophical (Zagzebski, 2017) and psychological (Damon & Colby, 2015), which have turned increasingly towards the emulation of virtuous exemplars (cf. Grossmann, 2017a, on wisdom exemplars; Jameel, 2022).

We embarked on this detour of the conceptual terrain surrounding *phronesis* and wisdom in the broad field of Postformal Adult Thinking to explore and extend the eliminativist sentiments expressed by Lapsley (2019; 2021). Our ultimate insights at the end of this section tally essentially with those of Kallio (2020) that the literature on mature adult thinking is multifaceted and encompasses various research traditions that can be brought together under the umbrella of 'contextual integrative thinking'. Most of those research traditions seem to be running on parallel lines without significant interactions, however, except in the recent volume edited by Kallio (2020), which robustly tries to bring them closer together. The viability of that enterprise notwithstanding, what we have identified in this section are what Fowers et al. (2021) would call the 'rudiments' of the *phronesis* construct (e.g., executive functions and metacognition) and larger-scale theoretical models, such as paradigms of social cognition, that may well incorporate both the APM and the CWM. Yet there are ample grounds for exploring the specifics of those two models without becoming bogged down in a debate about eliminating or transcending one concept or another. Surely, it is too early to draw such conclusions.

Decathlon and *phronesis*: An instructive analogy

We hope our arguments have been persuasive that it would be premature to rule out the concept of *phronesis*, and that an ad hoc collection of psychological constructs cannot replace an integral capacity with a specific rather than generic purpose. An analogy we described previously (Kristjánsson & Fowers, 2023) might shed additional light on the inadvisability of the eliminativist approach to *phronesis*.

Most readers will know that decathlon is a complex, balanced, and challenging Olympic sport, comprising 10 track-and-field events that take place over 2 consecutive days. It harks back to the ancient pentathlon (five events, including wrestling), a competition at the ancient Greek Olympics. Success in the decathlon is all about balanced and combined performance in individual sports as different as shot put, 100 m and 400 m runs, and pole vault. The capacities that make a great decathlete include muscular strength, cardiovascular endurance, explosive speed, flexibility, and neuromuscular co-ordination. Some of these are complementary in terms of training regimes but others are competing. For example, training for the 100 m dash and training for the shot put are potentially detrimental to one another, as too much strength can reduce speed and vice versa. This is why relying on combined training in the individual sports only is not going to make a champion decathlete. What is needed is a coach that can oversee the overall training regime and ensure that the best balance between the different sports is achieved.

Perhaps no more needs to be said to explain why the redundancy thesis about *phronesis* reminded us of the false view that the structure of and training for the decathlon can simply be reduced to that of the 10 individual sports. Indeed, the more we happened to read up on the 'philosophy' (and that word is actually used in the Sports literature) behind decathlon, the more analogies we noticed. We discussed 17 analogies in our recent article (Kristjánsson & Fowers, 2023), but we provide only a sampling here. We are aware of the merely illustrative nature of analogies of this kind, as opposed to a full-blown argument, but we intend them here to illustrate the integrity central to both decathlon and *phronesis*.

First, an elementary observation one picks up from the Sports literature is that the decathlon has a 'logic' or 'philosophy' of its own. Analogously, according to the Aristotelian 'standard model',[9] *phronesis* has a logic of its own that cannot be reduced to that of the individual psychological constructs with which it has parallels. The true mark of excellence in a master decathlete is proper balance between the 10 sports. That this also holds true for the *phronimos* is almost a truism, given what *phronesis* is meant to be for.[10]

Second, once you have entered decathlon training, the technique required for success in that sport must supersede any techniques you have learned previously to succeed in individual sports. This is comparable to the insight that different virtue-education methods are required at the habituation level versus the *phronesis* level: a common insight in the current Character Education literature.

Third, an essential psychological asset of a decathlete is a capacity for flexibility and frequent code-switching. Shifting from the mindset of a shot putter to that of a 100 m sprinter is a tall order for an athlete for whom concentration

---

[9] When we speak about *phronesis* in this list of comparisons, we mean *phronesis* as understood on the 'standard model' and most specifically our Chapter 2 version of it.

[10] Arguably, however, *phronesis* requires one kind of discernment in the face of uncertainty that is not required of decathletes in their 'balancing acts'. This is because the *phronimos* never knows what challenge comes next. In that sense, *phronesis* resembles a kind of decathlon in which the order of the sports has been scrambled and new ones may be added in randomly.

on the specifics of the task at hand is a core attribute. This contains an obvious parallel to the ability of the *phronimos* to switch, flexibly and ideally effortlessly, from one code of attitude and behaviour to the next within a very short time span.

Fourth, experienced decathletes often refer to the emotional turmoil created by this sport as its 'eleventh event' (Blockburger, 2021). It is bad enough to experience the emotional swings related to success or failure in individual sports, but those pale in comparison with the emotional stress created by a collective sport with five different events on 1 day where, within the same hour or two, a huge achievement can turn into a desperate disappointment, or vice versa. Analogously, in the field of overall virtuous performance, the most emotionally charged moments tend to be experienced when a moral quandary emerges, involving a conflict between different worthy considerations. A quandary can even turn into a traumatic event when it constitutes a true dilemma: namely, where all the options seem equally bad. This is one reason why emotional regulation is included as a component of *phronesis*.

Fifth, in addition to the physical skills required both for each event and for the balancing of those, decathletes rely on a battery of more general personal skills, such as versatility, all-roundedness, and metacognition. Similarly, *phronesis* requires, in addition to the components it combines synergistically, several other general skills, including the metacognitions foregrounded by Lapsley (2021).

The last point of comparison notwithstanding, the decathlon champion is often described as 'the world's greatest athlete' at the Olympics (perhaps alongside the winners of the marathon runs). Similarly, a person who excels at *phronesis*, such as King Solomon, is sometimes seen as the true virtue *virtuoso*, especially when some significant values have been at stake and the *phronimos* has saved the day.

In light of this account of decathlon, readers will realize that there would be something misguided about redundancy concerns when framed as concerns about decathlon rather than *phronesis*. We do not present these considerations here as a *reductio* of the redundancy thesis. As already noted, we are acutely aware of the limitations of analogies of this kind for making substantive philosophical points.[11] However, we hope they have helped to illuminate the inadvisability of attempting to eliminate something as complex and valuable as *phronesis*. Perhaps *phronesis* is not so redundant after all, any more than decathlon is as a sport.

---

[11] Aristotle himself relied heavily on analogies to make substantive points. However, this use has been criticized as a method (see, e.g., Bobonich, 2015).

4.5 Concluding Remarks

We have examined the viability of the APM with respect to several models and psychological constructs. We began by discussing three issues that arise in the general wisdom literature, that models and measures often (a) neglect emotions (in favour of cognition and metacognition), (b) disregard substantive aims (with a preference for formal aims or no aims at all), and (c) neglect actions (focusing instead on purely subjective psychological processes). We clarified that the CWM was subject to all three shortcomings.

Our discussion then turned to the ways that the APM manages the three issues prevalent in the wisdom literature, helping to make the APM distinctive and promising. Emotional processes are evident throughout the APM, but one of its components focuses explicitly on integrating emotion and reason. The aims of *phronesis* are also prevalent throughout the model, with the blueprint component giving the aims of *phronesis* a central place. The APM integrates behaviour with reason, emotion, and behaviour to form action. This is a unique strength of the APM, as wisdom models tend to separate behaviour from subjective psychological processes.

We then juxtaposed several contemporary psychological concepts (metacognition, social-cognitive processes, moral identity, executive functions, tacit knowledge, and expertise) with *phronesis* to investigate the redundancy claims Lapsley (2019; 2021) makes. Consequently, we see Lapsley's views as helpful in sparking a useful analysis, but we find his redundancy claims premature. The first reason for this is that we agree with his more modest claim that *phronesis* scholarship has much to learn from the decades of empirical research and theory in these areas. There is considerable overlap among these domains of study themselves, as well as significant intersections between these domains and *phronesis*. The second reason is that *phronesis* is an integrated form of activity that cannot simply be parcelled up in several pre-existing broad domains. All that Lapsley demonstrates is that there is some overlap between extant psychological concepts and *phronesis*, but then he leaps to the conclusion that *phronesis* is unnecessary, without adequately considering *phronesis* in its entirety. We concluded the chapter with the decathlon-*phronesis* analogy to clarify why it is important to see *phronesis* as an integrated whole rather than an ad hoc collection of operations.

5
The 'Gappiness Problem' in Moral Psychology and the Relevance of *Phronesis*

5.1 The Historical Backdrop: From Kohlberg Onwards

Clarifying concepts in Moral Psychology and proposing models that make sense of complex, underexplored processes is a laudable aim. Readers may have come to think, after reading the first four chapters, that this is the fundamental aim of the present book. Both current authors happen to be great fans of conceptual analysis and consider it a worthy enterprise. However, as we indicated at the outset, this book also has a more practical aim: to elicit a number of practical implications of our model for the development and education of *phronesis* and its application in areas of professional practice and daily conduct.

Chronologically and autobiographically speaking, our interest in *phronesis* was not aroused initially by philosophical or conceptual concerns but rather in the context of thinking about a specific practical problem in Moral Psychology and Moral Education: the so-called gappiness problem (Darnell et al., 2019). Indeed, the whole enterprise undertaken in this book project can best be understood as a sustained attempt to find a solution to that problem. The present chapter explains what the problem is, sketches some standard solutions to it and their shortcomings, and then compares our Aristotelian *phronesis* model (APM) to what we consider its closest non-Aristotelian contender: the four-componential neo-Kohlbergian model suggested by Rest and colleagues (Rest, 1984; Rest et al., 2000).

The moral reasoning–action gap

The Apostle Paul (Romans 7:15) neatly sums up the perennial gap between moral knowledge and moral action that continues to haunt moral psychologists and moral educators: 'I do not understand what I do. For what I want to do, I do not do. But what I hate, I do.' We offer below a critical review of the literatures on two single-component solutions to the 'gappiness problem' that emerged after Kohlberg's well-known single-component solution of *moral reasoning* fell by the wayside: the *moral identity* and the *moral emotions* solutions, respectively. Lurking in the background of this discussion is the hope, or at least the possibility, that by, inter alia, synthesizing the three single components in question, *phronesis* may help bridge the knowledge–action gap.[1] We will not argue here that Aristotelian *phronesis*, in general, or our APM, in particular, definitely can provide a robust answer to the 'gappiness problem' or that obeisance to all of Aristotle's conceptual tenets is required. Our motivation is, rather, simply to articulate this possibility in the present chapter by looking at the historical precedents and the lessons that can be drawn from them; it is not until the following Chapter 6 that we explore this possibility empirically.

Kohlberg's hard rationalism

In order to contextualize the 'gappiness problem', a quick historical rehearsal is in order. Once upon a time, Moral Psychology and Moral Education provided a safe haven for hard moral rationalists. For such rationalists, moral judgements can be justified independently of our sentiments and preferences, and those judgements can be grounded in reason alone (with emotions hindering rather than helping that process), as 'no moral principle is based [. . .] on any feeling whatsoever' (Kant, 1964, p. 33). Moreover, once correctly tracked, the moral judgements are seen as strongly motivating, for 'he who knows the good chooses the good' (Kohlberg, 1981, p. 189; this position is known as hard 'motivational internalism'). Moral Education is then all about helping young people learn to justify moral claims in the right, rational ways, and develop logical strategies to draw the right inferences from them in dealing with moral quandaries (Kohlberg, 1981).

---

[1] Cf. what Sternberg and Glück (2022, pp. 16–23) say about the contribution of a psychological construct of wisdom to bridge the gap in question.

It was actually Piaget's stage theory of development that provides the basis for Kohlberg's famous rationalist model of moral development. It ought to be acknowledged, however, that Piaget himself was less interested in the development from thought to action than he was in that from action to thought (Bergman, 2002, p. 105). Children act in the social world first. This crystallizes into new moral understanding after the fact: 'Thought always lags behind action and cooperation has to be practiced for a very long time before its consequences can be brought fully to light by reflective thought' (Piaget, 1997, p. 64). Thus the 'gap' between thought and action was not an issue for Piaget who, in effect, conceived of this relationship the other way around.

Influenced by Kant's rationalism (which he distilled mainly through the work of his fellow Harvard professor John Rawls) and Piaget's cognitivism, Kohlberg proposes that new ways of thinking (cognitive 'operations'), in terms of development, open the door to entertaining new courses of moral action. Kohlberg has, however, a slightly more subtle view of the interplay between cognition and emotion than Kant, acknowledging that 'the development of cognition and the development of affect have a common structural base' (1969, p. 389). Yet, inspired by the basic insights of rationalism, Kohlberg fails to adequately disentangle the complex relations between cognition, emotion, identity, and motivation—assimilating them in the end to a global stage theory. Kohlberg thus argues that moral reasoning goes through six sequential stages of development—in the same order for everyone although not at the same speed, and with most people not advancing past Stage 4 (Kohlberg, 1969; 1981). To determine an individual's level of moral reasoning, Kohlberg developed the 'moral judgement interview' (Kohlberg, 1958): a semistructured interview incorporating moral dilemmas, the most famous of which is the Heinz dilemma about a man who faces the choice of stealing an expensive drug as the only way to save his wife's life. To gauge a participant's level of moral reasoning against the six-stage schema, interviewees are asked a series of questions about what they consider the right course of action to be in the circumstances of the dilemma and why (i.e., what their moral justification is). The responses to the 'why' questions are scored, and an overall assessment of an individual's moral development (reasoning) is calculated across the vignettes.

The reason-responsiveness of emotion

However, in a set of seminal papers, Augusto Blasi (1980; 1983) challenged Kohlberg's approach empirically, in which Blasi reports that moral reasoning only accounts for about 10% of the variance in moral behaviour (cf. Walker, 2004). The inevitable corollary is to accept that some other factor (or factors) must be at work. The ensuing new proposals call the exclusive focus on moral reasoning into question. Nevertheless, Kohlberg's legacy in turning Moral Psychology into a respectable subdiscipline and attempting to provide theoretical gravitas to practices of Moral Education should not be underestimated.

Despite significant departures from hard rationalism in the two approaches that we explore presently, about the roles of moral identity and moral emotions, both retain an assumption about the essential *reason-responsiveness* of moral commitments. It thus tends to be assumed that young people can be taught to reason well about what sort of a moral identity they wish to adopt, and their emotions (in virtue of the cognitive component in emotions) are typically considered to be amenable to some reason-guided cultivation and coaching. However, recent times have seen more radical departures from any form of rationalism—be it 'hard' or 'soft' (see an overview of those options in Kristjánsson, 2018b, chap. 2)— towards forms of hard sentimentalism (Haidt, 2001) or moral situationism (Doris, 2002). According to the former, our moral responses *qua* emotional responses are genetically preprogrammed in noncognitive ways (with the role of reason reduced to justificatory afterthoughts). According to the latter, moral responses are essentially swayed one way or another by situational forces that have nothing to do with reason-informed decisions. In the case of either sentimentalism or situationism, the very idea of moral reason-responsiveness has virtually been done away with.

At the same time, however, we have seen a dramatic upsurge of interest in Aristotle-inspired virtue ethics, as charted in Chapters 1 and 2. Given the empirically friendly naturalism animating this approach, many social scientists see neo-Aristotelians as a group of philosophically grounded theorists they can finally do business with (e.g., Lapsley & Narvaez, 2008). Part of the allure of neo-Aristotelians is that they are not hard but soft rationalists—because they see moral facts as not only being tracked by emotions but some of those facts as being essentially constituted by emotions. Of particular interest for present purposes, the typical neo-Aristotelian view is that the pendulum of latter-day Moral Psychology and Moral Education to have swung too far away from reason. Notice that neo-Aristotelians are not even content with the sort of minimal reason-responsiveness still assumed by the moral identity and moral emotions models. Rather they insist that reason, as instantiated by the virtue of *phronesis*, plays a much more immediate and profound role in helping people figure out what to do in morally charged and complex situations, as we attempted to spell out in Chapter 2.

Our APM constitutes a multicomponent construct, which in many ways incorporates the insights of both the moral identity and moral emotions models (as we indicate further below). Neo-Aristotelians may also point out that the natural conclusion to draw from empirical research on the contributions of moral reasoning, moral identity, and moral emotions to moral behaviour is that while *each* of these elements is involved in moral behaviour, no *one* element can bridge the gap alone. This conclusion then naturally leads to the turning of the research lens towards *phronesis*. In order to motivate that move further, however, we need to look at the available single-component options, succeeding the (partly at least) discredited Kohlbergian moral reasoning.[2]

5.2 Moral Identity as a Gap-Stopper

Whereas Kohlberg holds that the essence of morality is commitment to moral principles, Blasi emphasizes the importance of fidelity to one's moral identity: 'Integrity and its failure cannot be studied without taking seriously into account the self and related constructs, such as self-definition, self-organization, self-awareness, and sensitivity to internal inconsistency' (1980, p. 41). This certainly seems at least intuitively correct, for as Bergman (2002, p. 120) points out, maintaining fidelity to one's moral identity is likely to have more motivational power in keeping people on the straight and narrow than not betraying an abstract moral principle. Thus, one alternative to Kohlberg's rationalism is to bridge the theoretical gap between knowing the good and doing the good by appeal to the concept of moral identity.

Moral identity is a complex concept (Hardy & Carlo, 2005); yet there is general consensus that it reflects the 'degree to which being a moral person is important to one's sense of self' (Hardy & Carlo, 2011, p. 212). As such, if individuals feel, for instance, that moral virtues define who they are, then they have a strong moral identity. For the past three decades, various theories and models have been posited to explain the processes behind moral identity as a source of moral motivation (e.g., Blasi, 1983; Colby & Damon, 1992; Gibbs, 2003; Narvaez & Lapsley, 2005). The first and indeed most influential of these is Blasi's (1983) Self-Model of moral functioning (see Walker, 2004).

---

[2] Moral reasoning is of course incorporated in the APM through its integrative/adjudicative function. Perhaps it is time for virtue ethicists and character educationists to put an end to the standard Kohlberg-bashing and to acknowledge his pioneering contributions to the field. At the moment, as indicated above, the danger in Moral Psychology lies in too little rationalism rather than too much. The field has moved on from the 1970s and 1980s.

Blasi's Self-Model

Blasi (1983) links moral judgement and moral action via three components: judgement of responsibility, moral identity, and self-consistency. He suggests that before embarking on a moral action, a moral judgement is filtered through a *judgement of responsibility* to decide if the action is necessary. Whether the individual feels obligated to carry out the judgement in action is dependent upon her *moral identity* and the extent to which she sees being moral as central to who she is. The drive to be *self-consistent* and act according to one's moral identity then acts as a motivator of the moral action.[3] Thus, moral judgements are more likely to predict moral actions if they are first categorized by a responsibility judgement based on moral identity and motivated into action via a drive for self-consistency (Hardy & Carlo, 2005). As Bergman (2002) writes: 'People sometimes fail to act on their moral beliefs because those beliefs are not really their own. Moral "oughts" may then seem oppressive and refusal to abide by them liberation' (p. 115).

Colby and Damon (1992) have built on the Self-Model, emphasizing the unity between the moral and self-systems (see also Damon, 1984). They suggest that moral identity reflects the integration of the moral and self-systems into a unified system. Individuals who are highly moral see themselves in moral terms so that their personal goals are unified with their view of morality. Acting morally accords with what they most want to do. Thus, it is not a failure of moral reasoning which lets us down in our attempt to bridge the gap between knowing what is right and doing what is right. Rather, it is a question of how important internalized moral beliefs are to individuals personally; and possibly this importance has been established through a series of existential decisions that the person takes, say, during early–late adolescence about who she wants to be, as well as through the influence of earlier upbringing. Becoming moral is therefore essentially a self-definitional rather than an entirely rational task.

Socio-cognitive approaches to moral identity

Two main limitations have been raised in relation to the Self-Model (Hardy & Carlo, 2005; see also Aquino & Freeman, 2009). First, it is hard

---

[3] Recall and compare our account of the secondary motivation stemming from the blueprint component of *phronesis*, in Chapter 2.

to apply the model to moral behaviours that are automatic or less deliberate and even possibly genetically preprogrammed. Second, it does not account for when and under what circumstances a particular identity will be experienced (Hardy & Carlo, 2005), hence underestimating the effects of contextual and situational factors (Doris, 2002). Recent socio-cognitive approaches have been advanced to try to explain why some moral behaviours can be tacit and automatic (Narvaez & Lapsley, 2005) and how an individual may display different aspects of selfhood across different situations (Aquino & Reed, 2002). The key aspect of a socio-cognitive approach is that the centrality of an individual's moral identity is related to the accessibility of so-called *schemas* (Aquino & Reed, 2002; Aquino et al., 2009; Lapsley & Hill, 2009; Lapsley & Narvaez, 2004). Schemas are conceptualized as knowledge structures stored in memory, consisting of values, traits, goals, and behavioural scripts (Cantor, 1990). Easily accessible schemas guide attention to relevant features of a situation and life tasks that are compatible with these schemas, are more likely to be chosen or sought, further reinforcing dispositional tendencies aligning with the schema. Behaviours related to these schemas become highly practised and thus provide an almost 'automatic plan of action' relating to the schema (Cantor, 1990, p. 738). These processes seem to correspond substantially to what neo-Aristotelians call 'habituated virtue'. The schema-dependent characteristics can also be understood in terms of knowledge activation or activation potential. The more readily accessible schemas are, the greater influence they have on behaviour.

From this perspective, an individual with a strong moral identity is an individual with a chronically accessible and easily activated moral schema or perhaps a network of readily available moral schemas (Aquino & Freeman, 2009; Lapsley & Narvaez, 2004). For a moral person, moral identity would be central to her self-concept *and* these moral schemas would be the ones that are most easily accessible for interpreting the social landscape (Lapsley & Narvaez, 2004). The schema concept leaves room for individual differences in how central these moral schemas are to the person, as well as situational differences in how easily accessible they are (Aquino et al., 2009). As such, while a socio-cognitive approach would agree that moral identity is fairly stable over time (Blasi, 2004; Colby & Damon, 1992), it also suggests that moral identity may be more salient in some situations than others (Aquino & Freeman, 2009; Aquino et al., 2009). In other words, the motivational effect of moral identity may be influenced by situational cues.

Moral identity research

Over the past 35 years there has been growing empirical support for the suggestion that an individual with a strong moral identity would engage more frequently in moral action, a suggestion relying on a variety of methods and approaches (for reviews see Hardy & Carlo, 2005; 2011; Hertz & Krettenauer, 2016). One method of exploring moral identity examines moral commitment in moral exemplars: individuals selected by expert panels (e.g., philosophers, scholars, theologians, and community and religious leaders; e.g., Colby & Damon, 1992; Hart & Fegley, 1995; Matsuba & Walker, 2004). Individuals who are dedicated to moral causes appear to demonstrate a unity between their self and moral goals, in that there is a clear integration between their moral principles and their own commitments and interests. Colby and Damon (1992) conducted in-depth interviews with adult moral exemplars and found that 'their own interests [are] synonymous with their own goals' (p. 299).

Interestingly, Colby and Damon (1992) report that many of the moral paragons they examined did not attain the highest levels of reasoning in the Heinz dilemma according to Kohlberg's criteria, suggesting that other factors must be implicated in reaching moral maturity. They propose that *the kind of person one wants to be* (one's ideal moral identity) is perhaps more important in translating moral thinking into moral action. Hart and Fegley (1995) found that adolescent moral exemplars were more likely to describe aspects of themselves, their personality, and their goals using moral personality traits than a non-exemplar comparison group (see also Reimer et al., 2009). Similarly, in narrative research among emerging adults, Pratt et al. (2009) suggest that moral identity (measured by investment in the needs and rights of others) is linked to prosocial[4] behaviours (e.g., community service) and generative concern (e.g., desires, actions, and commitments related to caring for future generations).

Researchers have also examined the relationship between moral identity and moral behaviour using correlational research (e.g., Aquino & Reed, 2002; Aquino et al., 2009; Barriga et al., 2001; Hardy, 2006). Pratt et al. (2003) conducted a longitudinal study on adolescents investigating the correlates of the moral self. Adolescents were given a moral self-scale and rated how important nonmoral and moral traits were to their lives, also rating how frequently they

---

[4] As we have noted, the term 'prosocial' is problematic because it is generally treated as a desirable, even moral kind of behaviour that leaves intention and motivation out. We use this term in this chapter because it is very widely used, although we would prefer to substitute the more descriptive and less loaded term 'other-benefitting'.

were involved in four different prosocial behaviours (e.g., community, political, responding, and helping activities). Pratt et al. (2003) reported higher moral self-scores to be associated with more prosocial behaviours across each of the categories. Aquino and Reed (2002) found positive correlations between moral identity and volunteerism in adults as well as positive attitudes towards out-group members (cf. Reed & Aquino, 2003). Moral identity has also been found to have a negative relationship with antisocial behaviour in adolescents, with reported moral self-relevance being negatively associated with scores on both parent and self-report measures of antisocial behaviour (Barriga et al., 2001). As a matter of fact, moral rationalists Kohlberg and Candee (1984) recognized that the action–judgement relationship is stronger in participants who somehow intuited or identified with the choice of high-stage reasoners although they did not reason at that level themselves.

Questions about moral identity

While moral identity seems a persuasive candidate for bridging the thought/action gap, it could be criticized for opening up a different sort of epistemological (Moshman, 2004) or ontological (Kristjánsson, 2010a, chap. 2) gap. People could construct false moral identities that do not accurately represent who they really are. A person may even possess a completely coherent and nondeceptive (as distinct from non-*self*-deceptive) self-identity that is nevertheless false. In his challenging paper, Moshman (2004) notes that false identities can easily be maintained through self-serving manipulations. He even claims that we may all have false moral identities. Notice that 'moral identity' does not refer to 'an actual self' that truly exists (Kristjánsson, 2010a); rather it is about one's own *theory* of what that self is.[5] Moral identity, then, is a self-theory, and identity formation is theory formation. But as Moshman correctly notes, theories (and thus identities) can be evaluated with respect to truth and may turn out to be false.

In a series of studies conducted by Batson et al., which seem to corroborate Moshman's insights, some individuals seem to be motivated to 'appear moral while, if possible, avoiding the cost of being moral' (Batson & Thompson, 2001, p. 54). In one study, participants were told to assign themselves and another participant to two tasks, one task where they would win tickets for a raffle (positive consequence) and the other task where no tickets could be

---

[5] We refer readers back to our earlier invocation of this problem in Chapter 2.

won (neutral consequence). Participants were then given written instructions which emphasized that the fairest way to assign the tasks would be to flip a coin. While in retrospect participants agreed that this would be the most moral thing to do, only around 50% of participants chose to do so. Even among those participants who chose to flip the coin, significantly more participants assigned themselves to the positive consequence task (option of winning raffle tickets) than would be expected by chance. So, if the coin did not land on the positive consequence outcome, most participants seemed to ignore the coin flip and follow their self-interest (Batson et al., 1999). In a result that would please schema theorists, participants were much more likely to use and follow the coin toss procedure if they were in a 'high self-awareness' condition that may have primed a moral identity schema.

Batson (2011) suggests that these studies demonstrate that many individuals are often not motivated by moral integrity but rather by 'moral hypocrisy'. This suggests that the proportion of college students with an active, chronically accessible moral identity schema may be relatively small. Similarly, Perugini and Leone (2009) note that while self-report measures of moral identity predicted responses to moral dilemmas, they did not predict responses to a 'live' moral dilemma (whether or not participants returned a 'mistaken' extra payment for their research participation). Thus, moral identity could simply constitute one's own overt self-theories *qua* self-confabulations or self-deceptions that may bear little resemblance to how one actually behaves in the world.[6]

The debate about false or true moral identities notwithstanding, in a meta-analysis of the Moral Identity literature, Hertz and Krettenauer (2016) report that despite the positive predictive relationship between moral identity and moral behaviour, this relationship is only small to moderate in size (similarly to moral reasoning). Based on these findings, Hertz and Krettenauer (2016, p. 136) conclude that 'it seems more appropriate to consider moral identity in a broader conceptualized framework where it interacts with other personological and situational factors to bring about moral action'. The upshot is that, if considered in isolation as a single-component construct, moral identity does not offer a definitive solution to the 'gappiness problem'.

To complicate matters further, Krettenauer (2022) identifies cases where moral identity can be counter-productive and motivate immoral behaviour, in an integrative review of the literature on moral identity. He points out that the goal of moral identity can vary along three axes: external versus internal motivation, prevention versus promotion orientation, and concreteness versus

---

[6] We also note that perhaps research respondents did not think of researchers as meriting moral treatment.

abstractness. Unfortunately, external motivation can foster moral hypocrisy; low levels of abstraction can promote moral licensing; and prevention orientation can foster moral disengagement. Moral identity is thus, at best, a two-edged sword.

5.3 Moral Emotions as a Gap-Stopper

While Blasi's (1980) paper inspired a turn towards moral identity as a contender for addressing the gappiness problem, another candidate has also appeared on the stage. Exponents suggest that an affective factor supplies the underlying motivational force to bridge the thought/action gap.

Most frequently, the term 'moral emotion' in the gappiness literature is used to refer to the affective states of empathy, sympathy, and compassion (Montada, 1993; Hoffman, 2000). Eisenberg and Miller (1987) define 'empathy' as 'an affective state that stems from the apprehension of another's emotional state that is congruent with it' (p. 91). In contrast, 'sympathy' is defined as 'an emotional response stemming from another's emotional state that is not identical to the other's emotion but consists of feelings of sorrow or concern for another's welfare' (p. 91). While being fully aware of the conceptual disarray in the field, Eisenberg and Miller's definition of 'empathy' is ambiguous between two common understandings of empathy: as *experiencing* the same emotion as another or being able to *understand* another's perspective with respect to that emotion. To add to the conceptual confusion, which can be traced all the way back to eighteenth-century philosophical accounts (see e.g. Hume, 1978), both Hoffman (2000) and Batson (1991) sometimes use the term 'empathy' when referring to 'sympathy'.[7] We try to overlook these ambiguities as much as possible in what follows by using the term 'empathy' unless authors specifically used the term 'sympathy'. In any case, this terminological ambiguity does not subvert the main point of the moral emotion solution, which is that a set of 'fellow-feelings' bridges the gap under discussion.

Research on moral emotions

Central to theories of moral emotion as bridging the gap is the idea that experiences of empathy can engender either helpful responses or personal distress,

---

[7] Hume on the other hand uses the term 'sympathy' to refer to what modern moral psychologists would call 'empathy'.

with the latter being a feeling of anxiety based on the recognition of another's emotional state (Batson, 1991; Eisenberg & Fabes, 1990). While empathy is associated with the other-oriented motive of helping the needs of others, personal distress is associated with the self-oriented motive of reducing one's own feeling of anxiety (Batson, 1991; Eisenberg & Fabes, 1990). For moral emotion to be a predictor of *moral* behaviour, feelings of empathy rather than personal distress must therefore be produced.

In Batson's (1991) empathy-altruism hypothesis, empathy plays a pivotal role and is seen as providing the impetus for engaging in prosocial behaviour. Similarly, Hoffman (2000) emphasizes the role of what he sometimes terms 'sympathy' in motivating moral action, and thereby extends Batson's (1991) hypothesis, suggesting that abstract moral principles, learned in 'cool' didactic contexts (e.g., lectures, sermons), lack motivational force. 'Empathy's contribution to moral principles is to transform them into prosocial hot cognitions—cognitive representations charged with empathic affect', thus giving them motivational force (Hoffman, 2000, p. 239). Empathy for an individual occurs alongside and is intensified by the judgement of having a responsibility to care about the individual's predicament. From this sociocognitive perspective, the motivational force of empathy (moral emotion) on moral action is likely moderated by moral judgement (Hoffman, 2000; Miller et al., 1996).

More recently, research has also begun to focus on moral emotion attributions (MEAs). 'MEAs' are defined as moral emotions that individuals 'attribute to an actor as a consequence of a morally relevant action' (Arsenio et al., 2006, p. 397; Malti & Krettenauer, 2013). MEAs are therefore considered as the emotions individuals expect to feel following a moral action, and those can include both negatively and positively valenced moral emotions. For example, an individual may interpret an emotion as the MEA of guilt or shame over a moral transgression or the MEA of pride over a prosocial deed (Malti & Krettenauer, 2013). MEAs are classified as self-conscious experiences (with one's own self as the emotions' intentional and attitudinal object) as they are felt when individuals reflect upon and evaluate the consequences of a moral action in relation to their own moral standards as well as those of others (Eisenberg, 2000; Malti et al., 2009; Tangney et al., 2007). Researchers suggest that empathy and MEAs may be conceptually related, with empathy giving rise to MEAs: for instance, (empathy-based) guilt (Daniel et al., 2014; Malti & Ongley, 2014). As a motivator for moral action, MEAs may thus help individuals predict the outcomes of moral actions and adjust their behaviour accordingly (Malti & Latzko, 2010).

Given that sympathy and empathy are thought to orient individuals towards the feelings and needs of others (Batson, 1991; Hoffman, 2000), it is perhaps not surprising that moral emotions have been linked to prosocial behaviour. In an early meta-analysis, Eisenberg and Miller (1987) report a positive relationship between empathy and prosocial behaviour, with numerous studies since supporting this conclusion (see Carlo, 2006). Unlike the relationship between moral identity and moral behaviour (typically thought to take shape in adolescence), the link between moral emotions and moral behaviour seems to occur much earlier, with some studies reporting correlations between moral emotions and moral behaviour in research participants as young as 2 years of age (see, Eisenberg et al., 2006; Spinrad & Eisenberg, 2017). The earlier developmental onset of moral emotions than of moral identity counts in favour of moral emotions because of the evident fact that the development of moral responsiveness in children begins well before adolescence.

This earlier development of moral emotions was documented by Trommsdorff et al. (2007), using an experimental paradigm wherein 5-year-olds' sympathy and prosocial behaviours were observed during a manipulated play situation. They found that 5-year-olds who demonstrated more sympathy towards a distressed adult also indicated more prosocial behaviours towards the adult. Similarly, observed facial sympathy has been linked to teacher reports of prosocial behaviour (Eisenberg et al., 1999), as well as observed helping behaviours (Trommsdorff & Friedlmeier, 1999), with teacher and parent reports of sympathy also being linked to higher scores on prosocial behaviour questionnaires (Malti et al., 2009).

This relationship between empathy and prosocial behaviour also seems to be fairly stable across time (Eisenberg et al., 1999). In a longitudinal study, spontaneous sharing in the early years predicts later prosocial behaviours and empathy-related responding up to 17 years later (Eisenberg et al., 1999). Importantly, empathy was also found to mediate the link between early spontaneous sharing and later prosocial behaviours, suggesting those children who were more likely to share spontaneously were prone to empathy from an early age (Eisenberg et al., 1999). Batson's research (1991) indicates that adults with heightened empathy were more likely to engage in helping behaviours even when it would be easy to avoid providing such help. Other researchers also report that adults with greater empathy to be more likely to engage in volunteering (e.g., Davis et al., 1999; Penner, 2002).

As well as providing evidence for a relationship between sympathy/empathy and moral behaviours, recent research also indicates an association between MEAs and prosocial behaviour. For example, Menesini and Camodeca (2008) reported on ratings of shame and guilt in 9- to 11-year-olds in hypothetical situations involving intentional or nonintentional harm. Children who had been identified by their peers as prosocial (e.g., children most likely to help or comfort others) were more likely than children identified as bullies or bystanders to report greater shame and guilt in the intentional hypothetical harm situations. That is, children who were seen in the classroom as prosocial were also more likely to feel guilt and shame when imagining committing a moral transgression. In a meta-analysis of 42 studies, Malti and Krettenauer (2013) note that MEAs were positively predictive of prosocial behaviour and negatively predictive of antisocial behaviour across development (4–20 years of age).

Moral emotions weakly predict moral behaviour: The need for an integrative approach

Although it is clear from the meta-analysis by Malti and Krettenauer (2013) and other empirical evidence that moral emotions have a role in motivating moral behaviour, the predictive relations between them still tend to be small to moderate in magnitude (Eisenberg & Miller, 1987; see Hardy, 2006). This suggests that moral emotions, like moral reasoning and moral identity, are an important part of the picture, but not sufficient to explain moral behaviour.

Thus, there seems to be a need for an integrated approach including all three sources of moral behaviour (see Arsenio et al., 2006; Malti & Latzo, 2010). The suggestion that these components may be interconnected when it comes to motivating moral behaviour is not a novel one. Using a range of self-report questionnaires, Hardy (2006) finds all three proposed sources of moral motivation (i.e., identity, reasoning, and emotion) to be predictive of prosocial behaviour in adults when different forms of prosocial behaviour are considered. Similarly, in children, research suggests that the predictive effect of empathy on moral behaviour is moderated by the role of moral reasoning (Miller et al., 1996). Likewise, researchers have reported predictive links between moral motivation (as measured by MEAs and their justifications after a moral transgression) and empathy on moral action in adolescents (Malti et al., 2009), with the suggestion that these associations between moral judgement and moral emotion may form the basis of moral identity development (Bergman, 2002; Krettenauer et al., 2008; see also Krettenauer et al., 2014). However, although the existing evidence suggests that these components may be related, it is not clear how they develop or indeed how or if they relate to each other when predicting moral action. In any case, the upshot is that moral emotions alone do not hold the key to a solution of the 'gappiness problem'—while they may do so in conjunction with other components.

Phronesis as an integrative concept

The discussion so far indicates that the logical step to take in the search for factors bridging the knowledge–action gap in Moral Psychology and Education is to look for multicomponent constructs. We nourish the hope that we have identified the right one, and we have called it *phronesis*.

From an empirical viewpoint, investigating whether *phronesis* can help solve the 'gappiness problem' is contingent on the development of a measure which allows *phronesis* to be empirically tested. Given the practical bent in Aristotle's ethical theory, and the recent resurgence in Character Education with an Aristotelian twist (Jubilee Centre, 2022), as well as burgeoning interest in Psychology for those matters (Fowers et al., 2021) and for research into the notion of wisdom (Grossmann, Westrate, Ardelt et al., 2020), it is curious that prior to 2019 (Darnell et al., 2019) no one had sought to conceptualize *phronesis* with a view to carrying out psychological research on it: understanding its psychological origins and development and laying out potential avenues for its cultivation.[8] Clearly, an instrument to measure *phronesis* would need to be a multifaceted one wherein researchers would measure each component with adapted existing measures or design new measures from scratch. From our viewpoint, what needs to be measured are the functions of moral sensitivity *qua* relevant-virtue recognition, moral adjudication *qua* virtue-conflict resolution, moral identity *qua* blueprint adherence, and emotion regulation *qua* proper reason-infusion of moral affect (recall Chapter 2).

The present authors have been working on a potential *phronesis* instrument: a work that is still in the stages of construct creation and trialling. We report on the current state of play in this research in Chapter 6. For present purposes, however, a salient preliminary question beckons. There already exists in the Moral Psychology literature a widely discussed neo-Kohlbergian four-component model of moral functioning, which also has the aim—if not always explicitly stated—of solving the 'gappiness problem'. Is there any

---

[8] This lack of empirical study of *phronesis* is the case, notwithstanding the 4 decades of research on generic wisdom we discussed in Chapter 3.

potential 'value-addedness' in the four-componential APM vis-à-vis the neo-Kohlbergian one?

5.4 Comparing the APM with the Neo-Kohlbergian Four-Componential Model of Moral Functioning

Kohlberg's enduring significance for Moral Education continues through the 'neo-Kohlbergians', especially James Rest, Darcia Narvaez, Stephen Thoma, and Muriel Bebeau (Rest et al., 2000). They propose a four-componential model of moral functioning (sometimes also referred to as Rest's model; cf. Rest, 1984) that is particularly germane to the current book. While other multicomponent constructs exist (e.g., Nucci, 2017), which could serve as potential reference points for our proposed four-componential model of *phronesis*, we confine our attention here to the neo-Kohlbergian model, both for reasons of space and because of its prominence in the history of Moral Psychology. Notice that we are solely interested in this model here as one of moral decision-making. Developmentally, the model is still rooted in the Kohlbergian assumption that moral development is the gradual natural ascendance of principled morality over convention. This flies in the face, for example, of moral domain theory (Turiel, 1983) and research (e.g., Turiel, 2006), which suggest that principled morality and convention are complementary. We take no stand on that debate here, as our interest for present purposes is on decision-making in a generally recognized moral domain, rather than in the contrast between a conventional domain and the moral domain.

The neo-Kohlbergians critique and refine Kohlberg's approach, taking some of his central elements on board while augmenting his work to include other dimensions of acting morally beyond Kohlberg's focus on moral judgement. According to Narvaez and Rest (1995), there are four psychological components of acting morally.[9] These are: moral sensitivity, moral judgement, moral motivation, and implementation—with cognition and affect being intertwined within each component. The failure to bring moral action to fruition can lie in deficiencies in any of these four components, either individually or collectively. For example, '*moral sensitivity*', defined as the ability to identify and attend to moral issues, could miscarry because of an individual's failure to draw inferences about how others might be affected by courses of moral

---

[9] Narvaez has continued to develop her views on moral development, but these are orthogonal to the focus of this book because she is most interested in normative development and nurturing environments (see Narvaez, 2008).

action or a failure to feel empathy for them. '*Moral judgement*', the ability to reason about and justify the morally ideal course of action, fails where reasoning abilities are compromised or perhaps simply remain undeveloped. '*Moral motivation*' 'implies that the person gives priority to the moral value above all other values and intends to fulfil it' (Narvaez & Rest, 1995, p. 386). A person who can perceive the relative merits of various goals but does not select the morally ideal choice will fail in moral action as a result of this deficiency in moral motivation. Narvaez and Rest (1995) identify a fourth component of acting morally as '*implementation*', alternatively labelled '*character*'. This component is, however, not moral in itself: it consists rather of qualities that enable the actor to stay on (moral) task, such as ego-strength and social and psychological skills (Narvaez & Rest, 1995). Thus, in the absence of such abilities, moral action also miscarries.

The neo-Kohlbergian model postulates that there may be one or more separate reasons for moral failure. The corollary of the model is that any attempt to predict moral behaviour from one component—and here one might have in mind Kohlberg's emphasis on moral judgement—is insufficient on its own. The pedagogical implications of the model are, in turn, that Moral Education needs to address all four components if the goal of implementing moral action is to be realized (Bebeau et al., 1999). More recently, Nucci (2017) drew similar pedagogical conclusions from his understanding of character as a multifaceted developmental system, also consisting of four components.

Although componential models have proved persuasive from a theoretical point of view, their empirical testing has only taken place in a limited way. While the moral judgement component of the neo-Kohlbergian model has been subjected to extensive testing via the well-known Defining Issue Test (DIT) and Intermediate Concept Measure (ICM) instruments (Thoma, 2014: Thoma et al., 2013), only one attempt seems to have been made to design an instrument homing in on all the components. You and Bebeau (2013) thus assessed the four components in a self-report instrument designed to measure dentists' moral skills (cf. Chambers, 2011, for a more rudimentary version). However, this instrument captures the four components in a specific applied professional context only, not in a more general way. This means that a potential instrument designed on the basis of our four-componential APM cannot be compared with an existing neo-Kohlbergian instrument in terms of incremental validity in predicting moral action. What we can do, however, is to reflect on the way in which the components in these two models overlap or contrast theoretically.

First, we defined the 'constitutive function' of *phronesis* in Chapter 2 as the ability to notice a given situation as ethically salient and identify the relevant virtue(s) germane to that situation. This maps onto the component of 'moral sensitivity' in the neo-Kohlbergian model, defined as 'the receptivity of the sensory perceptual system to social situations and the interpretation of the situation in terms of what actions are possible, who and what would be affected by each of the possible actions, and how the involved parties might react to possible outcomes' (Narvaez & Rest, 1995, p. 386). While the neo-Kohlbergian model is not couched in the language of virtue, it seems fair to suggest that the constitutive function of *phronesis* and moral sensitivity in this model are saliently similar, in that both fulfil the function of attending to, noticing, or perceiving a given situation as involving moral concerns.

Second, the 'integrative function' of *phronesis* (namely, the ability to weigh or adjudicate the relative priority of virtues in complex, dilemmatic situations) is arguably comparable with 'moral judgement' in the neo-Kohlbergian model. Narvaez and Rest (1995, p. 386) describe this component as enabling the agent to '[decide] which of the possible actions is most moral. The individual weighs the choices and determines what a person ought to do in such a situation.' Though neo-Aristotelians will no doubt point out that the neo-Kohlbergian model has its theoretical origins in a deontological approach to ethics, whereas the *phronesis* model presupposes a virtue-based approach, the two seem to be substantively parallel here, insofar as it is the task of this second component both to weigh, evaluate, and adjudicate over different actions or virtues, respectively.

We identified one more function of *phronesis* as that of possessing a blueprint of the good life that enables individuals to adjust their own moral identity to accord with the blueprint, thereby furnishing it with motivational force. This component can be compared with 'moral motivation' in the neo-Kohlbergian model. However, while 'giving priority to the moral value above all other values and intending to fulfil it' (Narvaez & Rest, 1995, p. 386) may be functionally similar to having a blueprint of the good life (as *eudaimonia*), which orders moral priorities, the notion of a blueprint of what counts as a life well lived suggests a different theoretical function than simply securing the overridingness of moral value. The good life could, in some cases, demand giving priority to nonmoral values (e.g., theoretical, aesthetic). The idea of the overridingness of morality is very much a deontological one that does not find a comfortable home in Aristotelian theory (as Aristotle did not possess a discrete concept of 'the moral'). Again, however, one could argue that what the neo-Kohlbergian model and the APM share is a similar *function* in the moral sphere of human association (ordering priorities), such that they may be practically, if not theoretically, parallel in terms of outcomes in most relevant cases of, say, everyday moral dilemmas.

Fourth, in turning to the final component of the two models, a more significant difference seems to emerge. For whereas the *phronesis* model speaks specifically of emotion regulation (i.e., fine-tuning the emotions motivating virtuous action in the given situation), the neo-Kohlbergian model's fourth component of 'implementation' emphasizes ego-strength and social and psychological skills which combine in order to carry through the chosen course of action, with no specific mention made of emotion generation or regulation. Such general executive abilities would be identified by neo-Aristotelians as performance skills: those character traits that have an instrumental value in enabling the intellectual, moral, and civic virtues (Jubilee Centre, 2022). Perhaps the defining difference between the two models is that Aristotle holds that *phronesis* presupposes that the agent already wants the good and does not need to force herself to attain it. What is required is, rather, the infusion of emotions with reason so that the relevant feelings can be fine-tuned as needed. The neo-Kohlbergian model seems to retain the imperative approach to ethics in deontological ethics, whereas the *phronesis* model focuses on cultivating proper motivation as a baseline. It will be recalled, however, that the former model incorporates both cognitive and affective elements across all of its four components (Narvaez & Rest, 1995, p. 387). As such, it might be argued that this model does not stand in need of a discrete emotion component; yet it is not entirely clear how emotions are integrated into the neo-Kohlbergian model. On occasions, neo-Kohlbergians refer to the fourth component as 'character' (e.g., Narvaez & Rest, 1995, p. 396), which would align the model with a fairly narrow, if common, understanding of the term 'character' as having to do with performance skills only. In that sense, Nucci's conception of character as a 'multifaceted dynamic developmental system' (2017, p. 2) has more affinities with an Aristotelian conception, although Nucci (2017, p. 2) rejects understanding character as made up of 'virtues' in an Aristotelian sense.

As long as the two models under discussion here have not been empirically tested, comparisons and contrasts between them can only take place at a level of theoretical abstraction—and remain fairly speculative. Theoretically inclined academics will no doubt insist on the significant differences between the two models in terms of their underlying philosophical provenance and orientation. Those are clearly grounded in different moral ontologies and epistemologies. Moreover, the components of the neo-Kohlbergian model are to be seen as 'internal processes necessary to produce a moral *act*' but not 'as personality traits or virtues' (Narvaez & Rest, 1995, p. 386). Of course, neo-Aristotelians do not claim that the components of *phronesis*, viewed in isolation, constitute virtues, but they will insist that as a combined 'ensemble of processes' (Narvaez & Rest, 1995, p. 387), they capture the psychological functions underlying the virtue of *phronesis*.

More practically minded academics may observe, however, that at the functional level, the similarity between the two models is abundant. The 'constitutive function' of *phronesis* and the component of 'moral sensitivity' in the neo-Kohlbergian model are substantively parallel since both fulfil the function of attending to, noticing, or perceiving a given situation as one which involves moral concerns. The task of the second component of both models (the 'integrative function' or 'moral judgement' components) is to weigh up and adjudicate different virtues or actions. Third, the neo-Kohlbergian model and the *phronesis* model share the task of ordering priorities, although they are grounded in different theoretical assumptions. However, the fourth component of the two models differs substantively, as we observed above, and that is where the neo-Kohlbergian model would need much more than a modest revision from the perspective of Aristotelian *phronesis*.

It is outside the purview of this chapter to adjudicate whether a deontological approach or a virtue-based approach to morality is more adequate, or to hypothesize whether an instrument based on the neo-Kohlbergian model would give a better account than a *phronesis*-based instrument of how the knowledge–action gap can be bridged. The ideal situation would seem to be one in which both sorts of instruments existed and could be compared in terms of conceptualizations and findings.

5.5 The Prospects of *Phronesis* as a Gap-Stopper

We have reviewed the literatures that have developed in the wake of the finding that moral reasoning alone only moderately predicts moral behaviour. Unfortunately, the other main contenders, moral identity and moral emotions, only predict moral behaviour moderately themselves, at least when examined independently. The logical conclusion seems to be to focus attention on multicomponent constructs as potential solutions to the 'gappiness problem'.

Because of the burgeoning interest in Aristotelian virtue ethics across various subareas of Social Science, with *phronesis* often given pride of place as a meta-virtue of moral adjudication, it seems reasonable to offer an account of how a *phronetic* model could solve the gappiness problem. We identified four components of *phronesis* in Chapter 2 and elaborated on those in order to offer hints about how they might be measured. In view of (at least) surface similarities with the well-known neo-Kohlbergian four-componential model, the key elements of that model were compared above with our APM. Everything that we have said so far indicates that developing a measure of the *phronesis* model would be a feasible and potentially fruitful enterprise—but so would empirically assessing the neo-Kohlbergian model. It is, in our view, a pity that the latter model has so far mostly been mined for its moral judgement component only.

In sum, in light of all the background history of Psychology recounted in Chapters 3–5, we consider *phronesis* a promising psycho-moral developmental construct, although it may appear fairly late in the developmental trajectory, and we believe that analysing it as a potential model of moral decision-making is a useful enterprise. That said, we have acknowledged throughout this book (and harp further on that point in Chapter 11) that most of what Aristotle himself said about the development leading up to *phronesis* requires some serious modern overhaul. Unfortunately, current neo-Aristotelians have not yet provided a revised, empirically grounded, account of *phronesis* development. Yet, despite the paucity of Aristotelian theory on how *phronesis qua* intellectual virtue is (best) developed, nurtured, and sustained, we hope that by identifying above the historical precursors of a *phronesis* solution to the 'gappiness problem', we have at least succeeded in introducing the concept of *phronesis* into the Moral Psychology literature on the 'gappiness problem', suggested its potential relevance there, and indicated what further research needs to be undertaken to gauge whether its potential is specious or real.

6
A New Measure of *Phronesis*
Empirical Findings

6.1 Introduction

We have discussed the substantial scholarly attention to wisdom in multiple disciplines in the first five chapters (cf. Arthur et al., 2015; 2021; Darnell et al., 2019; Fowers, 2005; 2015; Grossmann, Westrate, Ardelt et al., 2020; Schwartz & Sharpe, 2010). Although this literature is rich conceptually, its empirical testing is quite thin. In this book, we are providing a more systematic theoretical model, the Aristotelian *phronesis* model (APM), that is directly amenable to empirical assessment. In this chapter, we discuss the empirical work on the APM thus far. We used extant psychological measures to empirically examine this well-articulated model of practical wisdom in two proof of concept studies. We see this approach as a promising way to productively begin the empirical evaluation of the APM.

As we discussed in Chapter 3, the approximately 50 years of empirical wisdom research includes numerous wisdom conceptions based on 'thorough reviews of the literature'. Yet each set of investigators reads the literature uniquely, leading to the development of multiple intuitive, but mutually inconsistent, conceptions. We are taking a different approach, building a conception of practical wisdom from a more systematic, neo-Aristotelian perspective, but doing so in a way that can facilitate the empirical assessment of the model.

As we discuss our empirical work, it is important to remind readers (recall Chapter 1) that our use of terms such as 'virtue', '*phronesis*', and 'flourishing' is intentionally moral because Aristotle viewed these concepts as inherent elements of his ethics owing to the need for practical wisdom in the pursuit of a good human life. Empirical social scientists generally favour a strict separation of facts and values (Fowers et al., 2021; Richardson et al., 1999), believing that they can study topics, even moral topics, in a value-neutral manner. As we have done throughout the book, we use the term 'moral' in the context of

Aristotle's ethical theory rather than in its standard modern usage. Aristotle did not have a discrete concept of 'the moral' at his disposal; he talked about 'the ethical', however, as that pertaining to a person's character, which he saw, in turn, as a constitutive element of *eudaimonia* (flourishing). In modern usage, especially within Social Science, 'moral' has acquired a much narrower and more behavioural understanding, tantamount to 'prosocial', which is an exclusively behavioural concept, or the moral has been entirely subjectivized to relate to an individual's values and moral decisions.

Our initial approach to studying the APM has been to measure it with existing psychological measures (Darnell et al., 2022). Having found success in this endeavour, we think this research suggests the empirical viability of the APM, and this can encourage the more extensive and ambitious kind of research necessary to examine the APM more thoroughly with scales uniquely designed to measure it rather than relying on existing assessments. When we write this, in late 2023, such work is already underway in the Jubilee Centre.

The APM lends itself to empirical assessment through a latent model approach, with each of the four components comprised as a first-order latent factor (each based on multiple observed measures) that can be explained by *phronesis* as a second-order factor. Accordingly, we created latent variables of the four APM functions with extant scales and assessed these latent variables as elements of a unitary concept of *phronesis*. This procedure is known as a second-order confirmatory factor analysis.

One way this measurement is an advance on most studies of wisdom is that we included both self-report and 'performance measures' (Kunzmann, 2019; Wright et al., 2021). In performance assessments, research participants complete tasks, and their performance on that task completion is evaluated based on trained observers' ratings of that performance or compared to experts' responses as performance criteria. That means that the scores on the assessments are evaluations of the research participants' responses, rather than simple self-reports on the topic. The primary drawbacks of performance assessment are its complexity, time-intensity, and expense. We were encouraged in using performance measures by the fact that other wisdom researchers have done so with reasonable success (Baltes & Staudinger, 2000; Brienza et al., 2018; Sternberg, 1998). In the long run, our aim is to create a combination of performance and self-report measures specifically designed to assess the APM. We aim to provide expert responses to the performance measures to make comparisons with those expert ratings easy. This can make performance measurement somewhat more cumbersome than self-reports, but it will add significant value to the assessment by going beyond self-reported wisdom.

We also administered a prosocial tendencies measure as a reasonable (if not entirely satisfying) criterion measure. We reasoned that *phronesis* should be associated to some indicator of moral or beneficial behaviours, and prosociality is widely cited as a source of other benefit. The inclusion of this criterion measure constitutes the analysis as a structural equation model. Our view of this criterion variable is that it simply illustrates the moral relevance of practical wisdom, not that prosociality, as conceptualized and measured by most psychologists, has any role in defining *phronesis*. Figure 6.1 indicates our predicted model. We plan to use other outcome measures in future studies to broaden the predictive assessment of the APM.

A final consideration in this study was to rule out the possibility that *phronesis* is simply another way to assess personality. To do this, we tested whether controlling for the Big Five personality dimensions weakened the association between *phronesis* and prosocial tendencies. We emphasize that this is simply an initial study. If the proof of concept results support the APM, more rigorous research will be necessary to fully test it, with different cohorts in different contexts. We would be happy if some readers of this book took on that task or helped the Jubilee Centre with further instrument development and testing.

6.2 Methods

Participants

For the first study, the sample included 286 UK undergraduate participants (143 females) aged 18–50 years (mean = 27.69, SD = 10.02), recruited through a Psychology course or through the research firm Pure Profile. Participants from the Psychology course received course credit, and those recruited through Pure Profile were paid £2 for completing the study.

Measures

We approximated the four functions of the APM as latent variables with available measures in Moral Psychology. We estimated the *Constitutive Function* with moral sensitivity scales, the *Integrative Function* with moral adjudication measures, the *Blueprint Function* with moral identity scales, and the *Emotional Regulative Function* with moral emotion measures. This is consistent with our conclusions about these components in Chapters 2–5 and with the APM.

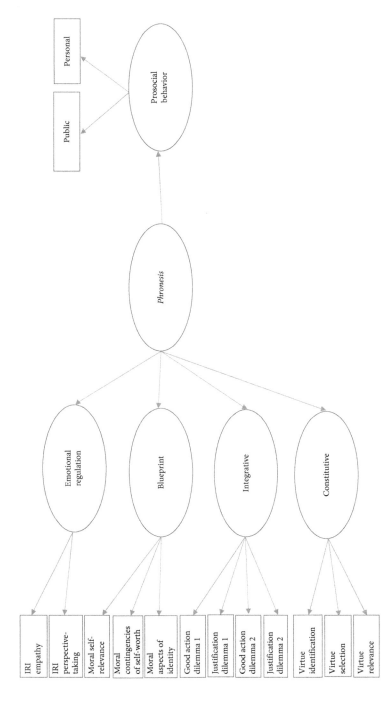

Figure 6.1 Predicted *Phronesis* Model

The *Constitutive Function*

We estimated the *Constitutive Function* latent variable with three moral sensitivity measures that were based on participants' responses to a series of tasks based on two dilemmas taken from the Adolescent Intermediate Concept Measure (AD-ICM) of moral reasoning (Thoma et al., 2013). The AD-ICM assesses adolescents' moral cognition, specifically their 'intermediate concepts' (i.e., the transition from thinking based on personal interests to conventional thinking). The full version of the AD-ICM includes seven vignettes depicting dilemmatic situations with high school and college student protagonists. We selected this measure, in part, to follow Kunzmann's (2019) recommendation to make measurement relevant to the sample. Each dilemma describes a situation in which one or more virtue concepts (e.g., courage) are in play. The two dilemmas used in this study emphasized (1) *honesty* (what to do when friends cheat in a test) and (2) *justice* (whether to fire a friend who is the weakest worker). The dilemma texts are available on request from the second author. Participants responded as if they were the protagonist in the story (e.g., 'If you were Nikki in this situation what would you do?').

The *Constitutive Function* latent was estimated by assessing three performance tasks in response to the two vignettes adapted from the AD-ICM. The first task, Virtue Identification, was assessed by whether participants identified a moral conflict (yes or no) and the relevant virtue(s) in the vignettes in an open-ended question. After reading the initial dilemma, participants were asked if the story characters 'faced any problems in this situation?' Participants answered 'yes' or 'no' and were then presented with an open-ended question. If they answered 'yes', they were asked to describe the problem and its most important considerations. If they answered 'no', they were asked to explain why there was no problem and what the most important considerations were. Two independent raters coded the participants' open-text box responses with ratings from 0 to 3. The ratings were based on whether the participants (a) recognized a conflict in the dilemma, (b) related the conflict to the relevant virtue(s), and (c) provided reasons explaining the problem with virtue-based justifications. Participants received a score of zero if their answers did not identify a conflict. If they did recognize a conflict, one point was assigned for each criterion that they met. For Dilemma 1, the inter-rater reliability was $k = .77, p < .001$, and for Dilemma 2, it was $k = .72, p < .001$. The Dilemma 1 and Dilemma 2 ratings were correlated ($rho = .65, p < .001$), so the participants' Virtue Identification score was the mean of the two dilemma scores.

The second task, Virtue Selection, was assessed after participants read and responded to a second dilemma section, which described the conflict explicitly. They then chose qualities from a list of eight virtues (i.e., honesty, compassion, loyalty, justice, respect, gratitude, humility, and integrity) that they thought were most relevant to the story. Participants could select any number of virtues and could add other unlisted characteristics. Virtue Selection assesses the ability to select the most pertinent virtues, compared to selections by an expert panel.[1] Pertinent virtues had unanimous endorsement from the expert panel. For example, for Dilemma 1, the panel selected five virtues as relevant to the story (i.e., honesty, integrity, justice, loyalty, and compassion). The participant's Virtue Selection score was a percentage of virtue selections that matched the panel's selections (0 to 100). For example, if a participant picked three out of the five virtues selected by the panel, their score was 60%. The percentages for Dilemmas 1 and 2 were correlated (rho =.55, $p < .001$), so the Virtue Selection score was the mean of the Dilemma 1 and Dilemma 2 scores.

For the third task, Virtue Relevance, independent raters coded the degree to which the selected virtues were relevant to participants' description in the Virtue Identification task. The score was the number of participant-selected virtues in the second task that were reflected in their Virtue Identification description (the first task), with a range of zero to 2. A score of two indicated that two or more of their selected virtues in the first task were reflected in the second task. The inter-rater reliability for Dilemma 1 was k =.71, $p < .001$, and for Dilemma 2, it was k =.66, $p < .001$. A mean rating was calculated for each dilemma. A significant correlation was found between Dilemma 1 and Dilemma 2 ratings (rho =.59, $p < .001$), so the mean of the two dilemma scores provided the Virtue Relevance score.

The *Integrative Function*

We estimated the *Integrative Function* latent with four observed measures.[2] These four performance measures were based on the AD-ICM. For each dilemma, participants responded to a list of action choices we provided that

---

[1] The panel consisted of two Psychology professors and a research fellow working in the field of Moral Psychology and one Philosophy professor and one research fellow working in the field of Virtue Ethics. This included one of the authors of the AD-ICM (Thoma).

[2] We initially intended to include the Situated Wise Reasoning Scale (SWIS; Brienza et al., 2018), as an observed measure of the *Integrative Function*. The SWIS is a 21-item self-report wisdom questionnaire. In our initial analyses (reported below as an assessment of the measurement model), the SWIS cross-loaded on three factors and was therefore unsuitable for the measurement model of the confirmatory factor analysis. In hindsight, we should have expected this cross-loading because the SWIS is a broad measure of wisdom that we should not have expected to be limited to the *Integrative Function*.

the protagonist might make (e.g., 'Danielle should send an anonymous note to the teacher about what happened'). Response choices were on a five-point scale from 'I strongly believe this is a bad choice' to 'I strongly believe this is a good choice'. Then participants ranked the three *best* action choices for each dilemma.[3] Having participants rate the items before ranking them ensures they have considered each item individually before choosing the best actions (Thoma et al., 2013).

Participants then rated and ranked a list of possible justifications we provided for the actions in response to the dilemma (e.g., 'Those that received information were not likely to remember it anyway'). Response choices were on a five-point scale from 'I strongly believe this is a bad reason' to 'I strongly believe this is a good reason'. Following standard AD-ICM scoring procedures, participants then ranked the three *best* justifications for each dilemma.

Each of the action and justification items used in the AD-ICM has been categorized as 'acceptable', 'unacceptable', or 'neutral' by an expert panel (Thoma et al., 2013). The scores for 'good action' were based on the degree of match between the participant's ranking and the expert panel's ranking, ranging from -12 to 12 (correctly selecting all 'acceptable' items as the *best choices*). There was a good action score for Dilemma 1 and for Dilemma 2. We used the same set of calculations to obtain the justification score for each Dilemma. The action and justification scores were not statistically significantly correlated across the two dilemmas, so each dilemma was retained as a distinct observed measure. The construct validity of the AD-ICM expert scoring system was reported by Thoma et al. (2013). We scored participants' choices according to that pre-established expert scoring system.

Emotional Regulative Function

In default of any off-the-shelf measures of an Aristotelian notion of regulated emotions, we estimated the *Emotional Regulative Function* with two self-report scales from the Interpersonal Reactivity Index (IRI) focused on moral emotions Davis, 1983). The complete IRI assesses four aspects of empathy (i.e., perspective-taking, fantasy, empathic concern, and personal distress). Participants completed the Perspective-Taking (i.e., adoption of

---

[3] The original AD-ICM also asks participants to rate the two worst action choices and the two worst justifications, but we found that scores on these worst action and justification choices were uncorrelated with the best action and justification scores, so we did not include the worst action and justification choices in our modelling.

others' viewpoints) and Empathic Concern (i.e., compassion and concern for others) subscales as the two scales that best reflected the *Emotional Regulative Function*. The subscales consist of seven Perspective-Taking items (e.g., 'I sometimes try to understand my friends better by imagining how things look from their perspective') and seven Empathic Concern items (e.g., 'I am often quite touched by things that I see happen'). The response choices have a five-point scale ranging from 'Does not describe me very well' to 'Describes me very well'. Four of the items were reverse scored and we used a mean item score for each subscale (range 0–4).

Blueprint Function

We estimated the *Blueprint Function* with three self-report scales of moral identity. First, we used the Moral Self-Relevance (MSR) measure and its scoring procedure (Patrick & Gibbs, 2012). Participants rated how important moral and nonmoral qualities are to themselves. Participants first rated the importance of 16 qualities on a five-point scale from 'not important to me' to 'extremely important to me' (e.g., 'How important is it to you that you are kind?'). These 16 qualities consist of eight moral (e.g., honest, kind, and fair) and eight nonmoral items (e.g., imaginative, cautious, and athletic). We computed a mean item score for this section of the MSR. Then participants chose 8 qualities from a list of 32 qualities that they see as most important to them as a person. The 32 qualities consisted of the same 8 moral qualities (e.g., generous, helpful, and sincere) and 24 nonmoral qualities (e.g., popular, talkative, and strong). Then the number of moral items picked from the 32 qualities are summed (range 0–8) and divided by two. The MSR score was the mean of the two sections (range of 1–9).

The second observed measure was the Virtue subscale of the Contingencies of Self-Worth scale (CSW; Crocker et al., 2003). This subscale focuses on the importance of virtuous living to one's self-esteem. Participants rated five items (e.g., 'My self-esteem depends on whether or not I follow my moral/ethical principles') on a seven-point scale ranging from 'strongly disagree' to 'strongly agree'. The CSW score is the item mean (range 1–7).

The third observed measure was a single item from the Aspects of Identity scale (Cheek et al., 2002). Following Morgan and Fowers (2021), we chose this single item because it is the only item of the Aspects of Identity scale that directly assesses moral identity (distinguished from other sources of identity).

On a five-point scale, participants rated how important 'my personal values and moral standards are . . .' from 'not at all important to my sense of who I am' to 'extremely important to my sense of who I am'.

Personality control variables

Participants completed the 44-item Big Five Inventory Scale (John & Srivastava, 1999), which assesses neuroticism, extraversion, openness, conscientiousness, and agreeableness. Participants rated how well each item described them on a five-point scale from 'disagree strongly' to 'strongly agree'. Sixteen of the items were reversed scored. This measure has been used frequently in studies of personality dimensions. We used the item mean for each personality dimension (range 1–5).

Prosocial tendencies criterion variable

We estimated the *Prosocial* latent variable with the Prosocial Tendencies Measured—Revised scale (PTM-R; Carlo et al., 2010), a 21-item measure of prosocial behaviour with six subscales: public, anonymous, dire, emotional, altruism, and compliant. Response choices are on a five-point scale from 'does not describe me at all' to 'describes me greatly'. Altruistic items are reverse scored.

When we analysed the reliability of the PTM-R (Carlo et al., 2010), we found that two items in the compliant subscale were unexpectedly negatively related to the scale. The PTM-R was initially developed based on focus groups and a literature review, resulting in six conceptually developed, moderately to strongly correlated scales (Carlo et al., 2003). This measure has been used in many studies, and to date, it has only been assessed with correlational analyses and confirmatory factor analyses (Carlo et al., 2010; Mestre et al., 2015). Its original 25 items were reduced to 21 because of poor confirmatory factor analysis (CFA) model fit by Carlo et al. (2010), and these researchers assessed CFA models with 4–6 factor configurations, all of which had similar relative fit statistics, with six factors having slightly better absolute fit indices. Because the six PTM-R scales were moderately to strongly correlated and the CFA modelling was less than conclusive, the evidence for a six-factor structure is not strong. For these reasons, along with the negative correlation of the two compliant subscale items, we re-evaluated this measure's structure with exploratory factor analysis.

We began with a parallel analysis for ordinal data (Lubbe, 2019) and used Mplus version 8 with the WLSMV[4] estimator (Muthén, & Muthén, 1998–2017) to conduct an exploratory factor analysis (EFA). This allowed us to assess the factor structure for this sample. In both the parallel analysis and the EFA, we found that the PTM-R was best understood as having two factors, which we termed 'Personal' (14 items) and 'Public' (7 items). These two sets of items formed the observed variables for the *Prosocial* latent variable. It is important to note that we are not claiming that this factor structure for the PTM-R is definitive in general. Our interest in prosocial behaviour in this study was simply as a criterion measure for our hypothesized *Phronesis* latent variable. Further research on the most appropriate structure for the PTM-R seems warranted.

Procedures

We collected the data online, with participants completing the questionnaires in one session. The order remained the same for each participant, following the order in the measures section. We obtained informed consent for all participants prior to completing the questionnaire.

Data analytic strategy

We analysed the data with structural equation modelling (SEM) to examine the hypothesized second-order factor model of *phronesis*, with its four first-order latent factors, and its relationship to prosocial behaviour. To facilitate the modelling, we modified the scaling of the measures arithmetically to make the scaling similar across measures (which is necessary for interpretable SEM estimation). For the self-report scales, we used the mean item scores. For the performance measures, this required dividing by an integer to make the scaling range from 0 to 5. We anticipated four latent variables explained by a second-order latent variable we termed '*Phronesis*'. We estimated these four functions as follows: *Constitutive Function* latent variable with the Virtue Identification, Virtue Selection, and Virtue Relevance observed ratings. We estimated the *Integrative Function* latent variable from the Good Action and Good Justification observed scores from each of the two dilemmas based on the AD-ICM (Thoma et al.,

---

[4] The WLSMV estimator stands for the 'weighted least squares mean and variance adjusted' estimator. We used this estimator instead of the more common maximum likelihood estimator because the item level observed data from the PTM-R were ordinal variables, rendering the maximum likelihood estimator inappropriate.

2013). We estimated the *Emotional Regulative Function* latent variable with the Empathic Concern and Perspective-Taking observed scales (Davis, 1983). We estimated the *Blueprint Function* latent with the MSR (Patrick & Gibbs, 2012), CSW (Crocker et al., 2003) and Aspects of Identity (Cheek et al., 2002) observed measures. We measured the *Prosocial* latent variable with the PTM-R (Carlo et al., 2010) observed scores we termed Public and Personal. We followed Kline's (2015) recommendations in evaluating the fit of our models. This meant generally disregarding the χ^2 statistic because we have very complex models. The other fit index recommendations are to have RMSEA less than or equal to .08, CFI greater than or equal to .90, and SRMR less than or equal to .10. The hypothesized model is presented in Figure 6.1.

6.3 Results and Discussion

Preliminary analyses

We first tested the sample for univariate normality and multicollinearity with SPSS 25 (IBM Corp, 2016). Histograms, skewness, and kurtosis analyses indicated that the variables did not violate the normality assumption. All variable inflation values were less than 5, below Kline's (2015) criterion of lower than 10, thereby meeting the multicollinearity assumption. Cronbach alphas were conducted with all study measures for which that was feasible. Descriptive statistics are presented in Table 6.1.

Structural equation modelling

We predicted a second-order factor analysis result with the first-order latent variables of *Constitutive Function, Integrative Function, Emotion Regulation Function,* and *Blueprint Function,* and a second-order latent variable we termed *Phronesis*. We expected the *Prosocial* latent to regress onto the *Phronesis* latent, assessing whether *Phronesis* is associated with a reasonable criterion variable. All SEM analyses were maximum likelihood analyses conducted with Mplus version 8 (Muthén & Muthén, 1998–2017).

We first created and assessed a measurement model of the expected second-order confirmatory factor analysis. Modification indices suggested allowing covariance of the (1) Good Action and Good Justification observed variables for Dilemma 1 and Good Action and Good Justification observed variables for Dilemma 2. Because each pair of variables is describing participants'

Table 6.1 Descriptive statistics of observed variables in the model

Variable	Range	Adult Sample[a]				Adolescent Sample[b]			
		Chronbach α	M (SD)	Skewness	Kurtosis	Cronbach α	M (SD)	Skewness	Kurtosis
IRI Empathy	1–7	0.75	2.80 (0.74)	−0.08	−0.21	0.77	2.37 (0.76)	−1.19	1.72
IRI Perspective-Taking	1–7	0.63	2.80 (0.64)	0.05	0.09	0.47	2.73 (0.76)	−0.19	−0.24
Moral Self-Relevance	0–9	0.89	3.85 (0.77)	0.00	−1.00	.89	2.45 (0.93)	0.22	−.021
Contingencies of Self-Worth	1–7	0.88	5.00 (1.22)	−0.82	0.82	0.7	4.95 (1.13)	−0.93	1.09
Aspects of Identity	1–5	—	3.77 (1.07)	−0.73	−0.10	—	3.85 (0.90)	−0.54	0.19
Good Action Dilemma 1	−12–12	—	1.17 (5.09)	−0.33	−0.47	—	0.74 (6.21)	−0.44	−0.86
Justification Dilemma 1	−9–9	—	2.10 (4.48)	−.43	−.71	—	2.12 (4.92)	−.53	−.73
Good Action Dilemma 2	−12–12	—	4.61 (4.89)	−.64	−.40	—	4.67 (4.12)	−.03	−1.37
Justification Dilemma 2	−9–9	—	2.99 (4.33)	−.50	−.35	—	4.04 (3.39)	−.18	−.79
Virtue Identification	0–3	—	0.68 (0.71)	0.61	−0.89	—	1.22 (0.74)	0.15	−0.68
Virtue Selection	0–5	—	2.40 (1.15)	−0.21	−0.91	—	2.67 (0.95)	−0.35	−0.29
Virtue Relevance	0–2	—	0.59 (0.68)	0.81	−0.73	—	1.07 (0.57)	−0.21	−0.86
Personal[c]	1–5	.83	3.35 (0.64)	−0.65	0.74	.76	3.38 (0.65)	−0.55	0.39
Public	1–5	.57	3.12 (0.38)	−0.08	−0.70	.62	3.17 (0.48)	−0.58	1.63

[a] n = 284
[b] n = 207
[c] The PTM-R was altered in conformity with exploratory factor analysis results in the two studies reported here.

performance with respect to a specific vignette, this covariance seemed reasonable. In addition, the indicator of Virtue Relevance had a small negative residual variance. In such cases, Kline (2015) recommends setting the residual variance to zero. Following these respecifications, the measurement model fit the data ($\chi^2(50) = 92.64, p < .001$, CFI = .93; SRMR = .08; RMSEA = .08, 90% CI = .06–.11). We created a structural model by adding the *Prosocial* latent variable to the model and regressed it onto *Phronesis*. The resulting structural model fit the data well ($\chi^2(72) = 228.76, p < .001$, CFI = .94; SRMR = .08; RMSEA = .09, 90% CI = .07–.10). The relationship between the *Phronesis* and *Prosocial* latent variables was significant ($b = .80, p < .001$). This model is available as Figure 6.2.

We also assessed whether the relationship between the *Phronesis* and *Prosocial* latent variables would be weakened when the BFI-44 personality scales were included as control variables. We used the same structural model as above and regressed *Prosocial* simultaneously on the BFI-44 scales and *Phronesis*. The model fit declined ($\chi^2(137) = 474.93, p < .001$, CFI = .85, SRMR = .14; RMSEA = .09, 90% CI = .08–.10), as expected. The result of interest was that the standardized association between the *Phronesis* and *Prosocial* latent variables remained strong with the inclusion of the Big Five scales ($b = .83$), indicating that this relationship was not weakened by the addition of the Big Five variables.

These results indicate that *phronesis* can be adequately modelled as a second-order factor with existing measures approximating the four functions of the APM. This successful empirical model presents the first empirical study of a systematic theoretical wisdom model, the APM (Darnell et al., 2019). Although other wisdom models have been corroborated to varying degrees empirically, these models were constructed based on less well-specified literature reviews and intuitions. There are currently multiple, divergent wisdom models, with low intercorrelations (Glück et al., 2013), as reviewed in Chapter 3. The current study also indicates that the APM was moderately strongly related to the criterion variable of *Prosocial Behaviour Tendencies-Revised*, and this relationship was not weakened when we controlled for Big Five dimensions.

This successful proof of concept study of the APM is consistent with existing wisdom models in three key ways. First, virtually all wisdom models are multidimensional, although there is disagreement about how many and which dimensions are necessary. Second, although wisdom theorists disagree about which functions to include, all theorists argue that the functions they include are necessary for wisdom. Third, virtually all wisdom theorists agree that cognition in some form plays a critical role in wisdom.

In contrast to existing wisdom models, the APM is more comprehensive by incorporating affect, aims, and actions (discussed in Chapter 4) and provides a

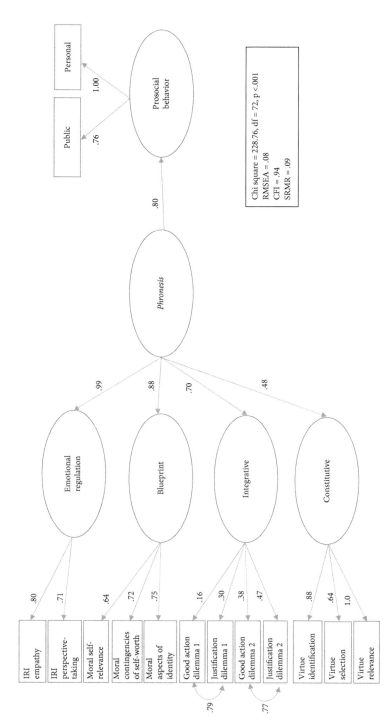

Figure 6.2 *Phronesis* among Adults (Standardized Coefficients)

systematic theoretical model of wisdom. Because *phronesis* is so integral and central to Aristotle's ethical theory, *phronesis* has a clearer and more systematic basis than we see in other wisdom models. Aristotle systematically related moral cognition, emotion, aims, and action. His theory, as appropriated by Darnell et al. (2019), conceptually organizes four functions (recall Chapter 2). This is distinct from other wisdom research in which intuitive and disparate elements have been aggregated into a model of wisdom. Therefore, the APM appears to be an empirically viable model. We understand the APM to be an interlocking, multidimensional model and take *phronesis* to be *constituted* by the four functions. Although SEM is not a direct test of constitutive relations, the results of our study are consistent with seeing the four functions as constituents of *phronesis*.

This initial study is limited in three ways. First, we used a convenience sample of UK undergraduates, and this leaves questions of generalisability open. Second, because our results are based on a single sample, and because model fit may be partly sample-dependent, replication is necessary to improve our confidence in the findings. Third, we used already available measures (mostly without any Aristotelian provenance) to approximate the APM's four functions, which allowed us to conduct this initial proof of concept. We recommend, however, that measures be specifically designed to assess the four functions more precisely.

6.4 A Replication of the Proof of Concept Study

To increase our confidence in the results of the initial study, a replication study is necessary. Some scholars have theorized that *phronesis* may begin to develop during later adolescence as part of the development of postformal operations (Kallio, 2020; Richardson & Pasupathi, 2005).[5] Therefore, we replicated the results with an adolescent sample.

Method: Participants

The sample for this study included 207 adolescents recruited from 15 UK secondary schools (females = 112) aged between 15 and 17 years (mean = 15.59, SD = 1.2). Secondary schools were offered presentations on Psychology and Character Education in exchange for students' participation in the study.

---

[5] We did not choose different age groups for the two cohorts to gauge whether *phronesis* increases from adolescence to early adulthood, as previous wisdom research has yielded little in terms of statistically significant age differences (Grossmann, Westrate, Ardelt et al., 2020), but rather simply to test our *phronesis* model on heterogenous populations.

Measures

We used the same measures and scoring calculations in this study as we employed in the first study. We calculated a mean score across the two dilemmas for Virtue Identification, Virtue Relevance, and Virtue Selection. For Virtue Identification, inter-rater reliabilities for Dilemma 1 were $k = .66$, $p < .001$, and for Dilemma 2, were $k = .69$, $p < .001$. The raters' mean Virtue Identification scores for each Dilemma were significantly correlated ($rho = .36$, $p < .01$), so these were combined. For Virtue Selection, a significant correlation was found between the raters' means of the dilemma scores ($rho = .30$, $p < .01$), so these were combined. For Virtue Relevance, inter-rater reliabilities for Dilemma 1 were $k = .58$, $p < .001$, and for Dilemma 2, were $k = .52$, $p < .001$). We found a significant correlation between the means of the dilemma scores ($rho = .32$, $p < .01$), so we combined them into a mean score. Neither the action nor justification scores were correlated across the dilemmas. Therefore, we retained the score for each dilemma as a distinct observed measure of the *Integrative Function*.

We repeated the procedures we used with the adult sample to assess the adolescent sample on the PTM-R scale. We identified the same two factors with parallel analysis and EFA. This resulted in the same item loadings on the two factors as well.

Procedure

Participants completed the questionnaires in one session either online or in a paper format, depending on the preference of the school. The procedure and content remained the same for both formats, and participants completed the questionnaires in the same order as the adult sample. We obtained informed consent from parents/caregivers and informed assent from all adolescents prior to the completion of the questionnaires.

Analytical strategy

Consistent with the first study, we fitted a structural equation model to the data to assess the hypothesized second-order factor model of *Phronesis* and its relationship to prosocial behaviour. The four latent functions of *Phronesis* were the *Constitutive, Integrative, Emotional Regulative*, and *Blueprint Functions*.

The latent variables were initially estimated with the same observed variables as the first study. Consistent with the first study, we arithmetically reduced the ranges of the observed variables to similar magnitudes (to range from 0 to 5), prior to conducting the SEM analyses. We also used the same criteria for model fit as in the first study. The descriptive results for this study are found in Table 6.1.

Results: structural equation modelling

In our attempt to replicate the first study with the adolescent sample, we began with the same measurement model we used in the first study. The latent variable covariance matrix was not positive definite owing to a linear dependency between the *Blueprint Function* and *Phronesis*. This dependency occurred because the MSR variable (initially designated as a *Blueprint Function* observed measure) cross-loaded on the *Phronesis* and *Emotion Regulation* latent variables. On inspection, the MSR score seems to indicate the *Emotion Regulation* rather than the *Blueprint* latent, in the adolescent sample. Accordingly, we moved the MSR observed scale to the *Emotion Regulation* latent. Similar to the first study, it was appropriate to allow the errors of the Good Action and Good Justification observed variables to correlate within each of the two dilemmas. In addition, there was a small negative residual variance in the indicator of Virtue Relevance. Following Kline's (2015) recommendation, we set that residual variance to zero. The revised measurement model fit the data well ($\chi^2(49) = 143.81$, $p < .001$, CFI = .95; SRMR = .08; RMSEA = .08, 90% CI = .06–.09). We then added the *Prosocial* latent to create a structural model, and that model also fulfilled Kline's (2015) criteria for good fit ($\chi^2(72) = 121.29$, $p < .01$, CFI = .94; SRMR = .08; RMSEA = .07, 90% CI = .04– .09). The link between the *Phronesis* and *Prosocial* latent variables was also strong ($b = .77$, $p < .001$). The results are depicted in Figure 6.3.

Finally, we examined whether the relationship between the *Phronesis* and *Prosocial* latent variables was robust when controlling for the Big Five personality dimensions. We regressed *Prosocial* simultaneously on each of the BFI-44 scales and on *Phronesis* with the adolescent sample. The model fit declined ($\chi^2(137) = 250.49$, $p < .001$, CFI = .85, SRMR = .12; RMSEA = .09, 90% CI = .07–.10]), as expected. The only result of interest was the standardized association between the *Phronesis* and *Prosocial* latent variables, which remained strong ($b = .73$, $p < .001$) when we controlled for the Big Five dimensions.

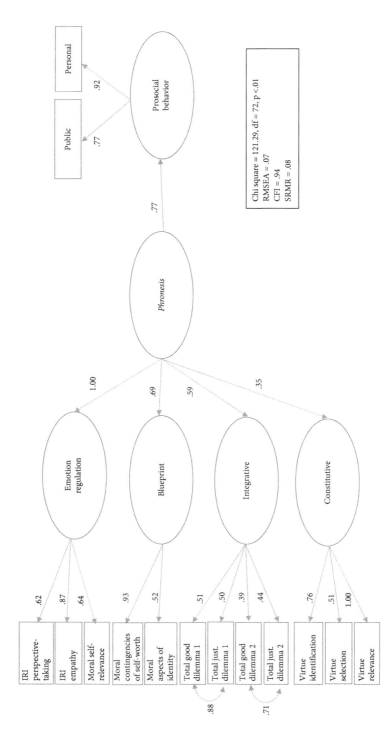

Figure 6.3 *Phronesis* among Adolescents (Standardized Coefficients)

Discussion

The results of the second study were consistent with the APM and its four functions, and the there was a strong relationship between the *Phronesis* and *Prosocial* latent variables, even when we controlled for the Big Five dimensions. The second study increases our confidence in the APM because the four-function model of *Phronesis* provided a good fit to the data.

The replication of the first study results in the second study addressed two limitations of the first study, the need for a replication and possible sample-dependent findings. Yet the second study remained subject to two additional limitations in that it relied on another convenience sample and on available measures that only approximated the functions of *phronesis*.[6]

6.5 Concluding Comments

In these two studies, the APM fitted the data well, suggesting that the model is empirically tractable. These are the first empirical assessments of the conceptual model of *phronesis* that many neo-Aristotelian philosophers and psychologists prefer (Darnell et al., 2019; Russell, 2009; Wright et al., 2021). The second-order factor model of *phronesis* we assessed is compatible with contemporary philosophical analyses of *phronesis*, in which it is portrayed as an umbrella concept encompassing several necessary functions (Russell, 2009; Wright et al., 2021; and as explained in detail earlier in Chapters 2 and 4). The APM is an appropriation of Aristotle's ethical theory, which rendered it quite distinct from the broader, and more intuitive models of wisdom studied recently by psychologists (Grossmann, Westrate, Ardelt et al., 2020). From a neo-Aristotelian perspective, the APM is preferable to the other wisdom models because it systematically includes cognition, affect, aims, and actions and focuses specifically on practical wisdom. This is especially important in that the four-function APM incorporates the key neo-Aristotelian concepts of the *Emotional Regulative* and *Blueprint Functions*.

The *Emotion Regulative Function* is necessary to assess the cognitive-affective harmony that is key to *phronetic* action (i.e., that wise actions are

---

[6] We have continued to analyse the data from those two studies, and some interesting initial findings have emerged, although those have not been peer-reviewed (see Kristjánsson, Pollard et al., 2021). For example, female participants outperformed male participants on all components of *phronesis* and on all APM measures targeting assumed subcomponents. Adults outperformed adolescents on moral reasoning *qua* moral adjudication. Adults outperformed adolescents on moral emotion. Adults had higher correspondence between chosen actions and justifications than adolescents. Higher action–justification correspondence predicted two kinds of self-reported pro-social behaviour. More unexpectedly, adolescents outperformed adults on moral perception and, indeed, on all its three presumed subcomponents.

accompanied by concordant cognition and emotion), according to Aristotle. For example, a true act of compassion must be accompanied by an appropriate understanding of compassion and suitable fellow-feeling and regret regarding someone's suffering. From our neo-Aristotelian perspective, *phronesis* is not meant to police or suppress problematic emotions. Instead, *phronesis* leads to an appraisal of situations that induces emotions that are consonant with virtuous actions. If the appraisal gives rise to a virtuous response, then the evocation of virtue-concordant emotions will also occur. We discussed this process in Chapter 4 in terms of harmonizing reason and emotions. This view is consonant with the resolution of the debate about the primacy of cognition and emotion within Psychology, which was resolved by recognizing that these psychological processes are thoroughly intertwined, and both are virtually continuously present.

There is one important caveat to this interpretation of the workings of the *Emotional Regulative Function* in our studies. We assessed this function with measures of empathy and perspective-taking. Although these two affective constructs will often track the appropriate emotional responses, they are not universally fitting. It is quite possible that empathy and perspective-taking may not be the most fitting forms of appraisal in some circumstances. For example, a firefighter often needs courage to contain a fire. In this case, a fitting appraisal would more likely be centred on measured risk taking rather than on empathy or perspective-taking. Therefore, it is important to develop more Aristotle-friendly and flexible measures to assess the *Emotional Regulative Function*. It seems to us that it is possible to construct a performance-based measure analogous to the measures of the *Constitutive* and *Integrative Functions* focused on vignettes wherein the appraisal of situations and the most appropriate affective responses could be examined.

Because we are reporting in this chapter on an empirical study, it is important to emphasize once again that Aristotle's concept of *phronesis* is an irreducibly normative concept, and moral aims (*Blueprint Function*) play a vital and substantive role in psycho-moral and sociopolitical pursuits (e.g., justice, social harmony). One of the shortcomings of most wisdom assessments is that they tend to neglect the substantive moral component of wisdom by leaving moral aims unspecified or by providing formal (contentless) aims, as we rued in Chapters 3 and 4. In the absence of specification about the aims of wisdom, it is difficult to differentiate between merely instrumentally clever actions and truly wise actions. An important advantage of a definition of wisdom that includes substantive moral aims is that we can stipulate that wise action is always aimed at praiseworthy ends. This prevents the awkward stand of allowing blameworthy actions to be the result of a kind of wise reasoning process that is separate from the ends or aims of the reasoner. Aristotle (1985) recognized that both clever and wise actions can involve high-quality reasoning. The difference, as we have repeatedly stressed, is that clever actions can have either blameworthy or praiseworthy aims, but *phronesis* is always directed towards praiseworthy aims.

As we noted in Chapters 4 and 5, the incorporation of an action choice as a constituent of wisdom eliminates the 'gappiness' problem in two ways. The first is that action is no longer viewed as an 'outcome' of a distinct and separate reasoning process. Instead, action is partly definitive of wise reasoning because *phronetic* reasoning always incorporates acting well. The second is that focusing on action strongly encourages assessments of *phronesis* that incorporate at least some performance-based assessments rather than a complete reliance on self-report scales.

These studies differ from most wisdom research in using both performance-based and self-report indicators of wisdom. We used self-report scales for the *Blueprint* and *Emotion Regulative Functions*, but we measured the *Constitutive* and *Integrative Functions* with performance assessments that examined how well participants' responses matched the responses of expert panels or raters. We see this as an important way to avoid merely asking participants how wise they think they are, which is subject to many forms of error.

One surprising and potentially important difference in our results with the adult and adolescent samples was that the MSR scale was a better measure of the *Emotion Regulative Function* for adolescents, but it assessed the *Blueprint Function* for the adults. A developmental explanation is likely most apt. Because adolescents are believed to be still developing their moral identities, it seems plausible that their moral identities may require more emotional regulation than the more settled identity of young adults (Darnell et al., 2019; Richardson & Pasupathi, 2005). This explanation is purely speculative and requires further empirical testing, however.

The value of these studies is in offering an empirical proof of concept for the APM. This empirical encouragement is useful because, as we have argued, the APM solves a set of conceptual confusions found in the wisdom literature. Inasmuch as it functions well empirically, even with measures that only approximate its elements, it shows great promise. We suggest that future researchers focus on creating measures specifically designed to examine the four APM functions directly. We are also encouraged that these studies suggest that performance-based and self-report scales can be successfully combined in research on *phronesis*.

7
Phronesis in Professional (Medical) Ethics

7.1 The *Phronesis* Bandwagon

The biggest growth industry in *phronesis* research in the last couple of decades has not been within Philosophy, Psychology, or even Moral/Character Education, but rather within *Professional Ethics*: the ethics of Medicine, Teaching, Nursing, Business, Social Work, Policing, the Military, and so forth. Schwartz and Sharpe's (2010) popular book on practical wisdom, which seems to have spurred some of the recent interest in *phronesis*, highlights particularly the use (or neglect) of *phronesis* within professional practice. We strongly recommend this book as a preliminary reading to any aspiring students of *phronesis*, and especially so within Professional Ethics. It neatly sets the background of the motivation to reclaim *phronesis* as an ideal, in an age of ever tighter and better regulated (but essentially fallible) audit cultures, in which professional wisdom has increasingly been deskilled and replaced with rules, codes, and incentives. The book is a goldmine of examples, many of which are derived from actual professional practice, of why the carrots-and-sticks method does not work and why it is essentially anti-professional.

To say that Schwartz and Sharpe's book created the surge of interest in *phronesis* within Professional Ethics would be to get hold of the wrong end of the stick, however. That interest dates at least a couple of decades further back, when papers about Virtue Ethics in general and *phronesis* in particular began to appear in Professional Ethics journals with almost dreary regularity: so much so that Virtue Ethics can now be seen as the moral theory of choice within many of those fields. Schwartz and Sharpe captured the mood rather than created it.

The shift from rule-based to virtue-based Professional Ethics

The reasons for the turning of the tide are, in our view, sociological as much as, or more than, ideological. Throughout most of the twentieth century, some sort of utilitarianism (or at least consequentialism) was the dominant moral framework justifying the role of professions in society,[1] complemented however with a deontological take on the practical ethics of professionals.[2] The way to keep professional agents on the straight and narrow—and strengthen their public reputation, acknowledged legitimacy, and communal support[3]—was seen to lie in ever-more detailed ethical codes, prescribing correct behaviour as well as procedures and sanctions to secure such behaviour. Repeated scandals within all the largest professions, often exposed by intra-professional whistleblowers, have shaken the foundations of this conviction. It suffices here to mention the 'banksters' responsible for the 2008 financial crisis and the recent revelations of corruption within police forces in countries such as the USA and the UK. As a consequence, focusing attention on the *phronesis* of practitioners is now seen by many as a helpful way to rescue Professional Ethics from the clutches of a stale rule-and-code-touting formalism and a culture of mere compliance: a culture that has not been properly internalized in any case in the way that one would expect moral virtues to be. Compliance aims at competence in professional behaviour rather than excellence, and it prompts ways to 'game the system' rather than developing professionalism (George et al., 2023). The turn away from mere compliance has created a fertile ground for theoretically minded virtue ethicists, operating within the field of Professional Ethics, as well as for empirical studies exploring the typical virtues and vices of different professions.

---

[1] For example, as Jameel notes correctly, the formation of the National Health Service (NHS) in Britain in 1948 represented an essentially utilitarian model of healthcare: improving the overall health of the nation as a single-denominator outcome (2022, chap. 1).

[2] In Medical Ethics, for example, this is best represented theoretically by Beauchamp and Childress's (2001) well-known four-principles model. What attracted professional ethicists to such models was their apparent universality and impartiality (see, e.g., Jameel, 2022, chap. 1).

[3] The history of the ideal of *police legitimacy* in the UK is fascinating in this respect, as it dates back to the formation of the Scotland Yard in the early nineteenth century and a certain obsession with the idea of the British police simply 'being the people'. This is very different from the ethical grounding of policing in countries such as France and may explain why Police Ethics in the UK has historically been more amenable to *phronesis* than that of many other countries, and why the British police tend to take a comparatively relaxed approach to public unrest. We return briefly to this issue in Chapter 11. See also Kristjánsson, Thompson et al. (2021).

Research on virtues and the professions

The most substantial and cohesive body of empirical work into virtues (or lack thereof) in different professions is probably that created by a series of studies conducted by the Jubilee Centre for Character and Virtues at the University of Birmingham into the characterological aspects of Medicine, Teaching, Law, Nursing, Business, the Military, and Policing in the UK.[4] Most of these studies have followed a uniform methods blueprint, which allows for salient comparisons and contrasts (Arthur, Earl et al., 2021). Three cohorts were typically studied: first-year undergraduate students, final-year undergraduate students, and established professionals with 5 years of or more experience in the field. In a survey, participants were asked to select their top character strengths and those they attribute to the ideal professional;[5] their moral reasoning strategies (i.e., deontological, utilitarian, virtue ethical, or self-serving) were gauged through responses to tailor-made professional dilemmas, created by an expert panel; and for the experienced professionals, workplace questions were used to identify their level of professional purpose, and the perceived threats to and facilitators of the development of virtuous professional character. About 10% of the participants in each cohort were then interviewed for further depth and clarity.

The findings of these studies are illuminating both in terms of similarities and contrasts. It is revealing, for example, how much the professions differ in terms of professionals' sense of purpose, with lawyers scoring far the lowest (Kristjánsson, Thompson et al., 2021, chart 5).[6] Comparisons of moral reasoning strategies reveal a certain trend towards a *U-curve*, where entrants to professional education rely substantially on virtue-based strategies; this lessens during their university years, perhaps because of the focus there on formal codes, but then picks up again after working in the field, perhaps (as at least Schwartz & Sharpe, 2010, would have it) because the professionals have

---

[4] Rather than referencing all the individual research reports here in detail, we direct readers to the Jubilee Centre website where all of them are available for free downloads: https://www.jubileecentre.ac.uk/1595/projects/virtues-in-the-professions. Extended and updated versions of the reports have also been coming out individually as short books published by Routledge. Cf. also Arthur, Earl et al. (2021).

[5] The participants were given a list of the 24 VIA strengths to choose from, which means that *phronesis* as such was not on offer. However, the three VIA strengths that McGrath (2019) considers collectively to replace *phronesis* (i.e., judgement, prudence, and perspective) did not get high scores from the participants. As indicated earlier in this book, we believe that many participants did not even understand what 'prudence' is typically taken to mean in the Virtue Ethical discourse and certainly did not share Aquinas' understanding of it.

[6] The police came out as second lowest. However, that finding may be an aberration as the study was conducted during the height of the challenging COVID pandemic, and the survey findings were not corroborated in subsequent interviews. Interestingly, the professionals that often complain most in the public media about a loss of purpose, teachers and nurses, scored fairly high on purpose in the surveys.

realized that a reliance on formal rules to replace their own moral compass often does not suffice to reach morally acceptable decisions.[7]

In a fairly complex subsequent analysis (Arthur, Earl et al., 2021), the professionals were clustered into four distinct profiles depending on the extent to which they self-ascribed virtuous moral character and good judgement. One profile consisted of practitioners who identified dimensions of moral character and judgement in balance; two separate profiles comprised professionals who either identified moral character at the expense of judgement, or vice versa; with a final profile displaying a lack of identification of both dimensions. Examination of these profiles revealed that, regardless of stage of career, practitioners valuing moral character reported greater experiences of professional purpose compared to groups that devalued moral character. Contrary to prior expectations, however, these differences were evident regardless of character being valued simultaneously with, or in isolation of, good judgement.[8] For present purposes, there are three ways to interpret this finding. One is that the measure of judgement was inadequate inasmuch as it relied on the VIA character strengths, which were not designed to assess *phronesis*. A second explanation could be that *phronesis* does not matter as much as we thought for virtuous professional practice; only the moral virtues do. The third interpretation—towards which the authors of the analysis seem to lean (Arthur, Earl et al., 2021)—is that professionals already see good moral character to be good-judgement-guided and do not make a distinction between merely habituated and *phronesis*-guided virtues.

Phronesis was not studied specifically in those reports. However, it often entered the stage during the interview phase when experienced professionals were asked about the Professional Ethics education they had been given. A common complaint, by those who had been provided with such education,[9] was that its content was either too *abstract* or too *concrete*. For example, in Medical Ethics education, there was seen to be too much emphasis on high-minded ideals, such as 'informed consent', or too-specific norms, such as 'good bedside manners', but too little on a critical exploration of the actual dilemmas that characterize the cut and thrust of much medical work, in the

---

[7] Nurses constituted an exception, however, as their reliance on virtue-based reasoning at the expense of rule-based one did not pick up again with experience, but rather lessened even further. This has been interpreted as a sign of a serious moral malaise within UK nursing (Varghese & Kristjánsson, 2018). For a wider perspective, cf. Jenkins et al. (2019); Ko et al. (2020).

[8] The scores fell in the expected direction, but the difference between moral character only and moral character and judgement was not statistically significant.

[9] All UK medical schools offer some modules on Medical Ethics, for instance, which is not the case in all Western countries. However, provisions differ widely in the other professional areas both between professions and between particular UK universities offering the relevant degree programmes.

operating room or the general/family practice. Through appeals for more education in this area of what one participant called 'the missing moral middle'—education ideally to be led by established professional role models who could share their relevant experiences—one could sense a clarion call for more focus on *phronesis* and how to develop it. We return to some of those educational implications in Section 7.5 and then again in Chapter 11.

Focusing on *phronesis* in Medical Ethics

Based on the above findings and many others that have been reported upon in journals of Professional Ethics in the first 2 decades of the twenty-first century, we could easily write a whole book just about professional *phronesis*. However, in order to keep to the constraints of a single chapter, we will focus in what follows on some fairly general considerations only and confine our examples to one subfield: that of Professional Medical Ethics.[10] The discourse there is fairly advanced, compared to the rest, and would allow for generalizations across other fields as well if needed (although we will mostly refrain from making those here). Hence, although we limit our examples to one subfield in what follows, we consider most of the arguments made to be applicable to other areas of Professional Ethics also.

While the *phronesis* discourse in Medical Ethics is well-entrenched and some of it is of a high academic calibre (see, e.g., Jameel, 2022; Kaldjian, 2014), it is not entirely free from a shortcoming that, in our view, mars quite a lot of recent discussions of *phronesis* within the professions. We have noticed a trend there either to present the concept of *phronesis* in a very general and bland way, eliding its conceptual problematics, or to endorse a particular conception of the concept as authoritative without paying attention to competing conceptualizations. The first route, unfortunately, leads to a concept that is bloated and amorphous and cannot serve the integrative function of Aristotelian *phronesis*. The second route may lead to a concept that is morally salient and practically useful, but one that will be seen as inherently controversial unless its contours are explicitly and persuasively argued for.

---

[10] We survey some of the relevant Business Ethics literature briefly in Chapter 9. See also Huo and Kristjánsson (2018).

Four key binaries in professional *phronesis*

After exploring some recent writings on *phronesis* in Medicine, we will use this discourse to explore four significant conceptual controversies about *phronesis*, all revolving around the choice of one of two binaries. The first is whether the MacIntyrean or Aristotelian understanding of the concept is more helpful for Medical Ethics (and, by extension, for other Professional Ethics). The second concerns the extent to which the content of the considerations informing a *phronetic* decision are culturally *universalist* or *relativist*; the third is about the extent to which *phronesis* is informed by *generalist* moral consideration versus considerations emerging gradually from *particularist* experiences; and the fourth binary is about the division between those who see the ideally successful acquisition of *phronesis* as relatively *painless* (e.g., learning a complex skill, say, piano playing, mastered through a gift of unified agency), and those who consider the development and display of *phronesis* an essentially *painful* process, fraught with ambivalence and struggle.

We do not shirk taking a stand on those issues; indeed, our own conception of *phronesis* is unabashedly one of an intellectual virtue that is *Aristotelian* (rather than MacIntyrean), *universalist*, *generalist*, and *painful*. However, while we consider it more engaging to invoke contrasting options by arguing for one over the other, the main aim of this discussion is not to make a case for our own positions, as we have already argued for most of those in previous chapters (and the 'painfulness' one will be addressed in more detail in Chapter 10). Rather, the aim is to demonstrate that failing to take a stand on the controversies in question robs accounts of *phronesis*—for example, within Medical Ethics—of their putative explanatory power. More specifically, we stipulate that any serviceable account of *phronesis* as an ideal in Professional Ethics needs to pay sufficient attention to the contested contours of the concept. Otherwise, it obscures rather than enlightens a virtue ethical approach to professional practice and blocks further progress.

7.2 *Phronesis* in Medical Ethics: Aristotle or MacIntyre?

Apart from Business Ethics, the area of Professional Ethics where most attention has been paid to *phronesis* is within Medical Ethics. Not all of it allows for easy conceptual categorizations, however.

An undifferentiated account

We have already mentioned the Jubilee Centre's work at the University of Birmingham. Another large but unrelated research project at the same university has been led by Mervin Conroy. He and his colleagues have published a number of papers; the latest one, an ethnographic study (Conroy et al., 2021), tracks the understanding of wise medical decision-making by 131 medical doctors and proposes to develop a theoretical understanding of *phronesis* from narrative interviews and observations. The study ends up thematizing 15 different virtues seen by doctors as contributing to wise decisions: a mixture of moral, intellectual, and performative virtues, one of which is *phronesis*. We discuss this study because it exemplifies the tendency to avoid choosing an Aristotelian or MacIntyrean perspective. We argued that MacIntyre's perspective on *phronesis* differs significantly from Aristotle's in Section 1.4, and those differences matter greatly in ethical decision-making and practice.

Despite each of these 15 virtues being specified as a mean on a spectrum from deficiency to excess, in an Aristotle-friendly way, it is difficult to categorize the theoretical orientation of the model that Conroy et al. elicit. *Phronesis* does not seem to be accorded a meta-status in it, although the title of the paper refers to *phronesis*.[11] The Aristotelian connection of the research is unclear, although the findings are said to 'align with' a neo-Aristotelian concept of Virtue Ethics. MacIntyre is mentioned in the background and discussion sections, however, so one presumes that the approach taken by the researchers in interpreting their data is MacIntyrean rather than Aristotelian. Yet this paper is representative of many others in the field that make use of the *phronesis* construct without situating it adequately within a research tradition and thus fail to make a significant contribution to a deeper theoretical understanding of *phronesis*. That said, the motivation of the authors is clearly the laudable one of countering the deontological trend that one of their participants describes as the 'protocolisation of medicine'.

---

[11] *Phronesis* is just listed as one of the 15 virtues. Its deficient form is characterized as rule-following, but its excess form as a blasé, overconfident attitude to problem-solving. *Phronesis* is thus presented more in line with the architectonic of a moral virtue; Aristotle did not categorize excess and deficiency forms for intellectual virtues.

The fish-school model

One more Birmingham-based research project has recently been completed by Jubilee-Centre-affiliated PhD student Sabena Jameel, who is also both a general practitioner and a university medical lecturer. Utilizing her unique multifaceted background, Jameel's (2022) PhD thesis is of exceptional quality, both in terms of breadth and depth (including originality). Not only does Jameel survey systematically almost all the available background literature (initially almost 800 sources) in considerable detail; she also reports upon findings of her extensive empirical research into doctors' understandings and then produces a new model of *phronesis*: the 'fish-school model' that we introduced briefly in Section 2.5. Jameel is particularly alert to the theoretical provenance of various conceptualizations of *phronesis*, and although she departs from the view of the present authors by explicitly preferring a MacIntyrean conceptualization to an Aristotelian one, she produces respectable arguments for that choice that we review presently.

Like most contributors to the *phronesis* discourse in Medical Ethics, Jameel worries that the historical moral grounding of Medicine has been eroded by industrialization, commercialization, micromanaged accountability processes, and technical rationality—and that what has been gained in knowledge (e.g., through reductionist evidence-based Medicine) has been lost in wisdom.[12] However, because of her immersion in the mainstream psychological literature on wisdom, as well as philosophical and bioethical sources, Jameel is in a stronger position than most medical ethicists to counter those trends. She initially administered Ardelt's (2003) wisdom survey to 211 medical doctors and then interviewed 16 of the highest-scoring ones as well as 2 of the lowest scoring ones through a biographic narrative inquiry. Because of the constant interplay in Jameel's research between philosophical and psychological theory, on the one hand, and her empirical findings, on the other, the 33 themes she identifies and the model she builds upon those themes have considerable face validity. We grant that it is different from our Aristotelian *phronesis* model (APM), but we do not see the two models as essentially incompatible. Jameel's fish-school model is simply much more extensive and detailed than ours, both because she includes more profession-relevant detail than we could obviously do in a general decision-making model, and because she builds unapologetically upon MacIntyre's conception, which is already broader than our more orthodox Aristotelian one. We also find her explicit

---

[12] Interestingly, what seems to have drawn Jameel (2022, chap. 1) herself to *phronesis* is its accommodation of emotional considerations, often blocked out by Kantian-derived, rule-based approaches.

and thoughtful adoption of a MacIntyrean position preferable to neglecting to respond to this binary.

Kaldjian's approach, and the differences between MacIntyrean and neo-Aristotelian *phronesis*

In the USA, Lauris Kaldjian (2014) is, in our view, the most accomplished writer on *phronesis* in Medical Ethics, not least because of his command of the philosophical history of the concept, from Aristotle, through Aquinas, to MacIntyre. We described his model of practical wisdom in Section 2.5, and how significantly it overlaps with our APM. Another reason for the credibility of Kaldjian's writings is how deftly he synthesizes the lessons from the philosophical tradition with the long-standing *care* tradition in Medical Ethics as well as the abundant literature on the nature of *clinical judgement* (Pellegrino & Thomasma, 1993). However, Kaldjian's prioritization of MacIntyrean considerations over Aristotelian ones—when combined with Jameel's analogous view—induces us to revisit the somewhat dismissive remarks we made about MacIntyrean *phronesis* in Chapter 1.

Perhaps the most important difference is that MacIntyreans bring a considerably wider range of activities under the rubric of *phronesis* than Aristotelians do. This seems to result from the MacIntyrean move of neglecting Aristotle's 'unofficial' concept of noncodifiable *techné* (Dunne, 2022).[13] The difficulty is that this move apparently violates a vital distinction by confusing processes that are valuable in themselves and those that are valuable only in terms of a separate outcome.[14] It baffles orthodox Aristotelians, for example, when the wise clinical judgement of doctors about complex technical (as distinct from complex moral) cases is typified as a kind of *phronesis* (see, e.g., Montgomery, 2006; Pellegrino & Thomasma, 1993)—not merely as structurally similar to *phronesis—unless*, that is, one understands all professional problems to be moral problems in disguise.[15] Let us now consider a conciliatory position, however: namely, that although MacIntyreans may be too accommodating in their definition of a 'practice' (the domain of *phronesis*) overall, Medicine

---

[13] Somewhat ironically, Dunne (1993), the die-hard MacIntyrean, also offers the best argument (the neglect of the unofficial concept of noncodifiable *techné*) for why we may not actually need the wide concept of MacIntyrean *phronesis*.

[14] We say 'MacIntyreans' here rather than 'MacIntyre', for as was mentioned in Chapter 1, MacIntyre himself is not always consistent in his MacIntyrean view of the distinction between *phronesis* and *techné*. He has also questioned some aspects of what we call here 'MacIntyreanism' (see, e.g., MacIntyre & Dunne, 2002).

[15] See W. Carr (1995) for a defence of that radical thesis in the case of the teaching profession.

constitutes an exception, with all medical/clinical decisions falling under the domain of *phronesis* rather than *techné*.

This sort of argument seems to be at least hinted at, if not explicitly made, by both Kaldjian and Jameel. Kaldjian (2014, p. 72) argues that the relationship between clinical judgement and *phronesis* in the medical context is too close to call because both depend on the same 'primary moral ground': the 'good of the patient'. Medical practice is essentially a 'moral enterprise', lock, stock, and barrel (Kaldjian, 2019, p. 700). Hence he concludes that clinical judgement simply *is* practical wisdom applied in the practice of Medicine (2014, p. 72). Jameel (2022, chap. 2), similarly—while acutely aware of the fact that Aristotle defined 'Medicine' as a *techné*, with health as its end rather than moral character (1985, p. 1 [1094a9]; cf. Hofmann, 2002; Waring, 2000)—argues that each encounter in Medicine involves a moral dimension and relates directly to the flourishing of the patient.[16] So, in the case of medical practice, these authors view it as simply impossible to separate the clinical from the moral, as the former includes a fusion of technical skill/experience/knowledge and a moral judgement. This way of thinking also harks back to older writings in Medical Ethics. Thus, Pellegrino (1979, p. 170) argues that a moral screen is, 'in a way, cast over the entire sequence' of a doctor's deliberation about the right action for a particular patient. For Pellegrino, the moral value of care and respect for a human person (ideally) permeates the whole doctor–patient relationship, and there is no way to separate the technical from the moral in that enterprise.

We are sympathetic to this argument but still do not find it entirely persuasive. We realize that the distinction between the 'merely clinical' and the 'clinical *and* moral' is considered suspect and artificial by some of the most accomplished virtue-minded medical ethicists, whose views must be taken seriously. Aristotle's own response—as suggested by his writings about the difference between *techné* and *phronesis*—would probably be to point out that saying *phronesis* ideally *guides* the work of good doctors and other professionals is one thing; claiming that it is the mode of thinking which *informs* all their specific practical decisions is quite another thing. For example, a doctor's choice of a unique combination of cancer drugs to cure a particular patient may partly be based on non-rule-governed insights about the particular constitution of the patient, and it may require considerable personal understanding of the patient's needs and wants. Yet the goal of the activity still lies outside of the activity, namely in the removal of the tumour, rather than in

---

[16] Jameel considers this to be the view of the overwhelming majority of clinicians, like herself, whereas nonclinical academics may favour the Aristotelian concept (Jameel, 2022, chap. 2).

the quality of the personal relationship itself. Obviously, if this process is executed without due respect and care for the patient, it will not count as virtuous or *phronetic* at all, but that moral judgement seems to be logically separable from the judgement about the likely removal or nonremoval of the tumour. Pellegrino, Kaldjian, and Jameel might complain that Aristotle is operating here with a narrow biological view of health, and that their MacIntyrean view is a more holistic one, which does not separate the human body from the human person. Yet questions remain as to whether it is sensible to (a) understand Medicine in its entirety as an irreducibly moral endeavour and (b) broaden the scope of Aristotle's *praxis* to include all (non-rule-governed) clinical decision-making, or whether such extensions obliterate certain morally and logically salient distinctions.[17]

The bottom line is that—contrary to the MacIntyrean view—Aristotle would consider the wise clinical judgement of a medical doctor, in cases where moral values are not *specifically* or *directly* at stake, as an instantiation of noncodifiable *techné*, not *phronesis*, although the dividing line may be thinner here than in most other domains. We are still inclined to support that view, although this section has brought out that there may be more to the MacIntyrean view—at least in the domain of Medical Ethics—than we gave it credit for in Chapter 1. Table 7.1 summarizes the differences between MacIntyrean and Aristotelian *phronesis*.

7.3 Relativist or Universalist *Phronesis*?

We have now seen how the initial question one needs to ask about any use of the concept of *phronesis* in Professional Ethics is *what* concept it is. Is it Aristotle's concept about the intellectual coordination of moral virtue(s) within a moral *praxis*, or is it MacIntyre's concept about the specific practical intelligence of noncodifiable deliberations within any social practice, be it focused upon moral or nonmoral ends? Yet in order to get a firmer grip on which *conception* of either concept is being applied, we also need to subject

---

[17] The example of Medicine is illuminating for the MacIntyrean/Aristotelian binary because Medicine includes both means-end and constituent-ends actions. However, Carr's (1995) argument for an Aristotelian approach to *phronesis* in teaching has important parallels to a field such as Psychotherapy as a professional activity as well. In psychotherapy, the person of the therapist (warmth, genuine interest in clients) and the therapeutic relationship or alliance are the central elements of successful therapy (Lambert & Barley, 2001). This means that psychotherapy also seems to have a constituent-ends dimension that is eliminable only at the cost of severely undermining its benefits.

Table 7.1 Different categorizations of modes of thinking, by Aristotle and MacIntyre

	Aristotle	MacIntyre
Noncodifiable moral thinking relating to oneself only	*Phronesis* in the domain of *praxis*	Unnamed, but the domain is not *practice*
Noncodifiable moral thinking relating to others/society	*Phronesis* in the domain of *praxis*	*Phronesis* in the domain of *practice*
Noncodifiable thinking relating to social practices, e.g. Medicine, teaching, creative pottery	Noncodifiable *techné*	*Phronesis* in the domain of *practice*
Codifiable thinking relating to social practices, e.g., commercial pottery	Codifiable *techné*	*Techné*

the understanding to which individual professional ethicists avail themselves to scrutiny in light of the remaining binaries introduced in Section 7.1.

MacIntyre's inconsistent relativism

For understanding the *universalism* versus *relativism* binary, MacIntyre's analysis becomes relevant again, representing the relativist camp, as long as we overlook temporarily the difference between '*praxis*' and '*practice*'. The first thing to notice is that Aristotle's concept seems to have a certain relativity to individual constitution, circumstance, and developmental level built into it, as explained in Chapter 1. Thus, the content of the relevant considerations that make up the ingredients of a *phronetic* decision will vary among individuals and societies, as will the outcome of the considerations. Yet this relativity is *nonessential* in the sense that if we know enough about the context in which a person *P* reached an appropriately *phronetic* decision, we will understand the rationale of the decision and why we might have acted similarly if we had been *P* (or been in *P*'s shoes). The content of the considerations is thus *commensurable*, and the nature of the process can be understood in universalist terms, based on Aristotle's (1985) remark that 'in our travels we can see how every human being is akin [. . .] to a human being' (p. 208 [1155a20–2]).[18] In *After*

---

[18] Admittedly, in other works, such as his *Politics*, Aristotle makes more relativistic remarks, about justice being relative to constitutions, etc. However, those remarks are typically understood to relate to political incarnations of virtues such as justice; not to justice as explained in the *Nicomachean Ethics* or the *Rhetoric*, nor to *phronesis* as presented in the *Nicomachean Ethics*.

Virtue, MacIntyre (1981), however, makes more dramatic claims about the relativity of virtues and virtuous decisions to different—in the strong sense of *incommensurable—moral* and cultural traditions. Thus, two practically wise human beings may inhabit two mutually impenetrable moral worlds, to the extent that a *phronetic* decision reached by one of them would remain essentially opaque and incomprehensible to the other. The basic question to ask about *phronesis*, on this interpretation, is 'Whose *phronesis*, which *phronimoi*?'

Two observations are in order here, however. One is that MacIntyre has not remained consistent in his adherence to relativism of this sort, as we noted in Chapter 1. His commitment to relativism differs between his various works, some of which make space for a constructive rational fusion of moral horizons. Moreover, he often says that some practices are features of all human societies, and that some virtues, such as justice, courage, honesty, and patience, are required for participation in all practices. Hence, when MacIntyre's Aristotelianism is being referred to, the question 'Whose MacIntyreanism, which MacIntyre?' may emerge.

The second observation is that MacIntyre has never claimed that his brand of social relativism is drawn from Aristotle. Indeed, it would be fair to say that it owes at least as much to the nineteenth century idealism of Hegel (see Carr, 2015) and the historicism of Collingwood. MacIntyre's escapades into neo-idealism and moral anti-realism signify radical departures from the realist-naturalist tenor of Aristotle's own moral philosophy, at least on the interpretation which has informed the mainstream of modern Virtue Ethics through such thinkers as Elizabeth Anscombe (1958a).

MacIntyre's relativism about moral virtues and *phronesis* has entered Professional Ethics discourse through a commonly espoused view, according to which the virtues and *phronetic* modes of thought endorsed by participants of a given practice are so thoroughly conditioned by local contingencies that they are immune from any external objective critique; more precisely, that insofar as professional practices such as Medicine are the products of rival historically conditioned normative traditions, there can be no theoretically objective criteria by which this or that local professional decision-making might be judged or found wanting.[19] However, as this view is more typically justified via particularism than the sort of socio-moral considerations that MacIntyre brings to bear, we postpone further scrutiny of it until Section 7.4.

---

[19] See Carr (2015) for a trenchant critique.

Nussbaum's naturalistic view

As an antidote to MacIntyre's relativism about virtue and deliberation, consider Martha Nussbaum's take on Aristotle. The basic idea behind her version of Aristotelianism is that we can construct an objective, universalist conception of human nature without invoking Aristotle's (or any controversial) metaphysics. What we need is simply a conception derived from the 'human experience of life and value': the shared ideas enshrined in the self-understandings of the 'many and the wise' (Nussbaum, 1988, p. 177). The notion of the virtue (as the ideal function or excellence) of human beings must be derived from the way in which such beings think, act, and feel when they function well and successfully, just as the *techné* of musicians must be observed from the manner in which they play well. But how do we ascertain that these excellences are characteristically human? The answer is: by exploring the evaluative, narrative beliefs of people at different times and places about what it means to be human. To find out what our nature is 'seems to be one and the same thing as to find out what we deeply believe to be most important and indispensable' (Nussbaum, 1995, p. 106).

The conception of human beings and their moral and intellectual virtues emerging from Nussbaum's (1990) analysis is one which she terms a 'thick vague conception' (p. 205): 'thick' as opposed to a liberal 'thin' conception in that it includes a much wider measure of essentially human characteristics; 'vague' in that it admits of various manifestations, since there can be many different ways to lead a good human life. In spite of its openness, what stands out in Nussbaum's account is her universalism about human nature, resting on empirical transcultural comparisons.[20] That said, the constitutive circumstances of human life, while broadly shared, can be realized in different ways in different societies and among different individuals, allowing for 'contextual particularity'. In the end, the *phronetic* decisions of a doctor operating in a war zone and in a rural English village can be equally sound—albeit not simply, as a relativist might think, because they have been *chosen* as ways of life in incommensurable contexts, but rather because they happen to be equally fruitful realizations of the same basic *phronetic* functions.[21] Most importantly

---

[20] Notably, just as with MacIntyre, Nussbaum's view continues to be a work in progress, and in some twenty-first-century writings, she has moved away from her 'thick, vague conception' to a conception that is more accommodating of 'thinner' liberal insights.

[21] We are assuming here that the two doctors have chosen to pursue the profession for the right moral reason and that they are virtuous agents. Otherwise, their deliberation about moral matters—even if it led to a good outcome for their patients—would not qualify as an exercise of *phronesis* in the first place but rather of the cunning capacity of calculation (*deinotes*).

for present purposes, the *phronetic* virtue adjudication of the two doctors would be mutually understandable and mutually condonable—if they made the effort to put themselves into each other's shoes (which is not the same as saying that it would be unproblematic or easy).[22]

7.4 The Two Remaining Binaries

As we already saw in Section 2.2, there is a strong *particularist* strand in much of contemporary Virtue Ethics that rejects any appeals to general, context-independent moral truths and relies rather on the virtuous agent's 'intuitive artistry' in coping with situational demands. How do we know, on this view, whether the intuitive shape that jumps out at us is really the correct one and not some kind of a perceptual illusion? We discover that allegedly by consulting the experienced *phronimoi* who ultimately provide the yardsticks for what is fine and pleasant. If our choice of action would also be theirs in the relevant situation, we know that we are on the right track. Instead of trusting principles, we trust persons (Dunne, 1993, pp. 258, 312).

A generalist approach based on the human good

Generalists such as the present authors will insist that the right (*phronetic*) thing to feel and do, in the Aristotelian view, is not only to be gauged by the facts of the given situation (the relevant *thats*) and the virtuous agent's particularist 'seeings-in-a-flash', but also, and more importantly, by overriding blueprint truths (the relevant *whys*) about human *eudaimonia* that bring important concerns to light in particular cases. Although Aristotle is at pains to stress that such illumination is itself not easily codifiable and requires considerable attention to situational details, he does not shrink from giving advice about how to solve difficult moral dilemmas. He also stresses that in order for full virtue to develop in moral agents, it is not only necessary that they have been brought up in good habits, but also that they have been exposed to this universal theory through teaching. To be sure, *phronesis* is not 'about universals only' (1985, p. 158 [1141b15]), but it nevertheless takes its cue from a generalist theory about the good life.

---

[22] Fowers (2015) has proposed a similarly universalistic view of virtues and the human good based on evolutionary science.

Aristotle (1985, pp. 1–5 [1094a1–1095a27]) obviously did not possess the modern concepts of 'scientific theory' and 'applied science', but if we explore his account of human nature and ethical conduct, what emerges is suspiciously like a 'theory' in that traditional sense which the particularists so ardently renounce. It is a teleological theory about flourishing as the ultimate good of human beings, for the sake of which we do all other things—a good that is complex but objective and knowable in principle, given our empirical access to the essential specific nature of human beings (Fowers et al., 2023). This is, more specifically, a universal 'ethical theory' (Irwin, 1990, p. 467)—a theory which transcends mere common beliefs and any particular human 'practices'. Hence, Aristotelian generalists will see *phronesis* as good deliberation guided by a correct general conception of worthwhile ends (Hacker-Wright, 2015).

What we have said in this section may seem to add little to what we argued already in Chapter 2; it simply offers variations on the same theme. The reason for bringing this argument up again in the present context is simply to remind readers that when we explore conceptions of *phronesis* within a professionalism discourse, such as Medical Ethics, we need to be mindful of the generalism–particularism binary and look for signs of one of these two positions in each piece of writing.

Pain in *phronesis*?

The final binary that we need to look for in accounts of *phronesis* within Medical Ethics is whether they acknowledge the possibility of enduring pain—and even existential crisis—after a *phronetic* decision, or whether they see such a decision as putting pain to rest and securing the psycho-moral unity of the *phronimos* (in this domain, the practically wise medical doctor). Now, why should a person with such a fixed psycho-moral anchor as *phronesis* ever succumb to an existential crisis? Indeed, there is little doubt that, given Aristotle's focus on the motivational unity of the *phronimoi*, his own view was quite close to the reassuring one espoused, for instance, by Julia Annas's (2011) holism about *phronesis* as a unified skill.[23]

The basic question to ask here, however, is whether or not Aristotle got his Moral Psychology right. Carr (2002b) suggests that enlightened Aristotelians

---

[23] Cf. MacIntyre (1981, p. 153), on the absence of the centrality of tragic conflict in Aristotle.

should reject the assumption of the motivational unity of virtuous persons and replace it with a richer but more complex understanding of their virtuous unity, mediated through *phronesis*: a unity which would make room for emotional ambivalence and personal conflict as part of a constructive learning curve towards greater virtue. One way to illuminate this point is in terms of the 'mystery of the missing motivation' that we elaborate upon further in Chapter 10. Once a virtuous agent has *phronetically* adjudicated a virtue conflict, say, between honesty and compassion—for example a doctor by deciding in favour of full disclosure of a tragic truth to a patient—what happens to the motivation animating the other virtue? Does *phronesis* simply 'silence' it, or does it remain as a painful 'moral remainder' because of competing moral commitments that cannot be harmonized (see, e.g., Hursthouse, 1999, pp. 45–7)?

Carr seems to want to argue that emotional ambivalence actually improves the agent's overall situation. One must avoid going too far in fetishizing the tragic, however, if one is to remain faithful to an Aristotle-inspired Virtue Ethics. It is, after all, the basic predicament of the *nonphronimoi* to be plagued by inner conflict and self-doubt. Perhaps only for a rare few *phronimoi* will emotional ambivalence ever work as a source of sensitization and character-perfection through 'constructive dividedness of mind' (Kristjánsson, 2013, chap. 7). That said, if pain and ambivalence will typically linger on, even after one has developed *phronesis* to a satisfactory degree, it may well be that *phronesis* cultivation, for instance in Medical Ethics courses, needs to be complemented by a series of coping mechanisms to prepare the learners for the realization that exasperation and despair will continue to accompany even the greatest *phronetic* achievements, in such a way that the absence of those feelings 'would lead us to call into question the genuineness of the [*phronetic*] commitment' (Hacker-Wright, 2015).

Revealingly, a sizeable portion of experienced doctors, in the Jubilee Centre's UK-based research project on virtuous medical practice (Arthur et al., 2015), said that they ('sometimes' or 'often') experience difficulties in living out their characters—that is, they fail to live up to their own ideals and moral expectations of themselves—owing to hindrances in the workplace. It is unlikely that this group of doctors, who experience virtuous character as a painful enterprise, were exclusively drawn from the category of the *nonphronimoi*. We would be inclined to suppose quite the opposite, as the doctors who made themselves available for interviewing after completing the relevant survey are likely to be ones already more inclined to virtue ethical considerations.

7.5 Which Conception of *Phronesis* in Medical Ethics and Education?

The primary aim of this chapter has not been to explore and evaluate specific accounts of *phronesis* in Medical Ethics but to offer a prolegomenon to any such exploration, which would, *mutatis mutandis*, be applicable to other areas of Professional Ethics. We have already suggested an analytical framework for classifying those accounts and making them amenable to scrutiny in light of further practical or moral considerations that theorists may want to bring to bear. This framework consists of the four binaries introduced in Section 7.1. The most fundamental of those is whether or not the relevant understanding of *phronesis* is based on MacIntyre's broad conception of a noncodifiable mode of thinking about internal goals within any complex social practice, or Aristotle's original conception of *phronesis* as a specific mode of thinking about moral ends within a moral *praxis*. The relationship between one's positioning on those binaries allows for a number of variations. For example, endorsing a generalist position does not necessarily make one a moral universalist; it would be possible to hold the position that *phronetic* considerations are theory-informed *within* particular traditions, but that the criteria legitimating those traditions are in the end incommensurable.

The serviceability of this framework needs to be gauged by applying it to some of the major works in the fields, for example the books by Pellegrino and Thomasma (1993), Montgomery (2006), Marcum (2012), and Kaldjian (2014), and to other professions. However, such exercises would require significant space and must await another day. To illustrate briefly how the framework could be used, we have chosen instead four short articles that are available online and might serve as a first port of call for students entering the field of Medical Ethics (Table 7.2).

Beresford's (1996) article is a classic. Written in the style of a critical review, it is not always easy to decipher the author's own voice, however. He seems to come down on the side of a broad MacIntyrean conception, while acknowledging that a pure *phronesis*-understanding of Medicine may neglect its technical, institutional structure (p. 220). A strong sense of the relativity of sociocultural commitments (p. 223) places him in the relativist camp, and a sympathetic view of the refocus from theory to particularities (p. 210) makes him a particularist. Finally, Beresford is unambiguous about the value of *phronetic* accounts in delivering us from 'the tyranny of the quest to elide the ambiguity and uncertainty that must be a part of all decision making' (p. 211)—a

Phronesis in Professional (Medical) Ethics   173

Table 7.2 Four examples of different conceptions of *phronesis* in the Medical Ethics literature

	MacIntyrean or Aristotelian *Phronesis*	Universalist or Relativist *Phronesis*	Generalist or Particularist *Phronesis*	Natural or Ambivalent/Painful *Phronesis*
Beresford (1996)	MacIntyrean (yet with doubts raised)	Relativist	Particularist	Painful
Hutson & Myers (1999)	MacIntyrean	Not discussed	Particularist	Not discussed
Tyreman (2000)	MacIntyrean	Not discussed	Particularist	Not discussed
Kaldjian (2010)	MacIntyrean	Not discussed	Generalist	Not discussed

clear indication of where he stands with regard to the final binary regarding pain in *phronesis*.

Hutson and Myers (1999) approach these questions from the perspective of practitioners. They are MacIntyrean in highlighting the relevance of *phronesis* for the general practice of Paediatric Surgical Medicine (p. 320), and they express particularist sensitivities with their claim that every situation needs to be 'individualized', requiring the doctor's 'common sense, his carpenter's eye, his lucky hand' (p. 322). They give no clues about their stand on the other two binaries.

Tyreman (2000) takes a similar tack on the first and second binaries (see Table 7.2) by arguing for a broad conception of *phronesis* as 'criticality' (p. 119) and against a rule-governed understanding (p. 121), defining *phronesis* as being 'without specific measurable goals' (p. 120). He ignores the other two binaries.

Finally, Kaldjian's (2010) is unique among those accounts in offering a generalist take on *phronesis*, stressing that the 'ultimate *telos* provides the criterion or compass by which one navigates through a given set of circumstances' (p. 558). Kaldjian does not discuss the deeper philosophical dichotomy between universalism and relativism. Like the other authors studied here, Kaldjian takes a broad MacIntyrean view of *phronesis* as relevant for *all* clinical judgement (pp. 558 and 560).

Unfortunately, in some of those writings, conceptions of *phronesis* tend to be staked out (or simply taken for granted), without much attention to alternative conceptualizations. That, in brief, is our main complaint about the Medical Ethics literature on *phronesis*. Table 7.2 summarizes the stands taken by the four sets of authors.

A cynical interpretation of these initial findings would be that at least some of the authors using '*phronesis*' simply latch onto a term which sounds to them like a fancy way of saying 'clinical judgement', or even 'professionalism',[24] and they then pack into it whatever they happen to think 'clinical judgement' means, without much awareness of the background thinking around the concept. Even if that interpretation is warranted, however, it does not necessarily speak against their use of '*phronesis*', for we have not made an argument in this chapter for the strong claim that a nuanced conceptual grasp of *phronesis* is an absolute necessity for Professional Medical Ethics. More specifically, this chapter has been preaching to the converted—those who do adopt a virtue ethical position and think that *phronesis* matters—arguing that, for *those* people, settling on which conception of *phronesis* they endorse is essential. Analysing accounts of *phronesis* in terms of their positions within the proposed analytical framework is obviously not the last word on judging their justifiability, but we hope to have shown that it is the necessary starting point.

Complaints about the lack of opportunity to hone *phronesis* in medical education and practice are getting more vocal. For example, the large Jubilee Centre research project, targeting aspiring and practising doctors at different career stages (Arthur et al., 2015), seemed to reveal a strange mismatch between general Medical Ethics, where Virtue Ethics is becoming the theory of choice, and Professional Medical Ethics which is still, in UK medical schools at least, strongly focused on formal rules, regulations, and codes of conduct. The doctors interviewed—especially the more experienced ones—complained that the rules they had learned were too general, with no attention to particularities such as special circumstances and special personal characteristics of individual patients. They also rued the overestimation of compliance and the underestimation of professional judgement. As many doctors correctly pointed out, medical *phronesis* is not inborn—it requires attention and training, both in medical education and further in the workplace. The research report makes a number of recommendations about the role of character-and-*phronesis* building in Medical Ethics education, echoing earlier calls from the literature (Boudreau & Fuks, 2015; Bryan & Babelay, 2009; Kinghorn, 2010). Some of those recommendations become relevant once we turn our attention more directly to educational issues in Chapter 11.

However, yet again, questions beckon: What *sort* of *phronesis* should be cultivated and why? The different conceptions of *phronesis* canvassed in this chapter clearly have divergent educational implications. A MacIntyrean

---

[24] Jameel (email correspondence) has told one of the authors that when explaining *phronesis* to medical students, she sometimes simply uses the term 'professionalism' as that is already familiar to them.

conception will call for an emphasis on general critical thinking skills and an exploration of the narrative unity of practices, as well as one's involvement in them, whereas Aristotle's conception will support training for the different functions in the APM model. A universalist will see nothing wrong with a unified curriculum to teach *phronesis* in Medical Ethics education across the globe, whereas a relativist will see the need for tradition-specific curricula. A generalist will favour the teaching of moral theory, about the specific *telos* of human beings—eudaimonia—whereas a particularist will understand *phronesis* training mostly in terms of moral casuistry (i.e., solving moral questions by extracting moral rules from specific cases and generalizing them). Finally, an advocate of the painful ambivalence understanding may see the need to complement *phronesis* training with a dose of Stoicism (e.g., in the form of resilience-oriented cognitive behavioural therapy) to provide practitioners with a way to understand and deal with residues of pain and regret that will accompany even the best *phronetic* decisions.

Again, then, we see no other option than to pave the way for a refocus on *phronesis* in Medical Ethics education with some serious thinking about what sort of *phronesis* we want to promote. For that preparatory work, the analytical framework offered in this chapter will, we hope, be useful. Similar chapters could be written, *mutatis mutandis*, for other fields of professional practice, but we consider Medical Ethics a helpful prism to exemplify the problematics and binaries at issue across the broader field of Professional Ethics.

8
Phronesis and the Civic Virtues

8.1 Why the Lack of Engagement with Civic *Phronesis*?

The recent academic interest in *phronesis*, insofar as it harks back to Aristotle (and most of it does), has been almost entirely confined to his treatment of the concept in the *Nicomachean Ethics* and its harmonizing role vis-à-vis the *moral* virtues. Meanwhile, papers on the role of *phronesis* in guiding *civic* virtues,[1] discussed in Aristotle's *Politics*, are few and far between. We aim to make amends in the present chapter by unpacking in some detail the relationship between the civic and the moral (characterological) in Aristotle's corpus, with a special focus on his *Politics*, and specifying the exact role of what we could call 'civic *phronesis*'. We will also use the opportunity of a juxtaposition of the *Nicomachean Ethics* and *Politics* to provide some reflections on the 'bigger picture': namely, Aristotle's general method for conducting Social Science, which Flyvbjerg (2001) calls '*phronetic* social science'. While this method is often referred to simply as Aristotle's 'naturalism' by those who endorse his take on character and virtue in the *Nicomachean Ethics*, most readers fail to appreciate how radical his method is and how it provides true competition, rather than just complementarity, to standard qualitative and quantitative methods. In comparison with his other works, Aristotle's *Politics* brings his '*phronetic*' method into sharper relief and would, if for no other reason, be worthy of a close study in this book. We say more about it in Section 8.2.[2]

---

[1] We remind readers of our decision (Chapter 1, note 3) to use the modern terminology of 'moral' versus 'civic' virtues in this book, although the terms 'ethical' versus 'political' virtues would be more faithfully Aristotelian.

[2] We do not propose to make the strong claim that what we have said about the more standard role of *phronesis* in previous chapters only makes sense against the background of Aristotle's overall methods explained in Section 8.2: a claim that might alienate some friends of the neo-Aristotelian 'standard model' who consider Aristotle's teleology outdated beyond redemption. That said, it is interesting to see how all of this fits into Aristotle's bigger system.

The neglect of civic *phronesis*

There are some possible explanations for the neglect of civic *phronesis*. First, compared to the *Nicomachean Ethics*, which contains many inspiring passages, the style of the *Politics* is dry, plodding, and digressive. Bogged down in the history of 158 past and present (in his day) city-states, most of which have long since been consigned to oblivion, Aristotle is so preoccupied with obscurantist details, as well as with reviewing various existing views and counterviews of his contemporaries, that he often forgets to tell readers what his own measured verdict is. This makes the *Politics* a very 'frustrating' read (see, e.g., Ober, 2005, p. 223).

Second, when this topic has been brought up at conferences, we have faced the rejoinder that Aristotelian scholars tend to assume that the *phronesis* concepts in the *Nicomachean Ethics* and the *Politics* are simply different concepts (although conveyed by the same word in ancient Greek) and do not lend themselves well to being studied through the same academic lens.[3] Although we are no experts in ancient Greek philology, we find this explanation implausible. Aristotle (1985, p. 154 [1140b7–11]) himself takes the political leader Pericles as an example, in the *Nicomachean Ethics*, of a paragon of *phronesis*—and he is clearly there referring to Pericles' well-ordered set of civic virtues, not (only) his moral virtues as an individual person. We argue later in this chapter that civic *phronesis* is, so to speak, *quantitatively* different from the standard *phronesis* described in the *Nicomachean Ethics*, but that does not mean that these are two essentially separable concepts.

Third, there is a more mundane explanation, which applies specifically to the contemporary Values Education literature. Within this literature, there is a very unfortunate tension between Character Education and Civic Education;[4] Boyd (2010) refers to it as a 'cancerous' relationship. An old Norse proverb says that relatives make the worst enemies; and, family-wise, Character Education and Civic Education must be considered close relatives. They are both members of the same relatively small 'family' of Values Education, and they both trace their historical lineage back to Aristotle, with Character Education typically drawing explicitly on themes in his *Nicomachean Ethics* and Civic Education (commonly, if more obliquely) being influenced by his *Politics*. As we spell out in Section 8.2, Aristotle saw his ethical and political

---

[3] Moss (2011, pp. 233–6), e.g., makes a distinction along those lines, between what she calls 'architectonic' *phronesis* in the *Nicomachean Ethics* and 'non-architectonic' *phronesis* in the *Politics*.

[4] The terms 'citizenship education' and 'civic education' tend to be used interchangeably in the literature (although there are exceptions). For convenience of exposition, and to relate the terminology to the focus of the present chapter on civic virtues, we just use the latter term in what follows.

treatises as inseparable parts of one grand, unified project, and he would thus most likely find the current contretemps between Character Education and Civic Education injudicious if not wholly incomprehensible.

That conception of concordance is not evident, however, in the real world of contemporary (academic) Education. Rather, with some notable exceptions (e.g., Peterson, 2020), character educationists tend to quietly elide Civic Education (Kristjánsson, 2015) or relegate it to an afterthought (Kristjánsson, 2020), thus creating the impression of assuming a view of the essential primacy of the psycho-moral over the sociopolitical in the sphere of Character Education. Proponents of Civic Education are often more explicit and vocal in their scepticism of the 'other camp', accusing Character Education of an individualistic and reactionary orientation, written off as politically naive (Suissa, 2015) or socially conservative (Jerome & Kisby, 2019; cf. Kristjánsson, 2021, for rejoinders). This antagonism has gradually led to a general resentment within the Civic Education camp towards utilizing a language of virtues at all—and that unfortunately includes not only civic virtues (which are then reconceptualized as sociopolitical 'values') but the intellectual virtue of *phronesis* as well.

These introductory comments lead us to what follows. Here is a quick roadmap. We begin, in Section 8.2, by explaining Aristotle's '*phronetic* method' and how it generates his teleological primacy thesis about the civic, in general, and statehood, in particular. We then offer a very brief rehearsal of his account of different constitutions, real and ideal, in Section 8.3. This is followed, in Section 8.4, by an analysis of the role of moral and civic virtues in actual states and the ideal one—as well as an elaboration of the political role of *phronesis*. We end, in Section 8.5, by teasing out some of the educational implications of Aristotle's theory, in particular insofar as those establish the proper relationship between, and indeed the unconflicted marriage of, Character and Civic Education,[5] although this is topic awaits a fuller treatment in Chapter 11.

We realize that, in this chapter, we sail perilously close to the shores of Aristotelian exegesis, which we have tried to navigate past in previous chapters. Our excuse is that given the paucity of writings about civic *phronesis*, the obvious entry point is to try to make sense of Aristotle's own view of the topic and some of his background assumptions. Any proposed form of

---

[5] Substantively, one could divide the *Politics* into four main parts where the first one is about the teleology of statehood, the second about the pros and cons of existing state constitutions, the third about the ideal state (of 'our prayers'), and the fourth about the educational curriculum in the ideal state. It so happens that this fourfold division coincides broadly with the division of the current chapter into Sections 8.2–8.5, although its aim is not to provide a comprehensive overview of the whole *Politics*. We assume a 'unitarian' reading of the *Politics*; the days are gone when the third part was considered a relic from an earlier Platonic period in Aristotle's thought (see Curren, 2000, p. 2).

'neo-Aristotelianism' in this area cannot get off the ground until we have at least a broad idea of what Aristotle's own view is.

8.2 *Phronetic* Method, Teleological Axiology, and Civic Primacy

The concept of civic virtue places some key demands on modern readers. In this section, we rehearse these demands in terms of Aristotle's *phronetic* method, his teleology, and the role of the civic.

Phronetic method

It is almost a platitude to say that Aristotle was an ethical naturalist and more interested in the practical applications of his ethical inquiry than its theoretical contribution. After all, the purpose of such inquiry 'is not to know what virtue is, but to become good, since otherwise the inquiry would be of no benefit to us' (Aristotle, 1985, p. 35 [1103b27–9]). Naturalism of this kind is often taken to imply what Flanagan (1991) calls 'minimal psychological realism': that all recommendations posited by moral theory must be attainable for creatures like us. Moreover, Aristotle's naturalism is typically understood— in the contemporary academic climate—as a clarion call for more interdisciplinary research on morality and for supporting theoretical positions by use of social scientific methods, both quantitative and qualitative. While all this is warranted up to a point, it is only half the story and not even the more interesting half.

The first thing to note is that Aristotle (1985) never describes himself as conducting ethical theorizing. He refers to the subject matter of both the *Nicomachean Ethics* and *Politics* as 'political science' (p. 2 [1094a27–8]), which in ancient Greek literally meant the science about the state (*polis*). Elsewhere he names this subject matter 'the philosophy of human affairs' (p. 298 [1181b15]). The important takeaway lesson is that he does not refer to his inquiry anywhere as 'Ethics' or 'Ethical Philosophy', although both terms were available to him (Vander Waerdt, 1991, p. 232). The most felicitous modern denotation of the kind of study Aristotle claims to be pursuing is simply 'Social Science' (or, perhaps more specifically as Flyvbjerg, 2001, suggests, '*phronetic* social science'); hence, Aristotle would probably find it puzzling that the *Nicomachean Ethics* is nowadays almost exclusively studied in

Philosophy departments, not Social Science ones, and that Virtue Ethics is considered a branch of Moral Philosophy, and rarely a social scientific theory (see Fowers et al., 2021, for an exception).[6]

A second thing to digest is what we could call Aristotle's (1985) 'sandwich conception' of the two books under examination here. They need to be read in conjunction with one another, but in a certain temporal order; for after first reading the *Nicomachean Ethics*, students will be able to 'grasp better' the wider political issues (p. 298 [1181b21–2]) and can thus serviceably proceed towards the *Politics*. Only by reading both books, in the correct order, can one hope to 'complete the philosophy of human affairs' (p. 298 [1181b15]). So without the grounding in the theory of flourishing and (individual development of) *phronetic* virtue that the *Nicomachean Ethics* provides, students will be impeded in their study of the *Politics*. But, conversely, studying only the *Nicomachean Ethics* precludes a proper understanding of the necessary political dimensions of morality. Thus, 'the scholarly practice of reading the ethical writings in isolation from the *Politics* has no foundation whatsoever in Aristotle's thought' (Vander Waerdt, 1991, p. 253). One way to put this is to say that although the *Nicomachean Ethics* has developmental/educational primacy over the *Politics* (and, by implication, Character Education over Civic Education), studying it in isolation has little value.

Now, if Aristotle is basically conducting Social Science in these two works, what is the method that he is applying?[7] Here we want to aver that very few people seem to have grasped how radically different his method is from those that are typically applied in contemporary Social Science, and what a tall order it would be to persuade most current social scientists of its credibility.[8] Everyone knows about the competing, but sometimes synergic, paradigms of quantitative versus qualitative studies in Social Science. The former aim for width and comprehensiveness, and the identification of causal (or at least correlational) links, while the latter aim for greater depth and understanding by

---

[6] This is why Aristotle would be sympathetic, in principle, to the contemporary appropriation of his theory by social scientists such as positive psychologists Peterson and Seligman (2004), who claim to be pursing the 'social science equivalent of virtue ethics' (p. 89)—although he would no doubt find fault with some of the assumptions behind their specific take on character strengths and virtues, such as their lack of appreciation of *phronesis*.

[7] We draw extensively on Salkever (2005) in the next few paragraphs, as his is probably the best overall account of Aristotle's unique brand of Social Science methods.

[8] There are a few exceptions. We keep mentioning Flyvbjerg (2001) who proposes a whole new comprehensive methodology of doing '*phronetic* social science' along Aristotelian lines. However, his work has not received the attention it deserves, and when it is referred to, theorists typically fail to grasp its radicality. One might expect developmental theorists to be most receptive to Aristotle's teleology, but that is sadly not the case, although Tomasello (2019) comes within a stone's throw of endorsing the sort of social science that Aristotle advocates.

probing the meaning that agents ascribe to events and activities and interpreting them through a discursive lens.

Although the quantitative–qualitative dichotomy was not available to Aristotle, at least not in the terms in which it is couched nowadays, one could argue that he captures the essence of these two different sources of information/knowledge through his frequent allusions to eliciting the views of both the 'many' and the 'wise'. However, he would find the notion odd that agents can be considered ultimate authorities about the meaning they ascribe to facets of their lives. Even if the researcher understands the agent's words correctly, that is surely not the end of the story. People lack self-transparency; hence, they can be systematically mistaken about what is true or meaningful. For instance, someone who is really worthy of great things can think herself unworthy of great things: a vice that Aristotle (1985) called 'pusillanimity' (p. 98 [1123b10–13]) but would probably be called a 'lack of self-esteem' by moderns. In such cases, the task of the social scientist will be to correct the self-deception and identify the relevant objective truth of the matter. More generally speaking, for Aristotle there would be no meaningful Social Science method that does not criticize and offer normative guidance. The true aim of Social Science must be the improvement of sociopolitical discussion and sociopolitical activity (cf. Salkever, 2005, p. 48), not just the systematic gathering of information.[9]

Axiological teleology

The unique feature that sets Aristotle's Social Science method apart can perhaps most felicitously be called *axiological teleology*. It contains two assumptions that would both be rejected by (most) post-Weberian social scientists. The axiological assumption is that Social Science is an inherently normative enterprise, in the sense of applying (i.e., assuming, making, identifying, and creating new) value judgements (Fowers, 2005; 2022). Aristotle thus completely rejects the Humean fact–value distinction or, perhaps better put, he has no sense of this distinction and writes as if it does not exist.[10] For Aristotle,

---

[9] Aristotle would probably acknowledge that there can be social scientists who are mainly in the business of collecting data. However, if that data gathering is not to be written off as completely haphazard and otiose, it must be done in the light of some hypothesis which itself is evaluative, critical, and aims at offering guidance. Normativity will thus enter any proper social scientific study at some juncture; so will the need for research-relevant *phronesis*.

[10] Rejecting the fact–value distinction does not necessarily imply rejecting the is–ought distinction (the other famous Humean distinction) also. However, Aristotle is unaware of either distinction, and he disregards both equally.

evaluative judgements are just a subcategory of factual judgements that describe an objective world of evaluations, rather than merely evaluating subjectively an independent objective world of description.

The whole *raison d'etre* of Social Science (or what Aristotle calls 'political science') is to study human flourishing (*eudaimonia*, i.e., how to live well, *eu zēn*), and in such a study, the truth of evaluative judgements (e.g., about physical incapacitation, humiliation, callousness, and loneliness being bad for people; but health, virtue, friendship, and understanding being good) is simply taken as given. When this focus is questioned, one can almost hear Aristotle's incredulous response: what academic purpose would be served by second-guessing the unanimous verdict of both the many and the wise about these features of human existence? What the student of Social Science needs is a deep experiential understanding of how those features play out in different contexts and different individuals, just as a doctor assesses the health of an individual patient rather than some average patient (Aristotle, 1985, p. 297 [1181b3–5]). What the student does not need, however, is antirealism or cynicism about the nature of goodness as such. If one refuses to accept the experientially grounded claim that a human being's best life, both as an individual and as a citizen, is a life of virtue, accompanied with those enjoyments which virtue usually procures (Aristotle, 1944, p. 535 [1323b1–5]), one is, by Aristotle's lights, not just a moral cynic but a bad social scientist.

This axiology of goodness is not only grounded in simple empirical observations about human affairs but in a much deeper probing into the different 'causes' steering the existence and development of all well-ordered natural beings. One of those is the final cause (the *telos*)[11]—the ideal realization to which a being is naturally drawn. So, for example, a plant seed has a nature inherent to it, and this nature determines its teleological ends. The plant is a good plant insofar as it reaches these ends and bad insofar as it does not, given a properly nurturing environment. The general idea here is that goodness is thought of in terms of fulfilment, and this fulfilment is one of inherent potential reaching its teleological end, its best manifestation (see, e.g., Page, 2021). The *telos* of the human person is an active state of moral maturity, health, and happiness, just as the *telos* of the human group is a well-ordered state. This is, for Aristotle, not an esoteric metaphysical claim but simply a naturalist one, derived from observing how two natural entities (i.e., a human person and a

---

[11] Social scientists make much of causation, but, from an Aristotelian viewpoint, they limit their interests to what he would have called 'efficient causation' of the sort that has primacy in classical (pre–quantum theory) physical sciences. The other two types of causation Aristotle discussed are material and formal causation, wherein the material properties or the formal arrangements of components induce motions or alterations. For a fuller discussion of Aristotelian teleology, see Johnson (2005).

human group) best develop and reach a mature, self-maintaining condition. He would probably have found Enlightenment antiteleological catechisms challenging theoretically but, in a practical sense, totally beside the point. A doctor who does not operate with a clear sense of the *telos* of human health, or a teacher who has no vision of the *telos* of good education, or a developmentalist who has no concept of human maturity, are simply bad professionals, unable to do their jobs well; the same, *mutatis mutandis*, applies to the social scientist who refuses to acknowledge an objective sense of the human good.

It must be remembered that when Aristotle is edifying students in 'Political Science' through his writings, these are not budding disinterested academics—as there were no research institutions of Social Science around— but rather future statesmen (legislators). So, the method of axiological teleology that we have been describing is not first and foremost the incarnation of an academic method (although Aristotle would probably say the same to Social Science students today) but rather a *modus operandi* of competent statecraft. This explains the frequent medical analogies upon which Aristotle draws and his allusions to the 'political scientist' (*qua* practitioner in Politics) as a *doctor*. Just as the medical doctor operates with a clear axiology of biological goodness and a teleology of health in order to cure a patient; the 'state doctor' operates with an axiology of societal goodness and a teleology of well-ordered statehood to improve the lives of the citizens. In modern parlance, the statesman is an 'action researcher', applying certain assumptions and testing hypotheses based on those, and at the same time honing experientially his *phronesis*, enabling him to make good decisions in difficult circumstances.

The medical analogy is helpful to illuminate another feature of Aristotle's brand of Social Science: his pragmatic *realism* (this time in a political rather than an ontological sense). Two medical doctors who share the same axiological teleology about psycho-physical goodness and health can still end up giving different advice to a patient. One of the doctors may favour radical interventions for cure while the other is more cautious. Aristotle's political advice tends to fall into to the latter category; he would have endorsed the famous policy of German statesman Willy Brandt: *die Politik der kleinen Schritte*. This small-steps approach has probably more to do with Aristotle's own personal constitution than any theoretical leanings, as well (perhaps) as a once-bitten-twice-shy reaction to the idealistic radicalism of his mentors Plato and Socrates.[12] Although far from being a quietist in the Stoic or

---

[12] In a clear dig at Socrates (although not named), Aristotle (1944) says: 'Of those who have put forward views about politics, some have taken no part in any political activities whatever but have passed their whole life as private citizens' (p. 165 [1273b27–9]).

Daoist mould, he has a deep antipathy to conflict, be it psychological or social, and generally favours a bad order to no order at all (as will be exemplified in Section 8.3).

It would be misleading to characterize this penchant unreservedly as *conservatism*; after all Aristotle (1944) says that what all seek is not the 'customary' but the 'good' (p. 129 [1269a3–4]), and he allows himself to philosophize about an ideal state with an ideal educational system. The reason lies rather in his strong psycho-moral leanings towards moderation (namely, the 'golden mean' in everything) and his pragmatic distrust of radical social engineering. Another related reason may be his narrow application of his own naturalistic method. True, he assumes that all theorizing about the human good is answerable to empirical research—which is precisely the assumption that draws some contemporary social scientists towards Virtue Ethics (e.g., Fowers, 2005). However, at the same time, he takes it for granted that existing city-states and those that preceded them have already yielded sufficient evidence of all possible experiments in living (Aristotle, 1944, p. 93 [1264a4–7]). He does not take into account the fact that future states might reveal new facts about human associations that would perhaps motivate a radical rethink of statecraft—as well as of the best execution of both Character and Civic Education.

All in all, what we have been describing so far in this section constitutes nothing less than a 'third way' of doing Social Science, in addition to standard quantitative and qualitative ways: '*phronetic* social science' (Flyvbjerg, 2001), grounded in a certain axiological teleology. The *phronesis* of the researcher ideally steers the whole research process, which—because of the very nature of Social Science as dealing with human beings—requires hard moral evaluations at almost every turn.

Civic primacy

It is now time to explore how Aristotle applies it to the relationship between the moral (characterological) and civic, and what its bearings are for the currently 'tense' relationship between Character and Civic Education. The whole trajectory of thought here starts with the premise that the human being is a 'political animal', repeated at various junctures in the *Politics* (e.g., Aristotle, 1944, p. 11 [1253a5–8]; also in 1985, p. 15 [1097b11]). This has a double meaning in ancient Greek: referring generally to the sociable nature of human beings and their inclination to live in communities, but also, more specifically, to this communitarian instinct being best satisfied within the state (*polis*).[13] At the outset of the *Politics*, Aristotle (1944) charts a social teleology of human associations from the family, through the village (clan, tribe), and towards the state. Temporally (historically), forms of associations have approximately followed this order, but teleologically, the state is 'prior by nature' to the previous forms (not to mention to the individual person) in the sense of being closer to their ideal fulfilment and in the sense in which the whole must necessarily be prior to the parts (p. 11 [1253a19–21]).[14]

Aristotle is aware of the ambiguities of the terms 'prior to' and 'primacy' (see Kraut 2002, pp. 256–73). It is one thing to be prior in existence and/or development, another thing to be analytically prior (in terms of explanation of composition), and yet another to be prior in nature and substance, namely what we call 'teleologically prior'.[15] Although Aristotle is preoccupied in the *Politics* with 'primacy' in the context of forms of human communities, it is perhaps easiest to exemplify his general thesis with respect to *personal justice* (as typically taught within Character Education) versus *social justice* (as emphasized in Civic Education). According to an Aristotelian analysis, personal justice is *developmentally prior* to social justice: it develops in personal encounters in the family before the child knows how to apply it to wider social contexts. It is also *motivationally prior*, in the sense that a person who has not learned aversion to unfairness as a child will hardly learn to internalize later, somehow out of the blue, a motivation towards countering wider societal injustice. Third, it is *analytically prior* in the sense, for example, that whereas it is intelligible to criticize theories of social justice for not accounting for the simple sense of fairness that children begin to develop already at the preschool level (Damon, 1981), it would be absurd to criticize a 6-year-old child's conception of justice as desert for not conforming to, say, a Rawlsian theory of social justice.[16] None of this changes the fact, however, that social justice has primacy over personal justice in another logical sense, which we have above called 'teleological'. Social justice is a more mature, more fully developed conception, characterizing a more fulfilled life form, than just close personal

---

[13] In the former sense, human beings share this inclination with bees and ants, but obviously not in the latter sense.

[14] If one sees hunter-gatherer groups or tribes as communities, these social structures entirely predate individuals, and individuals can only be formed within them. Evolutionarily, this temporal ordering goes back at least 6 million years.

[15] There are other possible types of priority relevant here, for example, motivational priority, as exemplified presently, although those are not explicitly mentioned by Aristotle himself.

[16] Indeed, this is precisely how Rawls's theory has often been criticized: namely, for not accommodating people's preinstitutional sense of desert or deservingness, arguably underlying analytically all later developed and more complicated/multifaceted conceptions of justice.

justice encounters within a small in-group. Analogously, Civic Education has primacy over Character Education in this teleological sense. It signals the further development of human excellences towards capacities that are prior in the order of fulfilment (although secondary in a developmental sense).

The practicalities of the civic

The distinctions drawn in the preceding paragraph are more than just pedantic conceptual ones. They have significant educational and moral/political implications. First, *educationally*, they mean that although Character Education must, in general, precede Civic Education, the latter has primacy in the (teleological) sense that is given pride of place in Aristotle's Virtue Ethics. Hence, not offering some sort of Civic Education in the wake of Character Education points to a significant deprivation of educational opportunities for growth. Teaching about the functions of *phronesis* in relation to moral quandaries is necessary, but the functions must also be related to political quandaries. Second, *morally* and *politically*, the thesis about the primacy of the civic over the moral (characterological)—again in the sense that matters most to Aristotle—is nothing less than the pillar of what is sometimes referred to, slightly misleadingly, as his 'collectivism': the idea that 'if a choice must be made between the good of a single individual and the good of the other members of the community, the latter alternative should be selected' (Kraut, 2002, p. 269).[17]

It would take us too far afield to elaborate further upon those educational and moral implications here; some of them reappear at later junctures in this chapter. What stands out at the end of this section, hopefully, is the unreasonableness of claims about Aristotelian Character Education signalling a conservative form of individualism (Jerome & Kisby, 2019) or 'the disappearance

---

[17] Aristotle (1944) puts it in the terms that the citizen does not belong to himself but rather to the state because each individual is part of the state (pp. 635–636 [1337a27–9]). That said, various other things Aristotle (1944) says about the nature of individual *phronetic* choice and the individualization of virtue in the *Nicomachean Ethics*, as well as the human propensity to cherish what is one's own, including private property, in the *Politics* (e.g., p. 83 [1262b18–25]), differentiate his Virtue Ethics from positions that tend to be characterized as 'collectivist', 'authoritarian', or even 'totalitarian' in modernity (see e.g. Swanson, 1992, pp. 1–8). Unfortunately, the capacity to discuss constructively many of the issues that Aristotle is interested in regarding conflicts between the individual and common good has been undermined in current educational discourse. For Aristotle, social justice *ex hypothesi* aims at the common good. Despite the omnipresence of the term 'social justice' in current educational discourse, postmodern and other relativistic assumptions have robbed the foundational concept of 'the common good' of any clear meaning in this discourse, with the justice discourse frequently degenerating into stale identity politics (Arthur, Kristjánsson et al., 2021). Yet interestingly, Sternberg and Glück (2022) make it a definitional feature of a viable psychological conception of wisdom that wisdom aims at 'the common good' (p. 3).

of the political' (Suissa, 2015), at least insofar far as the Character Education under scrutiny is Aristotelian in more than name only. However, what is true is that the concept of *phronesis* has mostly disappeared from political discourse, and it is seldom if ever brought up in standard forms of Civic Education. We were motivated to write this chapter to help correct some of these misinterpretations.

8.3 Interlude: Actual Constitutions and the Ideal State

The study of past and present city-states (*poleis*) in Greece and elsewhere, with the aim of eliciting the pros and cons of different kinds of 'constitutions' (meaning forms of government, not charters of foundational laws), takes up the largest part of the *Politics*. We will treat this topic very cursorily here, however, for two reasons. First, this is by far the best-known part of Aristotle's political writings, and it suffices to have done an elementary A-level (senior high school) course in Politics to have a smattering of knowledge about it. Second, this topic is mostly tangential to the remit of the present chapter, which is to explore the relationship between the civic and the moral in the field of Aristotle's Virtue Ethics and the precise role that *phronesis* plays with respect to civic virtue. In this section, which we call an 'Interlude', we therefore rehearse only those aspects of Aristotle's account of real and ideal constitutions that will have a bearing on our discussion of civic *phronesis* in the subsequent sections.

'Correct' and 'erroneous' constitutions

Famously, Aristotle makes a distinction between 'correct' (*orthai*) and 'erroneous' or 'flawed' (*hēmartēmenai*) constitutions. 'Correct' here means 'essentially just' (although not ideally perfect), whereas 'erroneous' means 'essentially unjust' (although not necessarily base beyond redemption). 'Erroneous' is sometimes translated as 'perverted', which is apt because those forms are deviant/degenerative versions of the 'correct' ones and, teleologically, contrary to the ideally fulfilled nature of civic associations. Aristotle's (1944) distinction between the two forms is deceptively simple: correct constitutions aim at the common good (i.e., serve the interests of the ruled), whereas the erroneous ones serve the interests of the ruler(s) only (p. 205 [1279a17–29]). Depending on whether the rulers are

Table 8.1 Constitutions (forms of government) in Aristotle's *Politics*

Ruled By	For the Sake of the Common Good ('Correct' Forms)	For the Sake of the Ruler(s) Only ('Erroneous' Forms)
One	Kingdom	Tyranny
Few	Aristocracy	Oligarchy
Many	Polity	Democracy

many, few or just one, we end up with the well-known list of options shown in Table 8.1.

Aristotle's examples of real constitutions exemplifying the two different forms and subforms are enlightening, if somewhat tortuous.[18] However, our paragon of clarity becomes uncharacteristically cryptic when it comes to rank-ordering the correct and erroneous forms. He seems to think that a kingdom is in principle the best of the 'correct' forms if a benevolent and *phronetic* enough ruler (with good enough sons to match, as successors) can be found; however, he struggles to find real-life examples of this. Hence, aristocracy (as in Sparta and Carthage) is probably the most decent real-life option, followed by polity (as in Syracuse and Mali), although both contain potential seeds of degeneration within them. The same applies to the perversions; Aristotle is not entirely unambiguous on which of those is the worst—apparently tyranny, with oligarchy more pathological than democracy, although the latter is bad enough, especially because of its proneness to demagoguery.[19]

Before turning to Aristotle's ideal state, we will just add a couple of quick observations that matter for what follows. First, Aristotle's aversion to conflict shines through in his assumption that even the worst of perverse constitutions is marginally better than no constitution—namely anarchy—and that efforts can and need to be made within all existing constitutions, good or bad, to make them gradually better.[20] While not going in a Hobbesian direction in legitimizing state

---

[18] There were more than 1000 city-states in ancient Greece, but most of them had less than 1000 inhabitants, functioning more like villages than states. Aristotle was therefore limited when it came to states large enough (e.g., Athens) to matter for his analysis, and even Athens had the population only of a modern-sized large town.

[19] In light of the positive modern connotations of the word 'democracy', it might be helpful to coin a new term, like 'rabblecracy', for the perverted form (as Aristotle specifies it as government in the hands of the meanest rabble: the uncouth *dêmos*), reserving the term 'democracy' rather for what he calls 'polity'. However, since Aristotle uses the standard Greek term for 'democracy' and simply happens to have a very low opinion of this form of government, we stick to the traditional translation here.

[20] For a different take on Aristotle and anarchy, see Keyt (2005).

power, Aristotle is no believer in revolutions. He basically applies his teleology of the civic here (recall Section 8.2). In order to reach its fulfilment *qua* statehood, the state must, first, be preserved and, second, improved from within. Even when there is no hope of turning a state's constitution into a correct form, its 'health' can at least be brought to a bearable level (i.e., some modicum of justice), as a doctor would do for a patient in palliative care. Second, Aristotle's (1985) pessimism about radical constitutional change mirrors his pessimism of moral transformation in an individual who has not been brought up in good habits. The effects of the antecedent circumstances of bad upbringing, or living under a perverted constitution, cannot be undone, because of the intractability of altering 'by argument what has long been absorbed by habit'. For a person in such a condition 'would not even listen to an argument turning him away, or comprehend it [if he did listen]; and in that state how could he be persuaded to change?' (1985, p. 292 [1179b11–31]). A bad politico-legal order, just like bad upbringing, compromises, stifles, and stunts.

The 'ideal' state

Given Aristotle's (1944) antipathy to utopian thinking, Platonic and otherwise, it is somewhat remarkable that he devotes Books VII and VIII of the *Politics* to illustrating the ideal of a state that that has never existed but we can still 'pray for' (*kat' euchēn*) (p. 553 [1325b37]; we alter the translation slightly). However, Aristotle goes to some lengths to show that his ideal state is not unrealistically utopian but rather a viable option, subject to strict empirical constraints (see p. 553 [1325b39]).[21] It would have to be set up in a new place, preferably a coastal region, exclusively by a large group of unique *phronimoi* who decided to move from an existing *polis* and establish an autonomous colony elsewhere.[22]

The ideal state described by Aristotle—and which he must take to represent the final end of the natural teleology of statehood if that teleology ever succeeds in overcoming human imperfections and reaching its fulfilment—seems to combine the best of both aristocracy and the unpolluted form of what we would probably want to call 'democracy', but he called 'polity'. It is *aristocratic* in the sense that it is ruled by a select (namely self-selected) and

---

[21] According to Wolbert et al.'s (2019) distinction between 'utopian idealisation' and 'realistic idealism', Aristotle's ideal state clearly falls into the latter category.
[22] Cf. the fond hope nourished at the end of MacIntyre's (otherwise pessimistic) *After Virtue* (1981) of virtuous agents setting up socially isolated 'enclaves' or retreats of virtuous living.

well-off group of men of outstanding character; it is *democratic* in the sense that this group happens to include potentially all (i.e., male, permanent) residents of the new immigrant state, so that everyone has the option of—and capacity for—both ruling and being ruled by turns. Ober (2005) draws considerable mileage from the fact that the decision processes in the ideal state seem to be democratic and that Aristotle's teleology of statehood thus seems to point towards some sort of fairly egalitarian 'natural democracy'. Aristotle does not say what happens in this state if the *phronimoi* who happen to be ruling at a given time do not agree about a political decision, but Kraut (2002, p. 233) argues that he must assume that, in such cases, decisions will be made by majority voting—another nod to a democratic process.

We say more about the ideal state when analysing ideally combined moral and civic virtue at the end of Section 8.4. It is also relevant to the educational discussion in Section 8.5 and Chapter 11, as the educational system described by Aristotle is predicated upon the existence of the ideal state.

8.4 Moral and Civic Virtue, and the Role of *Phronesis*

What is the relationship between moral and civic virtues in Aristotle? Because we have been focused on moral virtues up to now, it is incumbent upon us to explore the relationship between the two forms of virtues.

The case of justice

Consider *justice* as an example, because that is sometimes treated as a moral virtue and sometimes as a civic one. However, Aristotle leads us here, in this case, into a blind alley. In the *Rhetoric*, Aristotle carefully analysed four justice-related (or, more specifically, desert-based) virtuous emotions: pain at another's undeserved bad or good fortune and pleasure at another's deserved bad or good fortune (see overview and references in Kristjánsson, 2006).[23] When he then fleshes out justice as a personal character virtue in the *Nicomachean Ethics*, one expects him to draw on this discussion for the

---

[23] The first two of those emotions have obvious designators in modern English and ancient Greek: compassion (*eleos*) and righteous indignation (*nemesis*); the second two have not. 'Schadenfreude' is more typically used, for example, in ordinary language to denote pleasure at someone's *undeserved* bad fortune—and Aristotle rightly considered that emotion vicious.

standard emotional component of the virtue. However, he says nothing there about its desert-basis nor indeed about its emotional concomitant(s). Indeed, the discussion of justice, while longer than of any other virtue apart from friendship, is uncharacteristically unclear and unpersuasive. Basically, Aristotle (1985) identifies two kinds of justice as a moral virtue where the first one seems to amount to little more than law-abidingness, for 'whatever is lawful is in some way just' (p. 118 [1129b11–14]). But hold on: surely there are unjust laws![24] The second kind of moral justice is about equality in the spheres of the distributive, the corrective and the reciprocal. But the examples he gives of this are lacking in cohesion. All in all, as Kraut (2002) notes, the long section on the moral virtue of justice seems to constitute an eclectic mixture of elements without a systematic structure (p. 99). To pile on the agony, when it comes to the *Politics*, Aristotle mostly discusses social justice without forging any logical links either to the account in the *Nicomachean Ethics* or the emotion analysis in the *Rhetoric*.

To mend matters, however, Aristotle does address the question of the relationship between moral and civic virtue head-on in the *Politics*, although he does so without invoking specifically his earlier accounts of the moral virtue of justice. Some of what he says is direct and unambiguous; other claims, such as about the four levels of civic virtue that we introduce presently, have to be teased out more indirectly from the text (in a way that has not been done previously). To begin with the direct and unambiguous claims, Aristotle (1944) asserts that moral and civic virtue, while overlapping, do not coincide except in the ideal state (p. 273 [1288a40–2]). In that state, civic virtue is nothing more than moral virtue applied to a wider societal context, and there is no possible conflict between the moral and the civic. In nonideal constitutions, however, be those of the 'correct' or 'erroneous' forms, civic virtues go beyond—and may even in some cases appear to conflict with—moral virtue. The main reason for this discrepancy is the fact that civic virtues are more context-sensitive and relative than moral virtues. Before explaining why this is the case, let us remember that one of the most conspicuous features of Aristotle's theory of moral virtue is how context-sensitive and individualized it is (as we explained in Chapter 1).

---

[24] Aristotle (e.g. 1944) acknowledges this in various places, both directly and indirectly (see pp. 129, 229–30 [1268b38–1269a3; 1282a41–b13]); cf. Kraut (2002, p. 104).

Context-sensitivity

However, even the context-sensitivity of moral virtue pales in comparison with the contextual and cultural sensitivity of civic virtue. Aristotle's (1985) idea here seems to be that the sphere where most moral virtues are played out is fairly uniform across cultures. Most people interact personally with family, friends, workmates, and casual strangers in ways that call for the same sort of moral virtues of honesty, compassion, agreeableness, etc.; and 'in our travels we can see how every human being is akin [. . .] to a human being' (p. 208 [1155a20–2]).[25] There are, however, two sorts of reasons why the civic virtues will need to function differently: an intra-constitutional reason and an inter-constitutional one (see Rosler, 2013). The *intra-constitutional* reason is that there is substantial division of labour within the civic sphere, just as in the different tasks that different sailors perform on a ship (Aristotle, 1944, p. 187 [1276b20–5]). Thus, the civic virtues of the person in charge of state finances will be radically different from those of the army general or the person overseeing agricultural matters—not to mention the more general differences between virtues of rulers and the ruled.

However—and here is the *inter-constitutional* reason—there are not only different tasks on the same 'ship'; there are also quite distinct types of 'ships' around: recall the account of all the discrete constitutions. The civic virtues of a person (a ruler or a citizen) in a polity will differ from the ones of a person in an aristocracy, for example. Aristotle (1944) is quite explicit here: 'If [. . .] there are various forms of constitution, it is clear that there cannot be one single goodness [virtue] which is the perfect goodness of the good citizen' (p. 187 [1276b32–6]). So, social justice as a virtue will vary, relative to constitutions, in ways that personal justice will not.[26] We say more later about how this discrepancy disappears in Aristotle's ideal state.

---

[25] While catchy, this often-cited phrase may seem a little naive and underestimate the cultural variance in moral virtue. Although Aristotle sees a lot of variance in different Greek political constitutions, he does not notice the same in in-group encounters. But then, he only looked at people brought up in a reasonably uniform Greek culture and saw no reason to consider non-Greek 'barbarian' cultures. This worry is reflected in the common misgiving that contemporary forms of neo-Aristotelian Character Education are not multiculturally sensitive enough. There are at least two ways to respond to this misgiving: by updating Aristotle's account of moral virtue to allow for more cultural variance, or by arguing that multicultural differences can be captured by the sort of Character Education that focuses more on the civic virtues, which even Aristotle acknowledged to be culturally relative to a significant extent. It is outside the current purview to offer a take on this question here, but we think that this is a worthwhile domain in which Aristotle needs updating. We also recommend various chapters in Darnell and Kristjánsson's (2021) edited volume as food for thought.

[26] One way to make sense of this claim regarding the simpler understanding of personal justice *qua* lawfulness is to say that the virtue of abiding by the law is essentially the same everywhere, in the sense of requiring the same state of law-abiding character; however, socially, it will manifest itself differently, having to do with different legal norms under different legislations.

A four-level structure for civic virtue

Although Aristotle is transparent in advancing and justifying the thesis of the separation of moral and civic virtues in actual constitutions, nowhere does he produce a comprehensive specification of what 'civic virtue' is (apart from truisms about its aiming at the common good), and how that specification will differ from the one given for moral virtue in general and discrete moral virtues in particular in the *Nicomachean Ethics*, as well as from that of the various virtuous emotions (while not full-blown virtues) in the *Rhetoric*. In what follows, we propose to elicit from Aristotle's *Politics* an account of four functional levels of civic virtue, ranging from the most rudimentary to the most advanced.

Level 1 civic virtue: uncritical 'law-abidingness'

According to Aristotle (1985), most people find themselves somewhere between the levels of incontinence (moral awareness but lack of self-control) and continence (self-control) (p. 190 [1150a15]). In other words, mainly because of defective upbringing, most people do not even reach the level of habituated moral virtue, let alone *phronetic* (i.e., *phronesis*-guided) moral virtue. Aristotle (1944) believes, however, that virtually every citizen in a state can learn to exhibit civic virtue—for 'all ought to possess the goodness [virtue] of a good citizen' (p. 189 [1277a2–4])—albeit at a fairly low level. It is clear that he relinquishes here the crucial demand made upon moral virtue that the agent enjoys its actualization; it suffices that the agent forces herself to act civically; hence, civic virtue at this lowest level is more akin to continence in the sphere of moral virtue.[27] The low-level civic virtue that Aristotle is talking about here, as available for everyone, is evidently just law-abidingness. The solution to the puzzle of why merely acting lawfully is a civic virtue, even if this is done mindlessly and without relishing it—and even when the law may not be just—lies again in Aristotle's deep-seated fear of anarchy.[28] A bad law is better than no law; for at least if there is a law, there will be processes in place

---

[27] Linn (2022) cleverly argues that the lower demands on virtue in the *Politics* may make Aristotle immune to the common accusation that he sets the bar for virtue too high. That said, since Aristotle is mainly talking about specifically civic virtues and civic friendships in the *Politics*, this may not necessarily save him from complaints lodged against his theory of moral virtues in the *Nicomachean Ethics*.

[28] It is also possible that Aristotle is here working implicitly on the (controversial) Socratic premise that deciding to continue to live in a state, and not to emigrate, somehow commits you to consider its laws just. Cf. Curren (2000), pp. 30–2.

to improve it (see level 2 civic virtue), which is not the case in a state of utter lawlessness.[29] The next worst thing after anarchy is that citizens consider the state their enemy (p. 509 [1320a14–17]); but being willing to follow its laws indicates that this is not the case. Aristotle (1944) bolsters his case with an army analogy; one cannot command cavalry well without having first learned to obey as a trooper (p. 193 [1277b7–16]).

To clarify, then, level 1 type of civic virtue is a virtue for citizens (not rulers) in both 'correct' and 'erroneous' states. It is simply about preserving the constitution and preventing it from falling into anarchy. It does not require the same mindset or intellectual capacity (*phronesis*) as moral virtue, and it can even at times, in principle, seem to contradict moral virtue (which would then call for level 2 civic virtue, as we see presently).[30] To take a modern example, a teenager may have come to the reasoned conclusion that a law prohibiting the personal use of a recreational drug like cannabis is unjust; his parents may agree with him, but it is nevertheless incumbent on the parents to persuade their child to obey the law and thereby execute a civic virtue. In a certain sense, then, education for level 1 civic virtue is 'training in conformity' (Curren, 2000, p. 98).

Level 2 civic virtue: critical law-abidingness

All the above claims about lawfulness as a civic virtue notwithstanding, once the citizens have contributed to the preservation of the constitution, they also need to try to improve it from within. This will be the case, in particular, when a specific law is considered unjust, for example when it clashes with the equity principles of moral justice. Aristotle is not explicit here; level 2 civic virtue needs to be drawn out by implication from his texts. *Criticality*, so to speak, shambles onto the stage rather than making a graceful entrance. The reason for this is that Aristotle (1944) is still dealing with ordinary citizens,

---

[29] Aristotle (e.g., 1944) seems to predicate his view on lawfulness being a civic virtue, even in 'erroneous' constitutions, on the premise that there is at least some legal structure at work there, albeit less than just. He would evidently not extend this requirement to obeying outrageous and evil commands by, say, a tinpot tyrant ruling on his whims (see pp. 459, 463–4 [1313a40–1, 1314a5–9]), as the constitution has then already sunk into complete lawlessness anyway; cf. Kraut (2002, p. 381).

[30] The discussion has so far identified two main differences between moral and civic virtue. The latter are more culturally relative and do not necessarily require *phronesis* to count as full-blown virtues. By implication also, exhibiting a civic virtue does not necessarily create the pleasant afterglow that the successful exhibition of a moral virtue does. Much of civic virtue is just about furthering smooth social interactions between relative strangers who happen to live in the same state. It would be odd, for instance, if one always felt a warm sense of personal accomplishment after passing through a green light at crossroads. Yet following traffic signals correctly is a civic virtue.

most of whom are not even budding, let alone full-blown, *phronimoi*. Some of those are, however, capable of holding 'right opinion' (*doxa alēthēs*) about socio-moral issues, although they are not in command of the bigger picture that the overarching meta-virtue of *phronesis* provides (p. 195 [1277b28-9]). Their condition is one in which they possess at best habituated moral virtue that has not yet been *phronesis*-infused. While incapable of making rational overall judgements about states of affairs, citizens at this stage are able to spot individual instances of unjust laws; in which case, it is incumbent on them as good citizens to execute civic virtue by trying to have those laws amended.[31] Aristotle (1944) even enters into cost-benefit analysis in considering whether the costs of repealing a bad law may outweigh the benefits, but the main point still remains that 'it is proper for some laws sometimes to be altered' (p. 131 [1269a12–20]).

To sum up, then, level 2 civic virtue operates in both 'correct' and 'erroneous' constitutions; it involves critical interventions by citizens to try to moderate the defects of the legal system. In many cases, this means making the law compatible with moral virtues. Yet most of the citizens in question, who are meant to execute this level of civic virtue, do not possess *phronesis*; hence their point of view will always be limited, and they are not fit to rule. To return to the modern example above, the consenting parents of the teenager who is opposed to current laws about recreational drugs will do well by supporting him to join demonstrations against the law. In that way they all execute their civic virtue—although it does not relieve them of the duty to follow the law while it is in existence.

It should be mentioned here as an aside that the fairly modest developmental demands placed upon people at levels 1 and 2 may provide an explanation of the claim frequently made by Aristotle (e.g., 1944) that the virtue of civic friendship, holding constitutions together as their greatest 'blessing' (p. 81 [1262b7-9]), even above and beyond justice, is a form of *utility friendships* (e.g., Irrera, 2005; Cooper, 2005). There are those who find Aristotle's description of civic friendships so exalted and demanding that it must be 'based in virtue and not merely utility' (Curren, 2000, p. 133): namely, it must be a form of the highest friendship type in Aristotle's theory: *character friendships*. However, character friendships can *ex hypothesi* only be implemented between developing or developed *phronimoi*; and this would limit civic

---

[31] Gustin Law (2017) gives an example of how this would mean, for instance, trying to counter some of the unsound extremisms of democracy in such a regime. See various other examples in Roberts (2009, pp. 561–2).

friendship to a subgroup of the population not big enough to safeguard the state against civic conflict.[32]

Level 3 civic virtue: *phronetic* civic virtue

Here we enter a level of civic virtue that is qualitatively different from the two earlier levels in being reserved for people endowed with *phronesis*. Although *phronesis* is always a good thing and a bonus if ordinary citizens possess it, Aristotle (1944) only talks about this level in the context of the metacognitive capacity that rulers in 'correct' constitutions need. They must possess mature *phronesis* (p. 63 [1260a14–17]), which also presupposes moral virtue—and it would be 'absurd' to think that the governance of a state should be in the hands of the base rather than the virtuous (p. 229 [1282a24–7]). While this level of civic virtue is confined to 'correct' constitutions, those are not perfect in the same way as the ideal state and have to control a populace that is defective in moral virtue. The ruler in a 'correct' state will make sure that his civic virtue is never at odds with moral virtue; yet there will be many procedures and laws in place in those regimes that are amoral or go beyond the moral. Moreover, the specific norms will differ as much as polities, aristocracies, and kingdoms differ, although they all aim at the common good. Thus, the civic virtues at level 3 are to a large degree extensions rather than applications of moral virtue.

To return to our modern example, the teenager should not dream of becoming a ruler in the state until he has reached the level of *phronetic* virtue. Whether he ever reaches that level is dependent upon not only his own acumen and good will but also various features of 'moral luck' that are beyond his control. Even if he achieves a position of power, he will need to take various contextual and local factors into consideration, other than merely moral ones, before he can change the law that he a opposes.

Level 4 civic virtue: *phronetic* (combined) moral and civic virtue

Here we move from the actual to the ideal. Let us assume that a group of *phronimoi* does, in fact, move and set up a new colony in a favourable place,

---

[32] This may not be as significant a concession as Curren would deem it to be, however, because it turns out that there are two sublevels of utility friendships in Aristotle, and one of them is quite close to character friendships. See Kristjánsson (2022b, chap. 6).

Table 8.2 Four levels of civic virtue in Aristotle's *Politics*

	For Whom?	The Same as Moral Virtue?	Includes *Phronesis?*	In What Kind of Constitutions?
1. Uncritical law-abidingness	The ruled	No, and at times evidently incompatible	No	Correct and erroneous
2. Critical law-abidingness	The ruled	No, but compatible	No	Correct and erroneous
3. *Phronetic* civic virtue	The rulers	No, incorporates moral virtue but goes beyond it	Yes	Correct
4. *Phronetic* combined (moral and civic) virtue	The rulers and the ruled	Yes	Yes	Ideal

establishing an ideal state. All the adult (male, for Aristotle) inhabitants of this colony will be equally capable of ruling and being ruled and will do so by turns. As all laws will be designed from scratch, a unique opportunity beckons to create a perfect concordance between the civic and the moral: laws and other civic ordinances will just be direct applications of moral virtues. We already explained the general contours of the ideal state above, and Aristotle adds little information about it in terms of practical application. That is understandable because most of his discussion of actual constitutions is drawn from real-life examples but there is obviously no such example available for the ideal state. Nevertheless, we include it in Table 8.2, summarizing the four levels of civic virtue, because although Aristotle talks about the fourth level as an idealization, it is meant to be a realistic idealization—hopefully to be approximated somewhere at some point in time.

Megalopsychia or *phronesis*?

Before leaving the discussion of the four levels, it is worth mentioning an interesting oddity. Aristotle (1944) twice refers to the *phronimoi* at level 4 (who can be either rulers or the ruled) as *megalopsychoi* (pp. 569; 645 [1328a9–10; 1338b2–4]). Now, Aristotle's great-souled persons (*megalopsychoi*) constitute a unique group of alpha males who, in addition to being full-fledged *phronimoi*, are endowed with an abundance of worldly riches and decide to use those to engage in philanthropy, public benefaction, and deeds of grandeur, requiring bravery and spectacular efforts. *Megalopsychia* is described as a moral meta-virtue that extends the sphere of the ordinary moral virtues and makes them greater (Aristotle, 1985, pp. 97–104 [1123b33–1125a35]). Yet, becoming *megalopsychoi* is a mixed blessing for the persons themselves for it requires sacrificing wonder and other intellectual pursuits, consigning the *megalopsychoi* to lives of philistinism where they are constantly at others' beck and call with no time left for many of life's niceties (see further in Fetter, 2015; Kristjánsson, 2020, chap. 4). As spelled out in the *Nicomachean Ethics*, being a *megalopsychos* seems to presuppose a community where most people are not *megalopsychoi*, and where those alpha-male characters can therefore make a significant contribution to the common good. It is difficult to imagine a community where all the males are *megalopsychoi*, however. It is like a community where everyone is an eager medical doctor but there are no patients to cure. So, one is left to wonder whether Aristotle has dropped in these *megalopsychoi*-comments about his utopia without thinking them through. On the other hand, there is some mileage in the point that the sort of civic virtue ascribed to the rulers signals an extension of ordinary civic virtue, just like great-souled virtue extends ordinary virtue.

Rather than thinking of this in terms of *megalopsychia*, it may be more instructive to revisit the idea of *phronesis*-guided civic virtue (at levels 3 and 4). We mentioned at the outset that despite the recent surge of interest in *phronesis* and its role in adjudicating virtue conflicts involving potentially clashing moral virtues (like honesty versus loyalty), little has been written since the time of Aristotle about the specific role that *phronesis* plays in relation to civic virtue. An initial hypothesis could be that there is no need to write specifically about *phronesis* in those contexts. It simply operates there as elsewhere by critically overseeing and deliberating about the best way to reach an overall wise decision, conducive to a flourishing life.

However, what Aristotle (1944) actually says about the *phronesis* of the ruler suggests a slightly more complicated picture. When he says in the *Politics* that *phronesis* is 'peculiar to a ruler' and the citizens do not need it (p. 195 [1277b25–9]), one may first read this cavalierly as referring to the majority of ordinary citizens who can survive and thrive to a certain extent by being self-controlled rather than *phronetically* virtuous. However, a deeper reading of this citation and the surrounding text reveals that Aristotle is clearly talking about *all* citizens barring the rulers not needing *phronesis*. But that seems a blatant contradiction with respect to the message from the *Nicomachean Ethics* according to which at least a small group of citizens are, in fact, already budding or fully developed *phronimoi* and those who are not should make an effort at getting there also if they possibly can.[33]

This apparent contradiction prompts a second look at what Aristotle (1985) says about *phronesis* in the *Nicomachean Ethics*. It so happens that he mentions Pericles and other politicians as paragons of *phronesis* because they take into account what is good not only for themselves but human beings more generally (p. 154 [1140b7–11]). It is not a big stretch to interpret Aristotle as claiming there that the sphere of *phronesis* differs between a *phronetic* ruler like Pericles and the ordinary *phronimos*—especially in light of what he says elsewhere about the difference between the good of the individual and of the whole state (p. 3 [1094b7–10]). One of the components of ordinary *phronesis* is some sort of a blueprint of flourishing (recall Chapter 2), but Aristotle nowhere says that it is the flourishing of all the citizens in the state, let alone of all humankind (he was not a utilitarian!), and although he was not a rational egoist either, confining his attention to the agent's own personal good, what he seems to be talking about as the blueprint for ordinary *phronesis* is the flourishing of oneself, one's friends, and family—or, more widely perhaps, of the people directly affected by one's decisions. However, Pericles has a wider blueprint component to accommodate, because his duty as a ruler is to execute civic virtue in the interest of the common good (Aristotle, 1944, p. 205 [1279a28–30]), and that will include *everyone* in the state.

This interpretation defangs the apparent contradiction identified earlier. The *phronesis* that is 'peculiar to the ruler' denotes a wider application of the concept of *phronesis* than that aspired to by ordinary citizens—so there actually is a unique level of civic *phronesis*: namely, *phronesis* needed to guide civic virtue. Gustin Law (2017) warns against this interpretation going too far, because Aristotle says that 'political science' (which we have interpreted earlier as meaning *phronetic* Social Science) is the 'same state' as ordinary *phronesis*, But Aristotle (1985) also says in the same place that their 'being is not the same' (p. 159 [1141b23–4]). What that could charitably be taken to mean is that civic *phronesis*—while not *qualitatively* different from ordinary *phronesis* applied to moral virtues only—is *quantitatively* different, by attaching itself to a wider range of issues and a wider group of people. So, what we end up with are two levels of *phronesis* (although not two distinct *phronesis* concepts) with civic *phronesis* being accorded a unique status.[34]

---

[33] Frede (2005, pp. 175–6) identifies this problem but does not suggest any clear-cut solution to it there. Later in her chapter, however, she toys with an idea of two levels of *phronesis*, as we suggest in what follows.

[34] Interestingly, Aristotle throws up at various junctures in the *Politics* the possibility that there might be people of super-human civic virtue, ideal to fill the role of a benevolent monarch. While this is just suggested as a theoretical possibility, without real-life examples, it creates conceptual space for an even higher level of *civic virtue* than those we have identified above. See further in Frede (2005, pp. 179–80). Notably,

There is a final twist to this narrative of potential *phronesis* augmentation. Aristotle (1944) also mentions the possibility that wise decisions reached by a group of partially *phronetic* persons may be better than a *phronetic* decision made by a single ruler, just as a dinner cooked by many may be better than one provided by a single chef (pp. 221–3 [1281a40–b10]). Aristotle does not bring this discussion to a clear conclusion (cf. Ober, 2005, pp. 237–40); however, it reminds us painfully of the fact that although the notion of 'collective *phronesis*' as the pooling of wisdom is not totally unheard of in the contemporary literature (e.g., Schwarz & Lappalainen, 2020), it is an area that is, so far, seriously underresearched and underdeveloped. This is why we have decided to devote the whole of the following chapter to it.

Unfortunately, as we have seen, some parts of this discourse have not moved much forward since Aristotle's time.

8.5 Some Educational Implications

Although the argument in this chapter has mainly proceeded by way of excavation into Aristotle's ancient texts, the original motivation for writing it was current and substantive rather than historical: namely, to make sense of the ongoing tensions between Character Education and Civic Education, especially regarding the priority of moral versus civic virtue as well as their cultivation, and to pave the way for the resurrection of the idea of civic *phronesis* as a moral and educational ideal. Aristotle's discussion is obviously not the last word on those issues, but, given his historical role as the forebear of both those forms of Values Education, it is reasonable to see it as the first word.

The conclusion we have reached is that there are no historical or substantive grounds for seeing Character Education and Civic Education as competitors, at least if we agree on following a broad Aristotelian script. Character Education comes, for developmental reasons, most naturally before Civic Education, because of the child's initial close familiarity with the in-group—although we identified one fairly primitive kind of civic virtue (uncritical law-abidingness) that can easily be taught alongside early Character Education. However, because of the teleological primacy of the civic, Civic Education is the more sophisticated and advanced of the two and also more demanding

---

Aristotle also mentions the possibility of super-human *moral virtue* in the *Nicomachean Ethics* but attributes it mostly to gods.

than Character Education except at level 1.[35] Yet that level is important because it allows everyone to internalise (*nonphronetic*) civic virtue, even those who do not go on to develop moral virtue.

Level 1 is also the only level at which the moral could potentially come into conflict with the civic. That can be made less likely by assisting the student in advancing as soon as possible to level 2 of critical law-abidingness where she is able to criticize the content of the level 1 civic virtue in light of a (habituated) moral virtue or a more general moral outlook. Kraut (2002, p. 380) considers civic virtue 'less exalted' than moral virtue because an agent can actualize it (at what we called levels 1 and 2) without possessing *phronetic* moral virtue. Nevertheless, once you advance to the higher levels, the teleological primacy of the civic begins to kick in, and civic virtue becomes more demanding than even *phronetic* moral virtue.

The above excavation also revealed a potentially more expansive kind of *phronesis*, civic *phronesis*, which augments ordinary *phronesis* and is invaluable for those in charge of ruling a state. It is somewhat remarkable, given the recent interest in a (neo)-Aristotelian conception of *phronesis* and all the buzz around wisdom more generally in Psychology (Grossmann, Westrate, Ardelt et al., 2020), that a thorough literature search revealed almost no articles exploring the difference between ordinary *phronesis* and civic *phronesis* in an Aristotelian context and its educational implications. We return to some further educational reverberations of civic *phronesis* in Chapter 11.

---

[35] A common assumption in civic educational critiques of Character Education is that the latter is somehow more conservative than Civic Education, while Civic Education is more radical (e.g., Jerome & Kisby, 2019). However, since Civic Education follows naturally in the wake of Character Education, it is difficult to avoid the conclusion that a truly radical change in moral make-up can more feasibly be accomplished if it takes place at the earlier developmental stage.

9
Collective *Phronesis*

9.1 Why Collective *Phronesis*?

The aim of this chapter is to provide a broad overview of various discourses relevant to developing a construct of collective *phronesis* from a broadly (neo)-Aristotelian perspective, with implications for professional practice, in general, and potentially for various of its subdomains in particular—although we have chosen in this chapter to focus exclusively on business practice and Business Ethics education.[1]

Despite the recent proliferation of interest in practical wisdom as *phronesis* within Professional Ethics, including Business Ethics, and more general areas of both Psychology and Philosophy, the focus has remained mostly on the construct at the level of individual decision-making, much as the forebear of the *phronesis* concept, Aristotle, did in the *Nicomachean Ethics*. However, he also made intriguing remarks about *phronesis* at the collective level in his *Politics*: remarks that have mostly eluded elaboration outside of small pockets of Aristotelian scholarship. The reason is, no doubt, related to the one unearthed in the preceding chapter: namely, a general lack of engagement with what Aristotle says about *phronesis* in the *Politics*.

In line with the general tenor of our book, the aim of this chapter is practical and revisionary, rather than exegetical and deferential, with respect to Aristotle. Nevertheless, just as most of the standard literature on *phronesis* takes its cue from Aristotle's exposition in the *Nicomachean Ethics*, the obvious first port of call for an analysis of collective *phronesis* is to explore the resources handed down to us by Aristotle himself. The lion's share of this chapter is, therefore, devoted to making sense of Aristotle's somewhat unsystematic remarks and the lessons we can draw from them: lessons that are,

---

[1] A prototypical context in which collective decisions are arrived at is within Business and Business Management; hence our choice of this domain. See also R. C. Solomon's remark, cited at later junctures, about how Aristotle's *Politics* would be an ideal reading for today's business managers rather than politicians.

arguably, quite different from the ones typically elicited in the scholarship on Aristotelian political theory.

Aims of the chapter

We begin with a critical overview of some of the recent literatures on *phronesis* and how those relate to various other discourses to which they are not normally connected, such as those on the 'wisdom of crowds'. Section 9.2 excavates those resources in Aristotle that might, initially at least, be considered most germane to the topic of *phronetic* joint decision-making: his account of friendships in the *Nicomachean Ethics* and of the 'wisdom of the multitude' in the *Politics*. Section 9.3 subjects those resources, and the secondary literature on them, to critical scrutiny, the upshot of which will be that whilst Aristotle's potential contribution to the ideal of deliberative democracy has been overemphasized, he does make some salutary claims about the nature of practically wise joint decision-making, whose relevance extends beyond political governance into areas of Business Ethics education, administration, and management. As Aristotle's account of *collective phronesis* is lacking in detail and nuance, Section 9.4 offers speculative hypotheses about how our componential model of individual *phronesis* could be extended to the joining of *phronetic* dots from different individuals to make up collective managerial *phronesis*. Finally, Section 9.5 elicits some practical, including educational, lessons about how collective *phronesis* could be enhanced and practised at the collective (Business Ethics educational and organizational) level.

When beginning research into the construct of collective *phronesis*, we were struck by the apparent absence of any comprehensive overview of the field or, more specifically, any study charting the outlines of a broad terrain, the subareas of which could then be mapped out in more targeted studies. The current chapter aims at providing such an overview or initiation into a potentially novel discourse, which other researchers would then be encouraged to flesh out and finesse.

Virtue Ethics and *phronesis* in Business Management

Let us begin, as often before in this book, with some history. In the last 25 years or so, Virtue Ethics has gradually equalled or even surpassed deontology and utilitarianism as the theory of choice within academic Business Ethics, although that scholarly interest has not always percolated down to actual business practice or even Business Ethics education (Huo & Kristjánsson, 2018). Solomon's (e.g., 1992) pioneering work acted as a catalyst for this development, but various formidable Business Ethics scholars have followed in his wake (see e.g., Alzola et al., 2020; Beadle & Moore, 2018; Koehn, 1995; Sison et al., 2018). Many of these scholars have given pride of place to *phronesis* in their virtue ethical theorizing, and that may be part of the explanation for the general appeal of such theorizing. This explanation would tie in, among other things, with a perception of escalating corporate scandals and organizational failures, culminating in the 2007–2008 financial crisis: events that have undermined beliefs both in scientific (e.g., Taylorite[2]) managerial structures and the power of formal rules and codes of conduct (be those deontological or modelled on Aristotle's skills of *techné* and *deinotes*) to guide professional behaviour. This perception has gone hand in hand with a growing concern—that we identified at the beginning of this book—among professionals about the loss of the ideal of professional expertise and its replacement with instrumentalist, managerialist orthodoxies that pander to a mistaken confidence in purported scientific certainties (Sellman, 2012), supplanting personal responsibility and contextual discernment with formalistic accountability and compliance. The concept of *phronesis* has thus been seen to fill a void in increasingly impoverished conceptualizations of the nature of professional work; recall Chapter 7 that focused mostly on the medical field.

As a case in point, various reports of ethical perceptions within UK professions have indicated a disillusionment with the content of Professional Ethics classes. Business students, for instance, complain about the content of Business Ethics classes being either too abstract (about lofty principles such as corporate social responsibility) or too mundane (just about compliance) with insufficient attention being paid to the moral crucible where business people encounter dilemmatic situations in dealings with customers, and how to navigate such situations through the use of personal character virtues, orchestrated by practical wisdom (Huo & Kristjánsson, 2018). This is a crucial point, because from the perspective of Aristotelian character education, *phronesis* development is the main goal of such education in early adulthood and must form the linchpin of all Business Ethics education.[3]

---

[2] The original Taylorite was Frederick Winslow Taylor who published important writings at the beginning of the twentieth century about scientific management methods.
[3] Notice that even social intuitionists like Jonathan Haidt might agree with the Aristotelian point about the fundamental role of *phronesis* cultivation in Business Ethics education. They would not, however, see the role of *phronesis* as that of helping students make good decisions, either individually or collectively (as those have already been made by nondeliberative intuitive thrusts from the emotional system), but rather

As we saw in the preceding chapter, in the *Politics* Aristotle extends his discussion to that of *phronetic* rulers grappling with civic virtues at the state level. Given that the 'states' Aristotle studied were city-states, most (apart from Athens and a few others) with less than 1000 citizens, those resembled more modern medium-sized companies or professional institutions, such as hospitals and universities, than contemporary mega-states. Indeed, one of the fathers of virtue-based Business Ethics, Bob Solomon (1992), very fittingly compared the city-states of ancient Greece to modern firms.[4] As corporate and professional decision-making currently takes place to a large extent at the collective rather than the individual level—through boards of directors or teams of professionals—Aristotle's reflections on collective *phronesis* seem at least as relevant to contemporary contexts as his account of individual *phronesis*. The two fundamental questions to be pondered in the following are, therefore, about (1) how *phronesis* (ideally) operates at the collective level and (2) how it can be enhanced at that level.

A focus on truly collective *phronesis*

Before delving into Aristotle's texts, some additional clarifications are needed about links that can—or cannot—be forged with contemporary literatures. First, what we are interested in here is collective *phronesis qua* joint *phronetic* decision-making. Conroy et al. (2021) use the term 'collective *phronesis*' profusely to describe the *aggregated phronesis* of a group of professionals across a series of different moral virtues they infuse with *phronesis* by finding their respective 'golden means'. Aggregated individual *phronesis* is an interesting topic but remains outside of the current purview which is about more than just the sum of parts. In contrast to aggregate *phronesis*, collective *phronesis* is about what Landemore (2012, p. 8) characterizes as 'an emergent phenomenon', not just 'the amplification of individual wisdom'. That is, we are

---

in helping them justify those decisions retrospectively. The salience of *phronesis* thus becomes social rather than epistemological or moral. See further in Sperber and Mercier (2012).

[4] Telling against this comparison are the frequent contrasts Aristotle draws between merely banausic and commercial enterprises versus the more elevated goals of the state (as a virtue-preserving and virtue-enhancing entity). However, in recent years more and more firms are incorporating virtue-relevant ESG goals into their mission statements, such as those of ethical responsibility and sustainability. This is why, in Section 9.4 below, we draw on the example of students who plan to establish an ethically responsible business venture. There is thus a case for arguing that Solomon's analogy is even more relevant today than it was in 1992.

exploring collective *phronesis* as a distinct level of decision-making, separate from the one than individual *phronesis* affords.

Second, Ames et al. (2020) draw a salient distinction between *phronetic* decisions in terms of 'amplitude': individual, group/organizational, and macro/societal. 'Amplitude' in this context can refer to the level at which decisions are taken, the set of people affected by the decision, whether the decision is jointly made or not, and then by whom. Since these four senses are not kept distinct by the authors, they miss the chance to address collective *phronesis* in the specific sense that we, the authors, are giving to it in this chapter. Hence, we do not count this review paper as an exception to the rule of failing to carve out a unique account of collective *phronesis* in the Business Ethics literature.

Third, especially for an author as interested in developmental issues as Aristotle was, there is a thin line between (a) truly joint *phronetic* decision-making and (b) individual *phronetic* decision-making, assisted by—or executed in collaboration with—a close friend or a mentor. Although it is, strictly speaking, only (a) that is on the current agenda, we cannot avoid saying something about (b) also at the beginning of Section 9.2.

Related literature

Rather than tarring the whole of the Professional Ethics literature with the same brush, it must be mentioned here that collective *phronesis*, in the true Aristotelian sense, has been explored in a few places before. For example, Schwarz and Lappalainen (2020) helpfully discuss joint decision-making in the context of Police Ethics and Police Ethics education, illustrating this with the way in which police partners control riots. Within the Business literature, the most direct exploration of collective *phronesis* has probably been through the work of the Japanese Business scholar Ikujiro Nonaka (e.g., Nonaka et al., 2008) on collaborative knowledge-creation within companies (see also, e.g., Scalzo & Fariñas, 2018). It is understandable that special attention is being paid to synergic features of *phronesis* in Asian cultures, already steeped in the idea of an interdependent self-concept (Markus & Kitayama, 1991). In any case, we will return to some of Nonaka's insights, especially about the corporate context or space required to facilitate collective *phronesis*, in Section 9.5.

Lurking outside the borders of the fairly narrowly circumscribed literature mentioned already lies a huge terrain of research within Business, Economics, and broader decision-theory upon which the concept of collective *phronesis* could be brought to bear. We only have space to mention some examples in passing here, but we will be returning to some of them in Section 9.5. The most obvious point of contact would be with the 'wisdom of crowds': an ideal harking back all the way to Galton (1907) but revived with considerable force, and given empirical backing, in Surowiecki's (2004) bestseller. Surowiecki makes a distinction between three senses of the term 'wisdom of crowds', which he refers to as *cognition, coordination*, and *cooperation*. The first two forms have to do with nondeliberative forms of collective wisdom: the ability of crowds to make better predictions about matters of fact, such as the weight of a fat ox or the true worth of a stock, than even expert individuals (through the so-called miracle of aggregation), and the capacity of people to coordinate their behaviours spontaneously (e.g., passing effortlessly through a busy railway station) to secure better outcomes than any intelligent external controller would. We could call those 'thin' wisdom procedures. 'Thicker' procedures involve deliberative collaboration between individuals, thus bringing the wisdom of crowds into the fold of Aristotelian *phronesis*. Surowiecki, however, spends less time exemplifying those processes in his book.

Even further afield lies a lively research field on Symbiotic or Collective Intelligence. (e.g., MIT runs a well-known 'Center for Collective Intelligence'). However, this discursive field is almost entirely confined to what Aristotle would call 'cleverness' (*deinotes*) and can thus be ignored with impunity here. Closer to present concerns is the field of 'Organizational Wisdom' (e.g., Rooney, 2013). However, that concept is considerably wider than 'collective *phronesis*', incorporating both deliberative and nondeliberative processes. Finally, at the highest level of philosophical abstraction, the concept of collective *phronesis* is theoretically parasitic on the very possibility of 'collective agency': a phenomenon studied within both standard Analytic Philosophy and Continental Phenomenology (Schwarz & Lappalainen, 2020).

What stands out at the end of this first section is that the concept of collective *phronesis* in Aristotelian Virtue Ethics potentially cuts across and ties together a motley array of theories and research standpoints both within and outside of Professional Ethics and the standard Business Ethics literature. While the following discussion will, by necessity, be selective and focus mainly on lessons to be learned from Aristotle himself, it is worth bearing in mind that any such lessons could potentially have repercussions that extend far beyond standard Business Ethics or even general ethical theorizing, more broadly construed.

9.2 What Is Aristotle's Take on Collective *Phronesis*?

The title of this section was deliberately framed to avoid indicating that it would summarize Aristotle's own *words* about collective *phronesis* because he never uses this term. An account of Aristotle's own *take* will thus have to be pieced together obliquely from various places in his corpus, especially the *Politics*. However, it is instructive to begin with his account of friendship from the *Nicomachean Ethics*, as that is the place where he is most explicit about interdependent character development.

Aristotelian *philia* (friendship) as a starting point

Aristotle famously makes a qualitative distinction between three kinds of friendship, but only the most 'complete' one need concern us presently: 'character friendship' (see further in Fowers & Anderson, 2018; Kristjánsson, 2022b). The most 'perfect' form of character friendships is enacted between fully and equally developed *phronimoi* who—while not having much left to learn from one another—mutually acknowledge, affirm, and enjoy each other's display of virtuous character.[5] For present purposes, however, the less 'perfect' subforms of character friendship are more relevant: namely, where the friends are either not equal in virtue or both aspiring, rather than fully developed, *phronimoi*. In the context of Business Ethics education, we can envisage a character friendship between a student and an experienced tutor as her moral exemplar, or between two students who aspire to ethical business practices but are still lacking in some of the relevant virtues and try to help each other progress characterologically.

Aristotle makes it abundantly clear that the *raison d'être* of such 'complete' but 'imperfect' friendships is *educational*. Indeed, his account of the educational value of character friendships may go some distance towards solving the puzzle of why he says so little about the methods of *phronesis* development in the sections of *phronesis* itself: namely, that he reserved it for his friendship theory. Character friends become 'better from their activities and their mutual correction' as 'each moulds the other', and through this mutual moulding

---

[5] There is an intriguing analogy drawn by Talbot Brewer (2021) between friendship and *phronesis* as 'dialectical activities', marked by their 'self-unveiling character' (p. 165). In our APM, the process of *phronesis* is already dialectical in virtue of the interactions of the four components. However, the notion of collective *phronesis* adds a self–other dialectic to the picture.

they become 'more capable of understanding and acting' (Aristotle, 1985, pp. 266 and 208 [1172a11–14 and 1155a15–16]). Friendship of this kind educates by being, in various ways, knowledge-enhancing, virtue-enhancing, and life-enhancing, through friends acting as each other's procreators on the trajectory towards full *phronesis* and helping each other make wise choices. Aristotle offers various helpful distinctions along the way, such as that of learning from an equal but not fully developed friend as a *soulmate*, and from a superior friend as a *mentor*, versus learning from a more distant (heroic) nonfriend as a *role model* (Kristjánsson, 2022b, chap. 5).

These lessons are highly relevant for modern Business Ethics education because, when probed about how such education could be improved and made more character-relevant, Business students, Business educators, and experienced business professionals in the UK agreed that a crucial step would be to bring more positive business role models into lecture rooms and to enlist tutors as character mentors. The role of equal (peer) character friends was not mentioned, however (Huo & Kristjánsson, 2018).[6] In response to the possible objection that Aristotle himself confines his specification of (even budding) character friendships to a small number of well brought-up people, and that most 'friendships' in the business world would be what he called 'friendships for utility', available to more agents, it must be pointed out that Aristotle (1985) also made a qualitative distinction between two subtypes of utility friendship where one type 'would seem to depend on character, and the other on rules', with the latter being confined to 'mercenary'-type associations, whereas the former is 'more generous' (pp. 233–4 [1162b23–7]). That former type includes the relationships that Aristotle notes often form between 'fellow-voyagers and fellow-soldiers' (p. 224 [1159b27–8]), and he would presumably have wanted to say the same about prospective business partners also.

From friendship to collective *phronesis*

We revisit briefly some of the 'methods' that learning from friends appear to involve, according to Aristotle, in Section 9.5. However, two observations are in order at the present juncture. The first is that, notwithstanding its historical and philosophical salience, Aristotle's friendship theory leaves many questions unanswered. For example, the frequent allusions to the (character)

---

[6] For reasons that remain unclear, the focus in most current forms of Aristotle-inspired character education (be it for school students or aspiring professionals) is on the emulation of superior moral exemplars rather than the role of peer character friendships (Hoyos-Valdés, 2018).

friend as 'another self' (1985, p. 246 [1166a30–3]; cf. pp. 260 and 265 [1170b6–7; 1172a32–4]) are problematic. It is not entirely clear whether Aristotle is (a) speaking *metaphorically*, (b) making a *moral* point about the essential substantive sharing of affection and purpose, and how what is in your best interest is also in your friend's best interest, and vice versa, or (c) making an *ontological* point about the inherently relational nature of selfhood. If (c) is what he means, that would obviously carry significant ramifications for the very idea of joint decision-making and its ideal *qua* collective *phronesis*.

Second, what Aristotle says about the educational value of friendships for developing good character and judgement falls short of being an account of the development of collective *phronesis*. To return to the example of the two Business Ethics students, Aristotle's theory explains how they can contribute to each other's individual *phronetic* development and prepare them for lives as ethically minded and responsible business professionals. However, he does not address the question of how developmental friendship processes can prepare them for truly joint decision-making. For example, if they decide to open a small business together, how could they run it fully collaboratively through equal, consensual managerial procedures? Relatedly, to what degree and in what ways would such procedures add value to the friends' merely aggregated individual *phronetic* capacities?

Insights on collective *phronesis* from the *Politics*

To elicit more explicit (if not always fully transparent) Aristotelian views about the value of collective *phronesis*, we need to turn to his *Politics*.[7] We ask readers, throughout the remainder of this section and the following interpretive Section 9.3, to remain mindful of Solomon's (1992) tip that because of the smallness and unique nature of the political entities Aristotle was talking about (Greek city-states), his theory of political governance may carry more immediate implications for the (ethical) running of small business firms or institutions than modern nation states (see also Sison, 2011).

It is worth reproducing here the much-cited and somewhat enigmatic passage by Aristotle in full about what is typically referred to as his 'argument about the wisdom of the multitude', but what Horn (2016) calls 'the accumulation argument':

---

[7] For the best overall exegesis of Aristotle's *Politics*, see Kraut (2002), of which we made ample use in Chapter 8.

For it is possible that the many, though not individually [virtuous],[8] yet when they come together may be better, not individually but collectively, than those who are so, just as public dinners to which many contribute are better than those supplied at one man's cost; for where there are many, each individual, it may be argued, has some portion of virtue and [*phronesis*], and when they have come together, just as the multitude becomes a single man with many feet and many hands and many senses, so also it becomes one personality as regards [character and thought] (Aristotle, 1944, pp. 221-2 [1281b1-8], minor amendments made to the translation).

At a later juncture, Aristotle (1944, p. 257 [1286a24–37]) complements this passage with an observation about the many being less corruptible than the few and also less likely to fall prey to an overbearing passion like anger. Notice that Aristotle is here going well beyond the message derived from his educational claims about character friendships and even the message from his passages on individual *phronesis* in the *Nicomachean Ethics*, where he observes that 'we enlist partners in deliberation on large issues when we distrust our own ability to discern [the right answer]' (Aristotle, 1985, p. 62 [1112b10–11]). The emphasis has now moved from enlisting help from others, to (learn how to) choose wisely, towards the synergic effect of joint *phronetic* decision-making.

Somewhat disappointingly, Aristotle backs up those accumulation claims (about the multitude being both ethically and intellectually stronger than the individual[9]) simply with a number of Socratic sounding analogies from daily life, rather than enlisting, as he usually does, the views of the many and the wise, and critiquing those. His analogies relate to (a) many cooks improving rather than spoiling the broth, (b) the many adding extra 'limbs' to the individual, (c) the many being better at judging poetry and music than a single critic, (d) great quantities of water being less easily polluted than a small amount, and (e) the 'users' of a product (here governance) being better judges of it than the 'makers'. Bobonich (2015) has subjected those analogies to critical scrutiny, both in themselves and as applied to the specific context of Athenian living and found them all wanting. That is, none of them, either individually or collectively, comes anywhere close to making a sound case for the collective wisdom of the multitude in terms of governance, especially

---

[8] It must be assumed that Aristotle is here referring to fully *phronesis*-guided virtue.
[9] Aristotle seems to be saying that the accumulation of individual capacities can boost the overall stock of both moral and intellectual (*phronetic*) virtue, beyond the mere aggregation of perspectives (e.g., Cammack, 2013).

the way in which the accumulation in question is meant to amplify the multitude's strengths only, but not their many deficiencies also. To move the discussion forward, we need to set the accumulation argument in the context of the overall theoretical argument that Aristotle is making in the *Politics*, about civic virtue and the specific *phronesis* of rulers/managers, rather than just relying on folksy analogies.

9.3 Interpreting the Accumulation Argument for Collective *Phronesis*

Interpreting 'the accumulation argument' correctly, especially in terms of eliciting its implications for Business Ethics and business practice, is a tall order, not only because the interpretative task has hitherto mostly been confined to a small group of Aristotelian scholars, but also because their interpretations have, in our view, typically highlighted very questionable aspects of the argument—namely, its relevance for ancient and modern *democratic theory*—rather than its more general implications for the collective *phronesis* of 'rulers', or what we could call 'collective managerial *phronesis*'.[10]

The wisdom of crowds

Two of the best-known Economics and Political Science scholars working on the wisdom of crowds, Hong and Page (2012), begin their study by claiming that in 'describing *the benefits of democracy*, Aristotle observed that when individuals see distinct parts of the whole, the collective appraisal can surpass that of individuals' (p. 56; italics added). These two are obviously not philosophers. However, philosophers have also perpetuated this received wisdom. For example, Waldron (2005), in a much-cited paper identifying a 'doctrine of the wisdom of the multitude' in Aristotle, pushes the concept in a radically democratic direction. This may seem decidedly odd at first sight since Aristotle (1944) was no friend of democracy, famously consigning it—as a seedbed of demagoguery—to one of the perverted forms of government. In response, prodemocracy scholars may argue that Aristotle did defend a more benign form of government, called *polity*, which bears some of the hallmarks of modern democracies although it was reserved for the rule of the middle

---

[10] For a typology of general managerial *phronesis* and an overview of the relevant literature, see Steyn and Sewchurran (2021).

class only, leaving out the poorest and least educated. However, as argued below, we doubt that the multitude (*plethos*) that Aristotle wants to franchise with his accumulation argument even covers all the middle class.

What seems to be forgotten in most of the prodemocracy interpretations is that part of the original passage which talks about the advantage of pooling the resources of those who have 'some portion of virtue and *phronesis*'. Given that Aristotle believed only a fraction of people ever develop any sort of *phronesis*, the accumulation argument may be much more circumscribed and elitist (albeit not necessarily in a negative sense) than it is often made out to be. In the context of the *Politics*, which is a treatise about the best governance/management of a very small state and who are fit to act as its rulers, we read the accumulation argument as simply stating that it is beneficial for such an entity to have relatively many people, who are already developing or mature *phronimoi*, coming together to manage it (in default of the earlier-mentioned 'god-among-men' single ruler who does not exist in the real world). The reason for this is that even the best of real-life *phronimoi* are fallible, and in adding together their intellectual and experiential resources, the benefits of collective *phronesis* (argued for through Aristotle's various analogies) are activated. In other words, we consider the accumulation argument to be exclusively about the pros of collective *phronesis* for good management, not about the pros of deliberative democratic practices, more broadly speaking.[11]

To substantiate our interpretation, let us remember that Aristotle does not mince his words about the *nonphronetic* masses. Having 'no taste' for the fine and truly pleasant, they have 'no notion' of what it is and find 'disorderly living' pleasanter than 'sober living' (Aristotle, 1985, p. 292 [1179b10]; 1944, p. [1319b30–3]). It would be very far-fetched to believe that Aristotle wanted to give this large multitude any seat at the high table, deliberating about the running of the city. That would, by his lights, not constitute an exercise in collective *phronesis* but rather in collective ignorance (cf. Tsouni, 2019),[12] just as if we allowed the person with no medical knowledge to independently evaluate the specialized work of physicians (Aristotle, 1944, pp. 226–7 [1282a1–10]).

---

[11] As Garsten (2013, p. 336) correctly reminds us, the modern assumption that the value of deliberation is somehow grounded in, and confined to, democratic practices would have been alien to Aristotle. We do not oppose the application of collective *phronesis* to democratic practices in principle. We simply see the application of collective wisdom to business management as more direct and simpler, making business a good place to start.

[12] In the words of Thomas Carlyle (cited in Surowiecki, 2004, p. xvi), 'I do not believe in the collective wisdom of individual ignorance.'

Civic virtue and *phronesis* in the *Politics*

When it comes to the *Politics*, where the focus turns from moral to civic virtue, Aristotle relinquishes the strict demands that virtue needs to be *phronesis*-guided to count as true virtue and enjoyable for the person actualizing it, as we explained in Chapter 8. For 'all ought to possess the goodness [virtue] of a good citizen' (Aristotle, 1944, p. 189 [1277a2–4])—albeit at a fairly low level. At this low level, he is for the most part referring to civic virtue *qua* mere law-abidingness, and there it suffices that the agent forces herself to act civically in following the law. Aristotle's aversion to conflict shines through in his assumption that even the worst of perverted constitutions is marginally better than no constitution—namely anarchy—and hence 'the many' (namely all citizens) need to be able at least to approve of decisions enshrined in law by acting in accordance with them. This is not the same, however, as playing a constitutive part in the actual deliberative process of state governance, as we have been explaining.

For present purposes, it is more important to consider higher forms of civic virtue, confined to rulers, with which Aristotle is more concerned and to which his accumulation argument is evidently tied. Aristotle does not believe any reasonable person can think it acceptable that the proper ruling of a state be in the hands of anyone except the *phronimoi*, and he would almost certainly have said the same about the management of modern-day business companies, at least those larger than small family-based ones. Instead of being *less* demanding than the criteria for moral virtue, the conditions of civic virtue at this managerial level become *more* demanding. In their decision-making, the rulers need to take into account what is good not only for themselves but for all citizens (Aristotle, 1985, p. 154 [1140b7–11]). This means that *phronesis* at the management level will have a wider scope than *phronesis* at the level of everyday affairs.[13]

This brings us back to the original question of who comprises the multitude under discussion in the accumulation argument. We hope it is now clearer than before that the multitude Aristotle has in mind, as potential collaborators in ruling, is a fairly small 'multitude', consisting solely of sufficiently educated people (Tsouni, 2019), intellectually and morally: namely, people who at least have some modicum of *phronesis* to contribute to the governance process. Two of the philosophers involved in Aristotelian exegesis, Bobonich (2015) and Irrera (2010), have suggested something of an intermediary position,

---

[13] We refer readers back to Chapter 8 for a fuller argument.

according to which *nonphronimoi* among the public may contribute to management processes because they may be privy to unique information and experiences that even all the relevant *phronimoi* lack, hence having important 'parts' of virtue and *phronesis* to add to the mix even if they lack the overall *phronetic* capacities. We do not think this argument works, at least not in the context of fleshing out the accumulation argument. To be sure, various citizens may be called to the table for guidance and information before collective decisions are taken, just as business managers may call in workers from the floor for consultation before agreeing on a new company policy. However, this does not thereby mean they have 'parts' of *phronesis* to contribute to the management process.[14] *Phronesis* does, according to Aristotle, have numerous components (see our Aristotelian *phronesis* model (APM)), but brute information about facts and brute experiences are not such components; *phronesis* is much more subtle and sophisticated than that. The basic problem that Aristotle is trying to solve in the *Politics* is how the quality of state governance can be made to approximate as far as possible to the quality of the utopian god-among-men ruler. His answer is that this is best done by collating the expertise of many *phronimoi*, at least minimally capable of ruling, because many wise heads are normally better than one, in a nonutopian world.

What explains, then, the staying power of the interpretation that Aristotle is, in his *Politics*, making an argument in favour of democratic deliberation and participation?[15] Some of it may simply be wishful thinking; it would have been nice if Aristotle had been a democrat! Some of it may be caused by inattention to modern democratic assumptions that were foreign to Aristotle, such that of the moral equality of all human beings, the idea of human rights, and the belief that individuals are themselves the best judges of their own interests. Finally, some of it may be derived from positive evaluations

---

[14] Consider, as a problematic intermediate example, the case of business managers calling in a not very *phronetic* accountant for consultation before making an important business decision. Does it really matter whether the 'part' contributed by the accountant can be defined as a component of *phronesis* or not? Well it does, for conceptual purposes at least, if we understand Aristotle's argument to be (as we argue) about the advantages of joint decision-making. Simply providing helpful information to a decision-making process is not the same as being actively involved in the process.

[15] None of what we have said above should be interpreted to mean that we reject the historic role that Aristotle has been seen to play in the development of the ideals of deliberative democracy: the school of thought in political theory that claims that political decisions should be the product of fair and reasonable discussion and debate among citizens. We are particularly referring here to work by Waldron (2005) and Schwartzberg (2016). The ideas of a thinker such as Aristotle may help develop a given discourse although they were not originally intended for that purpose. The point we have been making is simply that Aristotle's 'accumulation argument' was originally about what we have called the advantages of 'collective *phronesis*' rather than what would normally be called deliberative democracy on a modern understanding. Yet the general point he makes about the need to draw on as many sources of experience as possible, before making a decision, clearly allows for various extensions.

of various Aristotelian political ideas, many of which are uncharacteristically (for his time) egalitarian, state-interventionist, and, to use Nussbaum's provocative (1990) characterization, 'Scandinavian'. His strict demands for state-directed-and-funded public education were, for example, revolutionary in ancient Greece. Moderns may simply find it difficult to fathom that a person who was so egalitarian in one way could be so elitist in another.

Once we have got the prodemocracy reading of the *Politics* out of the way and direct our attention to the real core of the work, which is about how to rule a small unit of management (the city-state) in an ethically informed and *phronesis*-guided way by exploiting the advantages of collective *phronesis*, we realize that the *Politics* should more directly and easily be read and made use of by business ethicists and business managers than by democratic political theorists.

9.4 The Components of Collective Managerial *Phronesis*

What are the psycho-moral processes involved in Aristotelian collective managerial *phronesis*, as specified in the previous section? That is by no means an easy question, for Aristotle says next to nothing about it in the *Politics*. The only thing we can reasonably do is to revisit his extensive account of the functions of the different *phronesis* components in the *Nicomachean Ethics* and then offer speculative hypotheses about how the *intra-psychic* processes described for individual *phronesis* could be extended towards collective *inter-psychic* ones. Before embarking on that task, a few clarificatory remarks are in order.

Aristotle sometimes speaks in the *Nicomachean Ethics* as if virtue and *phronesis* are an all-or-nothing affair, and either one possesses the whole set—lock, stock, and barrel—or one has none of it. We rejected that unity thesis in Chapter 2. However, Aristotle also seems to assume that agents on a developmental trajectory towards *phronetic* virtue can already possess one portion of *phronesis* (*morion phroneseos*) but not others (e.g., Aristotle, 1985, p. 270 [1173a18–22]; 1944, pp. 223 and 533 [1281b4–5;1323a27–30]). The power of speech (*logos*) then allows us, in principle at least, to bring these virtue portions into a relationship with different portions from another individual and make them coalesce into a new broader whole (e.g., Garsten, 2013, p. 343). It is important to understand the 'portions' (*morion*) of *phronesis* not as mere fragments or crumbs, but rather as discrete psychological functions, where one ruler/manager can be stronger on one function but another ruler/manager stronger on another.[16] The natural place to look for those 'portions' is in the detailed account of individual *phronesis* from the *Nicomachean Ethics*, from which our APM, set out in Chapter 2, was derived.[17]

Let us now try to rhapsodize about how the four functions from the APM might operate and be enriched at the collective level.[18] Consider a group of recent Business graduates who, as fellow students and friends, decide to open an ethically responsible company together upon completion of their studies. As Business Ethics enthusiasts, and being virtue-ethically oriented, these friends and now business colleagues have been impressed by Aristotle's ideal of collective *phronesis* and want to enact it at the managerial level in running their company. All decisions will be taken on a collective basis and in line with the functions of *phronetic* decision-making. How could this work out and add incremental value in practice?

Blueprint component

Let us begin this time with the function of the *blueprint* component. Bear in mind that what Aristotle was after here is not an individual's idiosyncratic 'authentic', 'autonomous' sense of 'personal purpose', as such a conceptualization did not originate until the Enlightenment (although his insistence on the individualization of virtue might seem to suggest an embryonic form of those ideals). Rather, what is at stake is the overarching vision of the purpose (*telos*) of human life in general and a person's moral identity as it relates that purpose to her conception of flourishing (*eudaimonia*). The internal motivation for *phronetic* decision-making grows out of such deliberated desires (Aristotle, 1985, p. 64 [1113a12]), complementing the motivation from external sources: namely, the conative aspects of the specific moral and civic virtues that *phronesis* synthesizes.[19] Given that our business entrepreneurs are all virtue-ethically minded, they will most likely share a general common vision of flourishing, as well as the ethically responsible goals of their company. However, through a process of presenting their vision to one another,

---

[16] For a radical reminder of the value of cognitive diversity for *phronetic* decision-making, consider the argument by Jefferson and Sifferd (2022) that a person on the autistic spectrum may add an important ingredient to the decision-making processes favoured by 'neurotypicals'.

[17] Interestingly, our model bears a striking resemblance to the so-called Level of Connection in a model worked out independently (and not explicitly indebted to Aristotle) for Business education programmes by Intezari and Pauleen (2013).

[18] Steyn and Sewchurran (2021) helpfully elicit some relevant subcomponents/subfunctions (or what they call 'modes' and 'characteristics') of managerial *phronesis*.

[19] We are here summarizing very briefly the argument that we made in Chapter 2.

reflecting upon it and modifying it in light of the conclusions of their dialogue, they have a chance to come up with a blueprint that is more coherent and complete, and less easily corruptible, than any single person's vision.

Constitutive component

Next, we turn to the *constitutive* function (aka moral sensitivity). It is well known that people's perceptions of the same event differ considerably. One of the colleagues may notice a moral danger or a moral opportunity lurking in one of the business strategies that the group have come up with, while this has escaped the notice of others. This function of *phronesis* is perhaps the one most obviously augmentable through collective practice.

Emotional regulative component

The benefits of collective work on the *emotional regulation* function are more controversial. Aristotle's (1944, p. 257 [1286a31–6]) empirical observation that it is difficult for a whole group to be roused by a wayward emotion at the same time is not exactly in line with contemporary social psychological research about the effects of infectious mob psychology (cf. Cammack, 2013, p. 187). However, it is easy to understand where Aristotle is coming from if we remind ourselves that the collective in question includes people who are at least budding *phronimoi*. If one of the business partners becomes overly upset by a setback, or angry about a rebuff from a potential buyer, some of the other members of the group are likely to be less emotionally affected and thus able to calm her down. Similarly, if one of them loses courage and confidence in the venture, the rest may be able to help her renew and solidify her commitment to the endeavour.

Adjudicative component

Finally, the *adjudicative* function is the crucible through which potentially conflicting considerations are reconciled and channelled into ethically responsible action. As Garsten (2013, pp. 329–30) explains well, Aristotle has a strong view on this. He not only believes that collective *phronesis* can help coordinate independent deliberations from different agents, but rather that it can bring those deliberations 'into relation with one another in a manner that yields actions attributable to the whole of which each of them is a part'. For example, it is easy to imagine that, in collective decision-making, one or the collaborators recognizes the need for one virtue, and another recognizes the necessity of another virtue. The group could then deliberate together about how to harmonize or prioritize the two in a way that would be more fluid and complete than is possible for an individual *phronimos*. We must remember here that Aristotle's conception of selfhood was arguably more interdependent than the one we are used to in contemporary Western cultures (Markus & Kitayama, 1991)—witness for example Aristotle's earlier-cited remarks about the character friend as 'another self'.[20]

Some of the above musings about the synergies of collective managerial *phronesis* may sound like little more than platitudes about the working of human collaboration in general, probably better accounted for by more sophisticated models from modern Moral Psychology (e.g., Akrivou & Scalzo, 2020) or some more fancy academic labels, such as 'intersubjective co-creativity'. While that may be true, we must be mindful of the uniqueness of the Aristotelian conception of collective *phronesis*, in that its system of mutual checks and balances aims not so much at favourable collaborative outcomes—although those matter also—as for the ethical betterment of the agents involved. *Phronesis* may be an intellectual virtue, but it is inseparably tied to the moral virtues and the overall aspiration to (help each other) become better persons. As Aristotle (1944, p. 547 [1325a22–3]) himself puts it, *eupraxia* (doing well, inter alia as a result of *phronesis*) and *eudaimonia* are in the end one and the same thing.

9.5 Some Practical Business Applications

This chapter has so far proceeded at a fairly high level of abstraction, perhaps higher than Aristotle himself would have liked. After all, the purpose of an inquiry into virtue theory, such as this one, is ultimately 'not to know what virtue is, but to become good' (Aristotle, 1985, p. 35 [1103b27–9])—or to help others become good. It behoves us, therefore, to suggest some more practical applications for Business Ethics education and practice.

---

[20] It may well be that Confucian forms of virtue ethics come closer to Aristotle's self-concept than most modern Western forms, even so-called neo-Aristotelian ones (cf. Alzola et al., 2020; Huo & Kristjánsson, 2020).

Business Ethics education

The primary goal of Aristotle's ethical and political treatises is educational.[21] At the early adulthood level—where most Business Ethics students are situated—the fundamental virtue to be taught is *phronesis*, as one will expect the students to have been more or less habituated into the moral virtues already, and if they have not, there is not much that can be done in a single university course to rectify that anyway. Teaching *phronesis* does not just mean teaching *about phronesis* but rather providing students with practical opportunities to hone it through emulation and guided practice. This is why Aristotle would have been saddened by the already-cited finding that Business students, at least in the UK, do not consider themselves to have had the opportunity to develop *phronesis* in their studies, not even within discrete Business Ethics classes (Huo & Kristjánsson, 2018).

None of this will come as a surprise to virtue-ethically minded Business Ethics educators (e.g., Steyn & Sewchurran, 2021). What we have argued in this chapter and the preceding one, however, is that to do full justice to Aristotle's account of *phronesis*, it is not enough to study the *Nicomachean Ethics* on moral and intellectual virtues. We also need to pay attention to the account of collective managerial *phronesis* in the *Politics*, and how that links to the actualization of civic virtues (and through those to the 'common good'), especially for those who plan to run organizational entities, be it a city or a business. The problem is that Aristotle does not offer any new methods of instruction in the *Politics* for the cultivation of collective *phronesis* beyond those already adumbrated in his other works for virtue development more generally.[22] As suggested by Business students themselves (Huo & Kristjánsson, 2018), the role of moral exemplars will be invaluable, but in order to facilitate the positive impact of those role models on students, in terms of building up their collective *phronesis*, the exemplars must be brought into direct contact with the students and given a chance to interact with them constructively.

No less important for the development of collective *phronesis* would be the method of forming small teams of like-minded Business Ethics students—one could call them *phronesis* dyads or triads—and give them tasks that call for joint decision-making in the service of a higher ethical good. As Aristotle noted long before Dewey, 'learning by doing' is the fundamental method for

---

[21] We offer some educational suggestions specific to Business Ethics education below. A more general treatment of *phronesis* education awaits Chapter 11.

[22] A recent paper by Lawrence et al. (2021) describes methods to cultivate collective *phronetic* decision-making. However, disappointingly, for the *phronesis* part, they only draw on Aristotle's *Nicomachean Ethics*, not his more explicit inroads into this topic in his *Politics*.

moral education. Some guidance on how such student teams could operate can be gleaned from remarks Aristotle (1985, pp. 266 and 208 [1172a11–14 and 1155a15–16]) makes about the development of character friendships through the mutual 'moulding' of sensitivities. These arguably involve, in the first instance, the establishment of an *emotional connection* that is uniquely conducive to moral learning in terms of character improvement.

The pride of place that Aristotle gives to emotions as part of the good life is well known (Kristjánsson, 2018b). While he does not single out emotions that are specific to character friendships, some candidates readily suggest themselves. Trust is an emotionally imbued evaluation of others, and, in this context, the most important form of trust is *mutual trust*. 'Mutual trust' means not only that trust is bivalent, but that the individuals involved know that others trust them, that they know that their trust of others is recognized, and that this mutual trust is a vital shared value, one worthy of significant effort and protection. A moral learner can also place trust in an elevated role model, but in most cases such trust will not be mutual; the standard role model may not even be personally acquainted with the learner. Trust is essential in many non-friendship-based social relationships, such as in various complex market exchanges, but there it is grounded in quite different motivational and dispositional structures to friendship and manifests itself differently. The unique feature of mutual trust, which is grounded in psychological intimacy, soulmateship, and group membership, is that it steadies the mind, by providing what could be called existential security, and lowers psychological barriers of self-disclosure, self-receptivity, and risk-taking, some of which are inimical to any kind of moral learning.

We must not lose sight, however, of the difference between character friendship and collective *phronesis* that was already underlined: namely, that the former is typically about helping the friend to make informed decisions, whereas the latter is about facilitating the processes of truly joint decision-making. The friends may simply stare each other in the eye and give each other mental support (which is fine, as far as it goes), but partners in collective *phronesis* look forward, towards a shared moral vision, and try to achieve it collaboratively. Moreover, even if one wanted to exploit the empirical evidence on character friendship in the service of collective *phronesis*, very little of it unfortunately exists. The huge empirical mountain of literature on friendships notwithstanding (a lot of which is cited in the volume edited by Hojjat & Moyer, 2017), only a miniscule part of it deals with character friendships as a method of moral education (Kristjánsson, 2022b, chap. 5). That lacuna is obviously even more striking in the case of collective *phronesis* itself, as the concept is still not theoretically developed enough, let alone oven-ready for rigorous empirical scrutiny (yet see Schwarz & Lappalainen, 2020). So, for the time being, our best bet is to rely on the literature on *phronesis* development more generally, although that literature is also meagre, as we will see in Chapter 11.[23]

Business practice

Understandably, the construct of collective *phronesis* is not better developed for actual business practice than it is for Business (Ethics) education. One significant exception should be mentioned here, however, of a Business scholar who has made constructive use of this very concept in his theorizing: Ikujiro Nonaka (see, e.g., Nonaka et al., 2008). Best known for his work on the knowledge-creating firm, Nonaka draws on a number of Eastern and Western theoretical constructs, such as tacit learning, soft dialectical communication methods, and, most notably for present purposes, collective *phronesis*, which Nonaka seems to have derived through his own creative extension of Aristotle's concept from the *Nicomachean Ethics*, rather than gleaning it from its more specific context in the *Politics*. Nonaka's work is, in our view, a goldmine for Business scholars interested in further developing the concept of collective *phronesis*, especially in managerial contexts, and it means that they do not need to reinvent the wheel but can take Nonaka's writings as their starting point.

Particularly illuminating is Nonaka's setting of collective *phronesis* in the context of the Japanese concept of *ba*, which is ill-translatable into English but can be taken to refer to an ethos or a space in motion in which knowledge can be created (see further in Scalzo & Fariñas, 2018). While the ultimate goal is to create such space within every company, Nonaka sets the bar quite high by suggesting that, initially, companies need to create opportunities for their executives to cultivate character and integrity by interacting with scholars from the Humanities and Political Science to build up a humanist vision of the best goals of leadership. One may harbour doubts about the willingness of typical practically minded CEOs in the West to initiate such crossover discussions within their companies. Indeed, although we have already cited Solomon (1992) twice on similarities between ancient Greek city-states and the modern firm, someone might point out that, structural likeness aside,

---

[23] The best overview, in the context of *phronesis*-friendly Business education, is probably that by Grossmann (2021). Intezari and Pauleen (2013) also provide a helpful summary table of methods (p. 168).

the culture (ethos) in those city-states was radically different from today's corporate culture. That said, the corporate climate changes rapidly, and if a collective-*phronesis* forum, such as the one suggested by Nonaka, really produces results in terms of knowledge-creation that benefits firms, perhaps such forums will one day become standard business practice. Interestingly, Guiso et al. (2015) argue that corporate culture in the West may already be shifting in a more ethical and humanist direction, driven both by performance measures which show that such culture simply pays off and by the growing recognition that businesses must lead in many aspects of the common good, such as climate change.

In all events, Nonaka's focus on the necessary climate to foster collective *phronesis* within business companies leads us straight to discourses that are much better researched and evidenced that any applications of Aristotle's own repertoire. These are the discourses about team dynamics and ideal team composition. What we do know is that teams perform best when they are composed of individuals who are different in term of capacities (referred to as 'cognitive diversity') but still not too different so as to foster polarization (see, e.g., Surowiecki, 2004, chaps 2 and 8).[24] It is reasonable to suppose that these general findings will carry over into any study involving the creation of collective-*phronesis* forums or company teams.

Under the umbrella of organizational wisdom

We said earlier that collective *phronesis* could not be equated with organizational wisdom, as the latter construct is much broader, involving many nondeliberative variables. However, as we learn from Nonaka's work, the deliberative aspects of collective *phronesis* can only awaken and thrive within a climate that is conducive to innovation and knowledge-creation, and that climate includes certain mindsets of relevant actors that incorporate tacit knowledge which itself is not necessarily deliberative. To find a home somewhere, each academic pursuit requires the relevant pigeon-holing, and as 'organizational wisdom' is a better entrenched concept in the Business literature than 'collective *phronesis*', it might do the latter construct good to be studied under the umbrella of organizational wisdom, for example (Rooney, 2013).[25] This might also help connect research on collective *phronesis* to the even broader

---

[24] See Becker et al. (2017) for a more rigorous analysis of network dynamics, and Mannes et al. (2012) for some general findings about the psychology of crowd wisdom.

[25] See also Hays's (2013, p. 135) helpful model of dynamic organizational wisdom.

concept of *phronetic* Social Practice research (Flyvbjerg, 2001), which again represents a leaf taken straight out of Aristotle's book.

If we place collective *phronesis* in the context of 'organizational wisdom', there seems to be a short step from the current discourse about collective managerial *phronesis* to a discourse about 'wise organizations'. Apart from the general philosophical puzzle of ascribing agency to collectives, however, some important distinction must be made, which are somewhat overlooked in an otherwise informative study by Ardelt and Sharma (2021) about the link between wise organizations and employees' physical and subjective well-being. An organization can count as 'wise' because (a) its leaders possess individual *phronesis* and they happen, through good luck, to act in unison; (b) its leaders have got individual *phronesis*, and there are systematic processes and algorithms in place within the organization to coordinate the decisions made by those individuals; or (c) because the leaders engage in *phronetic* deliberative processes of joint decision-making, as the ones described above. Only (c) counts as true collective *phronesis*; yet the list of characteristics of 'wise organizations' compiled by Ardelt and Sharma (2021, Table 1) glosses over those distinctions.[26]

James Surowiecki (2004) remarks that the more important a decision is, 'the more important it is that it not be left in the hands of a single person' (p. 222). This chapter has perhaps constituted little more than a sustained reflection on that theme. However, we hope the main lesson learned is that there are underexploited resources within Aristotle's *Politics* enabling us to think this issue through more constructively than often happens to be the case in the current literature.

---

[26] We do not intend to dismiss cavalierly the whole academic field of Organizational Wisdom as underdeveloped conceptually. We consider it an important field of study, already with its own rich history. We are simply making the point here that (collective) *phronesis* tends not to be identified clearly within this field or distinguished from other senses of 'wisdom'.

10
Difficult Decisions and *Post-phronetic* Pain

10.1 What Is *Post-phronetic* Pain?

This chapter is about *post-phronetic* pain (PPP): namely, residual pain or psychological discomfort after a fully *phronetic* moral decision has been made. As David Carr (2009) correctly notes, the *phronetic* person is 'no more blessed than others with prescience', nor fully immune to factual errors and miscalculations (p. 41). Hence, an apparently sound moral decision may turn out to be faulty, and/or have grave, but unforeseeable, consequences, causing the agent pain. Here, however, we are not concerned with such cases of averse 'moral luck', but rather with ones where the decision was morally impeccable and had the intended consequences; yet the agent feels pain after making it. Another way of putting this is to say that ordinary *phronimoi* are fallible, imperfect humans who, in making the best decision possible, may have at least residual pain about the decision and its attendant actions.

How PPP may be unavoidable

To be more precise, we are thinking of moral decisions where the agent has identified and conceptualized the moral problem adequately, aligned her emotions with reason, considered the situation in the light of an understanding of what is conducive to flourishing, and arbitrated well between competing values and virtues. The image portrayed here is of the meta-virtue of *phronesis* having synthesized and harmonized various factors and considerations, in line with our model of *phronesis* (Aristotelian *phronesis* model, APM, from Chapter 2) as the locus and terminus of advanced ethical decision-making. Consider a physician who has to deliver a terrible diagnosis to a patient. There is no question about the correctness of the diagnosis or that the patient and her family must know about it. Any attempt to escape the pain of delivering the diagnosis will decrease the physician's humanity. Closer to home, another example would be to inform an eager, hard-working student that she had earned a lower grade than the one for which she had fervently hoped. This is an inherently painful situation and eliding that pain would undermine the teacher's character and have a destructive effect on the teacher–student relationship.

The orthodox Aristotelian non-PPP assumption

Nevertheless, from the perspective of orthodox Aristotelian theory, our title may seem to contain an oxymoron. The very *raison d'etre* of *phronesis* is that of a vehicle for psychological unity: an antidote to moral and emotional ambivalence. In contrast to the vicious, as well as to the incontinent and continent (the levels at which most people are at: Aristotle, 1985, p. 190 [1150a15]), and even to the successfully habituated but as yet *nonphronetically* virtuous, who all are variously awash with moral turmoil and emotional conflicts, many Aristotelians take Aristotle to be saying that *phronesis* signals either the permanent absence of such psychological disunity or at least its presently successful mitigation.[1]

The key to this understanding of *phronesis* lies in Aristotle's cognitive emotional theory (Kristjánsson, 2018b, chap. 1), a distinctive feature of which is the assumption that emotional reactions are essential ingredients in virtues. Hence, the role of *phronesis* is not only to direct actions but also to guide emotions: more specifically, as we argued in Chapter 2, to regulate them in accordance with reason—not in the sense of suppressing them but rather in harmonizing them with reason. Now, some of our morally justifiable emotions have 'negative valence': that is, they are painful. So, a virtuous reaction to a situation which the agent is incapable of altering may be painful; for example, compassion (*eleos*) as pain at somebody's undeserved bad fortune. However, if a discrete decision is called for, which involves a trade-off between that emotion and some other virtue or consideration, and the agent takes such a decision *phronetically* and is able to enact it, she should feel a sense of satisfaction at the decision without ambivalence or pain. That is because, *ex hypothesi*, the decision has brought the emotion into harmony with reason, issuing in a state of virtuous psychological unity. Any residual pain attached to the decision per se would, according to the view typically ascribed to Aristotle, be indicative

---

[1] As one of us has argued before, for example, those who have not found such an arrangement are 'likely to experience frequent, paralyzing conflicts, frustration, and a disorienting tendency to lurch back and forth' (Fowers, 2005, p. 63).

of a lack of virtuous unity and hence be symptomatic of something less than a *phronetic* decision having been made.

This is why our title appears oxymoronic, at least if understood as restrictively as it is meant to be here. One way scholars have argued against PPP is to suggest that a fully fledged *phronimos* can, of course, experience warranted pain about various remaining contextual facets of situation S, after taking a *phronetic* decision related to S, as well as about various actions required by that decision.[2] However, if she continues to experience pain about the *content* of the soundly made decision itself, then something is amiss with her *phronesis*.[3] In the context of true *phronesis*, as Aristotle apparently understands it, PPP therefore does not exist.

Aristotle himself nowhere formulates the non-PPP claim explicitly. It is commonly assumed in contemporary Virtue Ethics that this was his view given, on the one hand, the strict distinction he wants to draw between virtuous decisions (as fully harmonized with reason and psychologically unified) versus continent ones, and, on the other hand, his claim that virtue has 'its pleasure within itself' (Aristotle, 1985, pp. 20–1 [1099a15–23]). However, it could be argued that there is no ground for supposing that 'harmonizing with reason' carries an additional entailment that says that the decision is totally painless and to the agent's liking. Moreover, the unique pleasure of virtue does not entail that it is exclusively or smoothly pleasant. As often before, we refuse to be drawn into orthodox Aristotelian exegesis, and we eschew claims about what may have been Aristotle's own measured view.[4] It suffices for present purposes that the non-PPP claim is typically assumed in current Aristotelian virtue theory. We refer to it in what follows, therefore, simply as an 'Aristotelian assumption'.[5]

---

[2] This would be the standard explanation of Aristotle's claim that the virtue of bravery is 'painful' (1985, p. 78 [1117a33–b16]). It is not the content of the brave decision that is painful, because that decision aims at an 'end' that 'seems to be pleasant'. Yet the bravery calls for various actions that may be painful.

[3] Admittedly, the distinction between the *content* and *context* of a decision is not always crystal clear. Why should the circumstances of the decision and the foregone alternatives not register in the content of the decision? That would, at first sight, seem to fit well with Aristotle's own emphasis on the particularity of practical decisions. Aristotle's text does, indeed, make plenty of room for the possibility that, although the *phronimos* never regrets the fact that she made the decision that she did under the circumstances, she is and continues to be pained by having been faultlessly embroiled in circumstances that made it the case that the right decision was a difficult one. Nevertheless, we take it that there is a distinction to be made between this sort of pain and feeling (residual) pain over the content of the decision itself. Otherwise, all difficult decisions would, *ex hypothesi*, be painful, content-wise, because that is then what defines them as difficult in the first place. An important, if subtle, conceptual distinction would thus be lost.

[4] Nevertheless, below we canvass various bits and pieces of Aristotle's own texts, and none of them happens to contain an explicit accommodation of PPP or indicate that the standard picture of Aristotle should be retired.

[5] It might also be referred to as a 'thesis' or an 'implication' of the more explicit thesis of the psychological unity of the (fully) virtuous (to which we took exception in Chapter 2). However, the somewhat loose term 'assumption' serves our present purposes best here.

This assumption of full *post-phronetic* psychological unity and a lack of anguish appears to distinguish Aristotelian moral decision-making in many ways from its Kantian and utilitarian competitors. For Kantians, far from psychological unity signalling full moral maturity, the state of fully cooperating emotions following a moral decision compromises its moral worth. On that account, it is the Aristotelian continent agent who is the true paragon of morality, whereas the *phronimos* is simply a morally lightweight conformist. For utilitarians, the extreme demand of maximizing the overall happiness of all sentient beings keeps the moral agent constantly on her toes and prohibits any comforting psychological equilibrium. Each decision reached is, in a way, dissatisfying because one could always have done better, and this realization then becomes a spur to continued moral progress.[6]

Human imperfection and PPP

In comparison with these theories, the Aristotelian assumption of the nature of apt ethical decision-making sounds distinctively *therapeutic* (Carr, 2002b), tying in nicely (or suspiciously, depending on one's philosophical allegiances) with Aristotle's teleological view of psycho-social homeostasis. According to the teleological view, the parts of the soul are arranged such that it may adjust successfully to the various situations in which individuals will find themselves, *inter alia*, by adopting medial emotional states of character (Kristjánsson, 2007, chap. 4). The adoption of such medial emotional states seems to 'smooth over' emotional rough patches that could lead to PPP. But there are situations that cannot be resolved by adjusting to them, such as living in a manifestly unjust community or in a society ruled by tyranny.

It is no wonder, perhaps, that one of the most powerful paradigms of emotional cultivation as therapeutic in modernity, that of 'emotional intelligence', cites Aristotle as its progenitor and claims to be doing little more than repackaging his theory for contemporary consumption (Goleman, 1995). While emotion-intelligence theorists ignore the moral dimension of Aristotle's emotional homeostasis theory (with EQ being an amoral construct), thus undermining their own claims about an Aristotelian heritage (Kristjánsson, 2007, chap. 6), they do seem to have a point about a psychological-harmony thesis uniting them.

---

[6] There are obviously huge literatures on these particular aspects of Kantianism and utilitarianism, and not all authors will agree with the interpretation on offer here.

Whatever the true relationship between Aristotle's theory and the paradigm of emotional intelligence, there is a serious difficulty with the non-PPP assumption held by many Aristotelians. It simply seems to fall afoul of the principle of 'minimal psychological realism', often ascribed to Aristotle himself, which asserts that moral theories must ensure that the character, decision-processing, and behaviour they prescribe are 'possible, or are perceived to be possible, for creatures like us' (Flanagan, 1991, p. 32). This is, indeed, a serious problem for any naturalistic theory, like Aristotelian Virtue Ethics, which is meant to be answerable to empirical evidence. It is an uncontested assumption of everyday psychology that people frequently agonize retrospectively over even the best of decisions they have made. Consider Sophie's choice of her son over her daughter in the concentration-camp scenario: the pain (eventually leading to her suicide) from which Sophie suffered was not caused by regret about having made the wrong decision. Her premise, that the boy would stand a better chance of survival in the camp than the daughter, was unfalteringly sound as such; yet she was prey to conflicting emotions—about her very choice—of such intensity and fecundity that they gradually destroyed her life. Acknowledging pain in such decisions simply recognizes that humans cannot master all situations.

The point does not depend on extreme scenarios; consider a *phronetic* decision after a deliberative trade-off between honesty and kindness to tell one's friend that the dress she intends to wear to the party looks awful—because the friend is strong enough to hear the truth and there are not sufficient grounds for a white lie. After the decision has been enacted, one can easily—or so it seems—experience PPP in which conflicting emotions run amok in one's mind, for example when faced with the friend's tears of pain and self-doubt (although anticipated and taken into account in the decision-making). What is more, it is not only evidently a common occurrence that both budding and seasoned *phronimoi* can experience such PPP; it would even seem to be a plausible assumption that the more intellectually nuanced the *phronimos* is, the more likely she would be to experience ambivalent emotions about the relevant decision.

One of our core assumptions that lead us to admit that PPP occurs despite well-honed *phronesis* is recognizing the imperfection in all *phronimoi*. A claim of non-PPP in difficult decisions requires one to see the *phronimos* as having much more control over the situations in which she finds herself than is reasonable. It assumes that one could never be in a Sophie's choice sort of dilemma or even a 'that-dress-is-awful' sort of dilemma. No one has that much control, and *phronimoi* are thrust into difficult situations through no fault of their own, just as other are. If one grants this lack of complete control over morally relevant situational factors, then one must assume that a *phronimos* has a virtually perfect ability to harmonize emotions with reason, such that one's emotions are never ambivalent or at odds with one's decisions. This is an inhuman degree of emotional regulation and altogether too much to expect of any human *phronimos*. It is conceivable that a god or a Vulcan could have such complete emotional control, but it is not conceivable that a human could do so. We are firmly committed to the imperfection of the *phronimos*, which seems to require some degree of PPP. We also believe that it is difficult to ascribe wisdom to someone who does not recognize her own imperfection.

One of us has previously addressed this problem in the context of trying to make sense (psychologically and morally) of the construct of 'ambivalent emotions' (Kristjánsson, 2010b; 2013, chap. 7). There, the focus was on Stark's (2001) solution to this problem from within the perspective of virtue theory, and Carr's (2009) criticisms of this solution. The argument was that although Carr's criticisms may miss the mark, Stark's solution fails to hold water for a different reason. The argument culminated in a broad agreement with Carr's conclusion that Aristotle's strict psychological unity thesis had to be abandoned.[7]

In the present chapter, we want to probe deeper. We begin, in Section 10.2, with a brief rehearsal of the structure of the argument from our previous foray, following which we examine three different attempts to render the PPP view compatible with Aristotle's own virtue theory, in Section 10.3. The fourth section delineates the nature of PPP by arguing that it comprises a number of distinguishable emotions of moral sadness. The final section probes a number of resources within neo-Aristotelian theory that would allow us to reconceptualize PPP as beneficial to a certain extent—without fetishizing it as a pure blessing in disguise.

10.2 The Mystery of the Missing Motivation

One way to conceptualize the problem of non-PPP in Aristotelian virtue theory is to couch it in terms of 'the mystery of the missing motivation' (Kristjánsson, 2010b; 2013, chap. 7). Consider a case slightly more intense than that of the friend's unattractive dress, while less dramatic than Sophie's fatal choice, and in fact one based on a real incident.[8] You work in a UK police

---

[7] We recommend Carr's (2002b; 2009) two articles about ambivalent, conflicting emotions as the ideal starting point for anyone who wants to get an initial hold on the problem under discussion.

[8] This story was used in a recent research project into police ethics in the UK; see Kristjánsson, Thompson, and Maile (2021).

response unit. A new female student officer of South Asian heritage joins your team. While alone with an experienced white, male colleague, who happens to be a close personal friend, he refers to the new officer in blatantly racist terms and makes offensive comments about her origin, appearance, and character. You consider it a moral quandary whether to report this case to your supervisor (sergeant), as required by your formal Ethical Code, or to have a quiet word with your colleague/friend and try to talk some sense into him. After a period of intense deliberation, applying effectively your metacognitive capacity of *phronesis*, you decide to report the case to the sergeant. However, you continue to feel compassion towards your friend and painful unease about your decision, although you firmly believe it was the right one.[9]

Aristotle's assumptions about emotion and motivation

Aristotle invokes various assumptions that seem relevant to a case like this one. Consider the following:

(1) *We cannot control the experience of episodic emotions once the relevant emotional disposition to experience them is established.* (This is the point of Aristotle's (1985, p. 41 [1105b20–1106a7]) observation that we blame or praise persons not for their emotions *qua* occurrent episodes—say, for simply being angry—but for their *qua* settled character states (*hexeis*) that constitute virtues or vices.)
(2) *Occurrent emotions are at least weakly motivating.* (This assumption seems to follow from Aristotle's (2007) definition of 'emotion' as always 'being accompanied by pain and pleasure', pp. 112–13 [1378a20–1], and his view of all emotions involving a goal-directed activity that can either be frustrated or satisfied; see Kristjánsson, 2018b.)
(3) *There is an optimal way to feel in each given situation, and the morally virtuous person is motivated to feel in that way.* (This is when an emotion hits the golden mean of being felt at the right time, about the right thing, towards the right person(s), for the right end and in the right way: Aristotle, 1985, p. 44 [1106b17–35].)

---

[9] It is worth noting that the other alternatives (having a quiet word with the colleague or ignoring his comments) do not free one from ambivalence: justice for the South Asian colleague versus compassion for the colleague who is a friend. We do not see a unified way out, only easy and hard choices, with the *phronetic* choice entailing the experience of a painful ambivalence.

(4) Virtuous persons—as distinct from the merely self-controlled (continent) ones—are motivationally unified. (This follows from Aristotle's well-known distinction between virtue and continence.)

(5) Virtuous persons—as distinct from the continent ones—do not need to suppress their nonoptimal emotions. (Again, this follows from Aristotle's distinction between virtue and continence.)

Assumptions *(1)–(5)* are not strictly incompatible but give rise to a puzzle: 'the mystery of the missing motivation'. Recall that the police officer's *phronetic* balancing act yielded the conclusion to report the colleague. Although both happiness (e.g., over doing one's duty, following the Code, and creating a good precedent) and compassion towards the friend are rationally warranted here, when viewed in isolation, the optimal way to feel (given the assumed aptness of the *phronetic* decision) is to be happy. *Ex hypothesi*, according to *(3)* above, the fully virtuous person is motivated to feel in that way. Yet, this person also presumably has a virtuous disposition to feel compassion when a friend gets into serious trouble. According to *(1)*, the person cannot help feeling that emotion, and that emotion is at least weakly motivating (see *(2)*). Nevertheless, being motivationally unified *(4)*, the virtuous person does not need to suppress the nonoptimal weak motivation *(5)*.

The remaining mystery, then, is what happens to that nonoptimal motivation? To reiterate an earlier point, there is nothing mysterious from an Aristotelian perspective about the police officer feeling compassion towards the colleague with respect to the punishment that he is likely to receive, as well as further painful feelings about various other aspects of his life and their friendship that may be affected by the case. What should not happen, however, is enduring pain about the *content of the decision itself* (recall note 3), given that it was fully *phronetic*.[10] Does *phronesis* silence the relevant motivation?[11] And, if so, how does *phronesis* silence the motivation?

---

[10] The orthodox Aristotelian might argue that the reason for the remaining pain in this story is most likely that the decision was not fully *phronetic*. Indeed, it is true that Aristotle would ascribe full *phronesis* only to a very small group of people. However, if we are not allowed to assume in a story like this that a fully *phronetic* decision has been reached, then it seems that *phronesis* is just a rarefied ideal that has no traction in the real world—which means that its naturalistic appeal for virtue ethics is lost. We revisit this consideration in the following section.

[11] For the concept of 'silencing' in virtue theory, see McDowell (1998).

Stark's non-PPP view and its difficulties

In an earlier stab at this problem—where it was approached from a different angle (Kristjánsson, 2013, chap. 7)—considerable space was allocated to a debate between Stark (2001) and Carr (2009) on whether it is possible so defuse the apparent mystery (which Stark believes can be done but Carr does not). For present purposes, we simply rehearse briefly Stark's argument. Stark (2001) suggests that we drop assumption *(2)*: that all episodic emotions are at least weakly motivating. When two conflicting but virtue-based reactions to a situation are potentially appropriate (as we assume for the police story), we do not simply want the considerations inherent in the overall less virtuous option to be silenced or unrecognized or pushed out of view. Such a manoeuvre would make the psychology of the virtuous person seem singularly one-dimensional and immune from the recognition of the tragic that permeates any mature human person. Nevertheless, we want that person to experience the morally proper emotion in the end and to be motivationally unified, and therefore distinguishable from the continent person. How can these claims be made compatible? Stark's suggestion is to reject motivational internalism and maintain instead that, in the case of virtuous agents, they can experience emotions (*qua* moral evaluations) as yielding normative reasons but without having intrinsic motivational force. The quest for overall virtue does not silence the nonoptimal normative reason, for its very nonoptimality continues to be experienced as a reason for a sense of loss, but rather silences that reason *qua* motivational reason.

There are widely differing views on whether Aristotle's virtue theory is to be understood as motivationally internalist across the board (Strandberg, 2000) or as mixing motivational internalism and externalism depending on the developmental level of the person passing the relevant moral judgement (Kristjánsson, 2013, chap. 5). Motivational externalists believe that persons can sincerely pass moral judgements without being intrinsically moved by them. The trouble with Stark's externalism, however, is that it is not an externalism about moral judgements of this kind (as mere detached evaluations, say: 'It is morally wrong to report a close friend and colleague to a superior for a fairly minor offence.') but about moral *emotions*. But emotions already contain within them a conative as well as a cognitive component. Emotions are thus intrinsically motivating (at least weakly) in the way that some other types of moral evaluations are not.[12] If that is so, one simply cannot be a moral

---

[12] See, for example, Greenspan's (1980) observation, albeit in a different context, that we 'cannot simply decide to treat emotions, like judgements, as merely prima facie' (p. 233).

externalist about emotions. The only way to deflect this concern would be to reject the consensus that emotions have a conative element and understand them as mere cognitions. Some philosophers of emotion do hold such a pure cognitive view (e.g., Nussbaum, 2001, and the Stoics), but for Aristotle, emotions are affective and conative as well as cognitive.

There is a further problem here. If the police officer in the story is a *phronimos*, then even on a mixed externalist–internalist reading of Aristotle, all of that particular person's moral judgements should be intrinsically motivating. He is, *ex hypothesi*, fully motivationally unified, meaning that all his moral beliefs are fully in line with his emotions, and he does not feel emotions that are not backed up by moral judgements, and emotions are intrinsically motivating, be it weakly or strongly. However, even if we allow that the police officer is not a full *phronimos*, though was able to take a *phronetic* decision in this particular case, then it is possible that he will continue to harbour detached moral beliefs that do not motivate him intrinsically, because of their lack of attachment to the corresponding emotional repertoire. In that case, then, it is indeed possible, for instance, that he continues to harbour (prima facie) beliefs about the wrongness of his particular decision. However, those beliefs would not explain the pain that he feels about the content of the *phronetic* decision. That pain is an emotional PPP, as understood here. So, unless one refuses to accept the very possibility of a fully *phronetic* decision accompanied by residual PPP, it does not matter whether the police officer is a fully fledged *phronimos* or not; the mystery of the missing motivation remains.

10.3 Some Possible Aristotelian Rejoinders

There are at least three rejoinders available to those who would want to argue that PPP is actually compatible with Aristotelian virtue theory about *phronesis*.

Rejoinder (1): *Phronesis* is an ideal, which real people can only approximate. *Phronesis* is, in fact, a threshold concept, and even for those who have crossed that threshold, they will still fall short of perfect *phronesis*. Hence, as they are not completely unified, they may still experience PPP.

Response: We agree that *phronesis*, for Aristotle, is a threshold concept (just like flourishing and many of his key naturalistic concepts are) or, more specifically, what Russell (2009, chap. 4) calls a 'satis concept'. We endorsed that point already in Chapter 2. Nevertheless, there are two problems with this rejoinder. The first is that the assumption of the psychological unity of the *phronimos* is such a vital part of Aristotle's own characterization of *phronesis* that if we confine that aspect to a never fully realized approximation, we run the risk of turning *phronesis* into a rarefied ideal—some sort of philosophical plaything—with little real-world relevance. The second and more significant problem is that it is so far from being the case that we would expect nonchalance and immunity to pain to increase with greater psycho-moral maturity that most people would consider the opposite true: namely, that the more discriminate and nuanced the moral make-up of a person becomes, the greater her scope will be for residual postoperative pain at foreclosed alternatives.

Rejoinder (2): When Aristotle talks about the pleasure that completes fully virtuous activity, he makes the pleasure conditional upon the end of virtue being successfully completed. However, *ex hypothesi*, because in a typical *phronetic* adjudication one moral virtue takes priority over another, the outweighed virtue is not brought to completion. Hence, residual PPP originates from the noncompleted virtue—even if psychological harmony has been achieved through that virtue being trumped in the particular instance.

Response: This rejoinder refers to Aristotle's comments about the specific type of pleasure signalling the completion of virtuous activity. Such activity is true '*en-ergeia*', the actualization of our true '*ergon*' or functional essence as human beings: a sign of development, progress, and fulfilment. Indeed, Aristotle does not seriously consider the possibility that anyone except the virtuous can experience this type of supervening pleasure, which is not pleasure *simpliciter*, but the feeling of complete non-frustration and lack of inner conflict. As it differs in species and value from all other pleasures (Aristotle, 1985, pp. 277–9 [1175a21–b24]), we could call it the specific experience of *phronetic* virtue and *eudaimonia* in action. Hence, Aristotle (1985) cleverly 'weaves pleasure' into virtue (p. 203 [1153b14–15]); pleasure 'completes' the activities of the virtuous 'like the bloom on youths' (pp. 7 [1095b19–20], 276 [1174b30–5]).

However, what *Rejoinder (2)* fastens on is an important caveat. It is not the case 'that the active exercise of every virtue is pleasant; it is pleasant only in so far as we attain the end [of the virtue]' (Aristotle, 1985, p. 79 [1117b15–16]). This caveat may seem to place an extreme limitation on Aristotelian pleasure in virtue. After all, there are arguably a number of virtuous flourishing-constituting activities that can never be 'completed' in a strict sense.[13] However, that observation aside, *Rejoinder (2)* focuses specifically on the motivational aspect of *phronesis*. At least according to our interpretation from Chapter 2, *phronesis* incorporates

---

[13] For instance, being a good parent. One never completes that activity.

both a primary and a secondary motivation. The primary motivation derives from each of the specific virtues that are perceived to be relevant to the given situation upon which *phronesis* is called to adjudicate: say honesty versus kindness. The secondary motivation, on the other hand, derives from the blueprint component of *phronesis* itself: the aim of enhancing flourishing through a *phronetic* decision. While a successful *phronetic* decision, *ex hypothesi*, completes the end of *phronesis*, it will typically leave one of the adjudicated-upon moral virtues (or even both in case some sort a middle-ground reaction is identified) uncompleted.[14] This would then explain the PPP.

We agree with the terms in which this rejoinder is couched but disagree with the conclusion. The focus in this chapter is not on various kinds of pain that may remain after a *phronetic* decision relating to unresolved contextual features of the situation and how it continues to unfold, but is specifically, and exclusively, about PPP directed at the *phronetic* decision itself. However, as that decision is by definition successful and complete, there is no obvious reason, in Aristotle's own picture of why it should give rise to pain.

Rejoinder (3): Aristotle considered all emotions to be of mixed valence (rather than only pleasant or only painful). Hence, although a *phronetic* decision creates an emotion that is overall pleasant, it will inevitably also be mixed with some painful elements, hence the possibility of PPP and the accompanying emotional ambivalence.

Response: This rejoinder makes an important and valid point: namely, that whereas Aristotle (2007) does characterize each emotion he describes as *overall* 'painful' or 'pleasant', he seems to have understood most, if not all, emotions to be of *mixed* valence: namely, to incorporate a mixture of pains/disturbance/frustration and pleasure/restoration/gratification (see Frede, 1996; cf. Konstan, 2006, pp. 33–4).[15] For example, in anger—which is overall painful—the pain is partly offset by the pleasant anticipation of possible justice re-establishment or, at least of retaliation.

There are two things to note about this observation, however. The first is that although Aristotle makes this comment about emotions related to specific virtues (e.g., justified anger as part of the virtue of mildness [of temper]), he does not say anything similar about the feelings associated with *phronetic* activity. Second, even if he did mean that the phenomenology of *phronesis* is

---

[14] The idea of perfectly harmonious 'honest kindness' or 'kind honesty' is idyllic but unrealistic. In most conflict situations, a trade-off takes place in which the demands of one or both of the virtues need to be mitigated.

[15] It would be very Aristotelian to assume that the nature of the exact valence mixture in each instance will be heavily dependent on context (both cultural and individual). Indeed, this is exactly what the current empirical evidence indicates (e.g., Morgan et al., 2014, on gratitude in different cultures).

also of mixed valence, he would still, *ex hypothesi*, have to say that it is overall pleasant. However, the salient issue about PPP is not that it may just mar slightly an overall pleasant emotion completing a sound decision; more seriously—at least in dramatic cases such as that of *Sophie's Choice*—the overall valence may actually be negative. Or, more precisely, the fact that Sophie associates her decision more with pain than pleasure would not, for most people, undermine the claim that her decision could still have been fully *phronetic*.

Here we seem to have run out of interpretative acrobatics that would enable PPP to be conveniently accommodated within any orthodox Aristotelian model of *phronesis*.

10.4 Types of Moral Sadness

If PPP is indeed real, how can we best account for it within a revised neo-Aristotelian model of *phronesis*? We are taking it for granted here that a broad Aristotelian model offers so many theoretical and practical advantages that we had better try to modify it rather than discarding it and starting afresh just because of one serious anomaly in Aristotle's own conceptualization (recall earlier Chapters 3–4).

The best approach is to examine what Aristotle says about postdecision pain at characterological levels lower than that of the *phronimoi*. Consider the vicious first. Some would argue that those may stay clear of emotional ambivalences as long as they remain coherent in their evil-doing. However, Aristotle dismisses this possibility. He thinks that consistently vicious decision-making instantiating a state of mental homeostasis is a chimera, both because the vicious are constantly pulled in different directions by impulsive desires and that, deep down, they will always have some vague sense of, and wish for, goodness that upsets their balance. As their 'soul is in conflict', between appetite for the bad and wish for the good, 'each part pulls in a different direction', gradually tearing them apart (Aristotle, 1985, p. 247 [1166b11–26]). The emotions of the vicious, be they painful or pleasant, are thus in a constant state of ambivalence, criss-crossing each other like mistimed fireworks.[16]

What Aristotle says about the incontinent and continent is more predictable. The incontinent, who know the good but fall to temptations, suffer from remorse and guilt. The continent, who force themselves to do the good and succeed in doing so, suffer from emotional ambivalence after each continent

---

[16] As Jacobs (2017) explains well, the vicious also have to engage in a great deal of psycho-moral 'editorializing' to bring the world into conformity with their vices and self-conceptions.

decision because the contra-continent motivation is still active. Aristotle (1985, p. 54 [1110a5–18]) is particularly interested in actions that are 'mixed', such as when a tyrant forces you to do something shameful to save your wife and children. After such a decision, under duress, one experiences a mixture of pleasure and pain; we could call it regret (at having been put in such a terrible position) rather than remorse.

If we want to create space for PPP, we must give an account of that pain as a different emotional pain, post moral decision, than for the *nonphronetic* character types delineated above. Here we are obviously entering uncharted territory, given Aristotle's own (apparent) non-PPP assumption. We do not propose to offer an exhaustive taxonomy of emotions that can represent PPP, but we will just quickly enumerate a few candidates that come to mind.[17] What unites them is that they are all types of *moral sadness* accompanying the *phronetic* decision: sadness about that decision *qua* decision rather than just about its context or subsequent ramifications.

The first overall painful emotion is what we could call *tragic sadness*. Consider a case where I am on a sinking ship and there is space in a remaining lifeboat only for one of my two children: twins of the same gender and indistinguishable in terms of health or other personal features.[18] A *phronetic* decision in this case seems limited to just tossing a coin to pick the twin to survive. An alternative way of looking at this case would be to say that its conditions rule out the very possibility of a *phronetic* decision. However, that seems to be too defeatist; a *phronetic* person would surely opt for saving one of her children rather than neither. At the same time, it seems absurd to claim that such a decision could be taken from anything that could be called a 'unified mind'. The choice is inherently tragic, however well-grounded it may be. This choice may seem to resemble the duress choice mentioned earlier. However, the agent is not, strictly speaking, operating under duress. This case is more similar to that of Sophie's choice, but her case included a number of other conditions that render it philosophically controversial what a *phronetic* choice amounts to for Sophie; the issue there is not about a choice that is fairly uncontroversially *phronetic* but nevertheless tragic.

In some cases, the very fact of how marginal the decision was, even if it is deemed to be *phronetic*, can be a source of pain. Let us say that the police

---

[17] The question of the individuation of emotions is a tricky one (Kristjánsson, 2007, chap. 4). If readers worry that specifying the emotional states described in this section as discrete emotions elicits the problem of an uncontrollable proliferation of emotions, we are quite happy to redescribe them simply as variants of the same emotion, moral sadness.

[18] For readers uncomfortable with 'unrealistic' examples, we encourage them to think of any more realistic example where there is nothing to choose between the two options.

officer who decided to report his colleague is convinced that he took the right decision. However, the fact of how tight and tenuous the reflection leading up to that decision was can issue in what we could call *marginality sadness*: sadness attached to the fact that the decision was not more clear-cut. The problem here is not so much that of a consideration that continues to bother him retrospectively but rather that the awareness of the marginal nature of the decision-making forecloses a complete unity of mind.

Consider next cases where the *phronetic* decision is more clear-cut but where the *phronimos* knows that the counter-weighing consideration can never be fully silenced because of its deep-seatedness in her psyche. This sort of *nonsilenceable sadness* is very common in cases of divorce after a long marriage. A woman may decide to leave her husband after realizing that their marriage is hopeless. Yet she knows that her abiding love for her husband will always remain as a backseat emotion in her mind. An orthodox Aristotelian might want to say that the existence of a non-silenceable contra-consideration simply rules out the categorization of the woman's decision as *phronetic*. However, that sounds again like theoretical overkill. Fully silencing a consideration such as the woman's abiding love would more plausibly be explained as suppression rather than reason-infusion, which would turn the decision into a continent rather than a *phronetic* one. This decision illustrates the importance of 'all things considered' decisions wherein there are abiding reasons to decide the matter in different ways. On balance, divorce appears to be the best choice, but that does not require the woman to immediately turn off her emotions, which would be quite psychologically unrealistic. If she could somehow turn her feelings of love off, we would not see that as elevating her decision to a *phronetic* one.

Another common set of cases revolve around what we could call *bystander sadness*. This is the sadness felt, for example, by the army officer who decides to bomb a terrorist compound, knowing that some innocent bystanders may be hurt by the blast. Once again, the alternative and more orthodox Aristotelian option would be to consider this an encumbered, tragic situation where no truly *phronetic* decision can be reached—reminiscent of Aristotle's anti-Socratic thesis (directed at Socrates's the-good-person-cannot-be-harmed mantra) that those who maintain that we can flourish 'when we are broken on the wheel, or fall into terrible misfortunes, provided that we are good [. . .] are talking nonsense' (Aristotle, 1985, p. 203 [1153b19–21]). However, what proves too much proves nothing. If we rule out any decision accompanied by 'bystander sadness' as potentially *phronetic*, we seem to be saying that almost no significant decisions taken in war can be *phronetic*—which is excessively restrictive. Once again, it is worth noting that collateral deaths are one of the important things to consider when deciding to attack an enemy. If those collateral deaths do not dissuade the officer from attacking, they will nonetheless die, and turning a blind eye to those deaths does not elevate one's decision to a *phronetic* one.

The final emotion on this nonexhaustive list of PPP is *no-brainer sadness*: sadness accompanying a decision that is so obviously sound that a *phronetic* deliberation will yield an almost instantaneous and indubitable result. Consider a doctor who has to choose between five badly injured survivors of an air crash (whose lives could all be saved in an hour) and one more badly injured one (whose rescue would also take an hour). Other things being equal (e.g., the most badly injured one is not the doctor's spouse or child), there is not much doubt that the correct *phronetic* decision is so save the five. To claim, however, that this decision cannot be deemed fully *phronetic* unless the doctor has managed to defuse (albeit not suppress) the haunting image of the single survivor 'sacrificed' to die seems to betray an unreasonably one-dimensional and unrealistic picture of human psychology. We suggest that the absence of sadness over the person who died would tell against seeing the doctor as a *phronimos* rather than telling in favour of his wisdom.

10.5 Does PPP Have Any Redeeming Features?

The cases explored in the preceding section all involved decisions that can arguably be deemed *phronetic* but were characterized by PPP rather than any idyllic unity of mind—and indeed pain that is not only felt retrospectively (*post-phronesis*) but can be felt before and during the actual decision-making also. Some of the cases suggested are so common that it seems possible to generalize them by claiming that almost all significant *phronetic* decisions are likely to be accompanied by some degree of pain, in some cases, pain that outweighs any positively felt emotions at having made a good decision.[19]

Recognizing this, it may still be possible to make the distinctions between the different levels of virtue (and/or previrtue) that Aristotle makes between incontinence, continence, and virtue. Thus, while the residual pain of the incontinent agent would be that of failure to do what she knows is right, and that of the continent agent over unsatisfied desire to which she is still attached, that of the virtuous agent would be on grounds of inability to act on virtues she

---

[19] We ask readers at this point also to recall our earlier argument in Section 1.4, directed against Bernard Williams's view of the uniqueness of the motivational structure of Virtue Ethics, as compared with Utilitarianism and Deontology.

still finds morally compelling. But it would no longer seem plausible to construe the difference between continence and virtue in terms of the presence or absence of PPP. The maturely virtuous could hardly avoid PPP in some, if not all, morally serious (especially conflicted) circumstances. So, if one is still disposed to persist with a broadly Aristotelian virtue theory, some serious revision of Aristotle's (apparent) account would seem inescapable at this point.

It is tempting, therefore, to simply expunge the non-PPP assumption from neo-Aristotelian virtue theory and rest content with the moral benefits only that a *phronetic* decision will elicit, rather than expecting any pleasure- (or freedom-from-pain) benefits also. Such an expungement may also tally with a more general rejection of a flourishing–happiness concordance thesis: a thesis that is often ascribed to Aristotle (Kristjánsson, 2020, chap. 3). It is tempting also, however, to take a different tack and ask whether the expungement of the non-PPP assumption could confer some benefits on Aristotelian virtue theory (and indeed on the *phronetic* agent) other than just making the theory more psychologically realistic. Is PPP some sort of a blessing in disguise for the *phronetic* agent? May enduring emotional ambivalence actually, as Greenspan (1988) suggests, 'improve the agent's overall situation' (p. 127)?

These questions bring us back to the two papers by Carr (2002b; 2009) that we cited at the outset. Carr emphatically rejects 'therapeutic accounts' of emotional regulation, such as 'emotional intelligence', for their insistence on 'complete emotional harmony' and unproblematic resolution of 'unease and conflict'. He considers such endeavours both psychologically disabling and morally untoward. In contrast, Carr (2002b) argues that 'emotional ambivalence, conflict and disquiet, even at the price of some practical dysfunctionality, cannot but be part and parcel of any recognisable human condition' (p. 20). On his alternative model of conflictual unity, the *phronimoi* are 'precisely those equipped with the richly complex—albeit conflicted—psychological life through which alternative possibilities of (virtuous) action remain available' (Carr, 2002b, pp. 18–20; 2009, p. 37).

We argued in Section 7.4 that in wanting to avoid fetishizing psychological unity, Carr (2002b; 2009) comes perilously close to fetishizing its disunity. However, on closer inspection, Carr escapes this criticism. His two papers offer a measured view of the pros and cons of what he calls 'the slings and arrows of emotional ambivalence and moral uncertainty' (Carr, 2009, p. 46). He tries to draw a distinction between an unhealthy (pathological, neurotic) state of ambivalence and a healthy appreciation of conflict that may enhance possibilities of virtuous character. While warning against therapeutic conceptions of emotional virtue, be those motivated by Aristotle, EQ, or what he rightly considers misguided understandings of psychoanalysis, he remains acutely aware of the Aristotelian challenge that it is difficult to envisage true virtue, or indeed any effective agency, in a person torn by conflict.

Carr (2002b; 2009) mentions in passing some benefits that the virtuous agent may derive from a constructive dividedness of mind. If we try to offer a more systematic account of those, it may be helpful to divide them into four categories. First are the *epistemic* benefits. Emotional ambivalence can possibly be intellectually character-building through the exploration of alternative possibilities that conflicting emotions are likely to evoke. Very much like the famous Millian argument about the need to have truth constantly challenged in order for it to retain its heartfelt vitality, one could argue that optimal emotions would lose their epistemic urgency and immediacy—and ultimately their motivational bite—if they did not regularly come into conflict with other (nonoptimal) emotions. Second are the *existential* benefits of understanding one's own existence better in the light of a deeper understanding of the human condition (as inevitably riven by conflict). Third are the *developmental/educational* benefits. What ensures our psychological equilibrium by insulating us from ambivalent and/or painful experiences may be the very enemy of what promotes developmentally needed psychological change (Reeve, 2005, p. 34). Fourth are the *moral* benefits (and here Carr, 2002b, has much to say) of reminding us of moral diversity and the reality of pluralistic approaches to moral truths in the world—as the ambivalent emotions may often be seen to represent a healthy plurality of moral options.

It is unclear to what extent Aristotle would be willing to accept these potential 'benefits' as benefits, and to what extent neo-Aristotelians should take them on board. *Epistemically*, one could argue that the acquisition of truth may be impeded rather than enhanced by the baptism of fire that comes from being constantly challenged by nonoptimal viewpoints. This is not how Aristotle describes the typical trajectory of character development, at any rate. *Existentially*, there is a thin line between constructive existential awareness and debilitating existential anxiety. *Developmentally*, it is well-known that what does not kill you does not always make you stronger. And *educationally*, too much appreciation of moral diversity can easily lead to self-doubt or cynicism rather than progress.[20]

We have simply presented those potential benefits as possible stepping-stones on the next part of the journey for neo-Aristotelian virtue ethicists—after the acknowledgement that *phronesis* is not always accompanied by psychological unity and a lack of emotional ambivalence. The philosophical

---

[20] Leonard Cohen may be right that 'There is a crack in everything; that's how the light gets in'. However, unfortunately, there are other things than just light that can force their way through the cracks.

task is getting the moral psychology of the *phronetic* agent right. What lies beyond that task is perhaps better left to the educationists than the philosophers. Indeed, many of the psychological and philosophical questions that we have pondered in this book so far are actually developmental or educational questions in disguise. It is now time to subject them to a more sustained scrutiny.

11
Educating *Phronesis*

11.1 Aristotle's Reticence about *Phronesis* Education—and a First Look at the Developmental Picture

> Although [. . .] it is fine [. . .] to attain knowledge of the various fine things, all the same [. . .] in the case of goodness it is not the knowledge of its essential nature that is most valuable but the *ascertainment of the sources that produce it*' (Aristotle, 1935, pp. 1216b19–20, our italics).

For some reason, the prominence of *phronesis* has not—until very recently at least—been reflected in the vast practical literature on Aristotelian character development and education; and prior to our own work (Chapter 6 in this book; cf. Darnell et al., 2019), no instrument to evaluate *phronesis* progress existed that could be used for pre and post testing of educational interventions. The account we offer in this chapter is an initial, rough, and fragmented description of the development and education of *phronesis*, reflecting the current lacunae and fragmentation in the literature. We nonetheless hope that this will be a step along the way to more complete and integrated accounts.

Reasons for lacunae

At best, educated guesses can be offered about the above-mentioned lacunae. First, much more teaching materials have been produced for the primary (elementary) and lower secondary (junior high school) levels of the school system than for the upper secondary (senior high school) and early college (undergraduate) levels where *phronesis* development is usually considered to emerge. This could be inter alia because it is easier to focus on cultivating individual virtues if the thorny issue of virtue conflicts can be avoided. Second, most of the copious Professional Ethics literature on *phronesis* has not been about the standard Aristotelian concept but rather, on the one hand, MacIntyrean and, on the other, intuitionist-cum-postmodern versions of it, as explained in Chapter 1. However, both of those concepts happen to prioritize other problematics over developmental ones. Third, as outspoken as Aristotle himself was about methods of early years Moral Education, especially habituation and role modelling, he was singularly unhelpful in delineating useful strategies for *phronesis* development, to the extent of simply trading in platitudes. For example, it is not very illuminating to assert that *phronesis* is developed through 'teaching and experience' (Aristotle, 1985, p. 33 [1103a14–16]); we want to know what kind of teaching; what sort of experience ? More specifically, Aristotle fails to elaborate on what *phronesis*-enhancing teaching would look like, when it should take place in an ideal developmental trajectory, how long it should last, and at which stage, if ever, the teaching is complete so that the learners will count as *phronimoi*. Most neo-Aristotelians take it for granted that he is talking about late adolescence–early adulthood and that the 'teaching' relates to critical discussions with mentors and peers (as 'character friends'). But those assumptions must largely be read into Aristotle's texts.

Before turning to educational issues in Sections 11.3–11.5, we will devote the first two sections of this chapter to the topic of Aristotelian development towards *phronesis*. Psychologist Dan Lapsley (2021) has argued that the dearth of any empirically credible developmental account of *phronesis* is symptomatic of a 'developmental inadequacy' in Aristotelian character theory that makes it surplus to requirements for contemporary Developmental Science.[1] Meanwhile, Silverstein and Trombetti (2013) think that Aristotle has a rich developmental account that urgently needs to be mined. The truth probably lies somewhere in a 'golden mean' between these two suggestions. On the one hand, it is important to mine and reconstruct what the academic father of *phronesis* had to say about its development, and to subject it to scrutiny; on the other hand, it is equally important to venture beyond Aristotle's texts and to explore what insights can be added to his developmental story in the light of contemporary research. We try to do both below.

As with the discourse on another of Aristotle's core concepts, that of flourishing (*eudaimonia*), which carries a risk of blandness and banality if the underlying variables are not populated with sufficient specificity (Kristjánsson, 2020; cf. Carr, 2021), the *phronesis* discourse loses practical resonance when

---

[1] Although we took exception in Chapter 4 to Lapsley's redundancy thesis about *phronesis*, we do agree with him that a satisfactory model of *phronesis* needs a developmental account. Cf. also philosopher Swanton's (2016) complaint about neo-Aristotelians' lack of engagement with developmental psychology. Yet see Annas (2011) for an exception.

it is pitched at too high a level of philosophical abstractness and carried out in isolation from developmental and educational concerns. In the present section, we offer some preliminary reflections on the presumed trajectory towards *phronesis*; in Section 11.2, however, we hazard to reconstruct a fuller developmental model and offer some research hypotheses that stand in need of further (future) explorations.

The 'basics' of Aristotelian moral development

So how does *phronesis*, broadly speaking, fit into an overall Aristotelian theory of moral development? According to Aristotle, virtue is developed from early childhood through role model–guided habituation into ways of recognizing patterns in, and responding to, moral situations, which in turn mould one's affective and motivational structures into concordance with how those who have the virtues behave. However, this sort of habituation is not sufficient for fully possessing virtue. Instead, as explained earlier in this book, having developed appropriate habits and virtuous affective-cum-motivational structures only amounts to possessing what Aristotle calls 'habituated' virtue. To possess virtues in a complete sense, it is necessary that the habits in question also be undergirded by a robust intellectual foundation, which includes good understanding and reasoning in practical matters.

This is where *phronesis* enters the picture, which (as we have repeatedly seen) Aristotle defines as excellence in practical deliberation about moral matters. Apart from its theoretical significance, this condition placed upon complete virtue has wide-ranging practical ramifications, as it excludes the possibility that complete virtue can be acquired mechanistically, for instance through behavioural conditioning or indoctrination. It also gives rise to the hypothesis—which we explored in Chapters 5 and 6—that what really bridges the gap between thought and action is the development of *phronesis*, rather than the development of moral perception, identity, reasoning, or emotions, viewed in isolation. *Phronesis* is meant to crown, as it were, virtuous habits with a cluster of intellectual abilities and experience that are both necessary and sufficient for ensuring that these habits will not go awry, will be reliable both over time and across different situations, and will be put into practice in a way that is reflective and motivationally robust.

The question remains how we transition from the formation of good habits all the way to the sophisticated virtuous agency that Aristotle envisages. How can role model–guided habituation, which in the way Aristotle describes it would be mostly uncritical (or, in modern jargon, heteronomous), prepare students for the autonomous critical engagement required for *phronesis*? Moreover, at what age is this radical transformation meant to materialize?

The classic two-stage answer, proposed by Burnyeat (1980), is that first-stage habituation 'prepares' agents psycho-morally for becoming virtuous in the full-blown sense, which includes *phronesis*. In contrast, Sherman (1989) rejects habituation as a noncognitive process of low-level imitation and repetition. What she adds to Burnyeat's account is the idea that habituation itself gradually engages one's rational capacities. It seems plausible that once one comes to see that others whom one imitates offer reasons for their behaviour, one comes to reflect similarly about oneself regarding one's habits. In this way, affect and intellect intertwine in moral development, without any clear transition from a first to a second stage. What we now know, from recent Developmental Psychology, is that by the age of 6 years, children can typically compare their personal perspectives on their actions with the more general perspective of their community (Tomasello, 2019). This allows them to evaluate their own cognition, emotion, and behaviour from a collective viewpoint, which may be the beginning of metacognition and lay the groundwork for the development of *phronesis*.

The difficulty in providing an account of *phronesis* development is compounded, however, by the multivocality of current Developmental Science. Consider the alternative conception of moral development from Social Domain Theory wherein the development of children's judgements about morality, issues of social convention, and personal matters follow independent courses of development (Turiel, 1983; Smetana et al., 2014). The problem here is not so much that Aristotle would disagree with this view (or that neo-Aristotelians should), but rather that Aristotelian theory relies on a different conceptualization of human life. Although Turiel (1983, p. 35) is right to point out that Aristotle does make a distinction between forms of justice grounded in universal characterological features (e.g., pain at undeserved outcomes), on the one hand, and social conventions (relative to constitutions), on the other, this distinction does not amount to one between morality and social conventions in the modern sense. Generally speaking, there is no distinction in Aristotle between 'moral' and 'nonmoral'; indeed, as we have noted many times, he had no concept of 'the moral' at his disposal. More than that, there is no distinction in Aristotle's works between (moral) character and (nonmoral) personality; ancient Greek had no specific word for 'personality' (Reiner, 1991). Aristotelian developmental theory thus relies on a rather different ontology of humans that is incompatible with Social Domain Theory.

This distinction in outlooks becomes clearer when we recognize that Turiel's (1983) concept of morality is heavily weighted toward a principle-based ethics that emphasizes justice (broadly conceived) and harm avoidance, with both most commonly discussed as universals (i.e., non-context-dependent). Although this is one possible way to frame ethics, it is far more restrictive than the Aristotelian focus on action conducive to a good life, which include friendship and citizenship within it, for example. Turiel's three-dimensional model is one contemporary interpretation of the moral/ethical domain, but it has been thoroughly contested as well (e.g., Shweder et al., 1997; Walker & Frimer, 2011). Although this model has been challenged, children do appear to understand moral standards as obligatory and binding for all but view conventional standards as binding only on members of the group that holds those conventions. Therefore, children seem to recognize the difference between general obligations and locally held conventions. Accordingly, research suggests that children generally distinguish between local, changeable conventions and broader moral standards. Turiel and Aristotle differ in multiple ways but, needless to say, Turiel's developmental theory cannot simply be dismissed by Aristotelians by picking and choosing contemporary developmental sources that happen to fit their model better. At the same time, the incompatibilities between Aristotelian and contemporary conceptualizations about ethics cannot be ignored.

On a more positive note, there is a strong emphasis in recent developmental literature on how contextualized and domain-specific moral development is (Turiel & Nucci, 2018). This tallies with the basic Aristotelian insight that *phronesis* is a capacity that develops through experiential engagement with specific situations (developing *qua* 'excellence of learning', cf. Segvic, 2009, p. 169), and that *phronesis* may differ between individuals depending on their environmental/societal conditions, professions, and general context-specific life experiences. This feature distinguishes *phronesis* as *practical* wisdom from the global decontextualized wisdom construct that typically used to feature in psychological research (cf. Grossmann, 2017b). Moreover, there is a constructivist undercurrent in the *phronesis* concept, which may appeal to many current developmental psychologists (see, e.g., Dahl, 2018), in that *phronesis* ideally becomes a lens through which young people learn to construct their understanding of the ethical world. So, although the best developmental story for *phronesis* is unclear at this point, there is hope that exploring the development of *phronesis* with the tools, concepts, and methods of contemporary Psychology might elevate it to the status of a respectable construct within Developmental Science.

We would even go further and argue that Aristotle's ancient model of development towards virtue already tallies surprisingly well with some current concepts of moral development (see, e.g., Fowers et al., forthcoming), at least if one adds to it Aristotle's more general remarks about the social context required for this developmental trajectory to be open to moral learners in the first place: remarks that undermine some persistent individualistic and politically conservative accounts of character development.[2] Nevertheless, as could be expected, many aspects of this model are subject to ongoing criticism, both from contemporary neo-Aristotelian and non-Aristotelian educators. Since many of those criticisms and concerns are relevant to the specific topic of this chapter—the development and education of *phronesis*—it is instructive to offer a brief list of them here.

The need for updating the Aristotelian 'basics'

First, Aristotle assumes that children are born morally neutral (i.e., without any budding dispositions to be either moral or immoral), meaning that moral development is fundamentally a result of upbringing and education.[3] In contrast, quite a lot of current empirical evidence indicates that newborn children are endowed with inclinations towards empathy and even more advanced moral capacities, perhaps as evolutionary adaptations (Fowers, 2015; Hare, 2017; Hoffman, 2000; McCullough, 2008). These evolutionary accounts provide no guarantees of moral action, only that young children appear to be prepared to learn about morality. The readiness of very young children is evidenced in studies suggesting that preverbal infants engage in third-party punishment of antisocial acts (Kanakogi et al., 2022; Tasimi & Wynn, 2016) and indicate sympathy for distressed others (Kanakogi et al., 2013). Aristotle makes the more modest claim that children are born with the potential to become moral (or immoral, for that matter), in the sense of possessing capacities to internalize moral traits, but that 'none of the virtues of character arises in us naturally' (1985, p. 33 [1103a17–19]). However, it seems reasonable to update the neo-Aristotelian conception of morality to include young children's unique readiness to learn moral ways of thinking, feeling, and acting if they are taught to do so.

Second, another controversial assumption is Aristotle's (1985, p. 292 [1179b11–31]) 'early years determinism' about moral development, suggesting

---

[2] Aristotle's Biology and Psychology obviously include various anachronistic and outdated concepts that simply tend to be passed over in silence by current neo-Aristotelians, given Aristotle's own reminder that we should always defer to the latest scientific findings. However, he has nothing but scorn for those who believe that character education is just about fixing individual children and that everyone can become good irrespective of political and economic circumstances (Aristotle, 1985, pp. 21 and 203 [1099a32 and 1153b19–21]; cf. Kristjánsson, 2020, chap. 2).

[3] Aristotle refers quite often to 'natural virtue', and some interpreters think such virtue is inborn. However, we agree with Curzer (2012, pp. 296–304) that 'natural' here simply means not-yet-*phronetic*, and that 'natural virtue' and 'habituated virtue' are thus more or less synonymous.

that children brought up under terrible conditions and not receiving any significant moral stimulation in their early years will never progress towards virtue at all (cf. Kristjánsson, 2015, chap. 5). Again, the contemporary evidence on this point is mixed, with some evidence indicating that Aristotle may have been wrong about this and that radical moral conversions, if rare, are possible later in life, even for those not brought up in a minimal sense as moral agents (Kristjánsson, 2020, chap. 6; Chappell, 2022). On the other hand, it has been documented that some environmental deprivations entail irreparable deficits in individuals. An update seems reasonable that there may be capacities (e.g., facial recognition, language) that are very difficult (albeit possible) to learn if they are not acquired in what has been termed 'sensitive periods' (e.g., Pascalis et al., 2020).

Third, and related to the second worry, Aristotle does not consider attraction to abstract moral ideals as a feasible source of moral motivation. Intent on killing off the idealism of his mentor Plato, and only wanting to acknowledge the guidance from the moral characteristics of persons (role models, mentors, close friends) rather than high-minded ideals, Aristotle's developmental theory runs the danger of appearing disenchanted and deflated (or at least too cheaply practical) regarding possible sources of moral awe and inspiration (Kristjánsson, 2020, chaps 5 and 7).

Fourth, the 'paradox of moral education' that Peters (1981) famously identified looms large here: how can one be trained heteronomously to become autonomous? This paradox arises because the early habituation stage in Aristotle's model mainly seems to involve arational imitation and repetition. How does one get from there to autonomously (i.e., *phronetically*) sought moral goodness? This worry seems related to some scholars' conception of young children's imitation as an exact and mechanistic repetition of what a model does, which these scholars term 'overimitation' (Clay & Tennie, 2017; Wood et al., 2012; 2013). They justify this term by referring to the exact mimicry of sequences of action, whether or not those actions are necessary to complete a given task. Other scholars reject the 'overimitation' term because young children clearly imitate rationally, in choosing the best models to imitate (e.g., Gergely et al., 2002), completing actions a model fails to complete (e.g., Meltzoff, 1995), and differentiating errors from appropriate modelling (e.g., Want & Harris, 2001). Moreover, an alternative conception of imitation, high fidelity imitation, appears to be necessary for some forms of human learning (Kenward, 2012). In other words, imitation is not just about 'what works', it is about learning complexities that are difficult to disentangle (e.g., language).

Peters's question about how individuals progress from heteronomous teaching to the capacity to act autonomously remains an important one. There is no consensus solution to this quandary, but there are three readily available possibilities. Self-Determination Theory (Ryan & Deci, 2017) provides a detailed description of a process of internalization through which individuals learn how to act from others, then gradually take ownership of the actions and standards that guide them. A second possibility is the well-known human capacity for innovation, which generally takes a currently available ability and transforms it into something previously unavailable (Tennie et al., 2009), such as using fire and the ability to boil water to create a steam engine.

Metacognitive development offers the third (and our preferred) possible answer. We disputed Lapsley's (2021) proposal to replace the adjudicative function of *phronesis* with metacognition in Chapter 4. The concept of metacognition can be enlightening, however, if we recognize exactly how *phronesis* is metacognitive. Metacognition can occur with virtually any object-level cognition, and we are interested in how it can enhance our understanding of cognition focused on moral concerns. As Thomas et al. (2022) put it, 'the overarching goal [of metacognition research] has centred on understanding how humans monitor their internal mental processes and exert control over these processes' (p. 1). Moreover, *phronetic* metacognition is based on perspectivity, which includes complexity and coherence (Bauer et al., 2019).[4] Neither complexity nor coherence are necessarily present in metacognition in general, which can be nothing more than simple self-monitoring. Also, as Schwarz (2015) makes clear, metacognition often leads to errors through the use of improper heuristics, but the enactment of *phronesis* does not, *ex hypothesi*, lead to error. Moreover, complexity and coherence are required for *phronesis* because the perspectivity involved in *phronesis* incorporates and adjudicates among multiple perspectives. However, complexity alone is insufficient because *phronesis* involves the (at least tentative) arrival at the best or most complete perspective on a situation, with the appropriate appraisal, affect, and behaviour.

In short, our understanding of *phronesis* is that it contains a suite of metacognitive functions. Simply put, the blueprint function provides a kind of template for a good life, against which one's actions, aims, and experiences can be compared. This comparison is a classic metacognitive operation. The adjudicative function involves sorting out more or less compatible moral concerns and determining which virtue(s) are most fitting to a situation. This is also a metacognitive task in that one is reflecting on one's various virtues and deciding how they are relevant to a circumstance. As Hennecke and Bürgler

---

[4] 'Complexity' refers to the number of differing perspectives that can be considered at the same time, and 'coherence' refers to whether they can be linked and combined meaningfully.

(2023) note, identifying a conflict in response tendencies is, by definition, metacognitive. Similarly, metacognition is central to integrating cognition and emotion, which we have termed 'emotional regulation'. Emotion has generally only been included in metacognitive scholarship in terms of how it affects metacognition, but we are encouraged by Thomas et al.'s (2022) innovative model, which integrates emotion and cognition within metacognition, and Hennecke and Bürgler's (2023) incorporation of motivation in metacognition. These scholars have taken a more integrative approach to cognition, emotion, and motivation. Although the constitutive function seems the simplest of the four *phronetic* functions, it, too, is a metacognitive process in comparing one's perception of the facts of a situation and deciding which virtues fit the situation best.

This brief rehearsal of some ways to account for agentic *phronesis* are mere outlines that require further explication. In addition, these three possibilities to counter the fourth concern are not mutually exclusive, and some further conceptual work is required to answer Peters' question fully, but we have indicated some viable pathways for doing so. Yet the space we have devoted to Peters's concern shows how crucial it is, and how urgently it calls for some empirical realignment of what we have called the 'Aristotelian basics'.

Fifth, Aristotle seems to be overly demanding about the intellectual nature of moral decision-making post habituation. This is basically the normative corollary of the psychological fourth point: doing the right thing does not have any moral value, according to Aristotle (1985, p. 40 [1105a30–4]), unless it is done for the right (*phronetic*) reasons and from the right motives. Mere prosociality (good social outcome) does not seem to matter at all. So, Aristotle appears to move here between two extremes: from a habituation period, which is all about socialization and habit-formation, towards a period of complete autonomy where habituation and socialization play only a developmental role (contrast Sanderse, 2020).[5] This normative version of Peters's question does not have a current solution that both of us are happy with, so an update of Aristotle here awaits a resolution of how individuals develop from norms that others provide to autonomously formulating and endorsing norms for their own actions.

Sixth, Aristotle—despite his aversion to idealism—seems to have an overly idealized view of the psychological unity of the fully virtuous person, and to lack a sense of the residues of pain that may remain even after a fully *phronetic*

---

[5] Admittedly, the civic virtues (including law-abidingness) are not subject to this strict autonomy condition. Nevertheless, even the greatest proponents of autonomous moral decision-making in modernity would hesitate to go as far as Aristotle does here.

decision has been reached: say, the pain that Sophie (in *Sophie's Choice*) continued to experience after choosing her son over her daughter in the Nazi concentration camp. We have encountered this weakness at length in Chapter 10, where we offered an update to Aristotle's view.

Seventh, after extolling all the advantages of the *phronetic* life, Aristotle suddenly changes gear in Book 10 of the *Nicomachean Ethics*, now telling us that actually an even better life is one of mere contemplation, away from the cut and thrust of everyday activities (Kristjánsson, 2015, chap. 5). Although it is possible to interpret him as saying that this sort of life is only possible once the *phronetic* life has already been achieved, most morally committed readers will find this message deflating and potentially counterproductive from the point of view of moral development and education. Does such development and education then only have value for the sake of something else that transcends it? For someone as practically minded as Aristotle one would presumably need to factor in opportunity costs and the law of diminishing returns for those aiming at this highest supra-moral level. We leave this question for another day, as a more practical focus on *phronesis* is as much as we can tackle in this book.

11.2 Developing towards Virtue: Mining and Transcending Aristotle's Model

The previous section may have sent a mixed message to readers. On the one hand, we acknowledged how underdeveloped Aristotle's own account of the trajectory towards *phronesis* is, and how far it is from constituting a developmental theory in the modern sense. On the other hand, we noted various ways to update his views with contemporary Developmental Science.

Aristotle's account clearly needs some reconstruction for it to constitute a developmental model in the modern sense. This is the aim of the current section, elaborating on the neo-Aristotelian model presented, for instance, by the Jubilee Centre (2022). Now, Aristotle obviously wrote his texts long before the advent of Developmental Psychology, and ideas such as the Kohlbergian one about distinct stages of moral development through which everyone needs to pass in a certain order were foreign to him. Aristotle does describe people at different levels of moral maturity and some scholars have tried to adapt those into an 'Aristotelian stage theory' (Curzer, 2012; Sanderse, 2015). We have come to believe, however, that Aristotle did not think everyone needed to pass through all the levels he describes. Moreover, stage theories have not fared well in recent psychological research, so this approach seems dubious, in any case. We conclude that Aristotle is, rather, presenting two possible but distinct routes to a fully virtuous life.

The routes constitute two trajectories towards moral development.[6] The ideal trajectory, which we could name Plan A, is for those fortunate enough to have been brought up by good people (as moral exemplars), exemplifying moral habits and endowed with sufficient material resources.[7] Those fortunate children are the ones most amenable to moral development. They internalize moral habits by copying what they see being done by their role models, and gain virtue knowledge and understanding, adapted to their temperamental dispositions.[8] Guided by mentors, they become, step-by-step, 'just by doing just actions' and 'brave by doing brave actions', for example (Aristotle, 1985, p. 34 [1103b1–2]). What is more, to draw on an analogy from the field of Nutrition, they eat their 'greens' because they enjoy their taste; they do not need to force themselves to 'eat' the right things, and their emotions harmonize with their action choices. At some stage,[9] then (Aristotle is mostly silent about when this happens, though one would presume in late adolescence and early adulthood), the young gradually begin to develop critical thinking and reflection and revisit critically the traits with which they were originally inculcated: subjecting their merely habituated virtues to revision.[10] They now advance towards the stage of full autonomous virtue, which Aristotle calls 'phronetic' (i.e., guided by the metacognitive capacity of *phronesis*).[11] While some of their actions will be guided by externalist reasons (e.g., prudential motivations towards peace and sociality), most of their actions will be internally motivated by the conception they have developed of virtuous traits of character being constitutive of their identity: their second nature, so to speak. Some people—endowed with extraordinary personal strengths and/or spurred by unusual social circumstances—will progress even further than simply being *phronimoi* towards the level of heroic virtue. Those are the

---

[6] For a helpful comparison, see Hatchimonji et al.'s 'Spiral Model of *Phronesis* Development' (2020, p. 136). It is also worth noting that there are likely more than two pathways (e.g., also the development of vice), but this adapted model provides a highly simplified way to chart neo-Aristotelian virtue development.

[7] The focus on external resources foregrounds the extent to which Aristotle, unlike Socrates and Plato, allows nonrational factors to occupy a primary role in moral development.

[8] For modern evidence of those developmental factors, Bandura's (1977) work is invaluable.

[9] Of course, it is possible that, for some internal or external reasons, some moral learners stagnate at this stage, never turning their habituated virtues into *phronetic* ones. That may, however, be even worse than advancing to continence according to Plan B, because those who stagnate at the level of habituated virtue have not yet asked themselves which virtue has priority in each case 'because they have not yet tried to organize their lives around a single highest end'. They are thus likely to 'go seriously astray in their day-to-day decision making' (Kraut, 1993, p. 373).

[10] As Russell (2009, chap. 12) explains well, this creates the critical distance from one's character that grounds responsibility for it.

[11] The progression in this Plan A trajectory is thus compatible with what Ferkany (2020) refers to as 'beginner, intermediate, and expert stages' of *phronesis* development (p. 122).

Nelson Mandelas and Martin Luther Kings of this world—but Aristotle does consider heroic deeds supererogatory and not necessary for counting as fully virtuous.

The less ideal trajectory, which we could name Plan B, is for those somewhat less fortunate, brought up under more mixed moral conditions and hence less amenable, originally, to character-virtue development. Given that they will still have some moral exemplars in their environment to seek guidance from[12]—even if those happen to be outside of their immediate social environment—they will develop a conception of the morally good. However, because of the patchy ways in which this conception is strengthened, these children will arguably lack self-regulation. To return to the nutritional analogy, they may understand the value of eating their 'greens,' but they may struggle because self-control is required for eating them, and this is an unreliable motivation because they do not really love the taste. This is the stage that Aristotle calls 'incontinence' (*akrasia*).

Unfortunately, the majority of people, according to Aristotle's (1985, p. 190 [1150a15]) fairly dim view of his contemporaries, stagnate at this stage, or between incontinence and the next stage of 'continence' (*enkrateia*). Through practical habituation—either motivated by friends/mentors or their own powers of insight—a significant group of people progress towards being well self-regulated morally; and that is a considerable moral achievement. However, it still falls short of full virtue because even if the continent now actually 'eat their greens,' they still do not particularly enjoy the experience. In other words, they have to force themselves to be good. What they end up doing may be behaviourally indistinguishable from the actions of the truly virtuous, but it is not *phronetically* motivated in the same way, but rather mostly instrumentally or extrinsically driven. Yet, some of the continent agents may succeed in climbing up to the level of full virtue (the Plan A-trajectory), especially if they are fortunate enough to be in the company of close friends occupying that level.

Developmental hypotheses

Although we believe that this model is faithful enough to Aristotle's own account to count as at least 'neo-Aristotelian' and that it carries significant value

---

[12] One of us (Fowers, 2015) has suggested that humans begin life as 'ethically minded' creatures, meaning that humans are prepared to learn about moral action and only need to be guided in their moral development.

in the context of contemporary Developmental Science, we still consider it a work in progress. It is based on various explicit and implicit hypotheses that need a fuller empirical scrutiny in years to come. As a nonexhaustive list of such hypotheses, we offer 11 below. We offer some information about the theoretical provenance of each relevant hypothesis, although some of those serve mostly as received, but often implicit and unarticulated, assumptions undergirding the whole *phronesis* tradition, including and succeeding Aristotle.

> *Hypothesis 1*: There is individual variance in people's capacity to perceive situations as involving a moral dilemma (e.g., a virtue conflict), and the level of perception influences the quality of the overall decision reached.

Some Aristotelians might want to argue that seeing a situation as standing in need of *phronetic* deliberation is a necessary precursor of *phronesis* rather than part of the construct. However, the structural equation modelling of data from our pilot study, reported on in Chapter 6, placed this capacity within the rubric of *phronesis* (as proposed in Chapter 2). One interesting question here is to what extent moral sensitivity can be enhanced simply via 'virtue literacy'. For example, a young person might not perceive the need for gratitude if she does not know what the term 'gratitude' means or implies. It would indeed be good news from an educational perspective if virtue literacy is a strong predictor of moral sensitivity, for virtue literacy is the form of virtue competence that seems easiest to develop (Davison et al., 2016). However, it is unlikely that virtue literacy as such bridges the gap between knowing the good and doing the good.

> *Hypothesis 2*: There is individual variance in people's capacity to reason about situations involving a moral dilemma (e.g., a virtue conflict), and the level of reasoning capacity influences the quality of the overall decision reached.

There is not much need to justify this hypothesis as such. Its provenance is firmly within Aristotle's own theory of *phronesis* and reinforced in our Aristotelian *phronesis* model (APM). Despite interpretive differences, all Aristotelians and neo-Aristotelians will agree that a core function of *phronesis*, *qua* meta-intellectual virtue, is to reason (reflect, deliberate, arbitrate) about what to do in complex situations, especially when virtues seem to collide.

> *Hypothesis 3*: There is individual variance in people's possession of a blueprint of the flourishing life and of their identity as moral agents. This variance explains some of the quality of the overall decision reached.

This hypothesis opens up a can of worms in Aristotelian scholarship, as was duly noted in Section 2.3. What is uncontroversial is that Aristotle considered the *phronetic* agent to be in command of a clear conception of a flourishing life (*eudaimonia*). While psychologists tend to be cagey about incorporating any comprehensive normative assumptions into their specifications, it is worth noting that Grossmann, Westrate, Ardelt et al.'s (2020) model of (practical) wisdom would accommodate Hypothesis 3, as being about what they call the 'moral aspirations' inherent in the construct. Fortunately, there is much psychological research on several topics related to the blueprint function, which we touch on here.

Tomasello (2019) argues that children develop towards a moral identity that links the child's self-understanding to the norms and standards of her community. As children become more able to self-evaluate and self-regulate, they come to see that they are accountable to others and to intersubjective standards. They begin to evaluate their own and others' actions in terms of rightness, not just conformity. This developmental process seems to resonate with the blueprint function, in broad strokes.

To build on what was already said in Chapter 5, moral identity is a kind of stable personal commitment to acting according to communal ethical standards that are also central to one's identity (Hart et al., 1998). Aquino et al. (2009) defined 'moral identity' as a cognitive schema, 'consisting of moral values, goals, traits, and behavioral scripts' (p. 124) that is linked to acting morally. As several authors have pointed out, schemata differ across individuals, generally operate automatically, and are relatively stable (Aquino & Reed, 2002; Hill & Lapsley, 2009; Lapsley & Narvaez, 2004). As we discussed in Section 5.2, the chronic accessibility and situational prompting of moral identity schema help to explain consistent moral action.

In a meta-analysis of 77 studies, Hertz and Krettenauer (2016) found that in participants aged 12 and up, moral identity was correlated with moral behaviour. Pratt et al. (2003) found that an authoritative parenting style and involvement in community activities predicted other benefiting values in older adolescents. They suggested that these effects may be due to role modelling, based on the similarities between adolescents' and parents' moral ideals. Similarly, Hardy et al. (2014) reported that adolescent endorsement of moral ideals was related to parents' reports of aggression, altruism, and environmentalism.

The social standards children learn from their families and communities are generally believed to be internalized by children (Tomasello, 2019). This internalization is central to both moral identity and virtue perspectives. Csibra and Gergeley (2009) outlined a natural pedagogy wherein children are receptive to being taught normative standards by adults. Starting at 3 years of age, children tend to generalize what they are taught because they interpret the teaching as reliable and important (Butler & Tomasello, 2016). Researchers also found that 3-year-olds engage in teaching one another generic rules and normative standards about action (Göckeritz et al., 2014; Köymen et al., 2014).

Both Barkley (2012) and Tomasello (2019) suggest that the capacity for teaching others makes it possible for children to give themselves directions about how to act. Children's self-direction emerges first in overt speech, but by age 5 or 6 years, they tend to internalize this speech (Winsler, 2009). This internalization of teaching and self-direction seems to be the point of the role-reversal involved in children's games and joint activities, such as peek-a-boo (Martin & Gillespie, 2010; Tomasello, 2019). Therefore, a child's self-direction is just the application of the ability to guide others' actions to oneself. Tomasello (2019) put it this way: 'children's internalizations of adult pedagogical interactions [...] constitutes a form of normative self-regulation in which children begin to evaluate whether their decisions are good and their knowledge is valid, using as points of comparison the normative standards of rational action [...] from their cultural group' (p. 159). Beginning at age 3 years, children can provide the intersubjective standard underlying their actions. They are therefore able to give acceptable reasons for their actions to others. Although children (and some adults) may not be able to articulate the rationale for a given standard beyond conventional justifications (e.g., 'that's the way we do it'), they typically recognize and conform to those expectations.

Although these results regarding moral identity and value commitments among children suggest promise for future research, there is much detail to fill in. We added those references to the contemporary literature in order to remind readers of how far Developmental Science has progressed since Aristotle's time. That said, contemporary research still leaves the developmental sequence and the person-level development of moral identity less than fully clear.

Hypothesis 4: There is individual variance in people's capacity to regulate their emotions and 'moralize' them by integrating them with reason. This variance explains some of the quality of the overall decision reached.

While assumptions about 'virtuous emotions' are uncontroversial from an Aristotelian perspective, there might be a case for considering the integration of emotion and cognition as operating external to *phronesis*: enabling it rather than being part of it. For instance, this component does not figure in Grossmann, Westrate, Ardelt et al.'s (2020) model of (practical) wisdom. This is therefore a hypothesis that needs to be tested further.

Emotion regulation, of course, is a very substantial research topic, but, as we have been at pains to clarify, we are referring to the integration of emotion and cognition, not to the direction from or control of emotion by cognition. What we have in mind is more like enactive accounts of emotions as *inseparable* from appraisals, aims, and beliefs than like emotions as *separate* from any cognition (Clark, 2015). In ordinary experience, emotions are intimately connected to perceptions, concerns, and personal projects. What happens in *phronesis*, then, is the excellent integration of cognition and emotion, such that they are aligned in a felicitous way and aimed toward one's concept of the best way to live. As Maiese (2017) puts it: 'Reflectiveness involves directing one's attention to how one is thinking, behaving, and feeling in a specific situation, and which aspects of self-experience are deemed worthy of examination has much to do with an individual's cares and concerns' (p. 208). Much more can be said about this integration, but space allows only this brief reference.[13]

> *Hypothesis 5*: Apart from the individual variance in the four specific components, there is also variance in the overall possession of *phronesis*, and it is a scalar concept.

This hypothesis may seem unnecessary, for if there is individual variance in the components of *phronesis* (between individuals and within the same individual, depending inter alia on age and experience), then surely the same will apply to the construct as a whole. However, this hypothesis is also relevant to the question of whether the components of *phronesis* typically develop simultaneously (Hatchimonji et al., 2020) or consecutively.

> *Hypothesis 6*: The development of *phronesis* takes off in late adolescence/early adulthood.

Aristotle (1985) says that 'the young' cannot develop *phronesis*, as they lack the relevant experience (p. 160 [1142a12–16]). He does not indicate, however, how young is young or when exactly *phronesis* begins to develop. Combining Aristotle's insights with modern knowledge about the development of adult integrative (metacognitive) thinking and identity formation (Kallio, 2020), most neo-Aristotelian theorists assume that *phronesis* development takes off in (late) adolescence to early adulthood. However, much more research is needed to assess that hypothesis. Indeed, this may be one of the less plausible of the Aristotelian and neo-Aristotelian hypotheses under scrutiny here. There is, for example, considerable psychological evidence indicating that

---

[13] We refer interested readers to several informative sources (Clark, 2015; Maiese, 2017; Stichter, 2021).

adolescents can reason about risk-taking dilemmas as effectively as adults from early adolescence. We have also cited considerable research indicating that the rudiments of *phronesis* (e.g., moral identity, metacognition) are established prior to adolescence. Generally, the current evidence indicates steep metacognitive development from early adolescence to late adolescence and then a gradual plateauing (Weil et al., 2013). Regarding further developments, psychological wisdom research indicates a dip in wisdom levels in middle-age, compared to younger and older adults, perhaps because of the prevalence of mental stressors for that age group (Grossmann, Westrate, Ardelt et al., 2020, p. 117).[14]

Hypothesis 7: The earlier that the foundations of *phronesis* are laid in childhood, the better for its future development.

This hypothesis departs substantially from Burnyeat's (1980) exegesis, according to which Aristotle considered the phases of early virtue-trait habituation and later *phronesis*-formation as separate. It leans rather towards Sherman's (1989) interpretation, according to which reason-responsiveness should ideally be cultivated from early childhood, through exposure to reasons and arguments (recall the previous section).

Although empirical data regarding this hypothesis is not entirely direct, it is suggestive. For example, Tomasello's (2019) work on the internalization of parental and community standards for self-evaluation suggests the importance of early exposure to parental 'reasons' underlying moral action. Other examples include research on the ways that children commit themselves to following parental direction, even when not being observed (e.g., Kochanska, 2002), the ways that offering reasons facilitates moral development (e.g., Hardy et al., 2008), and the development of moral identity (e.g., Kingsford et al., 2018). Chapters could be written about each of these topics, but simply mentioning them as generally supportive of this hypothesis is as much as we can do here.

Hypothesis 8: How *phronesis* develops and how (well) it functions depends partly on individual personality configurations.

Aristotle obviously did not know, as we do today, about our mostly genetically constituted (e.g., Big Five) personality traits and how these traits may partly condition the formation of moral character qualities (Kristjánsson, 2013,

---

[14] Jameel (2022) found such a middle-age dip in her studied cohort of UK general medical practitioners.

chap. 3). However, this current knowledge is fully in line with Aristotle's own strong emphasis on the individualization of virtue, which is fairly unique historically in character developmental theory. Thus, it is not a concession from an Aristotelian perspective to admit that honesty will come more naturally to a person with a strong personality trait of conscientiousness but compassion to a person who is strong on agreeableness. It is also consistent with personality psychological views of the relationships between personality and virtue traits (Jayawickreme & Fleeson, 2017; Wright et al., 2021). More than that, what counts as a *phronetic* decision for the person in question will be relative to her individuality, as virtue is in the specific person, not in 'the object' (Aristotle, 1985, p. 43 [1106b1–7]). This hypothesis obviously has dramatic implications for the idea of character education in schools, as such education then needs to be tailored to the individual constitution of each student.

Hypothesis 9: What counts as a *phronetic* decision depends on developmental level.

This hypothesis is a direct implication of the developmental strand that permeates the whole Aristotelian corpus and of his insistence on how different virtues and virtue constellations characterize different phases of one's life. More specifically, Aristotle seems to believe that in early adulthood, people need to rely strongly on their 'character friends' in order to reason wisely (namely, for honing and executing their *phronesis*), while this need will diminish with greater experience (Aristotle, 1985, pp. 266 and 208 [1172a11–14, 1155a15–16]).

Research on such developmental shifts is critical for the formulation of an adequate theory of *phronetic* development. In general, the question is how an individual can transition from compliance to internalization to more self-sufficient *phronetic* decision-making. We outlined a few models of internalization above in Hypothesis 4 (e.g., committed compliance, reasons facilitating internalization), but a fuller account is not possible here.

Hypothesis 10: What counts as a *phronetic* decision will depend considerably on culture and social position.

This hypothesis is most conspicuously brought out in Aristotle's discussion of the unique position of the great-hearted people: the *megalopsychoi*, blessed with abundant resources. What *phronesis* will dictate regarding the overall balance of virtue for the *megalopsychoi* (think of Bill Gates in the modern world) is drastically different from the balance for an ordinary *phronimos* with little material resources (1985, pp. 97–104 [1123a34–1125a35]). Different cultural expectations and norms will also presumably play a role here, as noted by

Grossmann, Westrate, Ardelt et al. (2020, p. 119) because what counts as good and wise likely varies in part by culture.

Hypothesis 11: The development and exhibition of *phronesis* is partly dependent on positive social circumstances and hence on 'moral luck'.

Aristotle's insistence on the need for certain (especially sociopolitical) external circumstances for the development and sustenance of one's virtue make-up is fairly strict—setting his theory apart, for instance, from the assumption that one finds in theorists as distinct as Socrates, Buddha, Confucius, and the Stoics of virtue being sovereign in the sense that nothing can harm the good person. Aristotle (1985) objects strongly, as we have pointed out before, saying that those who maintain that we can flourish 'when we are broken on the wheel, or fall into terrible misfortunes, provided that we are good [. . .] are talking nonsense' (p. 203 [1153b19–21]).[15] This view, as well as Aristotle's claim that *phronesis* requires civic virtues, not only (personal) moral ones, distinguishes his form of virtue theory and character education from more individualistic varieties that mostly eschew sociopolitical contexts. Virtue theory predicts this kind of variation across contexts (Fowers et al., forthcoming), and some evidence for this variability across contexts is available for decision-making (Briggs & Lumsdon, 2022; Kallio, 2020) and for virtues in general (Ferrari & Potworowski, 2010; Fowers et al., 2022; Thoma et al., 2019).

11.3 Some General Educational Hypotheses and Observations

> [. . .] whereas young people become accomplished in geometry and mathematics, and wise within these limits, [*phronetic*] young people do not seem to be found. The reason is that [*phronesis*] is concerned with particulars as well as universals, and particulars become known from experience, but a young person lacks experience, since

---

[15] For a focus on how *phronesis* development can be compromised by poverty, trauma, adversity, and marginalization, see Hatchimonji et al. (2020). While a certain amount of adversity may be likely to foster *phronesis*-developing processes, experiencing either too few or too many of such experiences is likely to have adverse consequences (Grossmann, Westrate, Ardelt et al., 2020, p. 116). Some studies indicate that lower-class individuals generally exhibit higher levels of wisdom than higher-class ones, perhaps because of greater interdependence, greater social vigilance, and a better navigation of their resource-poor environment (Grossmann, Westrate, Ardelt et al., 2020, p. 120).

> some length of time is needed to produce it. (Aristotle, 1985, p. 160 [1142a12–16])

The salience of the intellectual meta-virtue of *phronesis* for any Aristotelian or quasi-Aristotelian programme of character education can hardly be overstated. It must form the lynchpin of any sound, holistic programme that aims to target such education for older adolescents or budding professionals.[16] For instance, no decent programme of Professional Ethics in, say, teacher training could—from a neo-Aristotelian perspective—pass muster without primary attention being paid to *phronesis* (cf. Harðarson, 2019).

All that said, when turning from the development to the education of *phronesis*, we cannot avoid repeating our deflationary comment from the beginning of this chapter. Despite the abundance of teaching materials produced within the umbrella of so-called character education—and even more specifically 'Aristotelian character education'—in the last few decades,[17] very little of it is geared towards the cultivation of *phronesis*. A 2020 special issue of *Journal of Moral Education* (vol. 49.1) notwithstanding, individual research articles are also sparse and disparate, and meta-analyses are nonexistent. Indeed, even if we widen the lens to wisdom education more generally, the state of the current literature cannot be described otherwise than as fairly dire. It is not only that interventions to cultivate wisdom are much rarer than interventions to build many other character strengths and virtues, such as gratitude or forgiveness, the 'practical' or 'educational' literature is even more eclectic than the general psychological literature on wisdom (e.g., by drawing more commonly on religious perspectives), and it is often difficult to see what various scholars have in common (Ferrari & Potworowski, 2010).[18] Attempts to give an overview of this educational literature are also few and far between. It says a lot about the current state of play that the fairly brisk review by Grossmann, Westrate, Ardelt et al. (2020, pp. 117–19) is probably the best place to begin for researchers wanting to gain a comprehensive view of what has been done

---

[16] Hatchimonji et al. (2020) argue that *phronesis* can, even more broadly, serve as an overarching construct to pull together the different priorities of 'positive youth development'.

[17] See, for example, the huge list of free resources available here: https://www.jubileecentre.ac.uk/432/character-education. To rectify this imbalance somewhat, the Centre has recently produced a free teaching resource on *phronesis* within Professional Ethics: https://www.jubileecentre.ac.uk/2997/projects/virtues-in-the-professions/online-cpd-professional-ethics

[18] Interventions to enhance wisdom may seem to face an uphill battle, at least in public schools, when they go beyond the simple task of promoting critical 'expert knowledge' (Ferrari, 2010, p. 217). Ferrari comments that the aim to teach wisdom can only be achieved by radical personal transformations and epiphanies that run against the grain of state education in Western liberal democracies, which is meant to be neutral with regard to comprehensive conceptions of living well (Ferrari, 2010, p. 221). We agree that this may be part of the problem. However, it is difficult to envisage successful school interventions in the field of gratitude or forgiveness either that do not violate the idea of strict state neutrality on conceptions of the good life.

in this area (see also Huynh & Grossmann, 2020; Sternberg & Glück, 2022, chap. 6[19]).

Our survey of the relevant background literature suggests that the diffusion characteristic of extant wisdom interventions lies in the fact that most interventions do not take any distinct model of wisdom, such as the Common Wisdom Model (CWM) or the APM, as their starting point, and that they almost invariably work (implicitly) on just one, or maximum two, components of wisdom or *phronesis*, rather than the virtue as a whole.[20] For example, an interesting project on the development of social reasoning, based on dialogical and collaborative methods (Lin et al., 2019), might be good at developing the constitutive and integrative functions of *phronesis*, but it has little to do with the blueprint function or the emotional regulative one. A host of interventions to develop 'emotional intelligence' via 'social and emotional learning' exist (Durlak et al., 2011), but they usually do not target other aspects of *phronesis*, nor indeed see themselves as having anything to do with practical wisdom as such. Quite a lot is known about how to build a sense of purpose and moral identity in young people (Damon, 2008), but less is known about how such teaching can interact with work on the other components of *phronesis*. As Jeste et al. (2020) remind us, however, enhancing individual components of wisdom is not the same as increasing overall wisdom, and Grossmann, Westrate, Ferrari et al. (2020, p. 191) pile on the agony with their well-founded admission that 'little is known' about the salience of the *order* of teaching: for example (given the two pillars of their CWM), whether perspectival metacognition requires the moral aspirations to be taught first or vice versa.

Every cloud has a silver lining, however. We have found a lot of educational research, *under other designations*, that appears to be about the cultivation of what Aristotle called *phronesis* (or at least crucial components of it), either indirectly or directly. We are thinking here of research about metacognitions, postformal thinking, self-reflection, social reasoning, professional expertise, tacit knowledge, and various other related topics (cf. Kallio, 2020). For instance, when we reviewed precedents for a prospective *phronesis* intervention for secondary school students,[21] the most useful example was the

---

[19] Interestingly, Sternberg and Glück (2022, chap. 6) devote half of their chapter to exposing various fallacies that undermine wise thinking, motivated by the maxim that 'the first task of cultivating wisdom is to combat foolishness' (p. 130).

[20] This is not surprising. As Wright et al. (2021, chap. 2) correctly note, one of the biggest weaknesses of existing measures of virtues is the lack of theoretical depth behind the conceptions being employed. See further in Chapter 12.

[21] This intervention was begun twice in 2020 but had to be aborted both times because of Covid-related restrictions in the participating schools.

above-mentioned intervention by Lin et al. (2019) to enhance what they call 'social reasoning'.[22] The trick here, then, is not to reinvent the wheel but try to build on what other researchers have done in overlapping areas (cf. Sternberg, 2001).[23] In other words, new interventions will not need to be constructed *de novo*; the key will lie in combining them together correctly under the guidance of holistic models like the APM or the CWM. After that distillation work is done, the next step is to look at some of the remaining untested hypotheses about *phronesis*, which we listed in the previous section and will add to presently, addressing them one by one. There is every reason to believe that light will emerge at the end of this tunnel, as 96% of the wisdom researchers that Grossmann, Westrate. Ardelt et al. (2020) surveyed believed that wisdom is malleable in principle (p. 117).

We had originally planned to devote the current section to an educational intervention aimed at cultivating *phronesis* at the secondary school (high school) level, and Section 11.4 to *phronesis* initiatives at the university level: within Professional Ethics Education. However, because of the fragmented and diffuse nature of the existing literature, the current section must be hypothetical at this juncture. We turn now to some broad testable hypotheses about neo-Aristotelian *phronesis* education, and then add some scattered observations about such education that can be gleaned from the literature.

Educational hypotheses

Here are three hypotheses about the educational methods for teaching *phronesis*. Those hypothesized methods may seem to coincide with the methods of (moral) virtue in general, but they are still worth rehearsing here because of the close relationship between *phronesis* and the moral virtues: the former cannot exist without the latter and the latter can only exist when *phronesis* advances beyond a developmentally rudimentary form (as mere habituated virtues). We present those hypotheses here in the same form as we did for the developmental hypotheses in Section 11.2.

---

[22] This intervention utilizes real-life dilemmas to help students advance the four components of *phronesis*. Like Wright et al. (2021, chap. 3), we believe that moral dilemmas offer a fertile context in which to track the activity of practical wisdom. However, dilemmas need to be chosen wisely and be both relatable and relevant for the cohort in question (e.g., Briggs & Lumsdon, 2020, on dilemmas relevant to secondary-school students). See also what we say in the following section about developing *phronesis* in policing.

[23] For example, Bezanilla et al. (2019) offer a helpful overview of the abundant literature on teaching critical thinking in higher education. However, nowhere do the terms '*phronesis*' or 'practical wisdom' feature in their article: a telling example of how fragmented and siloed these apparent 'overlapping areas' are.

Hypothesis 12: A non-virtue-friendly ethos, for instance one steeped in rules, codes, and regulations, can hinder the development and execution of *phronesis*.

This was not a specific concern for Aristotle himself—apart from a more general threat to virtue-and-*phronesis* development that he identified in adverse social circumstances. However, this hypothesis is often raised by contemporary advocates of *phronesis* in professional contexts, and they have provided some evidence to support it (Schwartz & Sharpe, 2010). Harðarson's (2019) recent piece on teachers' *phronesis* (or lack thereof) is an extended variation on this theme. Although we mostly shelve further discussions of *phronesis* within Professional Ethics Education until the following section, this hypothesis has a wider application. *Phronesis* is unlikely to be acquired in a learning environment that is inimical to virtue development in general. As Russell notes (2021, p. 17), the difficulties in learning *phronesis* are not only caused by its 'high intrinsic load' (the need to synthesize cognitively different values and virtues) but also by a 'high extrinsic load' (environments typically full of misleading feedback, bad advice, and false friends). As Tomasello (2019) and others (e.g., Casler et al., 2009; Kenward, 2012) have pointed out, the context and its regular practices tend to recommend normative standards that are absorbed by learners.

Hypothesis 13: *Phronesis* is partly learned through teaching.

This hypothesis is simply based on Aristotle's (1985, p. 33 [1103a14–16]) claim that, distinct from the moral virtues which are (originally) learned through habituation, the intellectual virtues (including *phronesis*) grow from teaching and experience. The problem is once again that Aristotle does not tell us what sort of teaching is required, and this hypothesis thus clearly needs to be fleshed out with specifics before it can be made testable. Curzer (2012) frankly states that because 'specifics are frustratingly absent' in Aristotle's corpus, there is not much that the mere exegete can say: 'Aristotle leaves the nature of teaching unspecified, as will I' (p. 351). We do not give up as easily, and we mention some subhypotheses about *phronesis* teaching strategies below. We also return to the (limited) use of teaching *phronesis* in Section 11.4.

Hypothesis 14: *Phronesis* is best developed through a battery of interventions that target its different components.

We have complained repeatedly about Aristotle's reticence regarding the nuts and bolts of *phronesis* cultivation. However, he does suggest several different methods for virtue development more generally, and neo-Aristotelians have added considerably to that mix.[24] Let us just mention some of those methods and how they could possibly be hypothesized to target one or more of the components/functions of *phronesis* in the APM.[25] Consider those as four subhypotheses of Hypothesis 14:

(14.1) Moral identity can be fruitfully developed though exposure to art/literature, role models, and direct teaching; (14.2) moral sensitivity can be productively developed through exposure to moral quandaries (e.g., through literature or films[26]) and via service learning; (14.3) moral emotions can be developed through engagement with character friends, moral quandaries, and music; (14.4) moral reasoning can be fruitfully developed through grappling with moral quandaries, and learning from mentors and character friends.

It must be admitted that those subhypotheses have little else to recommend them at this stage beyond their (presumed) intuitive appeal and their provenance in some of Aristotle's texts. They are not sufficiently grounded in the empirical literature, and we present them here simply as food for thought—and for future testing. What we can simply say at this point that the most obvious instructional strategy that can be gleaned from our APM in Chapter 2 is to home in on the components/functions delineated there one by one and hope that added competencies, developed through the discrete methods suggested above, become synergized into an overall *phronesis* capacity. However, we know precious little yet about the best order in which to do this or the best overall plan of action.

We have combed the academic literature on *phronesis* (or wisdom more generally), trying to elicit specific pieces of practical advice on educational strategies, but this is a bit like looking for needles in a haystack. We present some scattered observations below, but they do not amount to any cohesive educational theory about *phronesis*.

---

[24] On specific *phronesis* interventions for online contexts, see Harrison (2022).
[25] Cf. also Hatchimonji et al.'s (2020) educational framework of a spiral staircase, according to which all the components of *phronesis* must be repeatedly reinforced via different methods and across multiple situations.
[26] When such sources are mentioned in the virtue ethical literature (often drawing on Iris Murdoch or Martha Nussbaum), the general assumption seems to be that psychologically 'thick' character descriptions from high-brow (often nineteenth-century) literature will be most salutary; and standard uses of 'thin', 'unpopulated' (Cigman, 2018) scenarios in Moral Philosophy and Moral Education is considered suspect. As Carr (2022) correctly points out, however, 'too much attention to the "thick" personal peculiarities of human nature may be more distracting than helpful in bringing key moral points to light', and apparently 'under-described' parables and allegories, such as Plato's Allegory of the Cave and Jesus's parables of the Prodigal Son and the Good Samaritan, may do the trick as well or even better. Standard references to King Solomon in the wisdom literature may be illustrative of the same point, as the stories about his *phronetic* skills are often seriously underdetermined, yet compelling.

Self-distancing
Various findings indicate that people are better at taking wise decisions on behalf of others than themselves (Huynh & Grossmann, 2020). A *phronesis* intervention using moral quandaries is more likely to work, therefore, when focusing on third-person scenarios in the first instance and only moving later in the programme, through ego-decentring, to first-person ones (Grossmann & Kross, 2014).

Role models
Role model education (or, as Aristotle would put it, learning frommoral exemplars) is a staple of early years character education (e.g., Osman, 2019). However, typically being fairly uncritical at that stage, this method comes with a known plethora of problems: moral inertia, moral over-stretching, and hero-worship (Kristjánsson, 2020, chap. 4; Swanton, 2003, chap. 3). Will those problems disappear if role model education is introduced as part of a more critical and reflective programme of *phronesis* education? Unfortunately, there is reason for caution here. The situations in which role models exhibit practical wisdom are often highly specific and far removed from the experiential worlds of the students. Moreover, lessons from stories about role models are often pitched at too high a level of generality, not taking account of the contextual/perspectival nature of practical wisdom. For example, King Solomon was unfortunately not wise across the board (Grossmann, 2017a). Hatchimonji et al. (2020) mention Malala Yousafzai and Maya Angelou as role models that should be 'culturally familiar' to middle-school students of colour in a US context. Although this has the laudable quality of transcending white exemplars of *phronesis*, there is more to relatability in terms of wisdom than just 'cultural familiarity' (cf. Han et al., 2017). Athanassoulis (2023) has even produced an extended two-pronged argument showing that the 'less-than-virtuous' may be better role models for moral learners than the *phronimoi* (contra the received wisdom from Hursthouse, 1999, and many other virtue ethicists). Her 'perspective argument' (which could also be called the 'opaqueness argument') is that the perspective of the *phronimos* is *ex hypothesi* opaque to the student much lower in the developmental ladder. Her 'context argument' is that the *phronimos* operates within a very different social context from the learner. In response to the worry that the learner will just pick up errors rather than wisdom from the less-than-virtuous, Athanassoulis points out that the latter have typically developed some elements of *phronesis* that are available for proper imitation as long as they are at least at a slightly higher level of maturity than the learner (cf. Stangle, 2020, p. 80).[27]

---

[27] While we agree with Athanassoulis that less than fully developed *phronimoi* probably make, in general, better role models for *phronimoi* beginners, we worry that she goes too far in arguing that the continent

Reflection

There are huge bodies of literature on reflection, both in school and professional contexts, although most of those do not forge any explicit link with wisdom or *phronesis* education, nor indeed define the term 'reflection' clearly.[28] Those who foreground the blueprint component of the APM are likely to encourage reflection on that component; conversely, scepticism about (the need for) a blueprint of the good life will elicit scepticism about reflection (Cokelet, 2022).[29] An interesting study by Bruya and Ardelt (2018) indicates that self-reflection on one's own character strengths through journal writing can enhance wisdom—more so than reflecting on the character strengths of a role model.[30] Other studies have shown that reflecting with the aim of advising or teaching others can be more beneficial than simply reflecting on your own (Huynh & Grossmann, 2020). However, the downside to all of this is that for reflection to work as a wisdom-enhancer, it needs to have reached a certain level of competence. Otherwise, bad reflection can simply perpetuate and reinforce existing errors of moral thought.

Related intellectual virtues

It is a fair bet that various other intellectual virtues, such as open-mindedness and intellectual humility, are related to *phronesis*, so that cultivating those further will bestow indirect benefits on *phronesis* also. The problem is that those virtues have been shown to vary as much or even more across situations than *phronesis* does (Huynh & Grossmann, 2020). One can be very open-minded regarding personal mores within one's family but close-minded politically; intellectually humble towards one's siblings but intellectually arrogant towards work colleagues. There is thus not much mileage to be had from relying on

---

would make good role models for such beginners. Recall that, in the Aristotelian developmental model, continence is not a natural steppingstone from habituated to *phronetic* virtue but a second-best tack for those who have not developed *phronesis* but need to exercise Kantian-like self-control to stay on the straight and narrow. We worry, therefore, that budding *phronimoi* will be led down the wrong path by the continent. As an illustration, consider that a solid second-division soccer coach may not make the best trainer for an aspiring premier-league player.

[28] For a philosophical reflection on 'reflection' and on the unhelpful dichotomy between reflection and intuition, see Bortolotti (2011).
[29] Although Warren et al. (2022) are less inclined to an Aristotelian conception of the blueprint component than we are, they refuse to go as far as Cokelet (2022) in their reflection scepticism.
[30] More generally on the use of self-or-other narratives for enhancing practical wisdom (this time in the context of medical education), see Kaldjian (2019); Jameel (2022, chap. 2.9).

other virtues doing the job that *phronesis* is meant to do, or on influencing *phronesis* positively—apart from the truism that virtues tend to 'hunt in packs'.

Leadership

Various performance virtues may also stand in a close relationship to *phronesis*. We would specifically like to mention leadership here—although leadership is sometimes presented as a moral virtue rather than just a performative one and would thus naturally fall under the jurisdiction of *phronesis* anyway. We recommend a recent article by Bohlin (2022) on how morally and intellectually minded school leaders can cultivate their own *phronesis* and contribute to the *phronesis* development of their staff and students by following certain procedures of *recognizing* (their initial reactions to quandaries), *reflecting*, *recalibrating*, and *responding* (more reflectively).

All in all, the literature on wisdom education, in general, and *phronesis* education, in particular—scattered and terminologically diverse as they are—seem to paint a pretty similar picture of the ingredients needed to progress in this area. To be sure, there is no short cut to cultivating *phronesis*, but as Hursthouse (2011) notes, 'there may be some ways that are shorter than others' (p. 54). Alternately, we say that there is no guaranteed way of cultivating *phronesis*, but some ways might be more promising than others.

11.4 Professional *Phronesis* Education and the Limited Role of Teaching

In this follow-up section to 11.3, we turn the lens once again to Aristotle's cryptic remarks about *phronesis* being cultivated through *experience* and *teaching*, and we now focus specifically on *phronesis* as part of Professional Ethics Education, with most of the discussion relating—as a case in point—to a recent intervention to cultivate *phronesis* in UK Police Science students, and to the role of teaching in that intervention.

It seems reasonable to suppose that the 'experience' required for *phronesis* development is experience of the sort of quandaries that *phronesis* is meant to solve: namely, by gradually becoming more adept at figuring out what to do about them and why. Obviously, those experiences cannot be induced artificially or pre-empted through any educational interventions,[31] so let us confine

---

[31] Some technically minded moral educators believe that virtual-reality technologies (e.g., the 'metaverse') will, in the near future, enable us to induce those experiences in students in class before they encounter them in real life.

our attention to the 'teaching' element. What is it precisely that we can teach students that helps them build up this intellectual virtue?

Police Ethics education

As already noted, Professional Ethics constitutes one of the growth areas in the recent resurgence of *phronesis* research. While professional codes of ethics tend to be essentially rule-based, the UK Police *Code of Ethics* (College of Policing, 2014) constitutes an exception. Although it employs the language of Police 'principles', 8 of those 9 'principles' happen to be virtues. Moreover, the Code produces a so-called National Decision Model for police officers that bears a striking resemblance to a neo-Aristotelian model of *phronesis*. The Code is replete with warnings about a belief in the unproblematic codifiability of Police activities, and it foregrounds what we could call three D's of *phronesis*—discernment, deliberation, and discretion—although it does not refer directly to the concept of *phronesis*. Recent scandals in UK policing have prompted a renewed focus on the ethical basis of the police force, and a new report on character virtues (or a lack thereof) in policing in England and Wales has provided considerable enlightenment about the current state of play in this area (Kristjánsson, Thompson, & Maile, 2021).

To cut a long story short, this report makes various recommendations about how Police Ethics education can be improved. Simultaneously, the Code of Ethics is undergoing a revision which—at least if the advice from the report is heeded—may lead to it becoming even more explicitly virtue ethical and *phronesis*-focused than before. In the spring of 2022, the authors of the report (including one of the present authors) trialled an intervention for Police Science students at a number of UK universities, aimed at cultivating *phronesis* through teaching. What matters for present purposes are some of the considerations and reflections that went into preparing the lesson plans for the relevant students. Those will be used, in the remainder of this section, as a platform from which to view the possibilities—but, no less importantly, the limitations—of *teaching* as a method to facilitate advanced moral functioning, such as that embodied in the intellectual virtue of *phronesis*.

The first constraint that we encountered was that of *time*. The most we could negotiate with the universities in question was an intervention taking up four 45-minute classes spread over 4–6 weeks. Typically, 'Professional Ethics' was not a special subject in those Police Science students' timetables so we had to negotiate an entry into 'related' taught subjects in the curriculum (such as 'Accountability'), where time is already limited.[32] This may seem like a fortuitous and non-academically relevant consideration, but in the light of Aristotle's own insistence that the development of good character is a practical rather than a theoretical enterprise, it is a highly relevant one. Given the way professional education is conducted, it is unrealistic to assume that the time allocated to direct teaching about *phronesis* will be anything other than strictly limited. We also decided that, since we could not assume that the students had any background in virtue theory, we would need to devote the first class mostly to teaching towards what is nowadays referred to as 'virtue literacy': simply explaining to them what terms such as 'character', 'virtue', 'virtue ethics', and '*phronesis*' mean, and how those might be related to the Police Code of Ethics and the National Decision Model.

This left us with three classes for the 'substantive' part of the intervention. We decided to devote those mostly to a deep discussion of topical Police dilemmas. The choice of those dilemmas was tricky—they would have to be *relevant*, *realistic*, and *relatable* (Han et al., 2017). However, we were aided here by the work of an Expert Panel who had already helped us create dilemmas for a previous study (Kristjánsson, Thompson, & Maile, 2021). Here is an example of one of the dilemmas chosen. We referred to this dilemma cursorily in Chapter 10, but now it is time to reproduce it in full:

> You work in a police response unit. A new female student officer of South Asian heritage joins your team under the degree holder's entry programme. Whilst you are alone with a close and experienced white, male colleague, he refers to the new officer and comments, 'I bet her parents are disappointed she's a copper. A Paki with a degree; there's not many of them—she should have done Law and become a lawyer, or Finance and been an accountant.' You have never previously heard your colleague express views like this and have worked alongside him for a number of years. What would you do?[33]

Through a guided discussion, the students were asked to discuss and reach a conclusion about various questions, including: (1) Which virtues or values are competing here and steering the police officer (later: 'you') in different

---

[32] There are no clear limits to the nature of courses into which *phronesis* can be incorporated. For instance, Goddiksen and Gjerris (2022) describe the introduction of *phronesis* into a Research Integrity course, aimed at replacing a legalistic compliance focus on research integrity.

[33] To make the dilemma realistic and engaging, the Expert Panel deemed it necessary to frame it in a language that may strike some readers as offensive. Notice that while this dilemma asks about what *you* would do, we followed the advice from Huynh and Grossmann (2020) by framing them in the third person: what should the *police officer* do? As we noted in the preceding section, research indicates that, at least at an early stage, a self-distancing strategy helps students focus more clear-headedly on the moral issue at hand.

directions? (2) What are the pros and cons of each action option? (3) Is the police officer experiencing strong emotions prior to the decision? (4) If so, what are those emotions? (5) What should the police officer do, in your view?

At the close of the intervention, the students were asked to relate their answers to the Police Code of Ethics and the National Decision Model—as well as reflecting further upon how those texts are related to the *phronesis* model, and what the possible synergies of those might be. A post-test with the *phronesis* measure from Chapter 6 was then administered to gauge whether progress had been made during the intervention in *phronetic* decision-making (compared to a pre-test with the same measure), with respect to one or more of the components/functions of *phronesis*.

The intervention, briefly sketched above, was no rocket science. The aim was, somewhat obviously, to help students develop the different components of *phronesis* in the APM, by taking them through some of the considerations that motivate and (ideally) strengthen each component. The method of teaching was a guided discussion about relevant dilemmas: a method that has a long history in approaches to Moral Education, as distinct as those of Kohlbergianism, neo-Kohlbergianism, and virtue-based character education. Without wanting to underplay the potential strengths of this approach, which are fairly well documented within these three traditions (e.g., Thoma et al., 2013), we will in the remainder of this section focus on its limitations.

To couch the rationale of the intervention in a slightly more academic educational language, it was set within what we deem to be the Police Science students' 'zone of proximal development' (ZPD) as *phronesis* learners. In line with Vygotsky (1978), we understand that zone to sit between two other zones, of (1) what students can learn by themselves without going through the actual future experiences and (3) what students will have learned after going through the actual future experiences. The ZPD marks the in-between zone of (2) what students can learn prior to the actual experiences through 'scaffolded teaching' by a skilled tutor.

Here is the first problem. Policing is—along with professions such as Medicine, Nursing, Teaching, and the Military—a *burdened profession* in the sense in which practitioners are likely to encounter various psychologically charged, and even life-changing, situations that are impossible to explain to students in sufficient depth before they encounter them. These are also professions with a high rate of burn-out, perhaps because of various factors that gradually seem to sap the practitioners' original moral purpose in entering them (Arthur, Earl et al., 2021). Ideally, in order to elicit the necessary trust between the tutor and the student, the former should be a trusted mentor or a 'character friend' who has already gone through some of the experiences that are being related to students. Otherwise, there is danger that the 'scaffolding' effect will not be activated. In our case, we simply did not have access to Police Science lecturers with sufficient knowledge of applied virtue ethics to steer a *phronesis* intervention themselves. The tutors were therefore academics without grounding in Police Science and without practical experience in working within a police force. That is a notable limitation—although, on the other hand, having the same tutors deliver the intervention across different cohorts/universities offered a layer of methodological robustness.

The second problem is that the dilemmas presented to the students involve experiences that are in a fundamental sense *embodied*. We are not using the term here in any obscure philosophical sense,[34] but simply as referring to the fact that the experiential context involves physical processes and feelings as well as mental reflection. To give an analogy, it is almost impossible to explain to a young child what sexual jealousy feels like and how those feelings will affect moral decision-making once the relevant adolescent hormones have kicked in. The child will perhaps know what sibling jealousy feels like, and analogies can be drawn with those experiences, but they are not the same as the experiences of sexual jealousy. Similarly, some of the dilemmas presented to the Police Science students involved situations that are bound to elicit strong physical and emotional reactions—but ones which cannot be known 'in one's skin' prior to the event (recall Athanassoulis' (2023) 'opaqueness argument' in Section 11.3).

In short, we are dealing here with a ZPD that is severely circumscribed by the fact that the situations for which the students are being prepared are experientially conditioned and embodied. All that can be achieved within the ZPD is an *intellectual* exercise that may, at best, stimulate certain discrete components of *phronesis* but can only partially account for the context in which the eventual decision will be set.[35] If we venture further than that, in attempting to expand the ZPD, two perils await us. One is *developmental naivety*, in which complex experiences are reduced to an intellectual exercise in an attempt to

---

[34] For instance, although we agree with Pickup's (2020) view of embodiment as antithetical to pure technical rationality, we are not in tune with his forging of a link between *phronesis* and what he calls 'the corporeal turn' in ontology towards a 'new materialism'.

[35] Unsurprisingly, therefore, Ardelt (2020) found that that a wisdom intervention that targeted 'the whole person' had a greater effect than more context-and-discipline-specific teaching. At the same time, Grossmann's (2017a) research indicates that teaching about how wisdom exemplars react to dilemmas is most beneficial to students if those examples are situated within specific contexts that the exemplars encountered and mastered. Those findings are not incompatible. If practical wisdom is a multi-component construct, as the APM assumes, it is likely that a broad approach to enhancing it will be the most effective *pedagogical strategy*. On the other hand, the *content* of the stories used to hone the different components may need to be highly situation-specific for it to resonate with the students.

articulate something that is inarticulable out of context[36]—possibly inducing the infamous Dunning-Kruger effect.[37] The second is *paternalism*, in which we cavalierly ignore the students' need to engage in their own Millian 'experiments in living' prior to becoming capable of making autonomous moral decisions, be those professional or personal.

That said, the temptation is very strong to expand the ZPD, especially if the tutors have gone through some of those experiences themselves and perhaps made mistakes that they want to pre-empt in students. The educational dilemma created here is a well-known one, with implications far beyond any interventions to cultivate Aristotelian *phronesis*. On the one hand, we may have tutors who know in their own skin what typically 'happens to the heart' in the relevant profession;[38] on the other hand, we have budding professionals who have not gone through those experiences and are full of idealism about their future work. The tutors do not want to curb the students' idealism, but they also want to convey to them a sense of the challenges ahead.

One of Leonard Cohen's most compelling lyrics (from the song 'Happens to the heart', released posthumously in 2018) is about this very dilemma—although it is set in a personal rather than a professional context. The song ponders the question of whether we should 'tell the young messiah / what happens to the heart'. Cohen charts his youthful exuberance in 'meeting Christ and reading Marx'. However, he describes the perils he encountered in trying to 'double park', namely pursue two incompatible values (in his case, presumably women!) at the same time, and how that left 'an ugly mark' on his heart. Gradually, he became more aware of how the exigencies and vicissitudes of life undermine one's unity, and how such experiences stifle and stunt: 'It ain't pretty, it ain't subtle / What happens to the heart'. The educational message of this song is clear, even if implicit. It remains an open question how much one can or should tell the young apprentice beforehand about 'what happens to the heart'.

Contrary to what Aristotle told us, direct teaching is probably quite a useful—even if limited—method of character education in early age. For example, teaching young children what the words 'gratitude' and 'grateful' mean—and how they can be distinguished from words such as 'appreciation'

---

[36] One further area of debate, which we gloss over here, is the extent to which an experienced *phronimos* needs to be linguistically articulate about her experiences and knowledge in order to be a good moral teacher/role model (Annas, 2011; Athanassoulis, 2023).

[37] The Dunning-Kruger effect is a cognitive bias through which people with limited knowledge or competence in a given intellectual or social domain greatly overestimate their own knowledge or competence in that domain.

[38] The *limitation* described earlier, in our intervention, of not having it led by a tutor with a police background may be partly offset by the current consideration.

and 'appreciative'—almost certainly helps them to understand the nuances of the terms and (possibly) to internalize the relevant virtuous emotions in their proper instantiations (cf. Gulliford, 2018). This section has, however, focused on the age of early adulthood where Aristotle himself presumably saw the greatest need for teaching—namely as a steppingstone towards *phronesis*—although he failed to tell us what form such teaching should take.

Drawing on an Aristotelian model of *phronesis*, we have described an attempt to prepare young Police Science students for the vagaries of police work through a short course on *phronetic* decision-making: a course attempting to hit a Vygotskyan ZPD, paving the ground for the embodied experiences that the students are likely to encounter as police officers. We have aimed in this section at dampening enthusiasm about the effectiveness of any such intervention by explaining how tantalizingly small this growth zone will be. That should not surprise those who have studied the more general development of mature adult thinking in the professional realm. Those studies tend to revolve around constructs such as 'professional reflection', 'skill acquisition', 'expertise', and 'tacit knowledge' (e.g., Kallio, 2020), and the growth of all of these is considered to be fundamentally experiential and sluggishly cumulative. It would be a miracle if *phronesis* development presented any radically different features.

Even the two most vocal champions of *phronesis* as part of Professional Ethics Education claim that it 'is not something that can be taught' (Schwartz & Sharpe, 2010, p. 271)—although they probably understand the term 'teaching' more narrowly in this context than Aristotle did. While we would not go as far as Schwartz and Sharpe, it is worth reminding readers of the well-known Chinese fable of the farmer who impatiently tried to pull up his rice shoots to make then grow faster, as a result of which they lost their rootedness and withered away. Young Police Science students, for instance, need to be fed a diet that does not exhaust their capacities for digestion—which is not the same as saying that they should not be provided with an intellectual initiation into some of the tough and discretionary choices that await them, and with a stark warning that no Police rule book will relieve them of the responsibility for making those choices themselves in the line of duty.

If this scepticism is well-grounded, it carries implications that go beyond any educational theories of *phronesis* cultivation. What the two mutual historic nemeses of all Moral Education, Kohlberg and Aristotle, seem to agree about is the reduced role of the environment or ethos for development as the moral learner matures, and an increased role for (what Vygotskyans would call) 'scaffolded teaching' and for autonomous decision-making.[39]

---

[39] This is not to underplay the vast differences between Kohlberg and Aristotle. Kohlberg does not understand this developmental process to be towards virtue, but rather towards higher stages of moral reasoning

In contrast, we hazard to conjecture that, at least in the area of Professional Ethics Education, such education never ceases to rely heavily on situational cues and other uncodifiable and essentially unpredictable lessons picked up in the cauldron of professional work: an essentially unsystematic moral environment. However well students are prepared through taught lessons—and however well motivated they are to seek the good of their own accord through varied work experiences—norms and values caught on the job will remain a powerful source of moral motivation. Perhaps, rather than either ignoring the 'caught' elements, or completely giving in to passive 'moral situationism' about them (Doris, 2002), *phronesis* education needs to prepare students for critically evaluating those influences. In the context of Police Ethics Education, for example, that means teaching students to be alert to norms issuing from the so-called blue code (Westmarland & Rowe, 2018) and to learn to subject those to scrutiny before they become an integral part of their moral identity.

We have taken an example in this section of a profession, the UK Police, which is for historical reasons fairly amenable to a focus on *phronesis*. There are obviously other professions where barriers to *phronesis* development seem to be higher, for various reasons. The strict top-down control of teaching in many countries has, for example, seriously limited the scope for *phronetic* decision-making in the classroom. Harðarson (2019) even wonders whether it is fair to expose teacher trainees to the ideal of *phronesis* if they are then debarred from using this mode of thinking when they enter the workplace. Similarly, Jameel (2022) despairs about the bureaucratic culture that has eroded the foundations of Family Medicine as a *phronetic* practice. While we do not want to underestimate those difficulties, we simply reiterate the Aristotelian point that insofar as general professional development includes a focus on moral character (Lamb et al., 2021), such development cannot be divorced from a focus on *phronesis* (Villacis et al., 2021). Siloed and merely habituated moral virtues in professional life, wandering alone without an intellectual integrator, can be as dangerous as no virtues at all.

11.5 Civic Education and Civic *Phronesis*

As frustratingly small and fragmented the literatures on general *phronesis* education are, they are even smaller for the cultivation of civic *phronesis*—to

---

per se, and he does not believe in the need for early years habituation either, except insofar as it can be described as the internalization of habits of rational (Kantian or quasi-Kantian) thinking.

the extent of virtually being nonexistent.[40] By saying that we are not casually denigrating the existing literature on Citizenship/Civic Education, many of which foreground the necessary reflective and critical elements of such education. However, they rarely, if ever, address the development and education of civic *phronesis* per se. Recall from Chapter 8 that in the Aristotelian model, civic *phronesis* occupies a higher level than ordinary *phronesis*, not in the sense of constituting a radically different construct but rather in the sense of being quantitatively different in being confined to rulers/managers and being geared towards the promotion of the common good. This means that the blueprint component of the construct cannot be confined to the agent's blueprint of her own good life and those who are usually affected by her daily decision-making (e.g., friends, family, neighbours, and colleagues) but has to include the wellbeing of the whole community.

One of the reasons for the scholarly silence about civic *phronesis* could be that, while many educationists are well versed in Aristotle's *Nicomachean Ethics* and cite it copiously, references to the *Politics* tend to be sparse—even by civic educationists who claim to draw upon it—and sometimes betray an inadequate grasp of fundamental issues (with some notable exceptions, e.g., Curren, 2000; Peterson, 2020). Given that the *Politics* offers much more detail on educational issues than the *Nicomachean Ethics*, and even outlines an 'ideal' curricular system, it must count as an underused resource in educational circles.[41]

What educational implications does Aristotle himself draw from his discussion in the *Politics* of civic virtue and how it differs from moral virtue? Surprisingly, few. He remains as reticent as in the *Nicomachean Ethics*, for example, about the exact ways in which to move a student from merely habituated to *phronetic* virtue. The strong thesis from the *Nicomachean Ethics* about the supreme importance of good education (above and beyond good laws) for psycho-moral and socio-moral development is still in full force in the *Politics* (see. e.g., Aristotle, 1944, pp. 275 and 435 [1288b1; 1310a12–14]).[42] Yet when Aristotle begins to describe in considerable detail the educational system in the ideal state, the focus seems to be more on the general contours of the

---

[40] A recent paper by Lawrence et al. (2021), on a Deliberation-Pedagogy course to develop citizenship capacities, constitutes a welcome exception.

[41] While the present chapter has mainly focused on the cultivation of individual *phronesis*, we refer readers back to Chapter 9 where we discussed collective *phronesis* (and how to cultivate it) in the context of Aristotle's *Politics*. There is also a sizable literature, which we cannot cover here, on nudging and other collective measures to encourage (groups of) people to make wiser choices. Cf. Sternberg and Glück (2022, pp. 35–40) on the importance of 'nontoxic' collective reward systems, national and international.

[42] Interestingly, Aristotle (1944, p. 637 [1337a39–41]) brings up the standard question, which still occupies the minds of many contemporary educators, on whether the ethical or the intellectual is more important in schooling. In matters of education, there may be nothing new under the sun!

curriculum, and what subject to teach at which age, than about the pedagogies of character or civic development specifically, let alone civic *phronesis*.[43] Not all may be what it seems here, though.

What we expect but fail to see in the educational chapters of the *Politics* is how students are prepared for *phronetic* moral and civic virtue through discursive methods, for instance critical discussions of moral quandaries, such as Aristotle conducts himself, particularly in the *Nicomachean Ethics*. However, what we get instead is an exclusive focus on what would be called, post-Dewey, 'learning by doing', especially learning through sports (gymnastic exercises) and music. The latter was a broad term in ancient Greece, which could include lyrics and poetry in addition to instrumental music, but Aristotle does insist that each student also learns to play a musical instrument. Although some of the uses of these curricular subjects are practical in an amoral sense—sport being instrumental for defence purposes and music for occupying leisure time—there is no doubt that Aristotle (1944) believed in their *character-forming* capacities. This emerges most clearly in his frequent references to how music can regulate the emotions and contribute to a homeostasis in the soul (e.g., pp. 659; 671 [1340b1–10; 1342a3–15]). He does not say this as explicitly, but there is little doubt that he would have thought the same about the balancing effects of music for civic concord in the state. Aristotle is, as always, motivated here by his strong belief in psycho-moral equilibrium and in hitting the 'golden mean' as a measure of moral competence.

The two most striking features of the educational discourse in the final chapters of the *Politics* are first, as already mentioned, the lack of focus on moral discussions and, second, the fact that the methods described seem to have more to do with the early habituation of virtue than its subsequent *phronesis*-infusion. One can only offer guesses as to why this is the case. Aristotle (1985, (p. 296 [1181a1–8]) inherited from Socrates and Plato a deep distrust of the sort of rhetorical teaching that was practised by the private teachers of their time, the sophists. This may be the reason why he is so quiet about formal discussions and debates with students. Moreover, one may divine from the long chapters on friendship in the *Nicomachean Ethics* that the second critical stage of Moral Education—the *phronesis*-guided one—is mainly stimulated through informal engagement with mentors and character

---

[43] To be sure, all the young students in the ideal state will have been brought up in good habits in the home, and hence need less formal education in moral matters. Yet one would have expected to see some specific guidance on the development of *phronesis*. Aristotle (1944, p. 633 [1336b38–41]) divides the school years into two main periods: age 7 years–puberty, and then puberty–21. A plausible modern character-education hypothesis would be that habituated virtue is mainly cultivated in the former period but *phronetic* virtue in the latter. If that was Aristotle's view, he, however, forgoes the chance to say so.

friends rather than formal methods of education (Kristjánsson, 2022b, chap. 5). Yet, when it comes to Levels 3 and 4 civic virtue (recall Chapter 8), it seems reasonable that some sort of instruction in Political Science would have to be provided, especially for prospective rulers. However, distinct from his mentor Plato (who obviously required the rulers in his utopian state to undergo strict and lengthy training), Aristotle does seem to think that the capacity for ruling comes naturally, through experience, to people who have succeeded in developing high levels of civic virtue, complementing their ordinary *phronesis*.

One well-known aspect of Aristotle's (1944) educational theory is his thesis that, once home schooling ends at the age of 7 years, education in the (ideal) state must be conducted along public, not private, lines and 'be one and the same for all' (pp. 635–6 [1337a1–34]) in order to secure cohesion and concord and ensure all get the same training in civic virtues. Curren (2000) has fleshed out this public education thesis in great detail and applied it to modern concerns in what remains the best work on the educational ramifications of Aristotle's political theorizing. He explains how Aristotle's demand for public schooling rests on the principle of respect for reason in us and others and the need to unite people under a common law. Public schooling requires a uniform curriculum delivered by state-sanctioned teachers in institutions to which all children have equal access, irrespective of socioeconomic status. We have nothing to add to Curren's detailed analysis except to note how uncharacteristically radical this thesis is, coming from the usually pragmatic realist Aristotle, as sending children from their homes to enter a common system of education was completely unheard of at his time in Athens (cf. Kraut, 2002, p. 207).

Looking past some of the unsavoury features of the *Politics*, especially regarding the status of slaves, women, and workers where Aristotle was too quick to endorse classical-era prejudices, Kraut projects a very appealing picture of Aristotle's ideal state:

> All citizens would be well educated. None would live in isolation. All would enjoy their families, friends, and households, but each would also be an active citizen impartially dedicated to the common good. Issues facing the whole community would be discussed openly and thoughtfully, and disagreements would be free of rancor. A sense of justice and friendship would pervade the community. All would have the material resources needed to live well, and inequalities would be too small to excite envy. Citizens would value themselves and each other for their qualities as human beings, not for their wealth and power. (Kraut, 2002, p. 481)

However, even if someone found this blueprint appealing enough to warrant a contemporary revival, mere replication will not suffice. First, current educators would have to be persuaded that the educational issues Aristotle was addressing in the context of ancient Greece are similar enough to the ones facing the modern world in Western liberal democracies to allow for solutions that are in any way similar. Second, as Aristotle fails to offer a clear pedagogical account of the major phases of socio-moral development, during which habituated virtue turns into *phronetic moral*, and later ideally also *phronetic civic*, virtue, there is no hope of lifting any 'off-the-shelf' strategies from his texts. As we have stressed repeatedly in this chapter, those will have to be reconceived and readapted for the needs of contemporary classrooms and lecture halls.

12
Concluding Remarks

12.1 An Overview of the Main Conclusions Reached

We have written this book as diverse academics have emerged, in the last decade or so, that are working with and celebrating the notion of *phronesis* or practical wisdom as a metacognitive capacity, guiding morally aspirational cognition and action. Although we have been delighted by this interest in *phronesis*, on closer inspection this new *phronesis* discourse is characterized by frequently unrecognized tensions, lacunae, and ambivalences.

This book has had five main aims. The *first* was to set the recently surging interest in *phronesis* in Psychology, Philosophy, and Professional Ethics in an historical and theoretical context. We did most of our philosophical context-setting in Chapters 1 and 2. In Chapter 1, we discussed the philosophical and historical context of *phronesis* scholarship by exploring the recent theoretical literatures about *phronesis* and, in particular, the so-called standard neo-Aristotelian model. We then discussed several alternative concepts of and approaches to *phronesis* (e.g., the MacIntyrean and postmodern approaches), that we have decided, for reasons we enumerated, to set aside in the remainder of the book (excepting Chapter 7). This overview settled on a definition of *phronesis* as an intellectual *meta-virtue* that orchestrates the moral and civic virtues and ultimately guides all mature moral decision-making. We have carefully differentiated *phronesis* from both *sophia* (theoretical wisdom) and *deinotes* (wisdom understood as mere instrumentalist calculation).

Throughout the book, we have been committed to taking Aristotle as having the first word about *phronesis*, but we have argued that certain lacunae and tensions in his work mean that he cannot have the last word on it. Therefore, we have not hesitated to add to or amend his views considering more recent philosophical, psychological, or educational scholarship—or simply because Aristotle left so many questions unanswered. In doing so, we take the 'neo' in neo-Aristotelian thought very seriously.

Chapter 2 continued the philosophical development of *phronesis* by discussing the 'standard neo-Aristotelian model' and its relation to contemporary research in Psychology and Philosophy. In this chapter, we argued for a four-componential neo-Aristotelian *phronesis* model (APM) that is an integration of neo-Aristotelian philosophy and current moral psychological research. It is important to test this model both theoretically and empirically. We concluded the chapter by examining other philosophical accounts of *phronesis* (e.g., De Caro & Vaccarezza, 2021; Wright et al., 2021). We also examined scepticism (e.g., expressed by Miller, 2021) about the philosophical need for a *phronesis* model. Therefore, beginning in Chapter 2, we attempted to fulfil our *second aim* of analysing and elaborating on Aristotle's standard model of *phronesis* to create a model that is both philosophically credible and empirically tractable.

We continued the context-setting in Chapter 3 by turning to the history of wisdom research in Psychology, which has burgeoned recently and culminated in the 'common [consensual] wisdom model' (CWM: Grossmann, Westrate, Ardelt et al., 2020) that has taken wisdom discourse much closer to *phronesis*. They defined wisdom briefly as the 'morally-grounded application of metacognition to reasoning and problem-solving'. The CWM successfully draws together many diverging themes of the wisdom construct, yet several wisdom researchers are critical of it. These critics focus on two primary disagreements with the CWM: 1) its neglect of emotionality and motivation, and 2) the vagueness of the morality one expects in wisdom. This helps to clarify that the CWM remains just a step in the development of wisdom research, with more conceptual development necessary.

In Chapter 4, we compared the APM with the CWM. This amounted to putting our APM in conversation with the current state of play in psychological wisdom research, which is the *third aim* of the book. We argued for the strengths of the APM, with its systematic philosophical sources, psychological practicability, realist focus, and integration of emotion, motivation, and cognition. It identifies two main sources of moral motivation, one sourced in specific virtues and the other in the blueprint function of *phronesis*. We detailed the synergistic integration of these motivations, focusing on how experiential knowledge gradually refines the blueprint function. Although the CWM advances the Psychology of Wisdom by better defining what is meant by wisdom (as practical, non-abstract), and by emphasizing moral aspirations as the core of perspectival metacognition, the model seems to stumble by lacking vital substantive content in its conception of morality. In contrast, the APM more directly addresses the moral aims, emotions, and actions, therein offering greater explanatory power than the CWM. The chapter ended by exploring why other constructs in Psychology, such as metacognition, do not render *phronesis* redundant, as well as responding to Lapsley's (2021) *phronesis* scepticism.

Chapter 5 continued to compare the APM to the current state of wisdom research through two objectives. First, we examined how well two well-known single-component solutions (moral identity and moral emotions) address the infamous gap between moral knowledge and moral action. We concluded that neither of the single-component responses to the 'gappiness problem' can, taken alone, account for moral behaviour. Second, we explored the extent to which a neo-Aristotelian framework of *phronesis* can bridge that gap. The APM is a multicomponent approach that includes moral identity and moral emotions, making it more likely to be successful. We recognized that the four-component neo-Kohlbergian model has many parallels with the APM, but the former incorporates a continence-style self-control that raises questions about the agent's complete commitment to moral action. We therefore suggested that the APM may be the best bet for solving the 'gappiness problem'.

Chapter 6 focused on the initial empirical assessment of the APM through two empirical 'proof of concept' studies with adolescents and adults. These studies evaluated our APM via a *phronesis* assessment battery that approximated the four components with the best available measures in Moral Psychology. The hypothesized *phronesis* model fitted the data well in both studies. A predicted second-order latent *phronesis* variable accounted well for the four first-order components and was strongly associated with a prosocial behaviour variable.

We addressed the *fourth aim*, to elicit several practical implications of our model for the development and education of *phronesis* and its application in areas of professional practice and daily conduct, primarily in Chapter 7. We noted that *phronesis* has been increasingly emphasized in contemporary Professional Ethics. Yet the use of this term hides diverging philosophical assumptions, including differing views on *phronesis* such as whether it is: universalist or relativist, generalist or particularist, and natural/painless or painful/ambivalent. This led to examining the differences between MacIntyre's and Aristotle's concepts of *phronesis*. We examined this difference concretely in Medical Ethics by using the three binaries just noted to evaluate several accounts of *phronesis* in the Medical Ethics literature.

Our *fifth* and final aim was to explore the relevance of *phronesis* in areas that have mostly eluded investigation so far, including civic/political virtues, collective decision-making, *postphronetic* pain, and the education of *phronesis*. We pursued this aim in Chapters 8–11. In Chapter 8, we expanded the renewed educational interest in *phronesis* to include civic virtues. We began by clarifying the similarities, differences, and tensions between civic and moral virtues in Aristotle's writings. These analyses revealed that the civic is (teleo)logically prior to the moral, but the civic is secondary developmentally and analytically. We concluded by illuminating that *phronesis* is also central to the civic virtues. Although *phronesis* has a similar relation to moral and civic virtues in many ways, *phronesis* differs in its more personal and interpersonal focus among moral virtues and its focus on the common good in civic *phronesis*.

Phronesis is generally described as a character strength possessed by an individual. In Chapter 9, we widened its scope to the collective level. We offered an overview of what collective *phronesis* might mean, including Aristotle's remarks about collective *phronesis* in his *Politics* that encourage elaboration and some revisionary thinking about neo-Aristotelian *phronesis*. We attempted to make sense of Aristotle's somewhat unsystematic remarks and chart a direction for the concept of collective *phronesis* by applying the concept to Professional Ethics Education.

We have emphasized, throughout the book, that *phronesis* oversees and adjudicates moral decisions in various complex, contested situations. In Chapter 10, we examined some potentially painful consequences of this complexity and tension following a *phronetic* decision. Orthodox Aristotelians standardly assume that a fully *phronetic* decision is always characterized by psychological unity, therein lacking ambivalent emotions and *postphronetic* pain (PPP). We argued that nonoptimal emotions do not simply vanish after a *phronetic* decision is made, thus challenging this orthodoxy. We found that three attempts to defang the PPP puzzle could not succeed. We then described PPP (when it occurs) in terms of emotions of moral sadness and argued that it is important to frankly acknowledge the inescapability of such emotions because of the imperfections of human reasoners. We concluded by exploring some ways to reconceptualize PPP as potentially beneficial.

We began Chapter 11 by examining the lack of clarity about how to educate *phronesis*, which included the well-known shortcomings of Aristotle's developmental views. We updated those views based on the empirical Moral Development literature. This led us to propose a set of testable hypotheses about the development of *phronesis* based on the Aristotelian, neo-Aristotelian, and Moral Development literature. Although these observations and hypotheses fall short of a full, systematic research programme for *phronesis* education, we endeavoured to provide useful starting points for such research. We then attempted to draw some lessons from an attempt to train police officers in *phronesis*. We concluded the chapter by returning to the topic of civic *phronesis* and how that may be fostered educationally.

12.2 Some Further Reflections on the Role of *Phronesis* in the Overall Flourishing Life

As we noted in Chapter 1, *phronesis* is important because it makes it possible to enact the virtues that enable one to live a good or flourishing life (*eudaimonia*). This Aristotelian formulation takes flourishing as the 'ultimate grounder' of virtue and *phronesis*. Unsurprisingly, the meaning and placement of 'flourishing' has been very contentious (e.g., Driver, 2001; Wright et al., 2021). For example, Wright et al. (2021) saw the connection among virtues, *phronesis*, and flourishing as sufficiently contentious that they chose to set it aside completely. In contrast, we see the topic as too important to set aside, but, given the absence of consensus about flourishing, we approach these relationships through a set of hypotheses rather than attempting to make a conceptual argument for a particular position. Although philosophical debate about the relations among virtues, *phronesis*, and flourishing is quite ancient, the efforts to understand these relations in an empirically tractable way are in their infancy (Fowers, Novak, Kiknadze, & Calder, 2023a).

This contention about the meaning and place of flourishing cannot be resolved here, so we will provide a simple definition rather than using this space to delve into this set of debates. Despite this contentiousness, a substantial and growing body of evidence indicates the value of viewing flourishing as a distinct form of wellbeing vis à vis subjective wellbeing (e.g., Bauer, 2022; Fredrickson et al., 2013; Thorsteinsen & Vittersø, 2020). For more extended discussion of this debate, see Fowers, Novak, Kiknadze, and Calder (2023a; 2023b); Haybron (2016); Kristjánsson (2020); Vittersø (2016).

Philosophers tend to translate the ancient Greek term '*eudaimonia*' as 'happiness', which works well enough when one has a sufficiently broad and rich understanding of 'happiness'. Unfortunately, for many people, 'happiness' connotes an emotional state that tends to be somewhat effervescent. We chose the term 'flourishing' because we think that it more clearly represents Aristotle's understanding of the kind of depth and richness that goes beyond a simple emotion or any other temporary experience to indicate a complete and felicitous life. That is, we see flourishing more as a way of living than as a state that can be achieved or as a subjective experience.[1] We see flourishing as living in a way that fulfils the best aspects of human being. We use this definition to

---

[1] It is important to emphasize here that this differs from a common psychological definition which claims that '*eudaimonia*' is the fulfilment of the individual's preferences and aims. This subjectification of *eudaimonia* is quite un-Aristotelian because his metric for *eudaimonia* is humanity rather than individual subjectivity.

meta-virtue like *phronesis*, whose very nature it is to be holistic and integrative and to latch itself onto the individual's complete characterological make-up.

Finally, there is good reason to believe that some underused empirical methods may pay excellent dividends, such as qualitative investigations into *phronesis* (e.g., Briggs & Lumsdon, 2022; Jameel, 2022), think-aloud research, which can follow decision-making in real time (e.g., Fan et al., 2023), and third-party reports of an individual's observable degree of *phronesis* (e.g., Hawkins et al., 2007; Vazire & Carlson, 2011). These methods may shed additional light on the complexities of *phronesis* and reduce our reliance on self-report questionnaires. We offer some further suggestions about the future of *phronesis* research, insofar as it relates to our own APM, in Section 12.5.

12.4 Interdisciplinary Work on *Phronesis*: The Pros and Cons

We are firm believers in the value of interdisciplinary scholarship on the important and complex topics of virtue, *eudaimonia*, and *phronesis*, as this book attests. There are many disciplines with a stake in the questions and promise raised by *phronesis*, and each of these disciplines has valuable perspectives and methods to add to the discussion and promotion of this vital meta-virtue. Yet interdisciplinary work on any topic is difficult and fraught with challenges. We do not think it is for everyone. We have several recommendations for those interested in entering this vibrant and maddening enterprise. These recommendations are based on our personal experiences and on observing some productive and inspiring collaborations.

Interdisciplinary teams of note

Some especially longstanding and productive collaborations deserve mention here for their contributions and as a testament to the fact that interdisciplinary research can be both productive and enormously enlightening. We cannot mention all such collaborations because they have multiplied a great deal, nor do we cite individuals who have reached across disciplinary lines. The latter is difficult and time-consuming, and we have recognized the efforts of many such individuals throughout this book.

First, the interdisciplinary research that has been conducted for the past 10 years at the Jubilee Centre in Birmingham, UK, is without peer in investigating topics related to virtue, *eudaimonia*, and *phronesis*. This assessment comes from one of us (Fowers) and will, no doubt, embarrass the other (Kristjánsson), but it is undeniable how productive the Centre has been with an interdisciplinary faculty of philosophers, educationists, psychologists, sociologists, and more. This work has been augmented by the highly successful series of truly interdisciplinary annual conferences at Oriel College, Oxford that has brought international scholars together to interact productively about topics such as virtue, *eudaimonia*, and *phronesis*.

We have frequently cited a second important and longstanding interdisciplinary collaboration conducted by Wright, Warren (psychologists), and Snow (a philosopher). Snow has collaborated with many social scientists and directed projects that have explicitly encouraged interdisciplinary scholarship through funding and conferences (e.g., Snow, 2015; Snow & Narvaez, 2019). The scholars at the *Aretai* Center in Italy have also promoted interdisciplinary scholarship through conferences and publications, notably Vaccarezza and De Caro (2021). Psychologist Howard Nusbaum has established an interdisciplinary Centre for Practical Wisdom at the University of Chicago. Fowers (another psychologist) has participated in multiple interdisciplinary collaborations, generally with philosophers, beginning with Richardson et al. (1999) and continuing to progress, as mutual understanding and degree of focus increased, to work focused on virtue (e.g., Fowers et al., 2021; 2023), and this book and its predecessor publications on *phronesis* (e.g., Darnell et al., 2022; Kristjánsson & Fowers, 2023). One additional and highly productive collaboration has occurred at Wake Forest University with a longstanding collaboration among philosophers and psychologists (e.g., Fleeson et al., 2022; Miller et al., 2015). This group has produced many illuminating publications and made many training opportunities available. This array of productive and longstanding collaborations indicates the value and fruitfulness of interdisciplinary work. What does it take to succeed in this endeavour?

What helps interdisciplinary teams succeed?

There has been much said about this topic. Indeed, interdisciplinary research has become a topic of its own (e.g., Cokelet & Fowers, 2019; National Research Council, 2015; Snow & Narvaez, 2019), but our experience and observation suggest several key elements. First, interdisciplinary teams require several personal characteristics in the team members, including patience, intellectual humility, flexibility, a capacity for character friendship, and need we say it, *phronesis*. Patience is necessary because interdisciplinary work takes time to come to fruition. It cannot be rushed, and it takes time to recognize the common ground people in different disciplines have and then to come to common understandings of the questions to ask and the methods available to answer those questions. Intellectual humility is a requirement because every discipline has its preferred set of questions and methods, and those approaches are typically valorized and protected within the discipline. Interdisciplinary work requires us to question those preferences and biases and to be open-minded about what can be learned from other disciplinary perspectives. That open-mindedness is not to be underestimated because accomplished scholars often have to recognize that they know little about another discipline's approach to the topic at hand. Flexibility in thinking and action is obviously needed as well. Without the ability to adopt or incorporate another discipline's methods, there is little point in interdisciplinary work.

The last two characteristics, character friendship and *phronesis*, are not typically mentioned by scholars who study interdisciplinary research, but we have observed their importance many times and we are particularly attuned to them as neo-Aristotelians. Along with having the patience to foster an interdisciplinary collaboration, the ability to act as a character friend with a collaborator is indispensable. Much has been written on character friendship both anciently and recently (Aristotle, 1985; Fowers & Anderson, 2018; Kristjánsson, 2022b), but the key elements are active in interdisciplinary scholarship. One is to allow time for a relationship of mutual respect and mutual well-wishing to develop. Interdisciplinary collaborations are personal as well as professional relationships, and cultivating a good relationship takes time and willing participation. Mutual respect facilitates the patience necessary and wanting the best for one's collaborator helps to open one's mind and gives motivation for the difficult work of mutual understanding and finding common ground. Finally, sharing goals such as producing valuable scholarship and formulating useful theory and methods provides additional motivation.

We hope that the previous paragraphs have been suggestive of *phronesis*, because we believe that successful interdisciplinary work depends on the ability to make good choices. Those choices relate to selecting good people with whom to collaborate, settling on important topics to explore, knowing when and how to be patient, flexible, and open-minded, on recognizing when and how to act as a character friend, and on recognizing the value of the overall aims of the collaboration.

There are also many impersonal factors that exert a substantial influence on the instantiation and success of interdisciplinary collaborations. We content ourselves with merely mentioning them here, as they will be familiar to any scholar who has contemplated or participated in such collaborations. In general, the question is whether there is institutional support for the time-consuming and arduous work involved. This includes departments and universities who encourage and support interdisciplinary research through hiring, promotion, merit raises, and funding. This includes the willing support of many colleagues and administrators. Many departments are oriented far more to policing disciplinary boundaries than to crossing them. Both disciplinary policing and interdisciplinary research are important, and it is vital to find a balance between them. External funding can be vital to nurturing interdisciplinary research, and it has played a large role in all the successful collaborations mentioned above. Young interdisciplinary scholars are advised to attend to these features when considering employment.

All this could seem like self-congratulation, but we do not intend it that way. We are well aware of our individual and collective shortcomings, and we have tried to keep them from getting in the way of our work. If anything, we feel that we have been extraordinarily fortunate to be in the right places at the right times to be able to work in such a vibrant and necessary endeavour. We have been the beneficiaries of institutional support, and we can attest to its value. In addition, we do not feel that we are in a position to judge the value of our work. We are just too close to it. It feels compelling and valuable, but that could be self-absorption or self-promotion as much as an accurate assessment. We leave those judgements to our colleagues and to history.

Some remaining concerns

Our own positive experience of interdisciplinary work notwithstanding, no one has ever claimed that crossover work between Philosophy and Psychology is a marriage made in heaven. There are significant differences in theoretical approaches, underlying motivations, methods, aims, and even presentational styles that separate the two disciplines and their practitioners, and such differences are not always easily reconcilable—although we have tried our best to overcome them in the preceding chapters. Our close collaboration in the formulation of individual chapters in this book may licence us to call it truly *trans*disciplinary rather than simply *inter*disciplinary; nevertheless, it will not have escaped readers' attention that some chapters are more characterized by the style and argumentation of one than the other of the two authors.

Not everyone will agree with these lessons, however, and we will use the remainder of this section to explore one such sceptical voice. David Carr (2023) has written an article questioning the credibility of much of recent virtue ethical and character-educational inroads into the Aristotelian territory of make it possible to focus our attention on the hypothesized relationships between *phronesis* and flourishing and because we think it unlikely that a fully consensual definition of 'flourishing' will be available in the near future.

In addition to this definition, we add a few distinctions that many flourishing scholars will welcome, although these distinctions may not be shared by all. First, neo-Aristotelians generally agree that there is a difference between subjective and objective forms of wellbeing. Subjective experiences of wellbeing are frequently empirically studied by psychologists with constructs like happiness, subjective wellbeing, and life satisfaction (e.g., Diener, 2012; Peterson et al., 2005), but psychologists also study flourishing in subjective terms under the heading of 'eudaimonic wellbeing', with constructs such as personal meaning, personal growth, and positive interpersonal relationships (e.g., Fowers, 2005; Ryff, 1989). In contrast, Aristotle is generally known as an 'objective wellbeing theorist',[2] meaning that he believed there were intersubjectively verifiable aspects of life that are good for humans whether those aspects are congruent with one's subjective preferences or not. These goods can include physical health, belonging, and a well-functioning community.

Second, most scholars of flourishing see it as a multidimensional concept rather than as a simple, unidimensional concept. This is because human life is complex, and a flourishing life likely consists in multiple goods rather than one. Therefore, neo-Aristotelians tend to be ethical pluralists rather than ethical monists. For this reason, we will phrase our hypotheses (following on from the 14 we advanced in Chapter 11) in terms of 'indicators of flourishing' rather than simply as 'flourishing'.

> *Hypothesis 15: Phronesis* will be positively correlated with indicators of subjective wellbeing.

Flourishing is obviously the ungrounded grounder of all human endeavours in Aristotle (1985), and subjective wellbeing tends to occupy a similar place for many psychologists. The importance of finding correlations between *phronesis* and subjective wellbeing can, therefore, not be overestimated. Fairly abundant research already exists on correlations between moral virtue(s) and wellbeing (Fowers et al., 2021, see their own Hypotheses 14–16 about virtues). There is also a good deal of research on the relationships among wisdom (generally considered) and subjective indicators of wellbeing, indicating positive

---

[2] Although we could use the phrase 'objective indicators of flourishing', we chose the phrase 'intersubjectively verifiable indicators of flourishing'. Despite the loss of felicity in the latter phrase, we have avoided the use of the bald term 'objective' in this book because it is so strongly freighted in the discipline of Psychology with connotations of 'real', 'true', and 'efficient causation'.

correlations (e.g., Ardelt & Jeste, 2018; Thomas et al., 2017). However, similar research is needed regarding the relationships among *phronesis* (rather than generic wisdom) and indicators of subjective wellbeing.

> *Hypothesis 16: Phronesis* will be positively correlated with subjective indicators of flourishing.

In contrast to the previous hypothesis, the relationships with *phronesis* in Hypothesis 16 focus on measures of flourishing, such as meaning,[3] purpose, and personal growth. Social scientists have also regularly found positive correlations among various generic wisdom measures and assessments of subjective aspects of flourishing (e.g., Glück et al., 2013; Taylor et al., 2011). Notably, *phronesis* has not been correlated with measures of subjective aspects of flourishing to date.

> *Hypothesis 17: Phronesis* will be positively correlated with indicators of intersubjectively verifiable wellbeing.

Hypothesis 17 is more challenging than Hypothesis 15 in two ways. First, relatively little research has been conducted on indicators of intersubjectively verifiable wellbeing. This is partly due to the greater simplicity and cost-effectiveness of using self-report scales of wellbeing than constructing measures that are intersubjectively verifiable. Assessing such variables is possible because there are multiple candidates for such measurement, from simple physical health to cellular markers of stress responses (e.g., Fredrickson et al., 2013) and to variables that are inherently intersubjective (e.g., well-functioning community, organizational ethos). This focus on the self-report measurement of wellbeing is also due to the fact that social scientists tend to subjectify such variables to avoid defining such value-laden terms themselves. The second reason that makes testing this hypothesis challenging is that *phronesis* itself has not, until very recently, been measured directly, with most empirical researchers focusing on a more generic form of wisdom. Consequently, the set of relationships among *phronesis* and intersubjectively verifiable indicators of wellbeing remains hypothetical at this point.

---

[3] We note that the concept of personal meaning is a relatively recent development as Aristotle did not discuss personal meaning explicitly in his ethical works. Instead, he seems to see meaning and purpose primarily as collective phenomena that were associated with being a citizen of a polis or community. We believe that personal meaning became essential for moderns as the cosmos became disenchanted, making meaning more of a personal matter. We suggest that both forms of meaning will be associated with *phronesis* in the relevant populations.

Despite the difficulties in assessing flourishing as intersubjectively verifiable, this is important for the reason Aristotle noted, that one can believe one is faring well or poorly but be mistaken in that belief. Although self-reports of flourishing clearly have a place, they are insufficient for indicating flourishing and should be complemented by intersubjectively verifiable indicators (Alexandrova, 2017; Bauer, 2022; Fowers, 2016; Fowers, Novak, Kiknadze, & Calder, 2023a). Fowers, Novak, Kiknadze, and Calder (2023a; Fowers et al. (in press, chap. 10) discussed other challenges in the assessment of flourishing, such as the ethnocentricity of contemporary measurement favouring North Atlantic cultures and the multivocality regarding the constituents of flourishing. They see these challenges as difficult, but surmountable. There remain redoubtable challenges in measuring *phronesis* as well, which we discuss in the next section.

12.3 Some Further Reflections on Measuring *Phronesis*

Although we presented a pair of proof of concept studies in Chapter 6 that provide reason to believe that the APM provides a promising approach to *phronesis* measurement, these studies are insufficient to fully support such an approach. We recount Swartwood's (2020) excellent critique of wisdom measurement here to highlight some important challenges for *phronesis* measurement and some ways that the APM may be responsive to those challenges, whereas previous wisdom research has not been. Then we discuss future directions for APM research that will hopefully capitalize on this promising approach.

Swartwood's critique of wisdom research

Swartwood (2020) clarifies some important obstacles to measuring *phronesis*. We admire his ability to discuss the measurement of *phronesis* in a thoroughly interdisciplinary and yet clear way, holding social scientific research accountable to a reasonable conception of *phronesis*, and expecting that philosophical concept to be answerable to data. This seems to be an excellent way to proceed. Ultimately, Swartwood concludes that measuring *phronesis* is impossible or at least highly dubious. He reaches this conclusion through a clear and systematic argument that we will recount here briefly.

Swartwood (2020) first asks the question of whether wisdom measures help to assess a 'minimal philosophical conception' (p. 77) of *phronesis*, which he states as 'the understanding that enables a person to make reliably excellent decisions about how they ought to live' (p. 72). He argues that satisfying such a reasonable minimum conception requires specifying the success conditions in which one could be said to have demonstrated *phronesis*. A related criterion is that a *phronimos* can be differentiated from someone who does not exercise *phronesis* with its defining features. He then argues that the wisdom measures extant at that time do not satisfy the minimal philosophical conception because they assess, at best, only necessary, but insufficient components of *phronesis*. For example, compassion is a key element of Ardelt's (2003) definition, but, as Swartwood clarifies, compassion is to be expected of the *phronimos* when it is appropriate, but there are many times when compassion is evidently unwise. Therefore, the presence or absence of compassion does not differentiate the *phronimos* from the less wise.

The core of Swartwood's (2020) argument seems to be that it is difficult to define and clearly demonstrate the success conditions of *phronesis*. He suggests a rather reasonable definition of these success conditions as 'the grasp that is conducive to living a good human life' (p. 79). He uses expertise in chess and teaching as instructive analogues for understanding *phronesis*, and states that 'Just as a person would not count as a chess expert if we found they did not, in fact, win many games, a person would not count as having practical wisdom if they did not have a reliably good grasp of what to do in particular cases' (p. 79). We find these two success criteria very congenial, and we are inclined to combine these two features, meaning that success in *phronesis* is having a good grasp on what to do in specific situations that conduces to a good life.

We see three reasons why this understanding of the success criteria could seem insurmountable for social scientists. First, Swartwood (2020) correctly notes that the philosophical concept of *phronesis* is normative in a prescriptive way, in that it provides guidance for how one *ought* to act. This will give many social scientists pause because they believe that the empirical world is comprised only of facts and that normative considerations have no place in Social Science. We do not share this squeamishness about normative concerns because we believe that Social Science is shot through with value commitments and that the idea of the good life that is central to *phronesis* is just as much a part of the world as the number of socks in one's sock drawer.[4] Therefore, we

---

[4] This argument has been made many times. We suggest Brinkmann (2011); Fowers et al. (in press, chap. 6); or Fowers (2022) as examples of such arguments.

think this difficulty is surmountable by discarding the fact/value dichotomy (which is, however, not necessarily tantamount to discarding the is/ought distinction if 'ought' is understood in an all-things-considered sort of way[5]).

Second, the concept of a good life is very difficult to clarify, and define, as we noted in the previous section, and is evident in the substantial debate about this central concept (Driver, 2001; Haybron, 2013; Wright et al., 2021). Although we doubt that full consensus on the question of the good life will ever be forthcoming, we do believe that substantial common ground can be reached on what constitutes a good life for humans, including that such common ground can be empirically tractable. In broad strokes, this would require defining some features that are necessary for living well for normally developing humans. Aristotle provided two very broad categories for these features, that humans are *reasoning social* beings. In contemporary terms, this would mean that a good life would be one in which there are good reasons for acting in particular ways (e.g., meaning, purpose) and that one is well situated in social attachments (e.g., close personal relationships, group belonging, and being part of an adequately well-functioning community). This seems like a reasonable starting point to us, and the details can be worked out. We have made an argument for just such constituents of the good life and presented the empirical evidence that supports these features as elements of a good life elsewhere (Fowers, 2015; Fowers et al., in press; Fowers et al., 2023; Kristjánsson, 2020). Therefore, although we have no illusions that complete agreement is possible (or even desirable) on a full picture of the good life, we do think there is a path forward on this question, and we see this worry as surmountable on that basis.

The third reason that it seems impossible to measure *phronesis* is that it is highly contextualized. Swartwood (2020) astutely points out that situations are unique and one daunting aspect of *phronesis* is that wise decisions will vary based on the specific characteristics of the situation at hand and on the particular person making the decisions. He illustrates this clearly with the relationship between chess expertise and the ability to 'choose the best move' given a board configuration. The best move assessment is superior to other obvious markers like thinking many moves ahead or memory for chess expertise. Nevertheless, the variation in situations is much more overwhelming

---

[5] This is a complicated issue. What we mean here is that it is possible to accept the objectivity of moral evaluations and action-guidance from a moral point of view without going as far as rejecting fully the distinction between descriptions and all-things-considered prescriptions. So, while we believe it is possible for a social scientist or a health professional to pass scientifically objective judgements about the best *phronetic* decision or the best dietary decision, we remain agnostic on whether questions such as Why be moral? or Why care about one's health? are scientific questions (see Kristjánsson, 2013).

than the variation in chess-board configurations, and a complete assessment of the nearly infinite possibilities for wise decisions and actions is clearly impossible. Here is one place where Social Science can be of assistance, however. The concept of sampling helps us deal with large variation because the idea is that no one can assess all the ways that intelligence or extraversion or goal-orientation can manifest, just as it is rare to assess an entire population. The social scientist does not attempt to assess all variations in situations or populations. Rather, the scientist determines what a reasonable sample of such variation would look like and assesses that sample. The argument needs to be made that it is a reasonable sample and that there are grounds for generalizing from that sampling of actions to the general variations in situations or populations. This approach is baked into Social Science, and it offers a way to manage the nearly infinite variation that Swartwood recognizes. Therefore, we see sampling as a way to manage this concern.

There is one more issue with Swartwood's (2020) analysis. He faults wisdom research in the Social Sciences for failing to address *phronesis* properly. We agree with this conclusion, but we have argued that this was entirely to be expected. With the possible exception of the Situated Wise Reasoning Scale (Brienza et al., 2018), we have noted that traditional wisdom measures do not even attempt to assess *phronesis*, and that they were not intended to do so (see Chapters 3–5). In this way, we believe that Swartwood has missed the mark because wisdom measures cannot be faulted for what they were not designed to do. This aim has only been approached recently (Brienza et al., 2018; Darnell et al., 2019; 2022; Grossmann, Weststrate, Ardelt et al., 2020). We have also argued that the Situated Wise Reasoning Scale and the CWM, two recent and substantial moves towards *phronesis*, fail because they do not define the success criteria for *phronesis*, to use Swartwood's useful terms. Accordingly, we have presented the APM as a more focused and systematic way to assess *phronesis*. It is now time to evaluate the degree to which the APM can address Swartwood's critique.

Evaluating how the APM responds to Swartwood's (2020) obstacles

The first question one should answer following Swartwood's critique of wisdom research is whether the model or measure that one is considering clarifies the success criteria for *phronesis*. The APM offers two sets of answers. First, as we noted, we agree with Swartwood's suggestion that successful *phronesis* should lead to a good human life. This should be a direct and planned result of *phronetic* activity rather than a fortuitous development. This is one of the reasons that we have included the blueprint function in the APM. We believe that having a reasonably clear idea about what a good life looks like is vital to guide *phronetic* activity. Our blueprint function can be criticized as too detailed and systematic, as Wright et al. (2021) worry that it is, or it can be faulted for being overly formal in failing to specify any content for a good life. We think that criticisms of these sorts suggest that we have proposed a good answer (not too far in either direction) to what a good life is. On one hand, no one is in a position to specify a good life so thoroughly that there is only one correct way to live, so it is necessary to have a concept of good living that is sufficiently capacious that it can accommodate many different versions. This is necessary, given historical, cultural, and individual variations in what a desirable life looks like. On the other hand, it is important to provide some basis for recognizing the similarities and commonalities among various versions of the good life. We believe that this is possible if we retain sufficient abstractness in those conceptions. From our viewpoint, the Aristotelian criteria of living well as a reasoning social being accomplishes this task well and it provides a definable set of domains for the blueprint function. We recognize that this is a bare beginning in this important discussion, but this is a book about *phronesis*, not one about the good life, so we will not delve further into this debate here.

The second answer to the question of success criteria is that the *phronimos* is reliably able to recruit and express appropriate virtues in response to situational considerations. The criterion then is that the *phronimos* generally gets it right about situations requiring courage, generosity, or kindness. This is another way of tying successful *phronesis* to the specifics of the current circumstance.

We were very taken with Swartwood's (2020) analysis of why specifying particular characteristics will not work for conceptualizing expertise in domains like chess, teaching, or *phronesis*. We think he is correct in citing the reason for this failure is that concepts such as 'best practices' are overly general whereas expertise always shows up in the best response to the particulars of situations. To return to the example of compassion and *phronesis*, he incisively points out that 'the biggest challenge is not working up concern for others but figuring out when, how, and why to express that concern' (p. 85). The answers to questions about when, how, and why to act compassionately (or courageously or fairly) depend on the specifics of the situation at hand. For this reason, the APM includes the constitutive function, which makes it possible for the *phronimos* to recognize the features of the situation that call for a particular virtue and to understand what would constitute that virtue in this situation. That is, what does it mean to be compassionate or fair in this specific moment?

Swartwood (2020) is also rightly concerned that there are often multiple goals relevant to any concrete situation, and, we would add, multiple virtues that are relevant to that situation and those goals. For this reason, the APM includes the integrative function, which allows a wise person to make the kinds of overall decisions that Swartwood calls for. We agree with him that this is a key aspect of *phronesis*, and that the ability to adjudicate among a variety of goals and the relevant virtues and harmonize those concerns in the best way is central to what it means to be a wise person. He also notes that 'living wisely requires evaluating and balancing the various goals one might have' (p. 78). We agree that this is vital 'because there is [often] no simple way to balance commitments to the various values at stake' (Swartwood, 2020, p. 80). The combination of the blueprint and integrative functions of *phronesis* allow the *phronimos* to evaluate and balance the goals that she sees as relevant.

The astute reader will have identified, in the preceding paragraphs, an important way that the APM and its measurement differs from most wisdom measurement. Rather than specifying the characteristics of the wise person (as compassionate, knowledgeable, or humble), our approach with the APM is to assess a set of functions that a *phronimos* reliably fulfils. We believe that this functional approach allows us to retain sufficient abstractness to be relevant to highly variable circumstances yet provides sufficient content to provide guidance and avoid the emptiness of merely formal criteria. The bottom line for us is that it seems entirely feasible (if daunting) to assess *phronesis*, contra Swartwood (2020). This means that we have adopted the optimistic response that Swartwood dismissed. We think this optimism is reasonable because we have adopted a radically different approach to assessing wisdom. We are unsure if it is revolutionary, but Swartwood certainly did not anticipate our approach in his critique. Our work so far only represents the beginning of demonstrating the value of the APM, and that much additional research is necessary before we can make our claims confidently, but we think this is a promising and plausible alternative for *phronesis* research.

The future of APM research

Here, we want to outline some of what seems necessary to empirically test the value of the APM. In Chapter 6, we presented a pair of proof of concept studies that suggested the feasibility and desirability of assessing *phronesis* in the form of an APM. What else is necessary to develop greater confidence in this approach? We present these recommendations as a series of hypotheses.

> *Hypothesis 18*: The APM will demonstrate its reliability and validity with samples outside the UK.

Although the proof of concept studies we have conducted so far provided a replication within the UK (adults and older adolescents), it is important to seek greater generalisability. This would include not only replications in the USA and other western, educated, industrialized, rich, and democratic (WEIRD) countries, but ideally, it will extend to many non-WEIRD societies to assess the generalisability of the APM. Studies with non-WEIRD populations may need to be preceded by qualitative explorations of what *phronesis* looks like in varying cultural contexts.

> *Hypothesis 19*: The APM can be better assessed with measures designed specifically to assess the four functions of the Model.

The current form of assessment associated with the APM is a set of existing measures that *approximated* the four functions of the APM. As we noted, this approach was pragmatic, making it possible to study the APM without the extensive effort needed to develop new measurement. It is now time to develop measures designed to assess those four functions directly (and such work has now started in the Jubilee Centre as we are finalising this chapter in late 2023). Presumably, better measurement will allow even more impressive results, which we propose as *Hypothesis 20*, but this awaits additional research. For practical purposes, those better measurements must also be less unwieldy to administer and score (and take less time to complete) than the current measure.

We outlined several hypotheses focused on the relationships among indicators of flourishing and indicators of *phronesis* in the previous section in hypothetical form. These hypotheses take on even more cogency in view of Swartwood's (2020) critique. Demonstrating relationships among these two sets of indicators is necessary for clarifying whether *phronesis*, as envisioned in the APM, relates to relevant success criteria such as flourishing. We can also suggest *Hypothesis 21* that *phronesis* ought to be associated with specific indicators of a good life as well, such as high-quality personal relationships, the presence of meaning and purpose in one's life, and so on.

One of the domains in which the measurement of *phronesis* and moral virtues is most important is in educational interventions, which are not credible unless there are some ways to evaluate their success. So far, evaluations of character and virtue have been the elephant in the room in most research on character education, but the recent book by Wright et al. (2021) may be a real game-changer in the field and even includes an extensive discussion of how to measure virtues. They provide concrete methods for assessing some aspects of virtues (e.g., attentional, recognition, and identification processes), and these research suggestions are relevant to both virtue and *phronesis*. They also mention a 'think-aloud' approach to having individuals discuss their thoughts, decisions, and likely actions in response to vignettes of morally complex situations to assess what we have called the integrative function of *phronesis*.

However, their discussion of *phronesis* development is conducted at a level of abstraction above that of providing practical advice about specific measures, new or off-the-shelf (Wright et al., 2021, esp. chap. 5). For example, these authors, like Russell (2009), divide *phronesis* into five parts (comprehension, sense, nous, deliberation, and cleverness) even though there are no extant measures of these parts, and they note that these divisions remain undeveloped conceptually and are hotly debated. We do not find this sort of abstraction useful, although it may prove to be important following more conceptual development and empirical research. To take a second example, Wright et al. helpfully suggest that *phronesis* develops out of children's ability to solve problems when they transition from seeing the 'solutions' to problems as simply instrumentally useful to coming to see these 'solutions' as constituents of a good life. This is a tantalizing suggestion, but they do not indicate how one could test such a hypothesis. This lack of concreteness about studying the development of *phronesis* is not a particular fault of these authors, and we have been at pains to detail just how difficult and rudimentary efforts regarding this topic have been for virtually all scholars. Wright and colleagues simply seem to share this challenge with us and others.

Wright et al. (2021) do make several useful suggestions about the measurement of virtues, which also apply to *phronesis*. They highlight the importance of attention by noting that a virtuous person or a *phronimos* will attend to features of situations that are opaque to those without *phronesis*. We endorse this suggestion and propose it as *Hypothesis 22*. Wright et al. also helpfully suggest that attention can be measured physiologically as well as through self-report. Physiological approaches include the measurement of gaze-tracking, pupil-dilation, heart rate, and electrodermal response. Wright et al. also suggest (what we will call)

Hypothesis 23, that the relationships between indicators of *phronesis* and attention should be moderated by distracting stimuli. That is, *phronimoi* are less likely to be distracted from virtue-related stimuli than those without *phronesis*.

Recommendations for future *phronesis* research

We have been observing the growing wisdom literature for many years and we have accumulated some experience in this domain as well. We offer several recommendations here that do not quite rise to the level of hypotheses, but bear mentioning, nonetheless. We make these recommendations tentatively and look forward to future assessments of their value. The first is that a complete reliance on self-report measures of wisdom seems inadequate currently. Kunzmann (2019) recommended the use of performance measures (where a respondent's output is assessed against expert raters' output), and this is one of the upshots of Swartwood's (2020) critique of the wisdom literature as well. Character educationists have rightly been wary of self-report tests, like the Values-in-Action inventory (VIA) because of people's lack of self-transparency and imperfect access to their 'real selves' (Kristjánsson, 2015; Wright et al., 2021).

Second, we believe that the study of *phronesis* is an interdisciplinary matter that is best handled with interdisciplinary teams. Some high-quality philosophical work has been done that takes psychological research into account (e.g., Haybron, 2016; Stichter, 2018; Swartwood, 2020), but including social scientists seems to be even more promising. We discuss this further in the next section.

Third, we recommend that *phronesis* assessment focus on first-person assessment of *phronetic* activity rather than third-person assessment, even though we know from previous research (e.g., Grossmann, Westrate, Ferrari et al., 2020) that people are generally better at making wise judgements in the third-person rather than the first-person. However, eventually, what we want to cultivate and evaluate is the person's ability to make wise, authentic, and autonomous choices about her own life.

Fourth, what matters for the effectiveness of a *phronesis* intervention is not so much the progress made in a post-test right after the intervention but the long-term benefits of the intervention. Unfortunately, most character-education interventions are short-term and longitudinal studies are sparse (Berkowitz & Bier, 2006; Brown et al., 2023). If this is a problem regarding the cultivation and evaluation of individual virtues, it must be even more so in the case of a *phronesis*. We are mainly interested here in the accusation of undue 'psychologizations' of the construct, but it is instructive to say something first about the other main foil of the article, which is Aristotle himself. Carr worries about various often-overlooked equivocations and ambiguities in Aristotle's account of virtue and *phronesis*. For example, for Aristotle, the ultimate goal of practical wisdom seems to be not only right or good conduct, but production of states of character whereby agents are not only able to do the right thing, but to do it with the right (pure or unambivalent) intention and emotions from firm states of character. Carr directs his animadversions at this unclearly articulated two-pronged role, especially its assumed second prong. He sees it as problematic for various reasons, including its reliance on a questionable architectonic of an identifiable 'golden mean' of every virtue, its failure to take account of the supposed individualization of virtue while promulgating single uniform programmes of character development, its antiliberal drive to 'mould' young people's character, and its failure to appreciate continued emotional ambivalence even in the so-called fully virtuous.

It would take us too far afield here to respond to all these new-found Aristotelian scepticisms from the erstwhile chief philosophical proponent of Aristotelian Character Education. We have discussed some of them, directly or indirectly, in other works (Fowers et al., 2021; Kristjánsson, 2015)—and we want to avoid turning this book into a wholesale apology of Aristotle. Indeed, as readers will recall, in Chapter 10 we largely endorsed Carr's criticism of the psychological unity thesis and Aristotle's subsequent lack of understanding of *postphronetic* pain. What is more relevant for present purposes is the claim that recent virtue ethical literature on *phronesis* has psychologized the construct overly and taken it in a direction that was foreign to Aristotle's own thoughts. According to Carr's narrative, Psychology, with its unique 'stratagems and methodologies', has been allowed to gate-crash a debate that is inherently philosophical and to import impure considerations.

His worries about various Aristotelian infelicities notwithstanding, Carr does believe that Aristotle's notion of *phronesis* provides a significantly better picture of the place and operations of reason in moral character and agency than anything to be found in latter-day (empirical) psychological theorizing. However, by running the two approaches together (as we have done shamelessly in this book!), Carr thinks that all the advantages of the Aristotelian picture will be lost. According to Carr's interpretation, much of recent theorizing about *phronesis* is problematically ambiguous between *phronesis* as a form of rational or intellectual moral inquiry versus a kind of (empirical) psycho-moral decision procedure. Aristotle insists that *phronesis* admits only of *deliberation* about judgement, precisely insofar as it cannot deliver the same conclusive verdicts that we expect of epistemic inquiry: 'In short, there can be no knowledge or truth of the matters with which *phronesis* is concerned' (2023, p. 141). This conclusion is motivated by the assumption that 'unlike the causally or contingently linked cogitations or other conscious experiences of empirical Psychology, relations between thoughts of logical or educational concern are fundamentally conceptual, semantic and inferential and it is primarily the business of teachers [. . .] to assist students to clear and/or critical appreciation, in the light of reasonable evidence, of the meaning of such thoughts and of sound inferential relations between them' (2023, p. 150). The deliberation that Aristotle ascribes to *phronesis* cannot, therefore, with impunity be translated into a language of quasi-empirical 'components' of virtue—as if these are parts for external psychological reconstruction or assembly—nor into the common psychological or social scientific vocabulary of 'intervention' or 'moulding'.

If Carr is right, the whole idea behind the present book, of identifying and analysing the 'components' of *phronesis* and aiding students in cultivating those in the service of good moral decision-making, is based on a category mistake. There is always a reason to take Carr seriously, and his observations invariably repay attention. However, in this case we think he has got Aristotle wrong. Firstly, the distinction that Carr invokes between conceptual and empirical inquiries is much more Wittgensteinian than Aristotelian; the methodological naturalist Aristotle (who was in many ways the father of contemporary Psychology) apparently saw no clear distinction between the two. Secondly, it is at best an exaggeration to say that Aristotle did not consider *phronesis* to aim at conclusive decisions (although those will be context-dependent and noncodifiable in practice). Just as for health, for moral conduct there is a 'ruling science' (Aristotle, 1985, p. 148 [1138b20–2]). Thirdly, while Aristotle was clearly concerned with the quality of good deliberation and reflection rather than with what today's social scientists call 'prosocial behaviour', he did insist that 'Olympic prizes are not for the finest and strongest, but for contestants, since it is only these who win; so also in life [only] the fine and good people who act correctly win the prize' (1985, p. 20 [1099a1–7]). In other words, the ultimate criterion of a person's moral stature is her action, as decided upon through *phronesis*; not just the quality of her deliberation about how to act.

We do take some salutary lessons from Carr's critique, however. He does warn decisively against what we could call 'codification envy' in Virtue Ethics, akin to 'physics envy' in Psychology. *Phronesis* does not present a decision procedure of *the same codifiable sort* as the utility calculus or Kant's categorical imperative. Moreover, although borrowing psychological methods and analyses of decision procedures to understand *phronesis* better is, in our view, an advantage rather than a drawback, we do agree with Carr that what must be avoided at all costs is a behaviouristic reading of *phronesis* that elides its cognitive and emotional consorts. Indeed, that is precisely what we have systematically attempted to do in this book.

12.5 Future Research on *Phronesis*

We have some further recommendations for future *phronesis* research that come from our own vantage points related to our theoretical, methods, and disciplinary perspectives.

APM-related recommendations

We believe that research on the APM is off to a good start, with a systematic theoretical basis and some promising empirical results. We are very cognisant, however, that this research has barely begun. As such, there are several ways the incremental explanatory value of the APM can be further tested. For one thing, replicating the pilot results and including broader sampling is necessary. Second, the APM can be tested for incremental validity vis-à-vis existing wisdom measures in predicting moral behaviour. We would expect the APM to predict moral behaviours better than more generic wisdom measures that tend to rely primarily on the subjective perception of wisdom or are limited to moral reasoning. We also envision this research to include person-centred measurement over time to assess the ongoing relationship of wisdom and moral behaviours. In addition, any model of wisdom must demonstrate its practical value in guiding the design and implementation of interventions designed to enhance *phronesis*.

As we have indicated, the APM must also be assessed regarding its relationship to many important criterion variables, including success criteria such as subjective wellbeing, *eudaimonia*, and virtue enactment. As Swartwood (2020) points out, the factuality of any expertise must be supported by its empirical relationship to recognizable and measurable success criteria. We have also suggested that relationships between *phronesis* and more detailed success criteria may also be worth investigating (e.g., quality of social relationships and how individuals reason about living well).

It is also important to allay the concern that APM research may be subject to a vicious circle of explaining fully motivated (observable) moral action by an assessment of fully motivated moral action (defined as *phronesis*). To break that circle, we recommend assessing simple moral behaviour without attention to its motives and reasoning as an outcome. Moreover, these assessments of moral behaviour can be made from several points of view (respondent, researcher observations, third-parties, and intervention outcomes) to transcend a vicious circle reliance on the respondent's perceptions alone. Indeed, this multimethod approach to *phronesis* seems invaluable to us as we can learn from the perspectives of different observers of *phronesis*, and we can learn from the use of a variety of conceptual analyses and data collection methods.

Given the enormous potential practical value of *phronesis*, research is also called for on the efficacy of interventions to improve *phronesis* among those who have not yet developed it. Ultimately, our desire is to craft a model, a set of assessments, and pedagogy that will teach people how to make good decisions about life, policy, and relationships. As we and others have pointed out, the future of our world depends, in so many ways, on wise decisions and actions. Consequently, this work feels portentous and promising. We cannot wait to see what the future holds for it.

References

Akrivou, K., & Scalzo, G. (2020). In search of a fitting moral psychology for practical wisdom: The missing link for virtuous management. *Business Ethics: A European Review*, *29*(1), 33–44.
Aldwin, C. M., Igarashi, H., & Levenson, M. R. (2019). Wisdom as self-transcendence. In R. J. Sternberg & J. Glück (Eds.), *Cambridge handbook of wisdom* (pp. 122–43). Cambridge University Press.
Aldwin, C. M., Igarashi, H., & Levenson, M. R. (2020). Only half the story. *Psychological Inquiry*, *31*(2), 151–2.
Alexandrova, A. (2017). *A philosophy for the science of well-being*. Oxford University Press.
Allport, G. W. (1937). *Personality: A psychological interpretation*. Holt.
Alvarez, J. A., & Emory, E. (2006). Executive function and the frontal lobes: A meta-analytic review. *Neuropsychology Review*, *16*(1), 17–42.
Alzola, M., Hennig, A., & Romar, E. (2020). Thematic symposium editorial: Virtue ethics between East and West. *Journal of Business Ethics*, *165*(2), 177–89.
Ames, M. C. F. D. C., Serafim, M. C., & Zappellini, M. B. (2020). *Phronesis* in administration and organizations: A literature review and future research agenda. *Business Ethics: A European Review*, *29*(S1), 65–83.
Annas, J. (2011). *Intelligent virtue*. Oxford University Press.
Anscombe, G. E. M. (1958a). Modern moral philosophy. *Philosophy*, *33*(1), 1–19.
Anscombe, G. E. M. (1958b). On brute facts. *Analysis*, *18*(3), 69–72.
Aquino, K., & Freeman, D. (2009). Moral identity in business situations: A social cognitive framework for understanding moral functioning. In D. Narvaez & D. K. Lapsley (Eds.), *Personality, identity and character: Explorations in moral psychology* (pp. 375–95). Cambridge University Press.
Aquino, K., Freeman, D., Reed, I. I., Lim, V. K., & Felps, W. (2009). Testing a social-cognitive model of moral behavior: The interactive influence of situations and moral identity centrality. *Journal of Personality and Social Psychology*, *97*(1), 123.
Aquino, K., & Reed, A. II. (2002). The self-importance of moral identity. *Journal of Personality and Social Psychology*, *83*(6), 1423–40.
Ardelt, M. (2003). Empirical assessment of a three-dimensional wisdom scale. *Research on Aging*, *25*(3), 275–324.
Ardelt, M. (2004). Wisdom as an expert knowledge system: A critical review of contemporary operationalizations of an ancient concept. *Human Development*, *47*(5), 257–85.
Ardelt, M. (2020). Can wisdom and psychosocial growth be learned in university courses? *Journal of Moral Education*, *49*(1), 30–45.
Ardelt, M., & Jeste, D. (2018). Wisdom and hard times: The ameliorating effect of wisdom on the negative association between adverse life events and well-being. *Journal of Gerontology, Series B: Psychological Sciences and Social Sciences*, *73*, 1374–83.
Ardelt, M., & Sharma, B. (2021). Linking wise organizations to wise leadership, job satisfaction, and well-being. *Frontiers in Communication*, *6*(235), 1–23.
Aristotle (1935). *The Athenian constitution, The eudemian ethics, On virtues and vices*. Trans. H. Rackham. William Heinemann.

Aristotle (1944). *Politics*. Trans. H. Rackham. W. Heinemann.
Aristotle (1985). *Nicomachean ethics*. Trans. T. Irwin. Hackett.
Aristotle (2007). *On rhetoric*. Trans. G. A. Kennedy. Oxford University Press.
Arsenio, W. F., Gold, J., & Adams, E. (2006). Children's conceptions and displays of moral emotions. In M. Killen & J. G. Smetana (Eds.), *Handbook of moral development* (pp. 581–609). Lawrence Erlbaum Associates.
Arthur, J., Earl, S. R., Thompson, A. P., & Ward, J. W. (2021). The value of character-based judgement in the professional domain. *Journal of Business Ethics, 169*(2), 293–308.
Arthur, J., Kristjánsson, K., Thomas, H., Kotzee, B., Ignatowicz, A. M., & Qiu, T. (2015). Virtuous medical practice: Research report. Birmingham: Jubilee Centre for Character and Virtues. http://www.jubileecentre.ac.uk/userfiles/jubileecentre/pdf/Research%20Reports/Virtuous_Medical_Practice.pdf
Arthur, J., Kristjánsson, K., & Vogler, C. (2021). Seeking the common good in education through a positive conception of social justice. *British Journal of Educational Studies, 69*(1), 101–17.
Asma, L. J. F. (2022). Habitual virtuous action and acting for reasons. *Philosophical Psychology, 35*(7), 1036–56.
Athanassoulis, N. (2023). The *phronimos* as a moral exemplar: Two internal objections and a proposed solution. *Journal of Value Inquiry*. https://link.springer.com/article/10.1007/s10790-021-09872-4
Austin, J. L. (1964). A plea for excuses. In V. C. Chappell (Ed.), *Ordinary language* (pp. 1–30). Prentice-Hall.
Baltes, P. B., & Staudinger, U. M. (2000). Wisdom: A metaheuristic (pragmatic) to orchestrate mind and virtue toward excellence. *American Psychologist, 55*(1), 122–36.
Baltes, P. B., & Smith, J. (2008). The fascination of wisdom: Its nature, ontogeny, and function. *Perspectives on Psychological Science, 3*(1), 56–64.
Bandura, A. (1977). *Social learning theory*. Prentice Hall.
Barkley, R. A. (2012). *Executive functions: What they are, how they work, and why they evolved*. Guilford.
Barriga, A. Q., Morrison, E. M., Liau, A. K., & Gibbs, J. C. (2001). Moral cognition: Explaining the gender difference in anti-social behaviour. *Merrill-Palmer Quarterly, 47*(4), 532–62.
Batson, C. D. (1991). *The altruism question: Toward a social-psychological answer*. Erlbaum.
Batson, C. D. (2011). What's wrong with morality? *Emotion Review, 3*(3), 230–36.
Batson, C. D., Thompson, E. R., Seuferling, G., Whitney, H., & Strongman, J. A. (1999). Moral hypocrisy: Appearing moral to oneself without being so. *Journal of Personality and Social Psychology, 77*(3), 525–37.
Batson, C. D., & Thompson, E. R. (2001). Why don't moral people act morally? *Motivational Considerations, 10*(2), 54–7.
Bauer, J. J. (2022). *Value and the good life story*. Presented at the 3rd Annual Network for Research on Morality Conference. https://www.youtube.com/watch?v=lnuVETJP-E0&t=7s
Bauer, J. J., King, L. A., & Steger, M. F. (2019). Meaning making, Self-Determination Theory, and the question of wisdom in personality. *Journal of Personality, 87*(1), 82–101.
Beadle, R., & Moore, G. (2018). MacIntyre on virtue and organization. In T. Angier (Ed.), *Virtue ethics* (pp. 323–40). Routledge.
Beauchamp, T., & Childress, J. (2001). *Principles of biomedical ethics*. Oxford University Press.
Bebeau, M. J., Rest, J. R., & Narvaez, D. (1999). Beyond the promise: A perspective on research in moral education. *Educational Researcher, 28*(4), 18–26.
Becker, J., Brackbill, D., & Centola, D. (2017). Network dynamics of social influence in the wisdom of crowds. *Proceedings of the National Academy of Sciences, 114*(26), 5070–6.

Beresford, E. B. (1996). Can *phronesis* save the life of medical ethics? *Theoretical Medicine*, *17*(3), 209–24.
Bergman, R. (2002). Why be moral? A conceptual model from developmental psychology. *Human Development*, *45*(2), 104–24.
Berkowitz, M. W., & Bier, M. C. (2006). *What works in character education: A research-driven guide for educators*. Character Education Partnership.
Best, J. R., & Miller, P. H. (2010). A developmental perspective on executive functions. *Child Development*, *81*(6), 1641–60.
Bezanilla, M. J., Fernández-Nogueira, D., Poblete, M., & Galindo-Domínguez, H. (2019). Methodologies for teaching-learning critical thinking in higher education: The teacher's view. *Thinking Skills and Creativity*, *33*(9), 1–10.
Blasi, A. (1980). Bridging moral cognition and moral action: A critical review of the literature. *Psychological Bulletin*, *88*(1), 1–45.
Blasi, A. (1983). Moral cognition and moral action: A theoretical perspective. *Developmental Review*, *3*(2), 178–210.
Blasi, A. (2004). Moral functioning: Moral understanding and personality. In D. K. Lapsley & D. Narvaez (Eds.), *Moral development, self and identity* (pp. 335–47). Erlbaum.
Blockburger, S. (2021). *Development and training for the decathlon*. http://coachr.org/deca.htm
Bobonich, C. (2015). Aristotle, political decision making, and the many. In T. Lockwood & T. Samaras (Eds.), *Aristotle's Politics: A critical guide* (pp. 142–62). Cambridge University Press.
Bohlin, K. (2022). The practical wisdom framework: A compass for school leaders. *Journal of Education*, *202*(2), 156–65.
Bortolotti, L. (2011). Does reflection lead to wise choices? *Philosophical Explorations*, *14*(3), 297–313.
Boudreau, J. D., & Fuks, A. (2015). The humanities in medical education: Ways of knowing, doing and being. *Journal of Medical Humanities*, *36*(4), 321–36.
Boyd, D. (2010). Character education and citizenship education: A case of a cancerous relationship. *Philosophy of Education Yearbook*, *2010*, 384–92.
Brewer, T. (2021). The aesthetic dimension of practical wisdom. In G. Pettigrove & C. Swanton (Eds.), *Neglected virtues* (pp. 163–78). Routledge.
Brienza, J. P., Kung, F. Y. H., Santos, H. C., Bobocel, D. R. R., & Grossmann, I. (2018). Wisdom, bias, and balance: Toward a process-sensitive measurement of wisdom-related cognition. *Journal of Personality and Social Psychology*, *115*(6), 1093–126.
Briggs, C., & Lumsdon, D. (2022). Practical wisdom: How do personal virtue beliefs and contextual factors interact in adolescents' moral decision-making? *Journal of Moral Education*, *51*(3), 293–311.
Brinkmann, S. (2011). *Psychology as a moral science: Perspectives on normativity*. Springer.
Broadie, S. (1991). *Ethics with Aristotle*. Oxford University Press.
Brown, M., McGrath, R. E., Bier, M. C., Johnson, K., & Berkowitz, M. W. (2023). A comprehensive meta-analysis of character education. *Journal of Moral Education*, *52*(2), 119–38.
Bruya, B., & Ardelt, M. (2018). Wisdom can be taught: A proof-of-concept study for fostering wisdom in the classroom. *Learning and Instruction*, *58*(1), 106–14.
Bryan, C. S., & Babelay, A. M. (2009). Building character: A model for reflective practice. *Academic Medicine*, *84*(9), 1283–8.
Burbules, N. C. (2019). Thoughts on *phronesis*. *Ethics and Education*, *14*(2), 126–37.
Burnyeat, F. M. (1980). Aristotle on learning to be good. In A. O. Rorty (Ed.), *Essays on Aristotle's ethics* (pp. 69–92). University of California Press.
Butler, L. P., & Tomasello, M. (2016). Two-and 3-year-olds integrate linguistic and pedagogical cues in guiding inductive generalization and exploration. *Journal of Experimental Child Psychology*, *145*(1), 64–78.

Cammack, D. (2013). Aristotle on the virtue of the multitude. *Political Theory*, 41(2), 175–202.
Cantor, N. (1990). From thought to behaviour: 'Having' and 'doing' in the study of personality and cognition. *American Psychologist*, 45(6), 735–50.
Caputo, J. D. (1993). *Against ethics*. Indiana University Press.
Carlo, G. (2006). Care based and altruistically based morality. In M. Killen & J. G. Smetana (Eds.), *Handbook of moral development* (pp. 551–79). Lawrence Erlbaum Associates.
Carlo, G., Hausmann, A., Christiansen, S., & Randall, B. A. (2003). Sociocognitive and behavioral correlates of a measure of prosocial tendencies for adolescents. *Journal of Early Adolescence*, 23(1), 107–34.
Carlo, G., Knight, G. P., McGinley, M., Zamboanga, B. L., & Hernandez-Jarvis, L. (2010). The multidimensionality of prosocial behaviors and evidence of measurement equivalence in Mexican American and European American early adolescents. *Journal of Research on Adolescence*, 20(2), 334–58.
Carr, D. (1995). Is understanding the professional knowledge of teachers a theory-practice problem? *Journal of Philosophy of Education*, 29(3), 311–31.
Carr, D. (2002a). Moral education and the perils of developmentalism. *Journal of Moral Education*, 31(1), 5–19.
Carr, D. (2002b). Feelings in moral conflict and the hazards of emotional intelligence. *Ethical Theory and Moral Practice*, 5(1), 3–21.
Carr, D. (2009). Virtue, mixed emotions and moral ambivalence. *Philosophy*, 84(1), 31–46.
Carr, D. (2015). *Educating for the wisdom of moral virtue*. http://www.jubileecentre.ac.uk/userfiles/jubileecentre/pdf/conference-papers/Varieties_of_Virtue_Ethics/Carr_David.pdf
Carr, D. (2021). What is the educational virtue in flourishing? *Educational Theory*, 71(3), 389–407.
Carr, D. (2022). From character to parable and allegory: Varieties of moral imagination in fictional literature. In E. Brooks et al. (Eds.), *Literature and character education in universities* (pp. 103–16). Routledge.
Carr, D. (2023). The practical wisdom of *phronesis* in the education of purported virtuous character. *Educational Theory*, 73(2), 137–52.
Carr, D., & Harrison, T. (2015). *Educating character through stories*. Imprint Academic.
Carr, W. (1995). *For education: Towards critical educational inquiry*. Open University Press.
Carroll, N. (2016). Fictional characters as social metaphors. In I. Fileva (Ed.), *Questions of character* (pp. 385–400). Oxford University Press.
Casler, K., Terziyan, T., & Greene, K. (2009). Toddlers view artifact function normatively. *Cognitive Development*, 24(3), 240–7.
Chambers, D. W. (2011). Developing a self-scoring comprehensive instrument to measure Rest's four-component model of moral behavior: The moral skills inventory. *Journal of Dental Education*, 75(1), 23–35.
Chappell, S. G. (2022). *Epiphanies*. Oxford University Press.
Cheek, J. M., Smith, S. M., & Tropp, L. R. (2002, February). *Relational identity orientation: A fourth scale for the AIQ*. Paper presented at the meeting of the Society for Personality and Social Psychology, Savannah, GA.
Chesterton, G. K. (1908). Orthodoxy. http://www.gkc.org.uk/gkc/books/orthodoxy/ch3.html
Cigman, R. (2018). *Cherishing and the good life of learning: Ethics, education, upbringing*. Bloomsbury.
Clark, A. (2015). *Surfing uncertainty: Prediction, action, and the embodied mind*. Oxford University Press.
Clay, Z., & Tennie, C. (2017). Is overimitation a uniquely human phenomenon? Insights from human children compared with bonobos. *Child Development*, 89(5), 1535–44.

Clayton, V. P., & Birren, J. E. (1980). The development of wisdom across the life-span: A reexamination of an ancient topic. In P. B. Baltes & O. G. Brim, Jr. (Eds.), *Life-span development and behavior* (Vol. 3, pp. 103–35). Academic Press.
Cohen L. (2018). Happens to the heart: Lyrics. https://genius.com/Leonard-cohen-happens-to-the-heart-lyrics
Cokelet, B. (2022). Virtue science and productive theoretical neutrality. *Journal of Moral Education*, 51(1), 104–10.
Cokelet, B., & Fowers, B. J. (2019). Realistic virtues and how to study them: Introducing the STRIVE-4 model. *Journal of Moral Education*, 48(1), 7–26.
Colby, A., & Damon, W. (1992). *Some do care: Contemporary lives of moral commitment*. Free Press.
College of Policing (2014). Code of ethics. https://www.college.police.uk/ethics/code-of-ethics
Conroy, M., Malik, A. Y., Hale, C., Weir, C., Brockie, A., & Turner, C. (2021). Using practical wisdom to facilitate ethical decision-making: A major empirical study of *phronesis* in the decision narratives of doctors. *BMC Medical Ethics*, 22(16), 1–13.
Cooper, J. M. (1977). Aristotle on the forms of friendship. *Review of Metaphysics*, 30(4), 619–48.
Cooper, J. M. (2005). Political animals and civic friendship. In R. Kraut & S. Skultety (Eds.), *Aristotle's Politics: Critical essays* (pp. 65–89). Rowman and Littlefield.
Crocker, J., Luhtanen, R. K., Cooper, M. L., & Bouvrette, A. (2003). Contingencies of self-worth in college students: Theory and measurement. *Journal of Personality and Social Psychology*, 85(5), 894–908.
Csibra, G., & Gergely, G. (2009). Natural pedagogy. *Trends in Cognitive Sciences*, 13(4), 148–53.
Curnow, T. (2011). *Sophia* and *phronesis*: Past, present, and future. *Research in Human Development*, 8(2), 95–108.
Curren, R. (2000). *Aristotle on the necessity of public education*. Rowman and Littlefield.
Curzer, H. J. (2005). How good people do bad things: Aristotle on the misdeeds of the virtuous. *Oxford Studies in Ancient Philosophy*, 28(1), 233–56.
Curzer, H. J. (2012). *Aristotle and the virtues*. Oxford University Press.
Curzer, H. J. (2017). *Practical wisdom and the time of your life*. Conference presentation. https://www.jubileecentre.ac.uk/userfiles/jubileecentre/pdf/conference-papers/CharacterWisdomandVirtue/Curzer_H.pdf
Curzer, H. J. (2022). Introducing the virtue of good timing and some surprising functions of practical reason. *Journal of Value Inquiry*, 56(3), 485–504.
Dahl, A. (2018). New beginnings: An interactionist and constructivist approach to early moral development. *Human Development*, 61(4–5), 232–47.
Damon, W. (1981). The development of justice and self-interest during childhood. In M. J. Lerner & S. C. Lerner (Eds.), *The justice motive in social behavior: Adapting to times of scarcity and change* (pp. 57–72). Plenum Press.
Damon, W. (1984). Self-understanding and moral development from childhood to adolescence. In W. M. Kurtines & J. L Gewirtz (Eds.), *Morality, moral behavior, and moral development* (pp. 109–127). John Wiley.
Damon, W. (2008). *The path to purpose: How young people find their calling in life*. Free Press.
Damon, W., & Colby, A. (2015). *The power of ideals*. Oxford University Press.
Daniel, E., Dys, S. P., Buchmann, M., & Malti, T. (2014). Developmental relations between sympathy, moral emotion attributions, moral reasoning and social justice values from childhood to early adolescence. *Journal of Adolescence*, 37(7), 1201–14.
Darnell, C., Fowers, B., & Kristjánsson, K. (2022). A multifunction approach to assessing Aristotelian *phronesis* (practical wisdom). *Personality and Individual Differences*, 196(October), 111684.

Darnell, C., Gulliford, L., Kristjánsson, K., & Paris, P. (2019). *Phronesis* and the knowledge-action gap in moral psychology and moral education: A new synthesis? *Human Development*, 62(3), 101–29.

Darnell, C., & Kristjánsson, K. (Eds.) (2021). *Virtues and virtue education in theory and practice: Are virtues local or universal?* Routledge.

Davis, M. H. (1983). Measuring individual differences in empathy: Evidence for a multidimensional approach. *Journal of Personality and Social Psychology*, 44(1), 113–26.

Davis, M., Mitchell, K., Hall, J., Lothert, J., Snapp, T., & Meyer, M. (1999). Empathy, expectations and situational preferences: Personality influences on the decision to participate in volunteering helping behaviours. *Journal of Personality*, 67(3), 469–503.

Davison, I., Harrison, T., Hayes, D., & Higgins, J. (2016). How to assess children's virtue literacy: Methodological lessons learnt from the Knightly Virtues programme. *Journal of Beliefs and Values*, 37(1), 16–28.

De Caro, M., Vaccarezza, M. S., & Niccoli, A. (2018). *Phronesis* as ethical expertise: Naturalism of second nature and the unity of virtue. *Journal of Value Inquiry*, 52(3), 287–305.

De Caro, M., Marraffa, M., & Vaccarezza, M. S. (2021). The priority of *phronesis*: How to rescue virtue theory from its critics. In M. S. Vaccarezza & De Caro, M. (Eds.), *Practical wisdom: Philosophical and psychological perspectives* (pp. 29–51). Routledge.

Diener, E. (2012). New findings and future directions for subjective well-being research. *American Psychologist*, 67(8), 590–97.

Dinsmore, D. L., Alexander, P. A., & Loughlin, S. M. (2008). Focusing the conceptual lens on metacognition, self-regulation, and self-regulated learning. *Educational Psychology Review*, 20(4), 391–409.

Dong, M., & Fournier, M. A. (2022). What are the necessary conditions for wisdom? Examining intelligence, creativity, meaning-making, and the Big-Five traits. *Collabra: Psychology*, 8(1), 33145.

Dong, M., Westrate, N. M., & Fournier, M. A. (2023). Thirty years of psychological wisdom research: What we know about an ancient concept. *Perspectives on Psychological Science*. http://doi:10.1177/17456916221114096

Doris, J. (2002). *Lack of character: Personality and moral behavior*. Cambridge University Press.

Driver, J. (2001). *Uneasy virtue*. Cambridge University Press.

Dunne, J. (1993). *Back to the rough ground: 'Phronesis' and 'techné' in modern philosophy and in Aristotle*. University of Notre Dame Press.

Dunne, J. (2022). Aristotle on techne: Two theses in search of a synthesis? In T. Angier & L. Raphals (Eds.), *Skill in ancient ethics: The legacy of China, Greece and Rome* (pp. 141–62). Bloomsbury.

Durlak, J. A., Weissberg, R. P., Dymnicki, A. B., Taylor, R. D., & Schellinger, K. B. (2011). The impact of enhancing students' social and emotional learning: A meta-analysis of school-based universal interventions. *Child Development*, 82(1), 405–32.

Eisenberg, N. (2000). Emotion, regulation and moral development. *Annual Review of Psychology*, 51(1), 665–97.

Eisenberg, N., & Fabes, R. A. (1990). Empathy: Conceptualization, measurement, and relation to prosocial behavior. *Motivation and Emotion*, 14(2), 131–49.

Eisenberg, N., & Fabes, R. A. (1998). Prosocial development. In W. Damon (Series Ed.) & N. Eisenberg (Vol. Ed.), *Handbook of child psychology, vol. 3: Social emotional and personality development* (pp. 701–78). Wiley.

Eisenberg, N., Guthrie, I. K., Murphy, B. C., Shepard, S. A., Cumberland, A., & Carlo, G. (1999). Consistency and development of prosocial dispositions: A longitudinal study. *Child Development*, 70(6), 1360–72.

Eisenberg, N., & Miller, P. A. (1987). The relation of empathy to prosocial and related behaviours. *Psychological Bulletin*, *101*(1), 91–119.
Eisenberg, N., Spinrad, T. L., & Sadovsky, A. (2006). Empathy related responding in children. In M. Killen & J. Smetana (Eds.), *Handbook of moral development* (pp. 517–49). Erlbaum.
Fan, Y., Rakovic, M., Graaf, J., Lim, L., Singh, S., Moore, J., Molenaar, I., Bannert, M., & Gašević, D. (2023). Towards a fuller picture: Triangulation and integration of the measurement of self-regulated learning based on trace and think aloud data. *Journal of Computer Assisted Learning*. https://doi.org/10.1111/jcal.12801
Farb, N. A. S. (2020). Meta-cognition with a heart: Mindfulness, therapy, and the cultivation of wisdom. *Psychological Inquiry*, *31*(2), 164–7.
Ferkany, M. (2020). A developmental theory for Aristotelian practical intelligence. *Journal of Moral Education*, *49*(1), 111–28.
Ferrari, M. (2010). Developing expert and transformative wisdom: Can either be taught in public schools? In M. Ferrari & G. Potworowski (Eds.), *Teaching for wisdom: Cross-cultural perspectives on fostering wisdom* (pp. 207–22). Springer.
Ferrari, M., & Potworowski, G. (Eds.) (2010). *Teaching for wisdom: Cross-cultural perspectives on fostering wisdom*. Springer.
Fetter, J. T. (2015). Aristotle's great-souled man: The limited perfection of the ethical values. *History of Political Thought*, *36*(1), 1–28.
Flaming, D. (2001). Using *phronesis* instead of 'research-based practice' as the guiding light for nursing practice. *Nursing Philosophy*, *2*(3), 251–8.
Flanagan, O. (1991). *Varieties of moral personality: Ethics and psychological realism*. Harvard University Press.
Flanagan, O. (2007). *The really hard problem: Meaning in a material world*. MIT Press.
Flavell, J. H. (1979). Metacognition and cognitive monitoring: A new area of cognitive-developmental inquiry. *American Psychologist*, *34*(10), 906–11.
Fleeson, W., & Jayawickreme, E. (2015). Whole trait theory. *Journal of Research in Personality*, *56*(1), 82–92.
Fleeson, W., Miller, C., Furr, R. M., Knobel, A., & Jayawickreme, E. (2022). Moral, extreme, and positive: What are the key issues for the study of the morally exceptional? In A. W. Kruglanski, C. Kopetz, & E. Szumowska (Eds.), *The psychology of extremism: A motivational perspective.* (pp. 230–58). Routledge.
Flyvbjerg, B. (2001). *Making social science matter*. Cambridge University Press.
Flyvbjerg, B. (2004). A Perestroikan straw man answers back: David Laitin and phronetic social science. *Politics & Society*, *32*(3), 389–416.
Flyvbjerg, B., Landman, T., & Schram, S. (Eds.) (2012). *Real social science: Applied phronesis*. Cambridge University Press.
Fowers, B. J. (2001). The limits of a technical concept of a good marriage: Examining the role of virtues in communication skills. *Journal of Marital and Family Therapy*, *27*(3), 327–40.
Fowers, B. (2005). *Virtue and psychology: Pursuing excellence in ordinary practices*. American Psychological Association.
Fowers, B. J. (2008). From continence to virtue: Recovering goodness, character unity, and character types for positive psychology. *Theory & Psychology, 18*, 629–53.
Fowers, B. J. (2010). Instrumentalism and psychology: Beyond using and being used. *Theory & Psychology, 20*(1), 102–24.
Fowers, B. J. (2015). *The evolution of ethics: Human sociality and the emergence of ethical mindedness*. Palgrave/McMillan.
Fowers, B. J. (2016). Aristotle on eudaimonia: On the virtue of returning to the source. In J. Vittersø (Ed.), *The handbook of eudaimonic well-being* (pp. 67–83). Springer.

Fowers, B. J. (2022). Social science as an inherently moral endeavor. *Journal of Moral Education*, *51*(1), 35–46.

Fowers, B. J., & Anderson, A. R. (2018). Aristotelian *philia*, contemporary friendship, and some resources for studying close relationships. In T. Harrison & D. I. Walker (Eds.), *The theory and practice of virtue education* (pp. 184–96). Routledge.

Fowers, B. J., Carroll, J. S., Leonhardt, N. D., & Cokelet, B. (2021). The emerging science of virtue. *Perspectives on Psychological Science*, *16*(1), 118–47.

Fowers, B. J., Cokelet, B., & Leonhardt, N. D. (in press). *The science of virtue: A framework for research*. Cambridge University Press.

Fowers, B. J., Lane, A. A., Lang, S. F., Cioffi, K., Anderson, A. R., & Cokelet, B. (2022). Does trait interpersonal fairness moderate situational influence on fairness behavior? *Personality and Individual Differences*, *193*(July), 111615.

Fowers, B. J., Novak, L. F., Calder, A. J., & Sommer, R. K. (2022). The distorting lens of psychology's individualism and a social realist alternative. In B. D. Slife, S. C. Yanchar, & F. C. Richardson (Eds.), *Routledge international handbook of theoretical and philosophical psychology* (pp. 78–97). Routledge.

Fowers, B. J., Novak, L. F., Kiknadze, N. C., & Calder, A. J. (2023a). Questioning contemporary universalist approaches to human flourishing. *Review of General Psychology*, *23*(2), 121–134. https://doi.org/10.1177/10892680221138230

Fowers, B. J., Novak, L. F., Kiknadze, N. C., & Calder, A. J. (2023b). Can a theory of *human flourishing* be formulated? Toward a science of flourishing. Manuscript in review.

Frede, D. (1996). Mixed feelings in Aristotle's *Rhetoric*. In A. E. Rorty (Ed.), *Essays on Aristotle's Rhetoric* (pp. 258–85). University of California Press.

Frede, D. (2005). Citizenship in Aristotle's *Politics*. In R. Kraut & S. Skultety (Eds.), *Aristotle's Politics: Critical essays* (pp. 167–84). Rowman and Littlefield.

Fredrickson, B. L., Grewen, K. M., Coffey, K. A., Algoe, S. B., Firestine, A. M., Arevalo, J. G., et al. (2013). A functional genomic perspective on human well-being. *PNAS*, *110*(33), 13684–9.

Frey, J. (Ed.) (2024). Practical wisdom. Oxford University Press.

Galton, F. (1907). Vox populi (The wisdom of crowds). *Nature*, *75*, 450–1.

Garsten, B. (2013). Deliberating and acting together. In M. Deslauriers and P. Destrée (Eds.), *The Cambridge companion to Aristotle's Politics* (pp. 324–49). Cambridge University Press.

Garver, E. (2006). *Confronting Aristotle's ethics: Ancient and modern morality*. University of Chicago Press.

George, A., Urch, C., & Cribb, A (2023). A virtuous framework for professional reflection. *Future Healthcare Journal*. http://doi:10.7861/fhj.2022-0121

Gergely, G., Bekkering, H., & Kiraly, I. (2002). Rational imitation in preverbal infants. *Nature*, *415*, 755.

Gibbs, J. C. (2003). *Moral development and reality: Beyond the theories of Kohlberg and Hoffman*. Sage.

Glück, J. (2020). The important difference between psychologists' labs and real life: Evaluating the validity of models of wisdom. *Psychological Inquiry*, *31*(2), 144–50.

Glück, J., & Bluck, S. (2013). The MORE life experience model: A theory of the development of personal wisdom. In M. Ferrrari & N. Weststrate (Eds.), *The scientific study of personal wisdom* (pp. 75–97). Springer.

Glück, J., König, S., Naschenweng, K., Redzanowski, U., Dorner, L., Strasser, I., & Wiedermann, W. (2013). How to measure wisdom: Content, reliability, and validity of five measures. *Frontiers in Psychology*, *4*(405), 1–13.

Göckeritz, S. M., Schmidt, F. H., & Tomasello, M. (2014). Young children's creation and transmission of social norms. *Cognitive Development*, *30*(1), 81–95.

Goddiksen, M. P., & Gjerris, M. (2022). Teaching phronesis in a research integrity course. *Facets*, 7(1), 139–52.
Goleman, D. (1995). *Emotional intelligence*. Bantam Books.
Grant, A. M., & Schwartz, B. (2011). Too much of a good thing: The challenge and opportunity of the inverted U. *Perspectives on Psychological Science*, 6(1), 61–76.
Greenspan, P. S. (1980). A case of mixed feelings: Ambivalence and the logic of emotion. In A. O. Rorty (Ed.), *Explaining emotions* (pp. 223–50). University of California Press.
Greenspan, P. S. (1988). *Emotions and reason: An inquiry into emotional justification*. Routledge.
Grossmann, I. (2017a). Wisdom and how to cultivate it. *European Psychologist*, 22(4), 233–46.
Grossmann, I. (2017b). Wisdom in context. *Perspectives on Psychological Science*, 12(2), 233–57.
Grossmann, I. (2021). Evidence-based training of wisdom in business and management: Use of scientific insights about malleability of practical wisdom for rigorous interventions. In B. Schwartz, C. Bernacchio, C. González-Cantón, & A. Robson, A. (Eds.), *Handbook of practical wisdom in business and management* (pp. 1–20). Springer.
Grossmann, I., & Kross, E. (2014). Exploring Solomon's paradox: Self-distancing eliminates the self-other asymmetry in wise reasoning about close relationships in younger and older adults. *Psychological Science*, 25(8), 1571–80.
Grossmann, I., Weststrate, N. M., Ardelt, M., Brienza, J. P., Dong, M., Ferrari, M., Fournier, M. A., Hu, C. S., Nusbaum, H. C., & Vervaeke, J. (2020a). The science of wisdom in a polarized world: Knowns and unknowns. *Psychological Inquiry*, 31(2), 103–33.
Grossmann, I., Weststrate, N. M., Ferrari, M., & Brienza, J. P. (2020b). A common model is essential for a cumulative science of wisdom. *Psychological Inquiry*, 31(2), 185–94.
Grossmann, I., Weststrate, N. M., Kara-Yakoubian, M., & Dong, M. (2020c). Points of divergence from the common wisdom model. https://osf.io/c37yh/
Guardian (2016). Parents disapprove of offspring marrying someone of different political persuasion. *Guardian*, Feb. 10. https://www.theguardian.com/politics/2016/feb/10/parents-disapprove-son-daughter-in-law-different-political-persuasion
Guiso, L., Sapienza, P., & Zingales, L. (2015). The value of corporate culture. *Journal of Financial Economics*, 117(1), 60–76.
Gulliford, L. (2017). Phronesis *and the integration of the virtues*. Conference presentation. https://www.jubileecentre.ac.uk/userfiles/jubileecentre/pdf/conference-papers/CharacterWisdomandVirtue/Gulliford_L.pdf
Gulliford, L. (2018). *Can I tell you about gratitude? A helpful introduction for everyone*. Jessica Kingsley.
Gustin Law, L. K. (2017). Is human virtue a civic virtue? A reading of Aristotle's *Politics* 3.4. In E. C. de Lara & R. Brouwer (Eds.), *Aristotle's practical philosophy: On the relationship between the Ethics and Politics* (pp. 93–118). Springer.
Hacker-Wright, J. (2015). Skill, practical wisdom, and ethical naturalism. *Ethical Theory and Moral Practice*, 18(5), 983–93.
Haidt, J. (2001). The emotional dog and its rational tail: A social intuitionist approach to moral judgment. *Psychological Review*, 108(4), 814–34.
Haldane, J. (2022). Knowledge of oneself and others: Aquinas, Wittgenstein and Rembrandt. *Philosophical Investigations*, 45(4), 388–413.
Han, H., Kim, J., Jeong, C., & Cohen, G. L. (2017). Attainable and relevant moral exemplars are more effective than extraordinary exemplars in promoting voluntary service engagement. *Frontiers in Psychology*, 8. http://doi:10.3389/fpsyg.2017.00283
Harðarson, A. (2019). Aristotle's conception of practical wisdom and what it means for moral education in schools. *Educational Philosophy and Theory*, 51(14), 1518–27.
Hardy, S. A. (2006). Identity, reasoning and emotion: An empirical comparison of three sources of moral motivation. *Motivation and Emotion*, 30(3), 207–15.

Hardy, S. A., & Carlo, G. (2005). Identity as a source of moral motivation. *Human Development*, 48(4), 232–56.

Hardy, S. A., & Carlo, G. (2011). Moral identity: What is it, how does it develop and is it linked to moral action? *Child Development Perspectives*, 5(3), 212–18.

Hardy, S. A., Padilla-Walker, L. M., & Carlo, G. (2008). Parenting dimensions and adolescents' internalisation of moral values. *Journal of Moral Education*, 37(2), 205–23.

Hardy, S. A., Walker, L. J., Olsen, J. A., Woodbury, R. D., & Hickman, J. R. (2014). Moral identity as moral ideal self: Links to adolescent outcomes. *Developmental Psychology*, 50(1), 45–57.

Hare, B. (2017). Survival of the friendliest: Homo sapiens evolved via selection for prosociality. *Annual Review of Psychology*, 68, 155–86.

Harrison, T. (2022). A new educational model for online flourishing: A pragmatic approach to integrating moral theory for cyber-flourishing. *Pastoral Care in Education*, 40(2), 128–51.

Harrison, T., & Polizzi, G. (2021). A cyber-wisdom approach to digital citizenship education: Insights from adolescents and parents: Research report. https://www.jubileecentre.ac.uk/userfiles/jubileecentre/pdf/news/ACyber-WisdomApproachtoDigitalCitizenshipEducation_Final.pdf

Hart, D., Atkins, R., & Ford, D. (1998). Urban America as a context for the development of moral identity in adolescence. *Journal of Social Issues*, 54(3), 513–30.

Hart, D., & Fegley, S. (1995). Prosocial behaviour and caring in adolescence: Relations to self-understanding and social judgement. *Child Development*, 66(5), 1346–59.

Hatchimonji, D. R., Linsky, A. C. V., Nayman, S. J., & Elias, M. J. (2020). Spiral model of phronesis development: Social-emotional and character development in low-resourced urban schools. *Journal of Moral Education*, 49(1), 129–42.

Hawkins, A. J., Fowers, B. J., Carroll, J. S., & Yang, C. (2007). Conceptualizing and measuring marital virtues. In S. Hofferth & L. Casper (Eds.), *Handbook of measurement issues in family research* (pp. 67–83). Erlbaum.

Haybron, D. M. (2016). The philosophical basis of eudaimonic psychology. In J. Vittersø (Ed.), *Handbook of eudaimonic well-being* (pp. 27–53). Springer.

Hays, J. (2013). Transformation and transcendence for wisdom: The emergence and sustainment of wise leaders and organizations. In W. Küpers & D. J. Pauleen (Eds.), *A handbook of practical wisdom: Leadership, organization and integral business practice* (pp. 134–54). Routledge.

Hennecke, M., & Bürgler, S. (2023). Metacognition and self-control: An integrative framework. *Psychological Review*. http://doi:10.1037/rev0000406.

Hertz, S. G., & Krettenauer, T. (2016). Does moral identity effectively predict moral behaviour? A meta-analysis. *Review of General Psychology*, 20(2), 129–40.

Hill, P. & Lapsley, D. K. (2009). Persons and situations in the moral domain. *Journal of Research in Personality*, 43(2), 245–46.

Hoffman, M. L. (2000). *Empathy and moral development: Implications for caring and justice*. Cambridge University Press.

Hofmann, B. (2002). Medicine as practical wisdom (*phronesis*). *Poiesis & Praxis*, 1(2), 135–49.

Hojjat, M., & Moyer, A. (Eds.) (2017). *The psychology of friendship*. Oxford University Press.

Hong, L., & Page, S. E. (2012). Some microfoundations of collective wisdom. In H. Landemore & J. Elster (Eds.), *Collective wisdom: Principles and mechanisms* (pp. 56–71). Cambridge University Press.

Horn, C. (2016). Individual competence and collective deliberation in Aristotle's *Politics*. In C. Arruzza & D. Nikulin (Eds.), *Philosophy and political power in antiquity* (pp. 94–113). Brill.

Hoyos-Valdés, D. (2018). The notion of character friendship and the cultivation of virtue. *Journal for the Theory of Social Behaviour*, 48(1), 66–82.

Hume, D. (1978). *A treatise of human nature*. Clarendon Press.

Huo, Y., & Kristjánsson, K. (2018). Why is there lack of growth in character virtues? An insight into business students across British business schools In D. Carr (Ed.), *Cultivating moral character and virtue in professional practice* (pp. 207–21). Routledge.

Huo, Y., & Kristjánsson, K. (2020). An explorative study of virtues in ethical consumption from a Confucian perspective in an urban-rural-fringe in China. *Business Ethics and Leadership*, 4(4), 105–22.

Hursthouse, R. (1999). *On virtue ethics*. Oxford University Press.

Hursthouse, R. (2006). Practical wisdom: A mundane account. *Proceedings of the Aristotelian Society*, 106, 285–309.

Hursthouse, R. (2011). What does the Aristotelian *phronimos* know? In L. Jost & J. Wuerth (Eds.), *Perfecting virtue: New essays on Kantian Ethics and Virtue Ethics* (pp. 38–57). Cambridge University Press.

Hutson, J. M., & Myers, N. A. (1999). The relationship between ethics and *phronesis*. *Pediatric Surgery International*, 15(5–6), 320–2.

Huynh, A. C., & Grossmann, I. (2020). A pathway for wisdom-focused education. *Journal of Moral Education*, 49(1), 9–29.

IBM Corp. (2016). *SPSS*. New York.

Intezari, A., & Pauleen D. J. (2013). Students of wisdom: An integral meta-competencies theory of practical wisdom. In In W. Küpers & D. J. Pauleen (Eds.), *A handbook of practical wisdom: Leadership, organization and integral business practice* (pp. 155–74). Routledge.

Irrera, E. (2005). Between advantage and virtue: Aristotle's theory of political friendship. *History of Political Thought*, 26(4), 565–85.

Irrera, E. (2010). Being a good ruler in a deviant community: Aristotle's account of the polity. *Polis*, 27(1), 58–79.

Irwin, T. H. (1975). Aristotle on reason, desire, and virtue. *Journal of Philosophy*, 72(17), 567–78.

Irwin, T. H. (1990). *Aristotle's first principles*. Clarendon Press.

Irwin, T. H. (2000). Ethics as an inexact science: Aristotle's ambitions for moral theory. In B. Hooker & M. O. Little (Eds.), *Moral particularism* (pp. 100–29). Oxford University Press.

Jacobs, J. (2017). Virtues, principles, and intuitions: Elements of an explication of phronesis. Conference presentation. https://www.jubileecentre.ac.uk/userfiles/jubileecentre/pdf/conference-papers/CharacterWisdomandVirtue/Jacobs_J.pdf

Jameel, S. Y. (2022). *Enacted phronesis in general practitioners*. Unpublished PhD thesis. University of Birmingham. https://etheses.bham.ac.uk/id/eprint/12197/

Jayawickreme, E., & Fleeson, W. (2017). Whole trait theory can explain virtues. In W. Sinnott-Armstrong & C. B. Miller (Eds.), *Moral psychology: Virtue and character, vol. 5.* (pp. 121–9). MIT Press.

Jayawickreme, E., Zachry, C. E., & Fleeson, W. (2019). Whole trait theory: An integrative approach to examining personality structure and process. *Personality and Individual Differences*, 136(1), 2–11.

Jefferson, A., & Sifferd, K. (2022). Practical wisdom and the value of cognitive diversity. In A. Jefferson, O. Palermos, P. Paris, & J. Webber (Eds.), *Values and virtues for a challenging world: RIP supplementary volume* (pp. 149–76). Cambridge University Press.

Jenkins, K., Kinsella, E. A., & DeLuca, S. (2019). Perspectives on phronesis in professional nursing practice. *Nursing Philosophy*, 20(1), 1–8.

Jerome, L., & Kisby, B. (2019). *The rise of character education in Britain: Heroes, dragons and the myths of character*. Palgrave-Macmillan.

Jeste, D. V., Lee, E. E., Palmer, B. W., & Treichler, E. B. H. (2020). Moving from humanities to sciences: A new model of wisdom fortified by sciences of neurobiology, medicine, and evolution. *Psychological Inquiry*, 31(2), 134–43.

John, O. P., & Srivastava, S. (1999). *The Big-Five trait taxonomy: History, measurement, and theoretical perspectives*. In L. A. Pervin & O. P. John (Eds.), *Handbook of personality: Theory and research, vol. 2* (pp. 102–38). Guilford Press.

Johnson, M. R. (2005). *Aristotle on teleology*. Clarendon Press.

Jubilee Centre for Character and Virtues (2022). *A framework for character education in schools*, 3rd ed. http://www.jubileecentre.ac.uk/userfiles/jubileecentre/pdf/character-education/Framework%20for%20Character%20Education.pdf

Kaldjian, L. C. (2010). Teaching practical wisdom in medicine through clinical judgement, goals of care, and ethical reasoning. *Journal of Medical Ethics*, 36(9), 558–62.

Kaldjian, L. C. (2014). *Practicing medicine and ethics: Integrating wisdom, conscience, and goals of care*. Cambridge University Press.

Kaldjian, L. C. (2019). Wisdom in medical decision-making. In R. J. Sternberg & J. Glück (Eds.), *The Cambridge handbook of wisdom* (pp. 698–720). Cambridge University Press.

Kallio, E. K. (2020). From multiperspective to contextual integrative thinking in adulthood: Considerations on theorisation of adult thinking and its place as a component of wisdom. In E. K. Kallio (Ed.), *Development of adult thinking: Interdisciplinary perspectives on cognitive development and adult thinking* (pp. 9–32). Routledge.

Kamtekar, R. (2004). Situationism and virtue ethics on the content of our character. *Ethics*, 114(3), 458–91.

Kanakogi, Y., Miyazaki, M., Takahashi, H., Yamamoto, H., Kobayashi, T., & Hiraki, K. (2022). Third-party punishment by preverbal infants. *Nature Human Behavior*, 6, 1234–42.

Kanakogi, Y., Okumura, Y., Inoue, Y., Kitazaki, M. & S. Itakura, S. (2013). Rudimentary sympathy in preverbal infants: Preference for others in distress. *PLoS ONE*, 8, e65292.

Kant, I. (1964). *Metaphysics of morals*. Trans. M. J. Gregor. Harper & Row.

Karami, S., Ghahremani, M., Parra-Martinez, F., & Gentry, M. (2020). A polyhedron model of wisdom: A systematic review of the wisdom studies in three different disciplines. *Roeper Review*, 42(4), 241–57.

Kayange, G. M. (2020). Restoration of *ubuntu* as an autocentric virtue-*phronesis* theory. *South African Journal of Philosophy*, 39(1), 1–12.

Keltner, D., & Piff, P. K. (2020). Self-transcendent awe as a moral grounding of wisdom. *Psychological Inquiry*, 31(2), 160–3.

Kemmis, S. (2012). Phronesis, experience, and the primacy of practice. In E. A. Kinsella & A. Pitman (Eds.), *Phronesis as professional knowledge: Practical wisdom in the professions* (pp. 147–61). Sense Publishers.

Kenward, B. (2012). Over-imitating preschoolers believe that unnecessary actions are normative and enforce their performance by a third party. *Journal of Experimental Child Psychology*, 112(2), 195–227.

Keyt, D. (2005). Aristotle and anarchism. In R. Kraut & S. Skultety (Eds.), *Aristotle's Politics: Critical essays* (pp. 203–22). Rowman and Littlefield.

Kinghorn, W. A. (2010). Medical education as moral formation: An Aristotelian account of medical professionalism. *Perspectives in Biology and Medicine*, 53(1), 87–105.

Kingsford, J. M., Hawes, D. J., & de Rosnay, M. (2018). The moral self and moral identity: Developmental questions and conceptual challenges. *British Journal of Developmental Psychology*, 36(4), 652–66.

Klaei, Y. A., & Reio, T. G. (2014). Goal pursuit and eudaimonic well-being among university students: Metacognition as the mediator. *Behavioral Development Bulletin*, 19(4), 91–104.

Kline, R. B. (2015). *Principles and practice of structural equation modeling*, 4th ed. Guilford.

Ko, H.-K., Tseng, H.-C., Chin, C.-C., & Hsu, M.-T. (2020). Phronesis of nurses: A response to moral distress. *Nursing Ethics*, 27(1), 67–76.

Kochanska, G. (2002). Committed compliance, moral self, and internalization: A mediational model. *Developmental Psychology*, *38*(3), 339–51.
Koehn, D. (1995). A role for virtue ethics in the analysis of business practice. *Business Ethics Quarterly*, *5*(3), 533–9.
Kohlberg, L. (1958). *The development of modes of thinking and choices in years 10 to 16*. Ph.D. Dissertation, University of Chicago.
Kohlberg, L. (1969). Stage and sequence: The cognitive developmental approach to socialization. In D. A. Goslin (Ed.), *Handbook of socialization theory and research* (pp. 347–480). Rand McNally.
Kohlberg, L. (1981). *Essays on moral development, vol. 1: The philosophy of moral development*. Harper & Row.
Kohlberg, L., & Candee, D. (1984). The relationship of moral judgment to moral action. In W. M. Kurtines & J. L. Gewirtz (Eds.), *Morality, moral behavior, and moral development* (pp. 53–73). Wiley.
Kohlberg, L., & Kramer, R. (1969). Continuities and discontinuities in childhood and adult moral development. *Human Development*, *12*(2), 3–120.
Konstan, D. (2006). *The emotions of the ancient Greeks: Studies in Aristotle and classical literature*. University of Toronto Press.
Köymen, B., Lieven, E. V. M., Engermann, D. A., Rackoczy, H., Warneken, F., & Tomasello, M. (2014). Children's norm enforcement in their interactions with peers. *Developmental Psychology*, *52*(3), 423–9.
Kraut, R. (1993). In defense of the grand end. *Ethics*, *103*(2), 361–74.
Kraut, R. (2002). *Aristotle: Political philosophy*. Oxford University Press.
Krettenauer, T. (2019). The gappiness of the 'gappiness problem'. *Human Development*, *62*(3), 142–5.
Krettenauer, T. (2022). When moral identity undermines moral behavior: An integrative framework. *Social and Personality Psychology Compass*, *16*(3), 12655.
Krettenauer, T., Malti, T., & Sokol, B. (2008). The development of moral emotion expectancies and the happy victimiser phenomenon: A critical review of theory and application. *European Journal of Developmental Science*, *2*(3), 221–35.
Krettenauer, T., Colasante, T., Buchman, M., & Malti, T. (2014). The development of moral emotions and decision-making from adolescence to early adulthood: A 6-year longitudinal study. *Journal of Youth Adolescence*, *43*(4), 583–96.
Krettenauer, T., & Hertz, S. (2015). What develops in moral identities? A critical review. *Human Development*, *58*(3), 137–53.
Kristjánsson, K. (2006). *Justice and desert-based emotions*. Ashgate/Routledge.
Kristjánsson, K. (2007). *Aristotle, emotions, and education*. Ashgate/Routledge.
Kristjánsson, K. (2010a). *The self and its emotions*. Cambridge University Press.
Kristjánsson, K. (2010b). The trouble with ambivalent emotions. *Philosophy*, *85*(334), 485–510.
Kristjánsson, K. (2013). *Virtues and vices in positive psychology: A philosophical critique*. Cambridge University Press.
Kristjánsson, K. (2015). *Aristotelian character education*. Routledge.
Kristjánsson, K. (2018a). Virtue from the perspective of psychology. In N. Snow (Ed.), *Oxford handbook of virtue* (pp. 546–69). Oxford University Press.
Kristjánsson, K. (2018b). *Virtuous emotions*. Oxford University Press.
Kristjánsson, K. (2020). *Flourishing as the aim of education: A neo-Aristotelian view*. Routledge.
Kristjánsson, K. (2021). Recent attacks on character education in a UK context: A case of mistaken identities? *Journal of Beliefs and Values*, *42*(3), 363–77.
Kristjánsson, K. (2022a). Reason and intuition in Aristotle's moral psychology: Why he was not a two-system dualist. *Philosophical Explorations*, *25*(1), 42–57.

Kristjánsson, K. (2022b). *Friendship for virtue*. Oxford University Press.

Kristjánsson, K., & Fowers, B. J. (2023). Phronesis as moral decathlon: Contesting the redundancy thesis about *phronesis*. *Philosophical Psychology*. http://doi: 10.1080/09515 089.2022.2055537

Kristjánsson, K., Pollard, D., Darnell, C., & Thoma, A. (2021). Phronesis: *Using an Aristotelian model as a research tool: Research report*. https://www.jubileecentre.ac.uk/userfiles/jubile ecentre/Phronesis%20Report.pdf

Kristjánsson, K., Thompson, A., & Maile, A. (2021). Character virtues in policing: Research report. https://www.jubileecentre.ac.uk/userfiles/jubileecentre/pdf/Research%20Reports/ CharacterVirtuesinPolicing_ResearchReport.pdf

Kumagal, A. K. (2014). From competencies to human interests: Ways of knowing and understanding in medical education. *Academic Medicine, 89*(7), 978–83.

Kunzmann, U. (2019). Performance-based measures of wisdom: State of the art and future directions. In R. J. Sternberg & J. Glück (Eds.), *Cambridge handbook of wisdom* (pp. 277–96). Cambridge University Press.

Lamb, M., Brant, J., & Brooks, E. (2021). How is virtue cultivated? Seven strategies for postgraduate character development. *Journal of Character Education,17*(1), 81–108.

Lambert, M. J., & Barley, D. E. (2001). Research summary on the therapeutic relationship and psychotherapy outcome. *Psychotherapy: Theory, Research, Practice, Training, 38*(4), 357–61.

Landemore, H. (2012). Collective wisdom: Old and new. In H. Landemore & J. Elster (Eds.), *Collective wisdom: Principles and mechanisms* (pp. 1–20). Cambridge University Press.

Lapsley, D. (2016). On the prospects for Aristotelian character education. *Journal of Moral Education, 45*(4), 502–15.

Lapsley, D. (2019). Phronesis, virtues and the developmental science of character. *Human Development, 62*(3), 130–41.

Lapsley, D. (2021). The developmental science of phronesis. In M. S. Vaccarezza & De Caro, M. (Eds.), *Practical wisdom: Philosophical and psychological perspectives* (pp. 138–59). Routledge.

Lapsley, D. K., & Narvaez, D. (2004). A social-cognitive approach to the moral personality. In D. K. Lapsley & D. Narvaez (Eds.), *Moral development, self and identity* (pp. 1–20). Lawrence Erlbaum.

Lapsley, D. K., & Narvaez, D. (2008). 'Psychologized morality' and its discontents, or, do good fences make good neighbours? In F. Oser & W. Veugelers (Eds.), *Getting involved: Global citizenship development and sources of moral value* (pp. 279–92). Sense Publishers.

Lapsley, D. K., & Hill, P. L. (2009). The development of moral personality. In D. Narvaez & D. K. Lapsley (Eds.), *Personality, identity and character: Explorations in moral psychology* (pp. 185–213). Cambridge University Press.

Lawrence, W. Y., Rountree, J., & Mehltretter Drury, S. A. (2021). Practical wisdom through deliberative pedagogy. *Journal of the Scholarship of Teaching and Learning, 21*(4), 225–38.

Lees, J., & Young, L. (2020). A theory of wisdom needs a theory of mind. *Psychological Inquiry, 31*(2), 168–73.

Lehman, M., Hagen, J., & Ettinger, U. (2022). Unity and diversity in metacognition. *Journal of Experimental Psychology: General, 151*(10), 2396–417.

Lerner, R. M. (2019). Character development: Four facets of virtue. *Child Development Perspectives, 13*(2), 79–84.

Levenson, M. R., Jennings, P. A., Aldwin, C. M., & Shiraishi, R. W. A. Y. W. (2005). Self-transcendence: Conceptualization and measurement. *International Journal of Aging & Human Development, 60*(2), 127–43.

Li, K., Wang, F., Wang, Z., Shi, J., & Xiong, M. (2019). A polycultural theory of wisdom based on Habermas's worldview. *Culture & Psychology, 26*(2), 252–73.

Lin, T.-J., Ha, S. Y., Li, W.-T., Chiu, Y.-J., Hong, Y.-R., & Tsai, C. C. (2019). Effects of collaborative small-group discussions on early adolescents' social reasoning. *Reading and Writing, 32*(9), 2223–49.

Linn, M. (2022). Aristotle on actual virtue and ordinary people. *Journal of Value Inquiry, 56*(4), 525–55.

Lubbe, D. (2019). Parallel analysis with categorical variables: Impact of category probability proportions on dimensionality assessment accuracy. *Psychological Methods, 24*(3), 339–51.

McCullough, M. E. (2008). *Beyond revenge: The evolution of the forgiveness instinct.* Jossey-Bass.

McDowell, J. (1998). Virtue and reason. In J. McDowell (Ed.), *Mind, value, and reality* (pp. 50–73). Harvard University Press.

McGrath. R. E. (2019). Refining our understanding of the VIA classification: Reflection on papers by Han, Miller, and Snow. *Journal of Positive Psychology, 14*(1), 41–50.

McGrath, R. E. (2022). The VIA virtue model: Half-baked or brilliant? *Journal of Positive Psychology, 17*(2), 250–56.

McGrath, R. E., & Brown, M. (2020). Using the VIA classification to advance a psychological science of virtue. *Frontiers in Psychology.* http://doi:/10.3389/fpsyg.2020.565953

MacIntyre, A. (1981). *After virtue.* University of Notre Dame Press.

MacIntyre, A. (1984). *After virtue*, 2nd ed. University of Notre Dame Press.

MacIntyre, A. (1998). Plain persons and moral philosophers: Rules, virtues and goods. In K. Knight (Ed.), *The MacIntyre reader* (pp. 136–52). University of Notre Dame Press.

MacIntyre A., & Dunne, J. (2002). Alasdair MacIntyre on education: In dialogue with Joseph Dunne. *Journal of Philosophy of Education, 36*(1), 1–19.

McMahon, J. M., & Good, D. J. (2015). The moral metacognition scale: Development and validation. *Ethics & Behavior, 26*(5), 357–94.

Maiese, M. (2017). Transformative learning, enactivism, and affectivity. *Studies in Philosophy and Education, 36,* 197–216.

Malti, T., Gummerum, M., Keller, M., & Buchmann, M. (2009). Children's moral motivation, sympathy and prosocial behaviour. *Child Development, 80*(2), 442–60.

Malti, T., & Latzko, B. (2010). Children's moral emotions and moral cognition: Towards an integrative perspective. *New Directions for Child and Adolescent Development, 129*(1), 1–10.

Malti, T., & Krettenauer, T. (2013). The relation of moral emotion attributions to prosocial and antisocial behaviour: A meta-analysis. *Child Development, 84*(2), 397–412.

Malti, T., & Ongley, S. E. (2014). The development of moral emotions and moral reasoning. In M. Killen & J. G. Smetana (Eds.), *Handbook of moral development* (pp. 163–83). Psychology Press.

Mannes, A. E., Larrick, R. P., & Soll, J. B. (2012). The social psychology of the wisdom of crowds. In J. I. Krueger (Ed.), *Frontiers of social psychology: Social judgment and decision making* (pp. 227–42). Psychology Press.

Marcum, J. A. (2012). *The virtuous physician: The role of virtue in medicine.* Springer.

Markus, H. R., & Kitayama, S. (1991). Culture and self: Implications for cognition, emotion, and motivation. *Psychological Review, 98*(2), 224–53.

Martin, J., & Gillespie, A. (2010). A neo-Median approach to human agency: Relating the social and the psychological in the ontogenesis of perspective-coordinating persons. *Integrative Psychological and Behavioral Science, 44*(3), 252–72.

Mata, A. (2019). Social metacognition in moral judgment: Decisional conflict promotes perspective taking. *Journal of Personality and Social Psychology, 117*(6), 1061–82.

Matsuba, M. K., & Walker, L. J. (2004). Extraordinary moral commitment: Young adults involved in social organisations. *Journal of Personality, 72*(2), 413–36.

Meltzoff, A. N. (1995). Understanding the intentions of others: Re-enactment of intended acts by 18-month-old children. *Developmental Psychology, 31*(5), 838–50.

Menesini, E., & Camodeca, M. (2008). Shame and guilt as behaviour regulators: Relationships with bullying, victimization and prosocial behaviour. *British Journal of Developmental Psychology*, *26*(2), 183–96.

Mestre, M. V., Carlo, G., Samper, P., Tur-Porcar, A. M., & Mestre, A. L. (2015). Psychometric evidence of a multidimensional measure of prosocial behaviors for Spanish adolescents. *Journal of Genetic Psychology: Research and Theory on Human Development*, *176*(4), 260–71.

Mill, J. S. (1972). *Utilitarianism, liberty, representative government*. E. P. Dutton & Co.

Miller, C. B. (2021). Flirting with skepticism about practical wisdom. In M. S. Vaccarezza & M. De Caro (Eds.), *Practical wisdom: Philosophical and psychological perspectives* (pp. 52–69). Routledge.

Miller, C. B., Furr, R. M., Knobel, A., & Fleeson, W. (Eds.) (2015). *Character: New directions from philosophy, psychology, and theology*. Oxford University Press.

Miller, P. A., Eisenberg, N., Fabes, R. A., & Shell, R. (1996). Relations of moral reasoning and vicarious emotions to young children's prosocial behaviour towards peers and adults. *Developmental Psychology*, *32*(2), 210–19.

Miyake, A., & Friedman, N. (2012). The nature and organization of individual differences in executive functions: Four general conclusions. *Current Directions in Psychological Science*, *21*(1), 8–14.

Montada, L. (1993). Understanding oughts by assessing moral reasoning or moral emotions. In G. G. Noam & T. E. Wren (Eds.), *The moral self* (pp. 292–303). MIT Press.

Montgomery, K. (2006). *How doctors think: Clinical judgment and the practice of medicine*. Oxford University Press.

Morgan, B., & Fowers, B. J. (2021). Empathy and authenticity online: The roles of moral identity, moral disengagement and parenting style. *Journal of Personality*, *90*(2), 183–202.

Morgan, B., Gulliford, L., & Kristjánsson, K. (2014). Gratitude in the UK: A new prototype analysis and a cross-cultural comparison. *Journal of Positive Psychology*, *9*(4), 281–94.

Morgan, B., Gulliford, L., & Kristjánsson, K. (2017). A new approach to examining moral virtue: The multi-component gratitude measure. *Personality and Individual Differences*, *107*(1), 179–89.

Moshman, D. (2004). False moral identity: Self-serving denial in the maintenance of moral self-conceptions. In D. K. Lapsley & D. Narvaez (Eds.), *Moral development, self, and identity* (pp. 83–110). Lawrence Erlbaum.

Moss, J. (2011). 'Virtue makes the goal right': Virtue and 'phronesis' in Aristotle's ethics. *Phronesis*, *56*(3), 204–61.

Müller, A. W. (2004). Aristotle's conception of ethical and natural virtue. In J. Szaif & M. Lutz-Bachmann (Eds.), *Was ist das für den Menschen Gute?/What is good for a human being?* (pp. 18–53). De Gruyter.

Muthén, L. K., & Muthén, B. O. (1998-2017). *Mplus User's Guide*, 8th ed. Muthén & Muthén.

Narvaez, D. (2008). Triune ethics: The neurobiological roots of our multiple moralities. *New Ideas in Psychology*, *26*(1), 95–119.

Narvaez, D. (2010). Moral complexity: The fatal attraction of truthiness and the importance of mature moral functioning. *Perspectives on Psychological Science*, *5*(2), 163–81.

Narvaez, D., & Rest, J. (1995). The four components of acting morally. In W. Kurtines & J. Gewirtz (Eds.), *Moral behavior and moral development: An introduction* (pp. 385–400). McGraw-Hill.

Narvaez, D., & Lapsley, D. K. (2005). The psychological foundations of moral expertise. In D. K. Lapsley & F. C. Powers (Eds.), *Character psychology and character education* (pp. 140–65). University of Notre Dame Press.

National Research Council. (2015). *Enhancing the effectiveness of team science*. The National Academies Press.

Navarini, C., Indraccolo, A., & Brunetti, R. (2021). Practical wisdom and generalization. In M. S. Vaccarezza & De Caro, M. (Eds.), *Practical wisdom: Philosophical and psychological perspectives* (pp. 114–37). Routledge.

Nelson, T. O. (1990). Meta-memory: A theoretical framework and new findings. *Psychology of Learning and Motivation, 26*, 125–73.

Ng, V., & Tay, L. (2020). Lost in translation: The construct representation of character virtues. *Perspectives on Psychological Science, 15*(2), 300–26.

Nonaka, I., Toyama, R., & Hirata, T. (2008). *Managing flow: A process theory of the knowledge-based firm*. Palgrave Macmillan.

Nucci, L. (2017). Character: A multifaceted developmental system. *Journal of Character Education, 13*(1), 1–16.

Nussbaum, M. C. (1988). Nature, function, and capability. *Oxford Studies in Ancient Philosophy, 1*(1), 145–84.

Nussbaum, M. C. (1990). Aristotelian social democracy. In R. B. Douglass, G. M. Mara, & H. S. Richardson (Eds.), *Liberalism and the good* (pp. 203–52). Routledge.

Nussbaum, M. C. (1995). Aristotle on human nature and the foundations of ethics. In J. E. J. Altham & R. Harrison (Eds.), *World, mind, and ethics: Essays on the ethical philosophy of Bernard Williams* (pp. 86–131). Cambridge University Press.

Nussbaum, M. C. (2001). *Upheavals of thought: The intelligence of emotions*. Cambridge University Press.

Ober, J. (2005). Aristotle's natural democracy. In R. Kraut & S. Skultety (Eds.), *Aristotle's Politics: Critical essays* (pp. 223–43). Rowman and Littlefield.

Ohtani, K., & Hisasaka, T. (2018). Beyond intelligence: A meta-analytic review of the relationship among metacognition, intelligence, and academic performance. *Metacognition and Learning, 13*(2), 179–212.

Osman, Y. (2019). The significance in using role models to influence primary school children's moral development: Pilot study. *Journal of Moral Education, 48*(3), 316–31.

Page, B. (2021). Powering up neo-Aristotelian natural goodness. *Philosophical Studies, 178*(11), 3755–75.

Pálsson, G., & Durrenberger, E. P. (1990). Systems of production and social discourse: The skipper effect revisited. *American Anthropologist, 92*(1), 130–41.

Pascalis, O., Fort, M., & Quinn, P. C. (2020). Development of face processing: Are there critical or sensitive periods? *Current Opinion in Behavioral Sciences, 36*(1), 7–12.

Patrick, R. B., & Gibbs, J. C. (2012). Inductive discipline, parental expression of disappointed expectations and moral identity in adolescence. *Journal of Youth Adolescence, 41*(8), 973–83.

Pellegrino, E. (1979). The anatomy of clinical judgment: Some notes on right reason and right action. In H. T. Engelhardt, S. F. Spicker, & B. Towers (Eds.), *Clinical judgment: A critical appraisal* (pp. 169–94). D. Reidel.

Pellegrino, E., & Thomasma, D. (1993). *The virtues in clinical practice*. Oxford University Press.

Penner, L. (2002). Dispositional and organizational influences on sustained volunteerism: An interactionist perspective. *Journal of Social Issues, 58*(3), 447–67.

Perugini, M., & Leone, L. (2009). Implicit self-concept and moral action. *Journal of Research in Personality, 43*(5), 747–54.

Peters, R. S. (1981). *Moral development and moral education*. George Allen and Unwin.

Peterson, A. (2020). Character education, the individual and the political. *Journal of Moral Education, 49*(2), 143–57.

Peterson, C., & Seligman, M. E. P. (2004). *Character strengths and virtues: A handbook and classification*. Oxford University Press.

Peterson, C., Park, N., & Seligman, M. E. P. (2005). Orientation to happiness and life satisfaction: The full life versus the empty life. *Journal of Happiness Studies, 6*(1) 25–41.

Phan, L. V., Blackie, L. E. R., Horstmann, K., & Jayawickreme, E. (2021). An integrative framework to study wisdom. In J. Rauthmann (Ed.), *Handbook of personality dynamics and processes* (pp. 1159–82). Elsevier.
Piaget, J. (1997). *The moral judgement of the child*. Free Press.
Pickup, A. (2020). Embodied phronesis. *Journal of Thought*, *54*(1/2), 4–22.
Polanyi, M. (1966). *Personal knowledge: Towards a post-critical philosophy*. Routledge.
Polizzi, G., & Harrison, T. (2022). Wisdom in the digital age: A conceptual and practical framework for understanding and cultivating cyber-wisdom. *Ethics and Information Technology*, *24*(1), 1–16.
Pratt, M. W., Hunsberger, B., Pancer, S. M., & Alisat, S. (2003). A longitudinal analysis of personal value socialisation: Correlates of moral self in adolescence. *Social Development*, *12*(4), 563–85.
Pratt, M. W., Arnold, M. L., & Lawford, H. (2009). Growing towards care: A narrative approach to prosocial moral identity and generativity of personality in emerging adulthood. In D. Narvaez & D. K. Lapsley (Eds.), *Personality, identity and character: Explorations in moral psychology* (pp. 295–315). Cambridge University Press.
Rabinoff, E. (2018). *Perception in Aristotle's ethics*. Northwestern University Press.
Railton, P. (2016). Intuitive guidance: Emotion, information and experience. In M. E. P. Seligman, P. Railton, R. F. Baumeister, & C. Sripade (Eds.), *Homo prospectus* (pp. 33–85). Oxford University Press.
Railton, P. (2017). Moral learning: Conceptual foundations and normative relevance. *Cognition*, *167*(1), 172–90.
Reed, A. II., & Aquino, K. F. (2003). Moral identity and the expanding circle of moral regard towards out-groups. *Journal of Personality and Social Psychology*, *84*(6), 1270–86.
Reeve, C. D. C. (2005). *Love's confusions*. Harvard University Press.
Reimer, K., Dewitt Goudelock, B. M., & Walker, L. J. (2009). Developing conceptions of moral maturity: Traits and identity in adolescent personality. *Journal of Positive Psychology*, *4*(5), 372–88.
Reiner, P. (1991). Aristotle on personality and some implications for friendship. *Ancient Philosophy*, *11*(1), 67–84.
Rest, J. (1984). The major components of morality. In W. M. Kurtines & J. L Gewirtz (Eds.), *Morality, moral behavior, and moral development* (pp. 24–40). Wiley.
Rest, J., Narvaez, D. Thoma, S. J., & Bebeau, M. J. (2000). A neo-Kohlbergian approach to morality research. *Journal of Moral Education*, *29*(4), 381–95.
Richardson, F. C., Fowers, B. J., & Guignon, C. B. (1999). *Re-envisioning psychology: Moral dimensions of theory and practice*. Jossey-Bass.
Richardson, M. J., & Pasupathi, M. (2005). Young and growing wiser: Wisdom during adolescence and young adulthood. In R. J. Sternberg & J. Jordan (Eds.), *A handbook of wisdom: Psychological perspectives* (pp. 139–59). Cambridge University Press.
Roberts, J. (2009). Excellences of the citizen and of the individual. In G. Anagnostopoulos (Ed.), *A companion to Aristotle* (pp. 555–65). Wiley-Blackwell.
Rooney, D. (2013). Being a wise organizational researcher: Ontology, epistemology and axology. In W. Küpers & D. J. Pauleen (Eds.), *A handbook of practical wisdom: Leadership, organization and integral business practice* (pp. 79–98). Routledge.
Rorty, A. O. (1986). The two faces of courage. *Philosophy*, *61*(236), 151–71.
Rosler, A. (2013). Civic virtue: Citizenship, ostracism, and war. In M. Deslauriers & P. Destrée (Eds.), *The Cambridge companion to Aristotle's Politics* (pp. 144–75). Cambridge University Press.
Rosling, H., Rosling, O., & Rönnlund, A. R. (2018). *Factfulness: Ten reasons we're wrong about the world—and why things are better than you think*. Sceptre.

Russell, D. C. (2009). *Practical intelligence and the virtues.* Oxford University Press.

Russell, D. C. (2014). What virtue ethics can learn from utilitarianism. In B. Eggleston & D. Miller (Eds.), *The Cambridge companion to utilitarianism* (pp. 258–79). Cambridge University Press.

Russell, D. C. (2017). *Practical unintelligence and the vices.* Conference presentation. https://www.jubileecentre.ac.uk/userfiles/jubileecentre/pdf/conference-papers/CharacterWisdomandVirtue/Russell_D.pdf

Russell, D. C. (2021). The reciprocity of the virtues. In In M. S. Vaccarezza & M. De Caro (Eds.), *Practical wisdom: Philosophical and psychological perspectives* (pp. 8–28). Routledge.

Ryan, R. M., Curren, R., & Deci, E. L. (2013). What humans need: Flourishing in Aristotelian philosophy and self-determination theory. In A. S. Waterman (Ed.), *The best within us: Positive psychology perspectives on eudaimonia* (pp. 57–75). American Psychological Association.

Ryan, R. M., & Deci, E. L. (2017). *Self-determination theory: Basic psychological needs in motivation, development, and wellness.* Guilford.

Ryff, C. D. (1989). Happiness is everything, or is it? Explorations on the meaning of psychological well-being. *Journal of Personality and Social Psychology, 57*, 1069–81.

Salkever, S. G. (2005). Aristotle's social science. In R. Kraut & S. Skultety (Eds.), *Aristotle's Politics: Critical essays* (pp. 27–64). Rowman and Littlefield.

Sandel, M. J. (1996). *Democracy's discontent.* Harvard University Press.

Sanderse, W. (2015). An Aristotelian model of moral development. *Journal of Philosophy of Education, 49*(3), 382–98.

Sanderse, W. (2020). Does Aristotle believe that habituation is only for children? *Journal of Moral Education, 49*(1), 98–110.

Sayer, A. (2011). *Why things matter to people: Social science, values and ethical life.* Cambridge University Press.

Scalzo, G., & Fariñas, G. (2018). Aristotelian *phronesis* as a key factor for leadership in the knowledge-creating company according to Ikujiro Nonaka. *Cuadernos de Administración, 31*(57), 19–44.

Schwartz, B., & Sharpe, K. E. (2006). Practical wisdom: Aristotle meets positive psychology. *Journal of Happiness Studies, 7*(3), 377–95.

Schwartz, B., & Sharpe, K. (2010). *Practical wisdom: The right way to do the right thing.* Riverhead Books.

Schwartzberg, M. (2016). Aristotle and the judgment of the many: Equality, not collective quality. *Journal of Politics, 78*(3), 733–45.

Schwarz, E., & Lappalainen, J. H. (2020). Collective *phronesis*? An investigation of collective judgement and professional action. In R. Giovagnoli & R. Lowe (Eds.), *The logic of social practices* (pp. 23–35). Springer.

Schwarz, N. (2015). Metacognition. In M. Mikulincer, P. R. Shaver, E. Borgida, & J. A. Bargh (Eds.), *APA handbook of personality and social psychology, volume 1: Attitudes and social cognition.* (pp. 203–29). American Psychological Association.

Segvic, H. (2009). *From Protogoras to Aristotle: Essays in ancient moral philosophy.* Princeton University Press.

Seligman, M. E. P. (2002). *Authentic happiness: Using the new positive psychology to realize your potential for lasting fulfillment.* Free Press.

Seligman, M. E. P. (2011). *Flourish: A visionary new understanding of happiness and well-being.* Free Press.

Sellman, D. (2012). Reclaiming competence for professional phronesis. In E. A. Kinsella & A. Pitman (Eds.), *Phronesis as professional knowledge: Practical wisdom in the professions* (pp. 115–30). Sense Publishers.

Sherman, N. (1987). Aristotle on friendship and the shared life. *Philosophy and Phenomenological Research*, *47*(4), 589–613.

Sherman, N. (1989). *The fabric of character: Aristotle's theory of virtue*. Oxford University Press.

Shweder, R. A., Much, N. C., Mahapatra, M., & Park, L. (1997). The 'big three' of morality (autonomy, community, divinity) and the 'big three' explanations of suffering. In A. M. Brandt & P. Rozin (Eds.), *Morality and health*. (pp. 119–69). Routledge.

Silverstein, A., & Trombetti, I. (2013). Aristotle's account of moral development. *Journal of Theoretical and Philosophical Psychology*, *33*(4), 233–52.

Sim, M. (2024). Benevolence/humaneness (*ren* 仁) as practical wisdom. In J. Frey (Ed.), *Practical wisdom* (in press). Oxford University Press.

Sison, A. J. G. (2011). Aristotelian citizenship and corporate citizenship: Who is a citizen of the corporate polis? *Journal of Business Ethics*, *100*(1), 3–9.

Sison, A. J. G., Ferrero, I., & Guitián, G. (2018). *Business ethics: A virtue ethics and common good approach*. Routledge.

Smetana, J., Jambon, M., & Ball, C. (2014). The social domain approach to children's moral and social judgments. In M. Killen & J. Smetana (Eds.), *Handbook of moral development* (pp. 23–45). Psychology Press.

Snow, N. (2006). Habitual virtuous action and automaticity. *Ethical Theory and Moral Practice*, *9*(5), 545–61.

Snow, N. (2015). Notes toward an empirical psychology of virtue: Exploring the personality scaffolding of virtue. In Peters, J. (Ed.), *Aristotelian ethics in contemporary perspective* (pp. 130–44). Routledge.

Snow, N. & Narvaez, D. (Eds.). (2019). *Self, motivation, and virtue: New findings from philosophy and the human sciences*. Routledge.

Snow, N., Wright, J. C., & Warren, M. T. (2021). Phronesis and whole-trait theory: An integration. In M. S. Vaccarezza & M. De Caro (Eds.), *Practical wisdom: Philosophical and psychological perspectives* (pp. 70–95). Routledge.

Solomon, R. C. (1992). Corporate roles, personal virtues: An Aristotelian approach to business ethics. *Business Ethics Quarterly*, *2*(3), 317–39.

Sperber, D., & Mercier, H. (2012). Reasoning as social competence. In In H. Landemore & J. Elster (Eds.), *Collective wisdom: Principles and mechanisms* (pp. 368–92). Cambridge University Press.

Spinrad, T. L., & Eisenberg, N. (2017). Compassion in children. In E. M. Seppala, E. Simon-Thomas, S. L. Brown, M. C. Worline, C. Daryl-Cameron, & J.R. Doty (Eds.), *The Oxford handbook of compassion science* (pp. 53–63). Oxford University Press.

Stangle, R. (2020). *Neither heroes nor saints: Ordinary virtue, extraordinary virtue, and self-cultivation*. Oxford University Press.

Stark, S. (2001). Virtue and emotion. *Noûs*, *35*(3), 440–55.

Staudinger, U. M., & Glück, J. (2011). Psychological wisdom research: Commonalities and differences in a growing field. *Annual Review of Psychology*, *62*(1), 215–41.

Sternberg, R. J. (1998). A balance theory of wisdom. *Review of General Psychology*, *2*(4), 347–65.

Sternberg, R. J. (2001). Why schools should teach for wisdom: The balance theory of wisdom in educational settings. *Educational Psychologist*, *36*(4), 227–45.

Sternberg, R. J. (2003). *Wisdom, intelligence, and creativity*. Cambridge University Press.

Sternberg, R. J. (2020). The missing links: Comments on 'The science of wisdom in a polarized world'. *Psychological Inquiry*, *31*(2), 153–9.

Sternberg, R. J., & Karami, S. (2021). What is wisdom? A unified 6P framework. *Review of General Psychology*, *25*(2), 134–51.

Sternberg, R. J., & Glück, J. (2022). *Wisdom: The psychology of wise thoughts, words, and deeds*. Cambridge University Press.

Sternberg, R. J., Glück, J., & Karami, S. (2022). Psychological theories of wisdom. In R. J. Sternberg & J. Glück (Eds.), *Wisdom: The psychology of wise thoughts, words, and deeds* (pp. 53–69). Cambridge University Press.

Steyn, F., & Sewchurran, K. (2021). Towards a grainier understanding of how to encourage morally responsible leadership through the development of phronesis: A typology of managerial phronesis. *Journal of Business Ethics, 170*(4), 673–95.

Stichter, M. (2018). *The skillfulness of virtue.* Cambridge University Press.

Stichter, M. (2021). Differentiating the skills of practical wisdom. In In M. S. Vaccarezza & M. De Caro (Eds.), *Practical wisdom: Philosophical and psychological perspectives* (pp. 96–113). Routledge.

Strandberg, C. (2000). Aristotle's internalism in the *Nicomachean Ethics. Journal of Value Inquiry, 34*(1), 71–87.

Suissa, J. (2015). Character education and the disappearance of the political. *Ethics and Education, 10*(1), 105–17.

Surowiecki, J. (2004). *The wisdom of crowds: Why the many are smarter than the few.* Abacus.

Sussman, W. I. (1973). *Culture as history.* Pantheon.

Svenaeus, F. (2014). Empathy as a necessary condition of phronesis: A line of thought for medical ethics. *Medicine, Health Care and Philosophy, 17*(2), 293–9.

Swanson, J. A. (1992). *The public and the private in Aristotle's political philosophy.* Cornell University Press.

Swanton, C. (2003). *Virtue ethics: A pluralistic view.* Oxford University Press.

Swanton, C. (2016). Developmental virtue ethics. In J. Annas, D. Narvaez, & N. E. Snow (Eds.), *Developing the virtues: Integrating perspectives* (pp. 116–34). Oxford University Press.

Swartwood, J. D. (2013). *Cultivating practical wisdom.* Unpublished doctoral thesis. University of Minnesota. https://conservancy.umn.edu/handle/11299/154543

Swartwood, J. (2020). Can we measure practical wisdom? *Journal of Moral Education, 49*(1), 71–97.

Tangney, J. P., Stuewig, J., & Mashek, D. J. (2007). What's moral about the self-conscious emotions? In J. L. Tracy, R. W. Robins, & J. P. Tangney (Eds.), *The self-conscious emotions: Theory and research* (pp. 21–37). Gulliford Press.

Tasimi, A. & Wynn, K. (2016). Costly rejection of wrongdoers by infants and children. *Cognition, 151*(1), 76–9.

Taylor, M., Bates, G., & Webster, J. D. (2011). Comparing the psychometric properties of two measures of wisdom: Predicting forgiveness and psychological well-being with the Self-Assessed Wisdom Scale (SAWS) and the Three-Dimensional Wisdom Scale (3D-WS). *Experimental Aging Research, 37*(1), 1–12.

Tennie, C., Call, J., & Tomasello, M. (2009). Ratcheting up the ratchet: On the evolution of cumulative culture. *Philosophical Transactions of the Royal Society B, 364,* 2405–15.

Thoma, S. (2014). Measuring moral thinking from a neo-Kohlbergian perspective. *Theory and Research in Education, 12*(3), 347–65.

Thoma, S., Derryberry, W. P., & Crowson, H. M. (2013). Describing and testing an intermediate concept measure of adolescent moral thinking. *Journal of Educational and Developmental Psychology, 10*(2), 239–52.

Thoma, S., Walker, D., Chen, Y.-H., Moulin-Stozek, D., Kristjánsson, K., & Frichand, A. (2019). Adolescents' application of the virtues across five cultural contexts. *Developmental Psychology, 55*(10), 2181–92.

Thomas, A. K., Wulff, A. N., Landinez, D., & Bulevich, J. B., (2022). Thinking about thinking about thinking . . . & feeling: A model for metacognitive and meta-affective processes in task engagement. *WIREs Cognitive Science,* 13(2), 301–4.

Thomas, M. L., Bangen, K. J., Ardelte, M., & Jeste, D. (2017). Developments of a 12-item abbreviated Three-Dimensional Wisdom Scale (3D-WS-12): Item selection and psychometric properties. *Assessment*, *24*(1), 71–82.

Thorsteinsen, K., & Vitterso, J. (2020) Now you see it, now you don't: Solid and subtle differences between hedonic and eudaimonic wellbeing. *Journal of Positive Psychology*, *15*(4), 519–30.

Tiberius, V., & Swartwood, J. (2011). Wisdom revisited: A case study in normative theorizing. *Philosophical Explorations*, *14*(3), 277–95.

Tomasello, M. (2019). *Becoming human: A theory of ontogeny*. Harvard University Press.

Toom, A., & Husu, J. (2020). Tacit knowledge and knowing at the core of individual and collective expertise and professional action. In E. K. Kallio (Ed.), *Development of adult thinking: Interdisciplinary perspectives on cognitive development and adult thinking* (pp. 141–55). Routledge.

Tosi, J., & Warmke, B. (2020). *Grandstanding: The use and abuse of moral talk*. Oxford University Press.

Trommsdorff, G., & Friedlmeier, W. (1999). Motivational conflict and prosocial behaviour of kindergarten children. *International Journal of Behavioral Development*, *23*(2), 413–29.

Trommsdorff, G., Friedlmeier, W., & Mayer, B. (2007). Sympathy, distress, and prosocial behavior of preschool children in four cultures. *International Journal of Behavioral Development*, *31*(3), 284–93.

Tsouni, G. (2019). Political wisdom as the virtue of the ruler and the defense of democratic participation in Aristotle's *Politics*. In *Philosophie für die Polis. Akten des 5. internationalen Kongresses der Gesellschaft für Antike Philosophie in Zürich* (pp. 279–99). De Gruyter.

Tsai, C. (2020). Phronesis and techne: The skill model of wisdom defended. *Australian Journal of Philosophy*, *98*(2), 234–47.

Tsai, C. (2022). Practical wisdom, well-being, and success. *Philosophy and Phenomenological Research*, *104*(3), 606–22.

Turiel, E. (1983). *The development of social knowledge: Morality and convention*. Cambridge University Press.

Turiel, E. (2006). The development of morality. In W. Damon, R. M. Lerner, & N. Eisenberg (Eds.), *Handbook of child psychology: Vol. 3. Social, emotional, and personality development*, 6th ed. (pp. 789–857). Wiley.

Turiel, E., & Nucci, L. (2018). Moral development in context. In A. Dick & U. Mueller (Eds.), *Advancing developmental science: Philosophy, theory, and method* (pp. 95–109). Psychology Press.

Tynjälä, P., Kallio, E. K., & Heikkinen, L. T. (2020). Professional expertise, integrative thinking, wisdom, and phronêsis. In E. K. Kallio (Ed.), *Development of adult thinking: Interdisciplinary perspectives on cognitive development and adult thinking* (pp. 156–74). Routledge.

Tyreman, S. (2000). Promoting critical thinking in health care: *Phronesis* and criticality. *Medicine, Health Care and Philosophy*, *3*(2), 117–24.

Vaccarezza, M. S. (2018). An eye on particulars with the end in sight: An account of Aristotelian phronesis. *Metaphilosophy*, *49*(3), 246–61.

Vaccarezza, M. S., & De Caro, M. (Eds.), (2019). *Practical wisdom: Philosophical and psychological perspectives*. Routledge.

Vander Waerdt, P. A. (1991). The plan and intention of Aristotle's ethical and political writings. *Illinois Classical Studies*, *16*(1–2), 231–53.

Varghese, J., & Kristjánsson, K. (2018). Experienced UK nurses and the missing u-curve of virtue-based reasoning. In D. Carr (Ed.), *Cultivating moral character and virtue in professional practice* (pp. 151–65). Routledge.

Vasalou, S. (2012). Educating virtue as a mastery of language. *Journal of Ethics*, *16*(1), 67–87.

Vazire, S., & Carlson, E. N. (2011). Others sometimes know us better than we know ourselves. *Current Directions in Psychological Science, 20*(2), 104–8.
Villacis, J. L., de la Fuente, J., & Naval, C. (2021). Good character at college: The combined role of second-order character strength factors and *phronesis* motivation in undergraduate academic outcomes. *International Journal of Environmental Research and Public Health, 18*(16), 8263. http://doi:10.3390/ijerph18168263
Vittersø, J. (Ed.), (2016). *Handbook of eudaimonic well-being.* Springer.
Vogler, C. (2020). *Phronesis.* Insight Series Paper. https://www.jubileecentre.ac.uk/userfiles/jubileecentre/pdf/insight-series/CV_Phronesis_May20.pdf
Vygotsky, L. S. (1978). *Mind in society: The development of higher psychological processes.* Harvard University Press.
Waggoner, M. (2021). The focus of virtue: Attention broadening in empirically informed accounts of virtue cultivation. *Philosophical Psychology, 34*(8), 1217–45.
Waldron, J. (2005). The wisdom of the multitude: Some reflections on Book III, Chapter 11 of Aristotle's *Politics*. In R. Kraut & S. Skultety (Eds.), *Aristotle's Politics: Critical essays* (pp. 145–65). Rowman and Littlefield.
Walker, L. J. (2004). Gus in the gap: Bridging the judgment-action gap in moral functioning. In D. K. Lapsley & D. Narvaez (Eds.), *Moral development, self, and identity* (pp. 1–20). Erlbaum.
Walker, L. J., & Frimer, J. A. (2011). The science of moral development. In M. K. Underwood & L. H. Rosen (Eds.), *Social development: Relationships in infancy, childhood, and adolescence.* (pp. 235–62). Guilford Press.
Walsh R. (2015). Wise ways of seeing: Wisdom and perspectives. *Integral Review, 11*(2), 156–74.
Want, S. C., & Harris, P. L. (2001). Learning from other people's mistakes: Causal understanding in learning to use a tool. *Child Development, 72*(2), 431–43.
Waring, D. (2000). Why the practice of medicine is not a phronetic activity. *Theoretical Medicine and Bioethics, 21*(2), 139–51.
Warren, M. T., Wright, J. C., & Snow, N. (2022). Against neutrality: Response to Cokelet. *Journal of Moral Education, 51*(1), 111–16.
Weber, M. (1949). *The methodology of the social sciences.* Free Press.
Webster, J. D. (2003). An exploratory analysis of a self-assessed Wisdom Scale. *Journal of Adult Development, 10*(1), 13–22.
Webster, J. D. (2007). Measuring the character strength of wisdom. *International Journal of Aging and Human Development, 65*(2), 163–83.
Webster, J. D. (2019). Self-report wisdom measures: Strengths, limitations, and future directions. In R. J. Sternberg & J. Glück (Eds.), *Cambridge handbook of wisdom* (pp. 297–320). Cambridge University Press.
Weil, L. G., Fleming, S. M., Dumontheil, I., Kilford, E. J., Weil, R. S., Rees, G., Dolan, R. J., & Blakemore, S. J. (2013). The development of metacognitive ability in adolescence. *Consciousness and Cognition, 22*(1), 264–71.
Westmarland, L., & Rowe, M. (2018). Police ethics and integrity: Can a new code overturn the blue code? *Policing and Society, 28*(7), 854–70.
Williams, B. (1981). *Moral luck: Philosophical papers 1973–1980.* Cambridge University Press.
Winsler, A. 2009. Still talking to ourselves after all these years: A review of current research on private speech. In A. Winsler, C. Fernyhough, & I. Montero (Eds.), *Private speech, executive functioning, and the development of verbal self-regulation,* (pp. 3–41). Cambridge University Press.
Wittgenstein, L. (1973). *Philosophical investigations.* Trans. G. E. M. Anscombe. Prentice-Hall.
Wolbert, L. S., de Ruyter, D. J., & Schinkel, A. (2019). What kind of theory should theory on education for human flourishing be? *British Journal of Educational Studies, 67*(1), 25–39.

Wolfe, C. J. (2016). Alasdair MacIntyre on the grand end conception of practical reasoning. *Polis*, *33*(2), 312–30.

Wood, L. A., Kendal, R. A., & Flynn, E. G. (2012). Context-dependent biases in cultural transmission: Children's imitation is affected by model age over model knowledge state. *Evolution and Human Behavior*, *33*(4), 387–94.

Wood, L. A., Kendal, R. A., & Flynn, E. G. (2013). Copy me or copy you? The effect of prior experience on social learning. *Cognition*, *127*(2), 203–13.

Wright, J., Warren, M., & Snow, N. (2021). *Understanding virtue: Theory and measurement*. Oxford University Press.

Yang, S.-Y. (2008). A process view of wisdom. *Journal of Adult Development*, *15*(2), 62–75.

You, D., & Bebeau, M. J. (2013). The independence of James Rest's components of morality: Evidence from a professional ethics curriculum. *Ethics and Education*, *8*(3), 202–16.

Yu, J. (2007). *The ethics of Confucius and Aristotle: Mirrors of virtue*. Routledge.

Zagzebski, L. (2017). *Exemplarist moral theory*. Oxford University Press.

Zheng, T. (2021). Effective deliberation, good deliberation, and the skill analogy. *Journal of Value Inquiry*, *55*(2), 213–28.

Index

For the benefit of digital users, indexed terms that span two pages (e.g., 52–53) may, on occasion, appear on only one of those pages.

Figures are indicated by *f* following the page number

accumulation argument 211–14, 212n.9, 215–16, 216n.15
Aldwin, C. M. 67, 80–81
Allport, G. W. 6, 89–90
Alvarez, J. A. 105
Alzola, M. 204–5, 220n.20
ambivalence 9–10, 22–23, 91–92, 160, 170–71, 174–75, 228–29, 233n.9, 238, 239–40, 243–45, 285, 304–5
Ames, M. C. F. D. C. 9, 207
Anderson, A. R. 209, 265, 303
Annas, J. 9, 12–13, 15–16, 17n.23, 34n.7, 47–48, 61–62, 170, 248n.1, 278n.36
Anscombe, G. E. M. 3n.3, 6–7, 12–13, 46, 48n.42
Aquinas, Thomas St. 2, 60–61, 60n.56, 157n.5, 162
Aquino, K. F. 103, 116–17, 118–19, 260
Ardelt, M. 9–11, 9n.13, 15, 19, 26–27, 36n.14, 66, 66n.1, 68, 69–70, 74–75, 76–77, 78, 79, 80, 81–82, 83–85, 88–93, 94, 101, 107, 125, 133, 147n.5, 151, 162–63, 202, 225, 260, 261, 262–63, 264–65, 265n.15, 266–68, 272, 277n.35, 286, 290–91, 293, 295
Aristotle 1, 2–5, 3n.3, 3n.4, 3n.5, 4n.8, 4n.9, 7–8, 9n.13, 10–11, 12–13, 13n.18, 13n.19, 14–18, 17n.23, 19, 19n.26, 19n.27, 20–25, 20n.29, 21n.31, 21n.32, 22n.33, 27–30, 31–35, 33n.5, 33n.6, 34n.7, 34n.8, 36n.11, 36n.12, 38–41, 39n.21, 40n.22, 41n.23, 42–44, 42n.25, 42n.27, 43n.28, 43n.32, 46n.41, 47–48, 49–50, 50n.45, 51, 51n.46, 52–54, 58–59, 58n.53, 59–60n.54, 60–62, 60n.56, 61n.57, 63–64, 70, 72–73, 76–77, 83–84, 84n.2, 88, 94–96, 96–97n.6, 97, 99, 101, 104–5, 109n.11, 112, 114, 125, 128–29, 130–31, 133–34, 145–47, 151–53, 159, 160, 161–62, 161n.11, 163–67, 164n.16, 165n.17, 166n.18, 168, 169–71, 170n.23, 172, 174–75, 177–202, 177n.1, 177n.2, 181n.6, 181n.7, 181n.8, 182n.9, 182n.10, 183n.11, 184n.12, 186n.15, 187n.17, 189n.18, 189n.19, 189n.20, 190n.21, 190n.22, 191n.23, 192n.24, 193n.25, 193n.26, 194n.27, 194n.28, 195n.29, 197n.32, 200–1n.34, 203–5, 203n.1, 205–6n.3, 206–22, 206n.4, 210n.6, 211n.7, 212n.8, 212n.9, 214n.11, 216n.14, 216n.15, 218n.17, 220n.20, 221n.22, 223, 224–25, 228–31, 229n.2, 229n.3, 229n.4, 232–34, 234n.10, 235–40, 238n.15, 241–44, 247–53, 252n.2, 252n.3, 255–59, 255n.5, 257n.6, 257n.7, 260, 261, 262–66, 267–68, 269–70, 271, 271–72n.27, 272n.29, 273, 274–75, 278–83, 279–80n.39, 281n.41, 281n.42, 282n.43, 284, 285–86, 287–91, 291n.3, 292, 294, 295–96, 303, 304–6
Arnold, M. L. 118
Arsenio, W. F. 122, 124–25
Arthur, J. 12n.16, 86n.4, 133, 157, 157n.4, 158, 171, 174, 187n.17, 276–77
Asma, L. J. F. 48n.42
Athanassoulis, N. 271, 271–72n.27, 277, 278n.36
Austin, J. L. 56

Babelay, A. M. 174
Ball, C. 250
Bandura, A. 257n.8
Barkley, R. A. 261
Barley, D. E. 165n.17
Barriga, A. Q. 118–19
Bates, G. 87, 291

Batson, C. D. 119–20, 121–22, 123
Bauer, J. J. 254, 289, 292
Beadle, R. 21n.30, 204–5
Beauchamp, T. 156n.2
Bebeau, M. J. 111, 126, 127
Becker, J. 224n.24
Beresford, E. B. 172–73
Bergman, R. 113, 115, 116, 124–25
Bezanilla, M. J. 268n.23
Bier, M. C. 300
Birren, J. E. 63–64
Blasi, A. 6–7, 83, 87, 92–93, 113–14, 115–16, 117, 121
Blockburger, S. 109
Bluck, S. 66, 68, 78, 81, 83–84, 85
Bobonich, C. 109n.11, 212–13, 215–16
Bohlin, K. 9, 273
Bortolotti, L. 272n.28
Boudreau, J. D. 174
Boyd, D. 178–79
Brackbill, D. 224n.24
Brant, J. 280
Brewer, T. 22n.33
Brienza, J. P. 9–10, 9n.13, 45n.36, 66, 67–68, 69–70, 74–75, 77, 80, 83–84, 85, 87, 88, 89–93, 101, 125, 133, 134, 138n.2, 147n.5, 151, 202, 260, 261, 262–63, 264–65, 265n.15, 266–68, 286, 295
Briggs, C. 41, 265, 300–1
Brinkmann, S. 71, 82, 293n.4
Broadie, S. 5, 10–11, 41–42, 53–54, 54n.48
Brooks, E. 280
Brown, M. 4n.8, 12–13, 15–16, 33–34, 72, 300
Brunetti, R. 43n.29, 45–46, 45–46n.38
Bruya, B. 272
Bryan, C. S. 174
Burbules, N. C. 9
Bürgler, S. 254–55
Burnyeat, F. M. 250, 263
business ethics 159n.10, 160, 203, 204–6, 205–6n.3, 207, 208, 209, 210, 211, 213, 217, 218, 220–22, 221n.21
Butler, L. P. 260–61

Cammack, D. 212n.9, 219
Camodeca, M. 123–24
Candee, D. 118–19
Cantor, N. 116–17
Caputo, J. D. 22
Carlo, G. 51–52, 115–17, 118, 123, 141, 142–43
Carr, D. 6–7, 37–38, 167, 170–71, 227, 230, 232, 235, 243–44, 248–49, 270, 304–6
Carr, W. 163–64
Carroll, N. 8, 9, 12–14, 12n.15, 15–16, 30, 33–34, 38n.20, 52–53, 72–73, 90–91, 107, 125, 133–34, 180–81, 290–91, 302, 305
Casler, K. 269
Centola, D. 224n.24
Chambers, D. W. 127
Chappell, S. G. 252–53
character education 4–5, 15–16, 29, 37–38, 41–42n.24, 57, 108, 115n.2, 125, 147, 155, 178–79, 181, 186–88, 193n.25, 201–2, 202n.35, 205, 210n.6, 252n.2, 263–64, 265, 266–67, 271, 276, 278–79, 298–99, 300, 304–5
Cheek, J. M. 140–41, 142–43
Chesterton, G. K. 8–9
Childress, J. 156n.2
Cigman, R. 270n.26
civic virtue 3n.3, 4–5, 29, 43, 50–51, 56–57, 58, 129, 177, 177n.1, 178, 178n.4, 179, 180, 188, 191, 192–200, 193n.25, 194n.27, 195n.29, 195n.30, 200–1n.34, 201–2, 206–7, 215, 218–19, 221, 255n.5, 265, 281–83, 284, 285, 287–88
civic/citizenship education 29, 178–79, 181, 185–88, 201–2, 280–84
Clark, A. 262, 262n.13
Clay, Z. 253
Clayton, V. P. 63–64
clinical judgement 163–65, 173, 174
codifiability 2, 17, 21–23, 45–46, 163–64, 165–69, 172, 274, 279–80, 306
Cohen L. 244n.20, 278
Cokelet, B. 8, 9, 12–14, 12n.15, 15–16, 30, 33–34, 34n.7, 36n.11, 46–47, 52–53, 72–73, 91–92, 107, 125, 133–34, 180–81, 272, 272n.29, 290–91, 302–3, 305
Colby, A. 107, 115, 116, 117–18
collective *phronesis* 201, 203–9, 209n.5, 210–11, 213, 214, 214n.11, 216n.15, 217, 218, 219–20, 221–25, 221n.22, 225n.26, 281n.41, 288
College of Policing 274
common model of wisdom (CWM) *see* wisdom, common model of
Confucius 2, 61, 61n.57, 220n.20, 265
Conroy, M. 161, 206–7
consequentialism 91, 156, *see also* utilitarianism

Cooper, J. M. 33–34, 196–97
Crocker, J. 140, 142–43
Crowson, H. M. 127, 137, 138–39, 142–43, 276
Csibra, G. 20
Curnow, T. 77
Curren, R. 179n.5, 194n.28, 195, 196–97, 283
Curzer, H. J. 5, 9, 12–13, 15, 18–19, 33–35, 36n.12, 43n.32, 45–46n.38, 50n.45, 252n.3, 256–57, 269

Dahl, A. 251
Damon, W. 107, 115, 116, 117–18, 186–87, 267
Daniel, E. 122
Darnell, C. 9, 16n.22, 36–37, 42n.25, 66, 68, 72–73, 77, 78, 83–84, 87, 92–93, 99, 103–4, 111, 133, 134, 145–47, 151, 153, 187n.17, 193n.25, 247, 295, 302
Davis, M. H. 123, 139–40
Davison, I. 259
De Caro, M. 10–11, 20n.28, 26, 32–33, 57, 57n.51, 57n.52, 58–59, 60–61, 285–86, 302
de la Fuente, J. 280
de Rosnay, M. 47–48, 103, 263
de Ruyter, D. J. 35n.10, 190n.21
Deci, E. 51n.46, 253–54
deinotes (instrumentalist calculation) 9–10, 18, 18n.24, 47–48, 61, 63–64, 77–78, 81–82, 85–86, 89–90, 105, 168n.21, 204–5, 208, 285
DeLuca, S. 158n.7
deontology 6–7, 23–24, 25, 91, 128–29, 130, 156–57, 161, 204–5, 242
Derryberry, W. P. 127, 137, 138–39, 142–43, 276
Diener, E. 290
dilemmas, 3n.2, 6, 33–34, 37–38, 38n.19, 39, 76, 113, 120, 128, 137–39, 142–43, 148, 149, 157, 158–59, 169, 262–63, 268n.22, 275, 277, 277n.35
Dinsmore, D. L. 37n.15
Dong, M. 67–68, 75, 91–92
Doris, J. , 13, 114, 116–17
Driver, J. 289, 294
Dunne, J. 17, 21n.30, 21n.31, 38–39, 163–64, 163n.13, 163n.14, 169
Durlak, J. A. 267
Durrenberger, E. P. 22n.33

Earl, S. 157, 157n.4, 158, 276–77
Eisenberg, N. 121–22, 123, 124
Emory, E. 105

emotion see *phronesis*, emotion-regulation function of
empathy 59–60, 59–60n.54, 68, 78–79, 85, 88, 104, 121–25, 121n.7, 126–27, 136f, 139–40, 142–43, 146f, 150f, 152, 252
Ettinger, U. 102
executive functions 98–99, 102, 105, 107, 110

Fabes, R. A. 121–22
Fan, Y. 300–1
Farb, N. A. S. 80
Fariñas, G. 207, 223–24
Fegley, S. 118
Ferkany, M. 33–34, 33n.6, 257n.11
Ferrari, M. 75–76, 77, 79, 86, 88–89, 90–91, 94–95, 265, 266–67, 266n.18, 300
Ferrero, I. 204–5
Fetter, J. T. 198–99
Flaming, D. 9
Flanagan, O. 42n.26
Flavell, J. H. 101, 102
Fleeson, W. 13–14, 100, 264, 302
flourishing 12–13, 13n.18, 13n.19, 14–15, 18–19, 21n.32, 41–43, 42n.26, 43n.28, 59, 93–94, 105, 133–34, 164, 170, 181, 183, 199, 200, 218–19, 227–28, 236–38, 241–42, 243, 248–49, 259–60, 265, 289–91, 290n.2, 292, 298
Flyvbjerg, B. 9–10, 177, 180–81, 181n.8, 185, 224–25
Fournier, M. A. 67–68
Fowers, B. J. 6–7, 8, 9, 12–13, 12n.15, 13n.18, 13n.19, 14–16, 14n.21, 30, 33–34, 34n.7, 42n.26, 44n.33, 49, 52–53, 70, 71, 72–73, 82, 89–90, 91–92, 103–4, 107, 125, 133–34, 140–41, 169n.22, 170, 180–81, 182–83, 185, 209, 228n.1, 251–52, 258n.12, 265, 289, 290–91, 292, 293n.4, 294, 295, 300–3, 305
Frede, D. 200n.33, 200–1n.34, 205n.2, 238
Fredrickson, B. L. 289, 291
Freeman, D. 116–17
Frey, J. 10–11
Friedman, N. 105
friendship 24–25, 96–97n.6, 183, 191–92, 194n.27, 196–97, 197n.32, 204, 209–11, 209n.5, 210n.6, 212, 221–23, 234, 251, 282–83, 302–3
Frimer, J. A. 251
Fuks, A. 174

Galton, F. 207–8
'gappiness problem' 27–28, 87, 111–12, 120, 121, 124–26, 130–31, 153, 287
Garsten, B. 214n.11, 217–18, 219–20
Garver, E. 42n.27
George, A. 156
Gibbs, J. C. 115, 118–19, 140, 142–43
Gillespie, A. 261
Gjerris, M. 275n.32
Glück, J. 9n.13, 37n.17, 64–66, 68, 74–75, 78–79, 81, 83–84, 85, 86n.3, 88–89, 95–96, 112n.1, 145, 187n.17, 266–67, 267n.19, 281n.41, 291
Göckeritz, S. M. 260–61
Goddiksen, M. P. 275n.32
Gold, J. 122, 124–25
Goleman, D. 230
Good, D. J. 101
Grant, A. M. 4–5, 70
Greenspan, P. S. 235n.12, 243
Grossmann, I. 45n.36, 66, 67–68, 70, 74–77, 78, 79, 80, 81–82, 83–84, 85, 86, 87, 88–95, 101, 104–5, 107, 125, 133, 134, 138n.2, 147n.5, 151, 202, 223n.23, 251, 260, 261, 262–63, 264–65, 265n.15, 266–68, 271–73, 275n.33, 286, 295, 300
Guignon, C. B. 6–7, 71, 82, 91–92, 133–34, 302
Guiso, L. 223–24
Guitián, G. 204–5
Gulliford, L. 9, 12n.15, 36–38, 42n.25, 56n.50, 66, 68, 72–73, 77, 78, 83–84, 87, 92–93, 99, 103–4, 111, 133, 145–47, 151, 153, 238n.15, 247, 278–79, 295, 302
Gustin Law, L. K. 196n.31, 200

habituation 2–4, 3n.3, 18–19, 18n.24, 24–25, 31–33, 40, 47–48, 48n.42, 49–50, 57, 58, 106, 108, 116–17, 158, 194–96, 202, 221, 228, 247–48, 249–50, 252n.3, 253, 255, 257–58, 257n.9, 263, 268, 269, 271–72n.27, 280, 281–83, 282n.43, 284
Hacker-Wright, J. 61–62, 170, 171
Hagen, J. 102
Haidt, J. 6–7, 13, 23, 103, 114, 116–17, 205–6n.3
Haldane, J. 41–42n.24, 44n.34
Han, H. 271, 275
Harðarson, A. 9, 266, 269, 280
Hardy, S. A. 51–52, 115–17, 118–19, 124–25, 260, 263

Hare, B. 252
Harrison, T. 8n.10, 36–38, 37n.18, 43, 270n.24
Hart, D. 118, 260
Hatchimonji, D. R. 257n.6, 265n.15, 266n.16, 270n.25, 271
Hawes, D. J. 103, 263
Hawkins, A. J. 300–1
Haybron, D. M. 13n.19, 289, 294, 300
Hays, J. 224n.25
Heikkinen, L. T. 95–96, 106
Hennecke, M. 254
Hennig, A. 204–5, 220n.20
Hertz, S. G. 103, 118, 120, 260
Hill, P. 116–17, 260
Hirata, T. 207, 223–25
Hoffman, M. L. 121, 122, 123, 252
Hofmann, B. 164
Hojjat, M. 222–23
Hong, L. 213–14, 267–68
Horn, C. 211
Hoyos-Valdés, D. 210n.6
Hume, D. 49–50, 89–90, 121, 121n.7, 182–83, 182n.10
Humean-ism 43, 49–51, 89–90, 182–83
Huo, Y. 159n.10, 204–5, 210, 220n.20, 221
Hursthouse, R. 4–5, 18n.24, 37–38, 39, 40n.22, 170–71, 273
Husu, J. 106
Hutson, J. M. 173
Huynh, A. C. 266–67, 271, 272–73, 275n.33

idealisation 33–34, 35, 177n.2, 197–98
Igarashi, H. 67, 80–81
Ignatowicz, A. M. 133, 171, 174
Indraccolo, A. 43n.29, 45–46, 45–46n.38
intellectual virtue 3–5, 17, 18, 31–32, 38, 55, 59–60n.54, 61–62, 61n.57, 74–75, 105, 131, 160, 161n.11, 168–69, 220, 259, 269, 272–74
Intezari, A. 218n.17, 223n.23
Irrera, E. 196–97, 215–16
Irwin, T. H. 39, 43n.32, 50, 170

Jacobs, J. 37n.17, 239n.16, 280, 300–1
Jambon, M. 250
Jameel, S. Y. 9, 21n.32, 156n.1, 156n.2, 159, 162–63, 162n.12, 164–65, 164n.16, 174n.24, 263n.14, 272n.30
Jayawickreme, E. 13–14, 68, 100, 103, 264, 302

Jefferson, A. 218n.16
Jenkins, K. 158n.7
Jerome, L. 179, 187–88, 202n.35
Jeste, D. V. 40–41, 77, 78, 267, 290–91
John, O. P. 141
Johnson, M. R. 183n.11

Kaldjian, L. C. 9, 59–60, 159, 163, 164–65, 172, 173, 272n.30
Kallio, E. K. 68, 95–96, 106, 107, 147, 262–63, 265, 267–68, 279
Kamtekar, R. 31–32
Kanakogi, Y. 252
Kant, I. 6–7, 45–46, 112, 113, 162n.12, 230, 230n.6, 271–72n.27, 279–80n.39, 306
Karami, S. 63–64, 65–66, 68–69, 78, 83–84, 85, 86, 86n.4
Kayange, G. M. 61n.57
Keltner, D. 78, 80–81
Kemmis, S. 22–23
Kenward, B. 253, 269
Keyt, D. 189n.20
Kinghorn, W. A. 174
Kingsford, J. M. 47–48, 103, 263
Kinsella, E. A. 158n.7
Kisby, B. 179, 187–88, 202n.35
Kitayama, S. 207, 219–20
Klaei, Y. A. 101
Kline, R. B. 143
Ko, H.-K. 158n.7
Kochanska, G. 263
Koehn, D. 204–5
Kohlberg, L. 6–7, 68, 83, 112–14, 115, 115n.2, 118–19, 126–27, 128, 256–57, 276, 279–80, 279–80n.39
Konstan, D. 238
Kotzee, B. 133, 171, 174
Köymen, B. 260–61
Kraut, R. 53–54, 54n.48, 186–87, 190–92, 192n.24, 195n.29, 202, 211n.7, 257n.9, 283
Krettenauer, T. 36n.11, 51–52, 52n.47, 103, 118, 120–21, 122, 123–25, 260
Kristjánsson, K. 4n.9, 5–6, 8, 9, 12–13, 12n.15, 12n.16, 13n.19, 15–16, 17, 19n.27, 21n.31, 23, 24, 25, 36–37, 39, 40n.22, 41n.23, 41–42n.24, 42n.25, 42n.26, 44n.34, 48, 50, 52–53, 58n.53, 61–62, 66, 68, 70, 72–73, 77, 78, 83–84, 84n.2, 86, 86n.4, 87, 89–90, 91–93, 96–97n.6, 99, 103–4, 107, 111, 114, 119, 133, 134, 145–47, 151, 151n.6, 153, 156n.3, 157–58, 157n.5, 159n.10, 171, 174, 179, 187n.17, 191–92, 197n.32, 198–99, 204–5, 209–10, 220n.20, 221, 222–23, 228–29, 230, 232–33, 232n.8, 235–36, 238n.15, 240n.17, 243, 247, 248–49, 252–53, 252n.2, 256, 263–64, 265, 271, 274, 275, 282–83, 289, 294, 294n.5, 295, 300, 301–2, 303, 305
Kross, E. 271
Kumagal, A. K. 51n.46
Kunzmann, U. 78, 83, 87, 134, 137, 300

Lamb, M. 280
Lambert, M. J. 165n.17
Landemore, H. 206–7
Lappalainen, J. H. 201, 207, 208, 222–23
Lapsley, D. 5, 15–16, 27, 33–34, 40–41, 41n.23, 42n.25, 55, 56–57, 56n.50, 98–101, 99n.8, 102–4, 107, 109, 110, 114, 115, 116–17, 248, 248n.1, 254, 260, 286–87
Larrick, R. P. 224n.24
Latzko, B. 122
Lawford, H. 118, 260
Lawrence, W. Y. 281n.40
Lees, J. 78, 80, 88–89, 96
Lehman, M. 102
Leone, L. 120
Lerner, R. M. 19, 67
Levenson, M. R. 67, 80–81
Lin, T.-J. 267–68
Linn, M. 194n.27
Lumsdon, D. 41, 265, 268n.22, 300–1

McCullough, M.E. 252
McDowell, J. 38
McGrath, R. E. 4n.8, 12–13, 15–16, 19n.27, 33–34, 71–72, 157n.5, 300
MacIntyre A. 2, 6, 12–13, 20–21, 20n.29, 21n.31, 28, 54n.48, 59, 158n.7, 160, 161–68, 163n.13, 163n.14, 165n.17, 170n.23, 173, 174–75, 190n.22, 247–48, 285, 287
McMahon, J. M. 101
Maile, A. 187n.17, 232n.8, 274, 275
Malti, T. 122, 123–25
Mannes, A. E. 224n.24
Marcum, J. A. 172
Markus, H. R. 207, 219–20
Marraffa, M. 57n.52
Martin, J. 261

Mashek, D. J. 122
Mata, A. 103
Matsuba, M. K. 118
Maiese, M. 262, 262n.13
medical ethics 28, 156n.2, 158–60, 158n.9, 162–63, 164, 165, 170, 171, 172, 173–75, 287
megalopsychia (great-heartedness) 4n.6, 19, 198–99
Mehltretter Drury, S. A. 221n.22, 281n.40
Meltzoff, A. N. 253
Menesini, E. 123–24
Mercier, H. 205–6n.3
Mestre, M. V. 141
metacognition 4–5, 23, 26–27, 37, 69–70, 72, 74–75, 76, 77, 78–79, 81, 83, 84–86, 88–89, 91, 94, 99, 101–2, 103–4, 105, 109, 110, 197, 232–33, 250, 254–55, 262–63, 267–68, 285, 286–87
meta-virtue 4–5, 4n.7, 7–8, 57n.51, 60n.55, 61n.57, 70, 71, 72, 77, 130–31, 195–96, 198–99, 227–28, 266, 285, 300, 301
Mill, J. S. 6–7
Miller, C. B. 15, 26, 32–33, 50, 55–58, 60–61, 285–86, 302
Miller, P. A. 105
Miller, P. H. 121, 122, 123, 124–25
Miyake, A.
Miyake, A. 105
Montada, L. 121
Montgomery, K. 163–64, 172
Moore, G. 21n.30, 204–5
moral development 52–53, 111–31, 249–65, 281–82, 288
moral identity 41–44, 115–98, 123, 124–25, 140–41, 218–19, 260–61, 263, 270, 287
moral reasoning 44–48, 83, 87, 111–31, 138–39, 157–58, 270, 279–80
moral virtue 3n.3, 4n.7, 4n.9, 8, 12n.15, 24–25, 29, 31–34, 40, 43, 43n.32, 44, 50–51, 51n.46, 55–56, 56n.50, 57, 58, 59, 61n.57, 93–94, 106, 111, 115, 156, 158, 161n.11, 165–66, 167, 177, 178, 191–93, 193n.25, 194–96, 194n.27, 195n.30, 197–99, 200, 200–1n.34, 201–2, 206–7, 215, 220, 221, 237–38, 268, 269, 273, 280, 281–82, 287–88, 290–91, 298–99
Morgan, B. 12n.15, 140–41, 238n.15
Moshman, D. 102, 119–20
Moss, J. 50n.45, 178n.3

Moyer, A. 222–23
Müller, A. W. 3–4, 24–25, 93–94
Muthén, B. O. 142, 143
Muthén, L. K. 142, 143
Myers, N. A. 173

Narvaez, D. 6, 12–13, 106, 114, 115, 116–17, 126–30, 126n.9, 260, 302–3
naturalism 15–16, 114, 167, 168–69, 177, 180, 183–84, 185, 231, 234, 306
Naval, C. 280
Navarini, C. 43n.29, 45–46, 45–46n.38
neo-Kohlbergianism 27–28, 111, 126–30, 276, 287
Ng, V. 3n.4, 4–5, 12–13, 48, 70
Niccoli, A. 32–33, 57, 58
Nonaka, I. 207, 223–25
Nucci, L. 126, 127, 129, 251
Nussbaum, M. C. 168–69, 168n.20, 216–17, 235–36, 270n.26

Ober, J. 178, 190–91, 201
Ohtani, K. 37n.15
Ongley, S. E. 122
Osman, Y. 271

Page, B. 183–84
Page, S. E. 213–14
Pálsson, G. 22n.33
'paradox of moral education' 253
Paris, P. 9, 36–37, 42n.25, 66, 68, 72–73, 77, 78, 83–84, 87, 92–93, 99, 103–4, 111, 133, 134, 145–47, 151, 153, 247, 295, 302
Pascalis, O. 252–53
Pasupathi, M. 147, 153
Patrick, R. B. 140, 142–43
Pellegrino, E. 163–65, 172
Penner, L. 123
performance measures 67, 87, 97, 134, 137, 138–39, 142–43, 152, 153, 223–24, 273, 300
personality 6, 14, 14n.21, 37n.17, 44–45, 74n.6, 99–100, 103, 118, 129–30, 135, 141, 145, 149, 212, 250, 263–64
Perugini, M. 120
Peters, R. S. 253–54, 255
Peterson, A. 179, 281
Peterson, C. 4–5, 12–13, 60–61, 70–72, 89–90, 180–81, 290
Phan, L. V. 68

phronesis adjudicative/integrative function/
  component of 18–19, 36, 44–48, 101–2,
  115, 128, 135, 138–39, 159,
  219–20, 254–55, 297
 Aristotelian model of (APM) 31–62,
  72–74, 93–109, 111, 115, 126–30,
  133–53, 162–63, 218, 227–28, 259,
  267–68, 272, 276, 286–87, 292
 blueprint function/component of , 12–13,
  27, 39, 41–44, 48–54, 59–60, 72, 73–74,
  93, 97, 102–4, 106, 110, 128, 135, 140–
  41, 148–49, 152–53, 169, 200, 218–19,
  254–55, 259–60, 272, 280–81, 286–87,
  295–96, 297
 and civic virtue 3–5, 10, 29, 58, 177–202,
  206, 215–17, 221, 265, 280–84, 287–88
 as collective 10, 29, 201, 203–25, 281, 287–88
 constitutive function/component of
  18–19, 36, 37–39, 59–60, 71–72, 97, 100,
  127–28, 130, 135, 137–38, 148–49, 219,
  267, 296–97
 emotion-regulation function/component
  of 18–19, 40–41, 49f, 59–60, 71–72, 73,
  75, 78–79, 83–85, 91, 93–94, 95–96, 97,
  110, 113–15, 121–24, 139–40, 151–52,
  219, 228–29, 230, 231–32, 243–44,
  254–55, 261–62, 286–87
 grand-end view of 53–54
 measurement of 16, 26, 28, 36–37, 66–68,
  87, 125, 133–53, 276, 292–97
 as painful 28, 160, 170–75, 227–45
 as particularist or generalist 21, 28, 38–39,
  42–43, 160, 165–71, 172–75, 287
 scepticism/eliminativism/redundancy
  thesis about 55–58, 99–109
 standard Aristotelian model of 10, 15–16,
  18–19, 20, 23, 31–48, 51, 285–86
 teaching of 247–84
 as universalist or relativist 21, 28, 160,
  165–69, 172–75
Piaget, J. 113
Pickup, A. 282n.43
Piff, P. K. 78, 80–81
Plato 4–5, 20, 58, 179, 184–85, 190, 253,
  257–58, 270, 282–83
Polany, M. 106
police ethics 4n.8, 156n.3, 207, 274, 279–80
Polizzi, G. 8n.10, 36–37
Pollard, D. 83–84, 86, 151n.6
positive psychology 4–5, 12–13, 70–73,
  89–90, 180–81

postmodernism 20, 22–23, 187, 247–48, 285
post-*phronetic* pain see *phronesis* as painful
Potworowski, G. 265, 266–67
practical wisdom see *phronesis*
Pratt, M. W. 118–19, 260
professional ethics 9, 12n.16, 20, 21, 21n.30,
  25, 28, 29, 73, 155–56, 156n.2, 158–59,
  160, 165–66, 167, 172, 175, 203, 205,
  207, 208, 247–48, 266, 268, 269, 273,
  274–75, 279–80, 285, 287, 288
professionalism 156, 170, 174
prosociality 3–4, 12–13, 22–23, 28, 48, 68,
  74, 90–91, 118–19, 122–25, 133–34, 135,
  141–45, 148–51, 255, 287, 306
prudence 60–61, 60n.55, 71–72, 157n.5
psychological unity 29–30, 33–34, 170–71,
  228–29, 230, 232, 236–37, 240–41, 242,
  243–45, 255–56, 288, 305

Rabinoff, E. 36
Railton, P. 23, 45n.35, 46–47
rationalism 6–7, 84n.2, 91, 112–13, 114, 115,
  115n.2, 118–19
Reed, A. II. 103, 116–17, 118–19, 260
Reeve, C. D. C. 244
reflection 23, 51, 52–53, 73, 75, 80, 95, 102,
  240–41, 248–49, 257–58, 267–68, 272,
  272n.28, 272n.29, 277, 279, 306
Reimer, K. 118
Reiner, P. 250
Reio, T. G. 101
Rest, J. 111, 126–30
Richardson, F. C. 6–7, 71, 82, 91–92,
  133–34, 302
Richardson, M. J. 147, 153
Roberts, J. 195–96
role-models 2–3, 19, 19n.26, 158–59, 209–10,
  221, 222, 247–48, 249–50, 253, 257–58,
  260, 270, 271–72, 271-72n.27, 278n.36
Romar, E. 204–5, 220n.20
Rönnlund, A. R. 8
Rooney, D. 208, 224–25
Rorty, A. O. 32–33
Rosler, A. 193
Rosling, H. 8
Rountree, J. 221n.22, 281n.40
Rowe, M. 279–80
Russell, D. C. 2, 2n.1, 3n.5, 9, 10–11, 12–13,
  15–16, 17, 18–19, 22n.33, 32–35, 37,
  42–43, 43n.29, 44–45, 46, 151, 236–37,
  257n.10, 269, 299

Ryan, R. M. 51n.46, 253–54
Ryff, C. D. 290

sadness 29–30, 232, 240–42, 240n.17, 288
Sadovsky, A. 123
Salkever, S. G. 181n.7, 182
Sandel, M. J. 86
Sanderse, W. 255, 256–57
Sapienza, P. 223–24
Sayer, A. 6–7
Scalzo, G. 207, 220, 223–24
Schinkel, A. 35n.10, 190n.21
Schwartz, B. 201, 207, 208, 222–23, 254
Schwartzberg, M. 216n.15
Schwarz, E. 201, 207, 208, 222–23
Schwarz, N. 254
Segvic, H. 41–42, 251
self-reports 66–68, 71, 83, 92–93, 118–19, 120, 124–25, 127, 134, 139–40, 142–43, 151, 153, 291–92, 299–301
Seligman, M. E. P. 4–5, 12–13, 12n.17, 60n.55, 70–72, 71n.4, 89–90, 181n.6, 290
Sellman, D. 204–5
Serafim, M. C. 9, 207
Sewchurran, K. 213n.10, 218n.18, 221
Sharma, B. 225
Sharpe, K. E. 8n.12, 9, 10–11, 12n.16, 56n.50, 70, 72, 73, 133, 155, 157–58, 269, 279
Sherman, N. 13n.18, 83–84, 250, 263
Shweder, R. A. 251
Sifferd, K. 218n.16
Silverstein, A. 248
Sim, M. 61n.57
Sison, A. J. G. 204–5, 211
skills 17, 22, 33–34, 61–62, 65, 109, 129, 160, 164, 170, 279
Smetana, J. 250–51
Smith, S. M. 140–41, 142–43
Snow, N. E. 43–44, 43n.31, 47–48, 51–53, 54, 70, 73–74, 74n.6, 100, 151, 302–3
Sokol, B 124–25
Soll, J. B. 224n.24
Solomon, R. C. 203n.1, 204–5, 206, 206n.4, 211, 223–24
sophia 9–10, 16–17, 61, 63–64, 65–66, 77, 80–82, 92–93, 94, 285
Sophie's Choice 3n.2, 231–33, 238–39, 240, 255–56
Sperber, D. 205–6n.3
Spinrad, T. L. 123

Srivastava, S. 141
Stangle, R. 271
Stark, S. 232, 235–36
Staudinger, U. M. 64–65, 90–91, 134
Sternberg, R. J. 9n.13, 37n.17, 63–64, 65–66, 68–69, 80, 83–84, 85, 86, 86n.3, 86n.4, 87, 90–91, 112n.1, 134, 187n.17, 266–68, 267n.19, 281n.41
Steyn, F. 213n.10, 217, 218n.18
Stichter, M. 17n.23, 37n.16, 42n.25, 61–62, 262n.13, 300
Strandberg, C. 235–36
STRIVE-4 model 14–15
Stuewig, J. 122
Suissa, J. 179, 187–88
Surowiecki, J. 207–8, 214n.12, 224, 225
Sussman, W. I. 6
Svenaeus, F. 59–60n.54
Swanson, J. A. 187n.17
Swanton, C. 248n.1, 271
Swartwood, J. D. 4–5, 18–19, 46n.39, 61–62, 95, 292–97, 298, 300, 307
sympathy 40, 74, 84–85, 94–95, 121, 121n.7, 122–24, 252

Tangney, J. P. 122
Tasimi, A. 252
Tay, L. 3n.4, 4–5, 12–13, 48, 70
Taylor, M. 87, 267, 291
techné 17, 21–23, 29–30, 163–66, 168, 204–5
teleology 95–96, 170, 179, 180–85, 201–2, 230
Tennie, C. 253–54
Thoma, S. 6, 83–84, 86, 126, 127, 137, 138–39, 138n.1, 142–43, 151n.6, 265, 276, 290–91
Thomas, A. K 102, 133, 171, 174, 254–55, 290–91
Thomasma, D. 163–64, 172
Thompson, A. 156, 157–58, 232–33, 274, 275
Thompson, E. R. 119–20
Thorsteinsen, K. 289
Tiberius, V. 18–19, 95
Tomasello, M. 47–48, 181n.8, 250, 253–54, 260–61, 263, 269
Toom, A. 106
Tosi, J. 8
Toyama, R. 207, 223–25
Trombetti, I. 248
Trommsdorff, G. 123
Tropp, L. R. 140–41, 142–43
Tsai, C. 61–62, 61n.58, 267–68

Tsouni, G. 214, 215–16
Turiel, E. 126, 250–51
Tyreman, S. 173

utilitarianism 6–7, 23–24, 25, 46, 60–61, 91, 156–57, 200, 204–5, 230, 242

Vaccarezza, M. S. 10–11, 20n.28, 26, 39, 39n.21, 57, 57n.51, 57n.52, 58, 60–61, 285–86, 302
Vander Waerdt, P. A. 180–81
Varghese, J. 158n.7
Vasalou, S. 37–38
Vazire, S. 300–1
Villacis, J. L. 280
virtue ethics 1, 2–5, 6, 9, 15–16, 23–24, 25, 27–28, 31–33, 39, 42–43, 46, 62, 81, 91, 94–95, 96, 107, 114, 130–31, 137–38, 155–58, 160, 161, 167, 169, 171, 174, 180–81, 185, 187, 204–6, 218–19, 229, 231, 242, 244–45, 270, 274–75, 276–77, 304–5, 306
Vittersø, J. 289
Vogler, C. 12n.16, 45n.37, 86n.4, 106, 133
Vygotsky, L. S. 276, 279–80

Waggoner, M. 37n.16
Waldron, J. 213–14, 216n.15
Walker, L. J. 6, 113–14, 115, 118, 251, 260, 265
Walsh, R. 68
Want, S. C. 253
Ward, L. A. 12n.16
Waring, D. 164
Warmke, B. 8
Warren, M. T. 11n.14, 12–13, 14, 14n.20, 14n.21, 15, 26, 30, 34, 36–37, 41, 43–44, 43n.31, 45–46n.38, 46–47, 51–53, 54, 58, 70, 73–74, 74n.6, 83–84, 100, 103, 134, 151, 252n.2, 263–64, 267n.20, 272n.29, 285–86, 289, 294, 295–96, 298–300, 302

Weber, M. 6–7, 89–90, 182–83
Webster, J. D. 67, 68, 83–84, 85, 87, 291
Weil, L. G. 262–63
Westmarland, L. 279–80
Westrate, N. M. 67–68, 69–70, 77, 83–84, 85, 86, 88–93, 94–95, 101, 125, 133, 147n.5, 151, 202, 260, 261, 262–63, 264–65, 265n.15, 266–68, 286, 300
Williams, B. 20, 23–24, 25, 242n.19, 252–53
Winsler, A. 261
wisdom, as organizational 204–5, 206–7, 208, 221, 224–25
  balance model of 65–66, 90–91
  Berlin model of 26–27, 64–65, 83
  common model of (CWM) 74–82, 83–110, 267–68, 286–87, 295
  of crowds 204, 207–8, 213–14
  in psychology 63–110
  as theoretical see *sophia*
Wittgenstein, L. 94, 306
Wolbert, L. S. 35n.10, 190n.21
Wolfe, C. J. 54n.48
Wood, L. A 253
Wright, J. C. 11n.14, 12–13, 14, 14n.20, 14n.21, 15, 26, 30, 34, 36–37, 41, 43–44, 43n.31, 45–46n.38, 46–47, 51–53, 54, 58, 70, 73–74, 74n.6, 83–84, 100, 103, 104, 134, 151, 263–64, 267n.20, 268n.22, 272n.29, 285–86, 289, 294, 295–96, 298–300, 302
Wynn, K. 252

You, D. 127
Young, L. 78, 80, 88–89, 96
Yu, J. 61

Zachry, C. E. 103
Zagzebski, L. 107
Zappellini, M. B. 9, 207
Zheng, T. 46n.39, 61–62
Zingales, L. 223–24